Rethinking Party Systems in the Third Wave of Democratization

THE CASE OF BRAZIL

SCOTT P. MAINWARING

Rethinking Party Systems in the Third Wave of Democratization

THE CASE OF BRAZIL

STANFORD UNIVERSITY PRESS

STANFORD, CALIFORNIA

Stanford University Press
Stanford, California

© 1999 by the Board of Trustees of the
Leland Stanford Junior University

Printed in the United States of America

CIP data are at the end of the book

For Sue

Acknowledgments

For a good part of the 1980s, Brazil was a home away from home for me. I was received graciously and generously, and I made valued friends. I am grateful to the countless individuals who made such positive experiences possible.

Antônio Kandir and his family have hosted me more times than I care to count, and with supreme graciousness. José Carlos Sebe, Jairo Nicolau, and Argelina Figueiredo have been generous friends and valuable critics. David Fleischer, then chairman of Political Science at the Universidade de Brasília; José Alvaro Moisés, who was then director of CEDEC in São Paulo; and José Artur Gianotti, then president of CEBRAP in São Paulo, were cordial hosts while I did my research in those cities. I am grateful to the institutions they led at those times, all three of which provided office space, intellectual stimulation, and other assistance. I am also grateful to IUPERJ, which has long been one of my intellectual homes in Brazil.

CESOP (Center for the Study of Public Opinion), DataFolha, and IBOPE provided survey data. I am grateful to these institutions and to the individuals who granted me the access to the data: Rachel Meneguello, Antonio Manuel Teixeira Mendes, and Orjan Olsen, respectively.

During the long gestation of this book, many other Brazilians contributed to it. They include Maria Hermínia Tavares de Almeida, Regis de Castro Andrade, George Avelino, Alexandre Barros, Renato Boschi, Ruth Cardoso, José Murilo de Carvalho, Eli Diniz, Vilmar Faria, Pedro Jacobi, Maria D'Alva Gil Kinzo, Bolivar Lamounier, Fernando Limongi, Rachel Meneguello, Judith Muszynski, Orjan Olsen, João Paulo Peixoto, Rogério Schmitt, João da Silveira, Lícia Valladares, and Francisco Weffort. I am also grateful to some old friends who have supported my work in Brazil: Luis Alberto Gómez de Souza, Julia Guivant, Paulo Krischke, Hector Leis, Vanilda Paiva, and Eduardo Viola.

I learned a tremendous amount from Brazilian politicians. Without their assistance, I could never have come to understand many aspects of Brazilian party politics. I am thankful to all those who gave their time for interviews. Countless conversations with Antônio Kandir were especially enlightening.

Marta Assumpção, John Carey, Frances Hagopian, Mark Jones, Jairo Nicolau, Guillermo O'Donnell, Robert Packenham, David Samuels, Thomas Skidmore, Alfred Stepan, and Kurt Weyland read the entire manuscript and provided invaluable criticisms. Their suggestions helped me reorganize the book, clarify some fundamental arguments, and rethink key issues.

As an undergraduate, I had the good fortune to study with Juan Linz and Alfred Stepan, both of whom nurtured my interest in Latin America, in questions of authoritarianism and democracy, and in a scholarly career. As a graduate student, I had the privilege of working with Robert Packenham, who taught me much of what I know about method in political science. At Notre Dame, I have worked with Guillermo O'Donnell, whose seminal contributions on democracy and authoritarianism have inspired me. My gratitude to these four mentors is enduring.

I've had a wonderful group of colleagues, friends, and critics at Notre Dame and elsewhere. Peri Arnold and Michael Coppedge have been excellent colleagues. David Collier has been a generous friend in the scholarly community. Ralph Della Cava inspired and supported my early work. Richard Fagen was a source of support and intellectual stimulation during my graduate education. Robert Fishman made intellectual and personal life better through his combination of scholarship, friendship, and unfailing good humor. Frances Hagopian has been a constant source of support. Without her detailed and penetrating criticisms, the flaws in the book would have been magnified and the contributions lessened. Charles Kenney, Timothy Power, and Nancy Powers were at first fine graduate students, then careful critics. Daniel Levine inspired me with his excellent work and his encouragement. James McAdams has been a great friend, colleague, and critic. Martha Merritt added a keen intellect and good cheer to my scholarly community. Timothy Scully has been a close friend and collaborator. I learned a great deal from Matthew Shugart in our work on political institutions in Latin America. Samuel Valenzuela has been an excellent colleague and critic, as was Alexander Wilde during the years we worked together.

I am grateful to Timothy Power for granting me access to his survey information on the Brazilian congress and to Barry Ames and Timothy Power for giving me a database on roll call votes in the constitutional congress of 1987–88. Jairo Nicolau, David Samuels, and Rogério Schmitt provided electoral data, and Argelina Figueiredo gave me data on party switching in the post–1989 period.

Peri Arnold, Mark Beissinger, Marjory Castle, Larry Diamond, Vilmar Faria, David Fleischer, Charles Kenney, Andrew Gould, Robert Kaufman, Herbert Kitschelt, Kevin Krause, Mary Ann Mahony, James McAdams, Scott Morgenstern, Robert Moser, Joan Nelson, Timothy Power, Nancy Powers, Richard Rose, David Samuels, Rogério Schmitt, Ben Schneider, Timothy Scully, Matthew Shugart, Mariano Torcal, Joseph Tulchin, Samuel Valenzuela, and Deborah Yashar read parts of the book. Their criticisms improved it immeasurably.

Daniel Brinks, Kalaya Chareonying, Charles Kenney, Marcelo Leiras, Juan Esteban Montes, Aníbal Pérez-Liñan, and Timothy Power provided research assistance. Rod Ganey, Stalbek Mishakov, Aníbal Pérez-Liñan, and David Steele helped process data.

Since 1983, I have been a member of the Government Department and the Kellogg Institute for International Studies at the University of Notre Dame. Dual citizenship of this type can mean additional burdens without augmented rewards. In my case, dual citizenship has been rewarding. I am grateful to my colleagues in both of these "homes." The Kellogg Institute staff, especially Martha Sue Abbott, Bettye Bielejewski, Caroline Domingo, Dolores Fairley, and Joetta Schlabach, enabled me to accomplish more than I otherwise could have, and with greater cheer. The Institute's executive director, Ernest Bartell, offered support throughout the project.

I received funding from the Department of Education (Fulbright-Hays), the Institute for the Study of World Politics, the Hoover Institute, and the Woodrow Wilson International Center for Scholars. I am grateful to all these institutions. Of course, none of these sources of funding bears responsibility for the ideas in the book. During my fellowship years, Terry Karl, then director of the Center for Latin American Studies at Stanford, and Cynthia Arnson, Ann Sheffield, and Joseph Tulchin of the Woodrow Wilson Center, were gracious hosts. Muriel Bell, Peter Kahn, and Norris Pope of Stanford University Press provided support and good advice.

I am thankful that I had parents who encouraged my intellectual interests, my desire to learn about the contemporary world, and my commitment to contribute to understanding it. I am also fortunate to have two wonderful young children, Benjamin and Grace, who helped me forget about this book for a few hours every day, rediscover the joys of playing, and focus on family life. Rod and Dorothy Elfin have been great friends, in-laws, and—for my children—grandparents.

I dedicate the book with gratitude to my wife, Sue Elfin, who provided love, support, good cheer, and a sense of humor throughout the many years that I worked on this project. Thanks in good measure to her, life was rich and rewarding even when writing was difficult.

Parts of Chapter 10 were previously published in Chapter 2 of Scott Mainwaring and Matthew Soberg Shugart, eds., *Presidentialism and Democracy in Latin America* (New York and Cambridge: Cambridge University Press, 1997), 55–109, and are reprinted here with the permission of Cambridge University Press. Parts of Chapter 2 were published in the *Journal of Democracy* 9 (July 1998) and are reprinted here with the permission of The Johns Hopkins University Press.

S. P. M.

Contents

TABLES   xiii

ABBREVIATIONS OF THE MAIN POLITICAL PARTIES, 1979–96   xvii

Part I: Rethinking Party Systems Theory

1. Introduction   3

2. Reexamining Party Systems Theory in the Third Wave
    of Democratization   21

Part II: The Brazilian Party Systems, Past and Present

3. A Legacy of Party Underdevelopment, 1822–1979   63

4. Elections, Parties, and Society, 1979–96   88

5. Weak Parties and Autonomous Politicians:
    Party Organization in the Catch-All Parties   136

6. Patronage, Clientelism, and Patrimonialism   175

Part III: Explaining Weak Party-System Institutionalization

7. Macrocomparative Factors and Post–1964 Developments   221

8. Institutional Rules and Weak Institutionalization:
Incentives for Legislators 243

9. Institutional Rules and the Party System: Federalism,
Malapportionment, and Presidentialism 263

Part IV: The Party System, Economic Reform,
and the Quality of Democracy

10. Political Institutions, State Reform, and
Economic Stabilization 283

11. Conclusion 322

NOTES 345

BIBLIOGRAPHY 359

INDEX 381

Tables

2-1 Lower-Chamber Electoral Volatility in 26 Countries   29

2-2 Presidential Vote Compared with Lower-Chamber Vote,
     Concurrent Elections   30

2-3 Percent of Recent Lower-Chamber Vote for Parties
     Founded by 1950   32

2-4 Years Since Founding of Parties with 10 Percent of the
     Lower-Chamber Vote, 1996   34

2-5 Vote Intention in the 1994 Presidential Election   43

2-6 Vote in the 1989 Presidential Election   44

3-1 Difference Between Presidential and Vice-Presidential
     Vote, 1950–60   79

3-2 National Results for Legislative Elections, 1966–78 (Percent
     of Popular Vote)   86

4-1 Brazilian Economic Indicators, 1979–96   90

4-2 Lower-Chamber Seats Won by Party, 1982–94   96

4-3   Senate Seats Won by Party, 1982–94   97

4-4   Senate Seats Held by Party, 1982–94   98

4-5   Governorships Won by Party, 1982–94   99

4-6   Results of Presidential Elections, 1989 and 1994   105

4-7   Party Identification, 1989–94   113

4-8   Party Identification in the City of São Paulo, 1974–93   114

4-9   Party Identification and Voter Behavior, São Paulo Mayoral
       Election, 1985   116

4-10   Party Identification and Voter Behavior, 1989 Presidential
       Election, First Round   117

4-11   Vote Correlation by State, 1978–94   121

4-12   Party Vote by State Correlated with
       GDP Per Capita   122

4-13   Left-Right Location of Brazilian Parties, 1990 (by Members
       of the National Congress)   132

4-14   Ideological Self-location of Brazilian
       Deputies by Party, 1987   133

5-1   Party Discipline in the National Congress, 1988–94   139

5-2   Party Switching, 1987–90   143

5-3   Party Switching and Ideological Family,
       Federal Deputies, 1991–94   144

5-4   Politicians' Perceptions of Party vs.
       Individual Campaign Effort   148

5-5   Politicians' Perceptions of What Gets Them Elected   149

5-6   Electoral Alliances by State: Gubernatorial Elections, 1994
       (Number of States in Which One Party Supported Another)   158

5-7   Politicians' Loyalty to State vs. Party   160

5-8   Attitudes of Brazilian Legislators on Party Discipline
       (Percent Agreeing with Statement)   168

8-1   Reelection in the Brazilian Chamber of
       Deputies, 1978–94   245

9-1   Actual and Proportional Number of
       Congressional Seats by Region   268

9-2   Voting by Region in the Constitutional
       Congress, Select Issues   271

Abbreviations of the Main Political Parties,
1979–96

Left

PC do B   Communist Party of Brazil. A Stalinist party. Created in 1958 as a schism of the Brazilian Communist Party.

PT   Workers' Party. A heterogeneous leftist party, ranging from some revolutionary groups to social democrats. Created in 1979.

PCB   Brazilian Communist Party. Created in 1922. Renamed the Popular Socialist Party (PPS) in 1992.

PSB   Brazilian Socialist Party. An independent leftist party created in 1986. Has a lineage going back to the PSB of the 1946–65 period.

PPS   Popular Socialist Party. The new name adopted by the former PCB in 1992.

Center Left

PDT   Democratic Labor Party. A populist party with predominantly social democratic tendencies. Created in 1979.

PSDB   Party of Brazilian Social Democracy. Created in 1988 by a dissident group of the PMDB. Follows the line of social democracy.

Center

PMDB   Party of the Brazilian Democratic Movement. Its precursor, the MDB (Brazilian Democratic Movement) was created in 1966 as the official party of opposition to the military regime. Renamed the PMDB in 1979. Since its inception, the PMDB has been a heterogeneous party, but its hegemonic group is centrist. Many conservatives have flocked to the party since 1982.

Center Right

PTB   Brazilian Labor Party. In contrast to the PTB of the 1945–65 period, a predominantly center-right party. Created in 1979.

PDC   Christian Democratic Party. Created in 1985. More conservative than its counterpart Christian Democratic parties in many countries. Merged with the PDS in 1993 to form the PPR.

PP   Progressive Party. Created in 1993 through a merger of the PST and PTR. Merged with the PPR to form the PPB in 1995.

Right

PL   Liberal Party. A conservative party known for its antistatist discourse. Created in 1985.

PRN   Party of National Reconstruction. Created in 1989 by Fernando Collor de Mello as a vehicle for running for president. Virtually disappeared after Collor's impeachment in 1992.

PFL   Party of the Liberal Front. A conservative party created by dissidents of the PDS. It was officially founded in January 1985, but for all practical purposes the party was created in 1984.

PDS   Democratic Social Party. Despite its name, a conservative party. The PDS and its predecessor, Arena (1966–79) provided the partisan support for the military regime. Merged with the PDC in 1993 to form the PPR.

PPR Reformist Progressive Party. Created in 1993 by the merger of the PDS and the PDC. Merged with the PP to form the PPB in 1995.

PPB Brazilian Progressive Party. Created by the merger of the PPR and PP in 1995.

PRONA National Order Reconstruction Party. Far-right party with a populist leader, Enéas Carneiro.

Rethinking Party Systems in the
Third Wave of Democratization

THE CASE OF BRAZIL

PART I

Rethinking Party Systems Theory

CHAPTER 1

Introduction

Until the late 1970s, the world had only a few dozen democracies. Since then, their numbers have exploded, and many excellent analyses about the distinctive nature of what Huntington (1991) called "third-wave" (i.e., post–1974) democracies have been published. However, our thinking about party systems in the third wave has lagged behind the literature on the distinctive nature of third-wave democracies. This book attempts to address that lacuna and contribute to rethinking theories of party systems in the third wave.

Using the Brazilian case and broader comparative evidence to illustrate my claims, I argue that most third-wave party systems have distinctive features that require us to reformulate theories about party systems. Because the theoretical literature has been so dominated by scholars whose empirical referents were Western Europe or the United States, the variance in the kinds of party systems that have been the basis for most theoretizing has been limited. As a result, three key issues in the comparative analysis of democratic party systems have been obscured or underemphasized. These three points are developed in detail in Chapter 2; here a brief look forward at these arguments suffices.

First, typologies of party systems have relied significantly on Giovanni Sartori's seminal *Parties and Party Systems: A Framework for Analysis* (1976). Sartori proposed comparing democratic party systems along two main axes: the number of parties and the degree of ideological polarization. These two axes make for a parsimonious and fruitful means of comparing older democratic party systems, but when we turn to third-wave party systems, an equally apposite dimension is the degree of institutionalization. A weakly institutionalized system is characterized by considerable instability in patterns of party competition, weak party roots in society, comparatively low legitimacy of parties, and weak party organizations. Weakly institutionalized party systems function very differently from highly institutionalized systems, with important implications for democracy.

Second, since the 1960s, and especially since the influential work of Lipset and Rokkan (1967), one major approach to the study of party systems has emphasized the way they are shaped by social cleavages. Despite many challenges in recent decades, the social-cleavage approach remains important for studying Latin American party systems. This book argues, however, that the evidence suggests that the social-cleavage approach is inadequate for understanding most Latin American and third-wave party systems.

Finally, many third-wave cases underscore the need to pay more attention to the capacity of the state and political elites in structuring and restructuring party systems from above. Two approaches have dominated our thinking about how party systems form. One has underscored the ways in which social cleavages such as class, religion, and ethnicity shape them. Another emphasizes the impact of electoral rules.

Neither approach has paid sufficient attention to the role of the state and political elites in shaping party systems. Most often, political elites create parties to further their own ends, and state actors often dissolve party systems, fearing that they represent a threat. Of course, political elites need to win support from below to remain electorally viable, and in their quest to do so they win loyalties among different social sectors, just as the cleavages approach would suggest. But the sociological pattern of support for parties should not obscure who created them: political elites, often those in command of the state.

In the Brazilian case, it is impossible to understand the formation of party systems and the difficulties of institutionalizing them without paying careful attention to the role of political elites and state actors. This is true for many third-wave cases, but theories of party-system formation have not paid sufficient attention to the state and political elites.

The Brazilian Case

This book is about the party system and the process of democratization in Brazil, focusing primarily on the 1979–96 period. To be more specific, it is about the weakness of the party system and some ensuing problems of democratization. The Brazilian party system is weakly institutionalized, and the book explores the reasons for the difficulties of party building and addresses the impacts of weak institutionalization. In an age of some skepticism about the importance of parties, it reaffirms their central significance by looking at the consequences of weak institutionalization.

I make three central arguments related to the Brazilian case. First, the party system is weakly institutionalized. For a nation that has had considerable experience with democratic government and that has attained a medium per capita income level, Brazil is an exceptional case of party weakness (Lamounier and Meneguello 1986). Brazilian parties are fragile not only compared to those in the other middle-income countries of Latin America—Argentina, Chile, Colombia, Costa Rica, Mexico, Uruguay, and Venezuela—but even compared to some poor nations that have had less experience with democracy, such as the Dominican Republic. Parties have appeared and disappeared with stunning frequency.

With the exception of three electorally insignificant organizations, the oldest party (the centrist PMDB, Party of the Brazilian Democratic Movement) has existed only since 1966—and has had its current name only since 1979. There have been frequent discontinuities from one party system to the next, and since the 1830s, when the first parties of notables emerged, the nation has had seven distinct party systems. Parties have weak roots in society and limited legitimacy, and exercise little influence over congressional representatives. These indicators and many others spelled out in Chapters 3 and 4 suggest that Brazil is a fascinating case for exploring the dynamics, causes, and consequences of weakly institutionalized party systems.

Why is the Brazilian party system weakly institutionalized? This is the second major issue explored. This question inevitably leads one to the larger questions of why party systems form as they do, why they change over time, and why they institutionalize to varying degrees. In examining these issues, I emphasize three kinds of factors. First, structural factors profoundly shape party system formation. In Brazil, such factors were inimical to the creation of modern mass parties until 1945 and continue to pose obstacles to party-system institutionalization. Second, political elites and state actors organize parties to further their own interests. As Lamounier and Meneguello (1986) have argued, state action has been a decisive factor in shaping the formation of the party system in Brazil. The state has repeatedly shaped party-system formation from above, and it dissolved party systems in 1889, 1930, 1937, 1965, and 1979, with disruptive consequences in each case. Finally, formal institutional rules help explain the nature of the party system. In Brazil, political elites have deliberately engineered institutional rules that favor decentralized, comparatively undisciplined, and comparatively individualistic catch-all parties.

The third major issue is the impact of weak institutionalization, which together with widespread reliance on clientelism contributed to the problems of Brazilian democracy. Weak institutions made it difficult for presidents to organize political support through party channels. Instead, they relied extensively on patronage, which had corrosive effects on public administration and policy implementation.

Weak parties limited popular representation in the political system, thereby
helping to sustain an elitist polity. Individual politicians became the main vehicle
for representation; this pattern favored powerful elites with connections to those
politicians. The problems generated by weak parties also undermined democratic legitimacy and made it difficult to establish accountability through parties.
Accountability through elections depends on the ability of voters to reward or
punish individual politicians and/or parties. But where party labels change
frequently, where major parties disappear and others come on the scene, where
politicians switch parties with impunity, where party discipline is limited, and
where interparty electoral alliances are common but neither national nor enduring, electoral accountability through parties is hampered.

Finally, party weakness contributed to leadership problems in Brazilian politics. With a more institutionalized party system, neither President Collor (1990–
92) nor President Franco (1992–94) could have ascended to the presidency.
Elected as an antiparty political outsider, Collor's victory would have been
unthinkable in a democracy with strong parties, and Franco became president
only because Collor had been impeached. Both presidents encountered grave
difficulties. Collor resigned to avoid impeachment because of corruption, and
Franco accomplished little until the implementation of the Real Economic Plan
in July 1994, six months before he left office.

My contention that an institutionalized party system is important comes at a
time when growing numbers of citizens around the world are cynical about
parties, and when many scholarly analyses of parties have emphasized their
demise as political actors (Pizzorno 1981; Sartori 1989). It is especially important
in the Latin American context, where many presidents and policy makers have
seen parties not as institutions that should be strengthened, but as obstacles that
impede effective governance. Parties in many democracies face new challenges
and have lost some of their centrality in political life. Nevertheless, parties
remain critical actors in democratic politics, more so than is often appreciated,
and their weakness has important consequences.

The Brazilian case suggests that democracy is likely to have shortcomings if a
moderately institutionalized party system does not emerge after democratic
government has been in place for some time. "Strong" parties with sharply
defined ideologies and social bases are not necessary, but parties that develop
allegiances among citizens, organized groups, and politicians are essential for
democracy to work well. Even though many kinds of parties and party systems
can be compatible with democracy, an institutionalized party system is important.

Among the many countries that underwent transitions to democracy in the
1970s, 1980s, and 1990s, very few—in fact, probably only Russia—are as impor-

tant to the United States and the world as Brazil. The fifth-largest country in the world geographically and demographically, with nearly one-half the inhabitants of Latin America, Brazil has the ninth-largest economy in the world. Given its size and influence, whether Brazil is able to achieve stable democracy and economic growth will have a major impact throughout Latin America as a whole. Understanding democracy in Brazil is therefore a crucial task. That is what I try to do here, from the vantage point of political parties.

Theoretical Approach

I rely on three theoretical approaches to comparative politics: comparative macroanalysis, institutionalism, and rational choice. The first compares class structures, states, political regimes, and patterns of economic and political development across cases and time. It is crucial for understanding broad factors that shape political developments in a given country, and it constitutes the starting point for my analysis of why Brazil lagged behind so many countries in generating modern mass parties (Chapter 2). Comparative macroanalysis is indispensable for understanding the formation and weak institutionalization of the Brazilian party system.

I complement comparative macroanalysis with historical institutionalism. Its adherents believe that institutions are relatively autonomous of social actors and are important actors in political life. They help shape the formation of political actors; they create incentives that shape actors' behavior. One of the reasons for studying parties here arises from a conception that they and other institutions are indeed important. The book calls attention to the importance of political institutions in understanding how democracy functions and how political actors behave.

As March and Olsen (1989) note, institutionalism rests upon two fundamental claims. First, political institutions must be more than an expression of societal interests or cultural patterns. If political institutions were little more than that, as several theoretical perspectives suggest, then analysis should focus primarily on them and treat institutions as secondary or epiphenomenal. As opposed to perspectives that see politics as determined by economic, social, or cultural factors, institutionalism posits the *relative* autonomy of politics vis-à-vis such factors. Second, institutions must be major actors in shaping political life.[1]— otherwise, there would be little point to studying them. If these two claims are correct, institutions provide an excellent lens for studying politics.

In studying Brazilian parties, historical institutionalism is useful in three ways. First, during democratic periods, institutional patterns are important for understanding politics. Party patterns, for example, have had profound consequences for democratic governance, for what actors are privileged in democratic politics, and for the forms of accountability and representation that prevail.

Second, drawing on rational-choice variants of institutionalism, formal institutions create incentives for actors, including policy makers, to behave in different ways. They structure the rules of the game, creating parameters within which actors establish their behavior. They provide regularity, stability, and predictability in political life. For these reasons, institutions have far-reaching effects; for example, the electoral system, the system of government (presidential, parliamentary, etc.), party legislation and rules, and the unitary or federal nature of the system shape the contours of politics. Although this is far from the first study to call attention to these issues, it does so more emphatically than most previous works on Latin American politics.

Finally, as I argue in Chapter 10, institutional arrangements shape policy outputs. Institutional structures make policy more or less difficult to implement, encourage greater or less responsiveness by policy makers to different actors, and encourage politicians to be more or less responsive to different problems and opportunities. In brief, formal institutions have far-reaching effects on the process of democratization. They have distributional effects and can affect the capacity to cope with the complex policy agenda that confronts a new democracy.

Although many of the major tenets of systems institutionalism are compelling, the Brazilian case also suggests that the power of institutionalism as a framework is contextual. Institutionalism is less useful for understanding Brazilian politics in the pre–1945 period because formal institutions had relatively little autonomy vis-à-vis social actors. For example, parties were organized and controlled by local elites to defend their own interests (R. Graham 1990; Lewin 1987; Hagopian 1996). For this lengthy period of Brazilian history, studying these traditional elites, rather than the parties they forged and closely controlled, is more meaningful. Moreover, before 1945, formal political institutions did not have great political import.

This study departs from some institutionalists by stressing the mutual interaction and linkages between societal patterns and institutions. Although it rejects "sociological reductionism," that is, the view that institutions are merely reflections of social actors, it argues that institutions reflect social patterns in addition to shaping them. A recurring theme throughout the book is the way Brazilian society shaped party systems, as well as vice versa. Focusing exclusively on institutions as shapers of political life without looking at the mutual interaction between institutions and social patterns is problematic. Institutions are relatively autonomous with respect to economic interests, social patterns, and cultural norms, but it is important to emphasize the *relative* and varying nature of autonomy. It is therefore important to examine linkages between structural and ideational/cultural factors and formal institutions.

The third theoretical approach that informs this book is rational choice. Such theories posit rational, self-interested actors as the fundamental unit of analysis in politics. According to rational-choice approaches, actors choose what they believe are relatively efficient means to attain their ends.[2] Rational actors have a set of preferences, take into account the rules of the game, and choose means that maximize their ability to accomplish these preferences and minimize the cost of doing so. They strive for an optimum outcome given the rules of the game.[3] Rational-choice analysis has important confluences with institutionalism, so much so that some scholars have treated it as a variant of institutionalism. Some rational-choice scholars may be considered institutionalists in the sense defined above, while others do not fully fit this bill.

The utility and power of rational choice depend on the context and actors. Where the latter have clearly defined objectives and believe they have relatively good information on how to further their goals, their behavior approximates that specified in rational-choice models (Tsebelis 1990). Actors then have more information, more interest in accomplishing their objectives, and more to gain by a successful intervention. Tsebelis (1990) argues that "rational choice is a better approach to situations in which the actors' identity and goals are established and the rules of the interaction are precise and known to the interacting agents. As the actors' goals become fuzzy, or as the rules of the interaction become more fluid and imprecise, rational-choice explanations will become less applicable." Tsebelis (1990) and Katz (1980: 118–19) both conclude that the assumption of rationality is more reasonable when we deal with elites.

Under democracy, these conditions are reasonably approximated by Brazilian (and most other) politicians. More so than most political actors, politicians usually have reasonably clear, defined objectives, even if they are complex and at times competing. Most politicians seek some combination of promoting their own careers and attempting to win their preferred policy outcomes. Most have comparatively good information about how to secure their political objectives because they know the system and its players and they have detailed information about the world of politics. Politicians tend toward rational action in politics because they are professionals, have better-defined objectives, have more to gain and lose, and have more information. In order to enhance their careers and promote the kinds of policies they prefer, they have instrumental reasons to seek to be well informed. Under these conditions, rational-choice approaches help explain important aspects of how politicians function and what this implies for parties.

In this book, rational-choice analysis is used to help explain Brazilian party weakness. Institutional rules of the game have given politicians incentives to cultivate a personalistic relationship with the electorate, to focus on local constituencies, and to pay attention to state and local politics. Politicians who fail to pay attention to the incentives created by formal rules usually do so at their own peril.

Politicians have strong incentives to abide by some rules even if they can get away with violating others. To become candidates, get elected, and advance their political careers, politicians must obey certain rules. If party legislation states that politicians must sign a paper proclaiming their intention in order to become a candidate, it generally behooves them to do so. If candidate selection takes place through primary elections, politicians need to cultivate broad public support; conversely, if the party's national executive committee determines candidate selection even for local elections, they need to cultivate the support of the top party leadership. In a similar vein, the way a candidate campaigns depends on the electoral system. A candidate who played by single-member-district plurality rules, limiting his/her campaign to one circumscribed electoral district, would be at a disadvantage in a multimembered district with proportional representation.

One implication of a rational-choice approach is that the nature of parties depends to a considerable extent upon how politicians act (and therefore indirectly on the rules that govern candidate selection and elections). In the first instance, then, my unit of analysis is the individual politician, not the party. Even in highly disciplined parties where individual politicians are subservient to the leadership, the party is made up of individual politicians in the first instance. The individual behavior induced by incentives shapes the nature of parties because the rules that govern how elections are conducted and how candidates are chosen affect the relationship between politicians and parties. In brief, formal rules shape the extent to which parties control individual politicians, whether parties are disciplined or loose, and whether they are centralized or decentralized.

Rational-choice perspectives provide a powerful explanation of important aspects of the behavior of Brazilian politicians—and by extension, important features of the parties. Brazilian politicians in catch-all parties usually behave like self-interested actors whose behavior is shaped by formal rules of the political game. Such rules help explain the individualism of politicians, the decentralization of parties, the weakness of national parties, the lack of party discipline, and the limited allegiance of politicians to their parties.

On some points, rational choice provides better insights into Brazilian parties and politicians than historical institutionalism. Rational-choice theorists believe that people adhere to institutions for instrumental purposes. In contrast, historical institutionalists argue that people and groups develop identities and allegiances that may outlive the instrumental purposes that led them initially to support the institution. In this perspective, people may value institutions beyond the instrumental benefits they provide (Selznick 1957: 1–22; Pizzorno 1985). Individuals do not constantly reassess the rationality of values, beliefs, and norms once these are institutionalized. Consequently, rules and norms can endure well beyond the rational objectives that initially inspired them. According to this view, such rules and norms can lead actors to pursue behavior that is counterproductive from a narrow conception of rationality. Institutional rules and norms give meaning to actors and events, and such meaning may outweigh and indeed shape perceptions of rationality (Pizzorno 1985).

Although this claim of systems institutionalists is valid in contexts of strong, well-entrenched institutions, it is not particularly insightful for Brazilian party politics from 1985 to 1997. Instrumental attitudes toward parties prevailed. Neither politicians nor voters were loyal to parties once the parties did not suit their interests. Politicians switched parties when their interests so dictated; voters changed allegiance frequently. Contrary to the claims of systems institutionalists, actors were often not loyal to institutions beyond instrumental logic. Historical institutionalists overgeneralize in their expectation of institutional loyalty; the Brazilian case shows that such loyalty does not always develop. The insistence of systems institutionalists upon actors' enduring loyalty to institutions may often be valid, but this perspective is not suitable in such cases as Brazilian party politics, where allegiance to parties (except on the left) was thin.

Parties as a Vehicle for Studying Democratization

Since the emergence of mass democracy in the nineteenth century, parties have been the major agents of representation and "channeling" (Sartori 1976) in democratic politics. Despite new challenges to parties, despite a growing sense in the scholarly world that parties are less dominant agents of representation than they were decades ago, and despite growing citizen disaffection with parties in many countries, parties have continued to be the main agents of representation and are virtually the only actors with access to elected positions in democratic politics. They may have lost some of their functions, but they are still crucial because they dominate electoral politics. Democratic governments are elected through parties, and in many parliamentary systems (those in which postelection negotiations determine who governs) they are also elected by parties. The way parties function affects such vital questions as the nature of representation, the way policies are formulated, and the capacity for policy implementation. Therefore, studying parties is an excellent way to study how democracies function.

Even where they are comparatively weak, parties provide a fascinating way to study democratization for several reasons. First, party weakness has important consequences for democracy; weak parties have opportunity costs. Party patterns matter not only where they are strong and well institutionalized, but also in democracies where they are weak actors. Parties reveal much about the political system even when they are not well institutionalized.

Second, even weak parties are important actors in some ways. Parties have become so ingrained in democratic politics that we easily lose sight of this fact. Parties are important agents of representation, above all because they have greatest access to state power. Despite personalistic campaigns and the increasing importance of individual candidates and television in many democracies, parties almost universally matter in the electoral arena. With few exceptions, even where campaigns are individualistic rather than party-based, elections are organized around competing parties. Candidates run through a party and on a party label. In this formal sense, parties virtually monopolize access to elected positions in most democracies. These labels are somewhat meaningful to most candidates; they do not arbitrarily choose a party, even if they are not deeply committed to a particular party.

Parties are vehicles to policy-making positions. In almost all democracies, the most important policy-making officials are either elected through parties or appointed by elected officials. The growing importance of a direct relationship between politicians and the mass public, made possible by television and the modern media, has not radically altered this fact.

In virtually all democracies, party labels are also meaningful to many voters, even if they are not attached to a party. In Brazil, a significant minority (nearly one-half) of voters identify with a party, and most can associate diffuse images with the major parties. Voters rely to some extent on party labels to orient their conceptual universe, and political elites rely on symbols and organizational linkages to win the sympathies of citizens. It would be impossible to begin every election anew, with no established party labels, without shortcuts that tell the electorate who is who. Party labels offer such a shortcut: they say something important about a candidate, even in personalistic, internally heterogeneous, and comparatively undisciplined parties. Parties take positions on key issues rending a society, and by doing so put order into what would otherwise be a cacophony of dissonant conflicts. Parties help reduce the information costs of voting, making it easier for citizens with little time and political information to vote (Downs 1957). In short, electoral competition takes place not only among individuals but also among parties.

Notwithstanding their weakness, in one regard parties are even more important in Brazil than they are in most established democracies. More so than is the case in most early democratizers, in many third-wave cases, the state has had a pervasive influence and the political system is characterized by extensive clientelism. In clientelistic polities, winning state power gives one access to control over vast resources. Mechanisms for influencing the polity from society (interest groups and social movements) are weaker than in the advanced industrial democracies. For this reason, obtaining access to state power is more important than it is in the advanced industrial democracies. In order to effect change, winning elections is essential. Moreover, in such cases, political connections are needed to gain access to state privileges and favors.

Leaders of the governing parties in clientelistic polities have access to valuable resources. They can appoint people to powerful positions in the bureaucracy and they are in a position to extract public resources. Parties remain the most important agents of representation in democratic politics because they provide greatest access to state power. Because the state is so important in many third-wave cases, even in this era of state shrinking, parties are valued first and foremost as routes to state power.

Parties also help order legislative life and sustain legislative support for presidents and governors, although they do so less where party discipline and loyalty are weak than in democracies with more institutionalized party systems. Without parties or coalitions to organize legislative life, a legislature with hundreds of members of very different political convictions could not function. Moreover, even in cases of weak party discipline and loyalty, there are systematic differences in how the main parties take positions on legislative issues (Kinzo 1990; Limongi and Figueiredo 1995). Almost universally, party affiliations reveal much about the political predilections of legislators.

Party competition—who wins elections—has a macro impact greater than that produced by social movements or interest associations. Winning executive power sets the whole policy agenda; social movements and interest groups affect specific items on the agenda. Social movements and interest groups are geared toward more specific objectives than most parties. They usually have fairly specific demands targeted for a fairly specific population. For example, social movements may press for better public housing, paved streets, access to land, or more day-care centers. For reasons of collective action (Olson 1965), they usually are satisfied with a state response for their specific group rather than broad entitlements. Interest groups generally seek delimited measures to benefit a specific organized actor.

Parties have a broader agenda. Even if they are motivated primarily by vote getting, in order to win votes they need proposals about public policy issues.

Parties have broad policy proposals about government, whereas social movements and interest groups usually focus their demands on specific government agencies. Social movements and interest groups may support political candidates, but parties ultimately sponsor them. Parties do not usually directly act as policy-making bodies, but through elections they place into office politicians who determine public policy. Because parties place representatives in government positions, their impact is ongoing.

Parties are not only vehicles for representing citizens. Because of their centrality in the competition for state power, their presence encourages groups to organize along party lines. This explains why party sympathies divided many social movements and the union movement.

Parties are key actors in other respects. They are crucial for establishing democratic legitimacy, which depends upon the performance of parties and of representatives and executives who are elected through parties. Parties and politicians must reasonably deliver what citizens expect of democratic government. Although democratic governments may be able to survive in the short run even in the face of eroding legitimacy, in the long term, stable democracy is unlikely in the absence of legitimacy.

Parties are the most important groups for inducing political actors to make compromises and accept some losses. If parties exert a moderating influence, democratic stability is likely. Conversely, if parties exert a sharply polarizing influence, democracy may be imperiled (Sartori 1976; Sani and Sartori 1983). Parties are thus key in the effort to represent popular interests and generate legitimacy while simultaneously channeling demands in nonpolarizing ways (Levine 1973; Kornblith and Levine 1995).

In the medium term, parties are also important in enabling governments to govern with a modicum of efficacy. To the extent that parties promote good leadership, successful democratic government is enhanced. Moreover, governments need the support of parties to accomplish their policy agenda. If governments lack party support, they may undermine or bypass legislatures, make direct appeals to the people, or create new bureaucratic agencies through which they can carry out their programs. But such measures have high costs in terms of democratic institution building, subjecting democracy to antidemocratic proclivities. Thus democracy depends on what kind of parties and party systems emerge.

A final way in which studying parties illuminates key aspects of democratization shifts the unit of analysis to the party *system*. Party systems establish a range of what is likely to happen in democratic politics. Because political leaders are chosen through parties, the nature of party competition determines what kind of leadership can emerge. For example, the two U.S. parties are sufficiently moderate that radical leadership at the presidential level is unlikely. In contemporary Brazil, the nature of party politics also shapes what kinds of leaders can emerge. But here, given considerable ideological breadth in the party system,[4] the range of possible leaders and policies is broader. Thus party systems affect the logic of nonparty actors.

Party systems shape whether political competition is centrifugal or centripetal (Levine 1973; Sani and Sartori 1983; Sartori 1976; Valenzuela 1978). Where parties enjoy legitimacy, they are able to channel demands of competing interests into the electoral arena and party politics. In this way, parties can blunt and shape the aggregation and articulation of societal interests. Parties are the primary agents for competing for state power. If, therefore, they agree to democratic rules of the game and encourage centripetal competition, prospects for democracy are enhanced.

The way in which parties shape the political agenda—giving voice to certain interests and conflicts while simultaneously muting others—enhances or diminishes prospects for effective government and stable democracy. Party systems thus affect not only elite political interactions, but have an impact on public policy, and by implication, on how ordinary people fare in different political systems.

Parties and party systems, then, shape the political landscape of different societies. Not only do they reflect features of a society's social structure, economy, and culture, but they also mold the political process, and through it shape the social structure, economy, and culture (Sartori 1969; Przeworski 1985: 99–132). Parties and party systems are key actors in understanding how democracy works, and why it sometimes fails to work.

Organization of the Book

The book proceeds from the general to the specific and then returns to the general. Chapter 2 reexamines the literature on party systems in light of the third wave of democratization. Most major theoretical contributions to understanding party systems have used Western Europe and the United States as empirical referents. When we analyze less-institutionalized party systems, some new questions come to the fore. As noted above, Chapter 2 discusses three such questions.

Chapter 3 summarizes the evolution of Brazilian parties and political regimes from the 1830s to the end of the 1970s, and explains the weak institutionalization of party systems during that period. Chapters 4 and 5 provide the empirical basis for the claim that the Brazilian party system is weakly institutionalized for a nation that has attained Brazil's level of development. Chapter 4 underscores the high volatility of the party system, the weak roots of parties in society, and the limited legitimacy of parties and elections. Chapter 5 emphasizes the weakness of the national party organizations and the individualistic nature of the catch-all parties. Chapter 6 completes the portrait of the major features of the contemporary party system by examining the widespread use of patronage and its consequences.

Chapters 7 to 9 discuss the causes of weak party-system institutionalization in Brazil. Chapter 7 discusses long-term and post–1964 development that have contributed to weak institutionalization since 1985. Although they are a necessary part of the explanation of weak institutionalization in the post–1985 period, they do not provide a full explanation. We also need to examine political institutions that have fostered autonomy on the part of individual politicians, decentralization, and weak national parties. I undertake this analysis in Chapters 8 and 9. Chapter 8 examines the effects of electoral and party legislation. Open-list proportional representation, the overrepresentation of the poor states, decentralization of candidate selection, and the comparatively low degree of control by leaders over candidate selection have contributed to party weakness. Chapter 9 analyzes the effects of federalism, malapportionment, and presidentialism.

Chapters 10 and 11 analyze consequences of party patterns in Brazil. Chapter 10 argues that Brazil's political institutions make it difficult for presidents to implement sweeping policy reform; this issue is examined particularly with respect to state reform and stabilization policies. Chapter 11 assesses the consequences of weak party-system institutionalization, presenting some general hypotheses and then addressing the Brazilian case. The overall argument is that the nature of democratic politics hinges significantly on how institutionalized the party system is. Chapter 11 also addresses the broader implications of this study for institutional design in new democracies. Institutional engineering is not a panacea that can overcome all problems, but those designing institutions in new democracies should be aware of the desirability of rules that favor institutionalizing a party system.

The Research

The book draws upon extensive field research in Brazil. I did field research from July 1987 to July 1988, in Brasília and São Paulo, with follow-up trips in August 1992, August 1993, October 1995, and January 1997.

The research strategy reflected the belief that it was important to look at parties at the three different levels—national, state, and local—at which Brazilian parties and governments are organized, and at the connections between these levels. More than any other Latin American country, Brazil has a decentralized federal system. Political careers are made or fail largely because of a politician's success at the state and local levels. At the same time, it is important to examine parties at the national level, for that is where their activities have the greatest impact. Consequently, I spent seven and a half months in Brasília, which is the best place to study parties at the national level, and where interviews with politicians and policy makers from all over the country suggested the diversity of how state party organizations function. I also did eight months of research in the state of São Paulo, including some small municípios in the interior of the state. This experience enabled me to look more closely at how state and local party organizations function, a key issue because of the weakness of national parties and the decentralized nature of the parties.

It was essential to look at parties through the lenses of individuals in different positions. Consequently, I conducted thirteen interviews with (federal) senators, thirty-seven with federal deputies and three with ex-deputies, nineteen with state deputies, three with municipal council representatives, ten with party leaders who were at the time not holding an elected post, twelve with staff members, and fifteen with (mostly high-ranking) state bureaucrats and policy makers. The interviews were open-ended, largely because they provided more detailed information on themes about which little has been written. Interviews varied in length from twenty minutes to three hours; most lasted an hour to an hour and a half. Newspapers and weeklies supplemented the information in interviews.

To quantify information on some issues, I designed a short (twenty-one-question) survey, which yielded 107 responses from the 559 congressional representatives. The survey was conducted in Brasília in February 1988. Although the response rate was low (19 percent), for many purposes getting 107 responses was extremely revealing. I also used a 1990 congressional survey conducted by Timothy Power, who generously provided access to his results.

The Superior Electoral Court and secondary sources yielded electoral data, use of which is made in Chapters 3 and 4, documenting some of the basic patterns in Brazilian party politics. DataFolha, CESOP (Center for the Study of Public Opinion), and IBOPE provided survey data. Surveys provide much of the information for points on the weakness of linkages between citizens and parties, as well as information on how citizens perceive parties.

Barry Ames and Timothy Power graciously provided a database on roll-call voting during the 1987–88 constitutional assembly; it contained valuable information on party discipline. I gathered information from the Chamber of Deputies and PRODASEN (Senate Data Processing Service) on party affiliations of Brazilian politicians. I used well-organized archives of newspaper clippings on political parties at the library of the Chamber of Deputies in Brasília and at the daily newspaper *Estado de São Paulo*.

As will be apparent throughout the text, the extensive secondary literature on Brazilian parties, produced largely by Brazilians, was a rich source. This corpus now includes a number of distinguished works.

Although the book focuses primarily on Brazil, it addresses problems of party-system formation and (weak) institutionalization in comparative perspective. The theoretical and comparative literature on parties and party systems was valuable. Although we need to reexamine party systems theory in light of the third wave of democratization, my understanding of the Brazilian party system has been informed by extensive reading on the United States and Western Europe. The literature on party systems in the United States and Western Europe is more developed and extensive than that on Latin America; it can illuminate much about third-wave cases.

The book moves back and forth between two main units of analysis: parties and the party system. It also embraces two other units of analysis: individual politicians and democratic institutions. In countries with cohesive, disciplined, more or less unitary parties, one might be able to analyze the party system without discussing individual politicians. However, the catch-all parties in Brazil are marked by decentralization and federalism, weak organization, limited loyalty and discipline, and comparatively high individualism. Many issues in Brazilian parties are therefore best examined by looking at the behavior of individual politicians. The parties themselves—with the important exception of the leftist parties—are comparatively weak actors; individual politicians and factions are comparatively powerful. The book also examines the interaction between the party system and other institutional arrangements—above all, electoral and party legislation, presidentialism, and federalism.

The year 1979 is a logical starting point for detailed analysis. Changes in party and electoral legislation that year led to the extinction of the two-party system that the military government had imposed in 1966. After 1979, the party system gradually returned to the fragmented pattern that had characterized it in Brazil's earlier experiment with democracy from 1945 to 1964. Moreover, in 1979 President João Figueiredo, the last of five military presidents, assumed office. He announced that one of the major goals of his administration would be to restore democracy. Despite some setbacks and reversals, the country gradually continued its long path toward democracy under his administration. As part of this path, elections became more important than they had been under military rule. As a consequence, party politics became more important. Although most of the book focuses on the post–1979 period, the analysis of the causes of party underdevelopment deals with the post–1945 period.

The book focuses mostly on what Kirchheimer (1966: 184–200) called catch-all parties. Such parties attempt to cast their appeals for votes in sufficiently broad terms that they can capture the sympathies of broad segments of the population, rather than concentrating on winning the support of a particular class. In Western Europe these parties are products of the post–World War II period, when class divisions softened. They focus on electoral goals rather than seeing themselves as the embodiment and representative of a given class; this focus has led them to tone down their class-based rhetoric (Przeworski 1985; Przeworski and Sprague 1986). Instead of aggressively pushing for entitlements that benefit a particular class or group at the expense of others, catch-all parties generally focus on less conflictual issues that do not stir up such broad resistance among other groups and classes. They eschew polarizing ideological positions and seek access to a variety of interest groups rather than relying heavily on one. They organize mostly for elections and are typically "internally created," in Duverger's (1954) terms—that is, they are created by parliamentary elites rather than by extraparliamentary groups.

In the Brazilian case, there are compelling reasons to focus on the catch-all parties. They have dominated the electoral scene and will continue to do so for the near future. The major parties of the 1945–64 period were catch-all, known for their ideologically diffuse character, the breadth of the groups they represented, and their internal ideological and social heterogeneity. The exception was the Communist Party, but it was declared illegal in 1947 and did not have a major impact on the party system as a whole. Catch-all parties have also dominated the post-1979 period, despite the growth of the four leftist parties (the Workers' Party, PT; the Brazilian Communist Party, PCB/PPS; the Communist Party of Brazil, PC do B; and the Brazilian Socialist Party, PSB), which are not catch-all organizations. Even so, as it grew, the largest of the leftist parties, the PT, changed somewhat in the direction of the catch-all parties, particularly in the sense of becoming more ideologically diffuse (Novaes 1993; Rodrigues 1990: 7–33). The four biggest leftist parties combined never managed to elect 10 percent of the National Congress until 1994, when their combined total was 11.8 percent. Consequently, notwithstanding their importance in challenging dominant party patterns, they are exceptional actors in a system dominated by malleable parties.

Among the many parties that won more than a few seats between 1982 and 1996, all except the leftist parties and perhaps the center-left PDT (Democratic Labor Party) qualify as catch-all parties. Despite some ideological differences among those parties, in terms of their conception of what a party is, the weakness of national organizations, their internal heterogeneity, comparatively low discipline, decentralization and federalism, the weak loyalty of politicians to their parties, and their willingness to rely on clientelism and patronage, they have important similarities. In many ways, the PDT also qualifies as a catch-all party, but it is more disciplined. Hence, it is not included in all generalizations about the catch-all parties. Because those parties have dominated electoral politics, they provide a good way of understanding mainstream politics in Brazil.

A final reason for focusing on such parties is that scholars have paid more attention to Brazil's leftist parties, which were electorally insignificant until 1985,[5] than to the catch-all parties. There are few works on the catch-all parties, and most of them focus on the 1945–64 period. In contrast, the literature on the communist parties is abundant, and more has been written about the Workers' Party than any other except the communist parties. The volume of literature on the communist parties and the PT, and the paucity on the catch-all parties, reflects a bias among social scientists and historians working on Latin America to study movements and parties of the left while paying less attention to those of the center and right. Yet the history of most Latin American countries, including Brazil, suggests compelling reasons to focus more on parties that block radical change than on those that have worked for it. Radical change has been the exception rather than the norm, and it has most often taken place through revolutionary movements that did not initially come to power through elections.

CHAPTER 2

Reexamining Party Systems Theory in the Third Wave of Democratization

Political parties created modern democracy and modern democracy is
unthinkable save in terms of the parties.
— E. E. Schattschneider (1942: 1)

The theoretical and comparative literature on parties and party systems
has been dominated by analyses of Western Europe and the United States. This
literature on the advanced industrial democracies has made major contributions
that are relevant for understanding party systems in what Huntington (1991)
called the "third wave" of democratization. But we cannot merely transport to
the study of third-wave party systems approaches that have been used in Western
Europe without paying attention to differences between party systems in old,
established democracies and those in new, unconsolidated regimes. These differences can be used to ask new questions that theoretically advance our thinking
about comparative party systems. Despite major advances in the work on
third-wave party systems in the past twenty years, little effort has been undertaken to rethink theories about party systems.

Three important issues related to our understanding of party systems need to
be rethought in light of the experience of new democracies around the world.
First, political scientists need to incorporate variance in institutionalization into
the comparative analysis of party systems. Weakly institutionalized party systems function differently from well-established systems, with significant implications for democracy. Yet political scientists have paid comparatively little
attention to this issue.

Second, the well-established social-cleavage approach explains some party
systems better than others, and its explanatory power varies over time. There
are reasons to expect that this approach will be less powerful in most third-wave
democracies than it was in the first-wave cases. The social-cleavage approach is
predicated on the idea that social identities such as class, religion, ethnicity, and
region provide the basis for common interests and thereby create enduring
partisan sympathies. In many new democracies, however, social classes are less

organized and more fragmented than was the case decades ago in earlier democracies. Not only are the party systems structured less by social cleavages, they are generally less structured than party systems in the earlier democracies.

The value of the social-cleavage approach has declined in recent decades as a tool for understanding Western European party systems, and in this sense there appears to be a convergence between party-systems theory based on the old democracies and the reality of the new ones. The power of social-cleavage approaches, however, remains greater for most Western European cases than for most third-wave cases. Moreover, whereas in Western Europe, new postmaterial values, especially among well-educated voters, represent the dominant cause of the waning predictive capacity of the social-cleavage model, in the third-wave democracies, other factors account for the difficulties in applying this theoretical approach.

Finally, many third-wave cases suggest that we need to pay more attention to the capacity of the state and of political elites to reshape party systems from above. Most important approaches to party system formation—social cleavage and spatial—have emphasized how society structures party systems from below. Third-wave cases show that we must be more attentive to examining how the state and political elites have shaped party systems from above. By suppressing parties and party systems, and by deliberately creating new ones, the state can decisively recast a party system. Political elites can alter party systems from above in a variety of ways, such as changing parties and inducing mergers and schisms.

Party-System Institutionalization

In thinking about party systems in new democracies, the notion of party-system institutionalization is crucial.[1] In order to explain why, a brief synthesis of the current wisdom on comparing and classifying party systems is appropriate. The most influential formulation comes from Giovanni Sartori's seminal *Parties and Party Systems: A Framework for Analysis* (1976). Sartori saw two dimensions of party systems as particularly important: the number of relevant parties and the degree of ideological polarization. In counting parties, Sartori included those that have "coalition potential," that is, that might form part of a governing coalition, as well as parties whose existence affects the tactics of party competition. His measure of ideological polarization, most clearly operationalized in Sani and Sartori (1983), focuses on the ideological distance among parties, that is, the breadth of ideological conflict. Using these two dimensions, his typology includes four types of democratic party systems: two-party, moderate pluralism (multipartism with low ideological polarization), polarized pluralism (multipartism with considerable polarization), and predominant (in which the same party consistently wins a majority of seats). Sartori also analyzed two kinds of nonde-mocratic systems, but they are of less concern here.

Although Sartori's work has been challenged in a variety of ways (e.g., I. Daalder 1983, Santos 1986), it is still the single most important broad theoretical treatise on party systems. His two dimensions for classifying party systems remain highly influential; his typology is still the most useful for classifying party systems in the advanced industrial democracies, even though the Laakso and Taagepera (1979) "effective number of parties" has superseded Sartori's less clearcut rules for counting parties.[2] Many other analysts (e.g., Blondel 1968, Duverger 1954) have focused primarily on the number of parties in their classi-fications of party systems.

In regions where democracy is not consolidated, the problem with classifying party systems mostly according to the number of parties is that it overlooks substantial differences in the level of institutionalization of the party systems, and hence in how democratic politics functions. Treating all multiparty systems as an undifferentiated category when there are vast differences in institutionali-zation is misleading. Brazil and Sweden have multiparty systems, but that in Sweden is much more institutionalized than the Brazilian variant. Lumping together all cases of multipartism conceals profound differences in the nature of the systems. Most of the literature has not recognized this fact; Sartori was one of the few analysts who did, but he failed to conceptualize it adequately.

The differences between democracies with more-institutionalized and those with fluid party systems are significant. Institutionalized party systems structure the political process to a high degree. In fluid systems, parties are important actors in some ways, but they do not have the same structuring effect. Assessing or comparing party systems among contemporary democracies without refer-ence to the level of institutionalization misses an aspect of party systems as important as the number of parties. If we restrict the analysis to the advanced industrial democracies, there is much less variance in levels of institutionaliza-tion than if we include democracies outside that restricted set. Therefore, there is less need to incorporate an analysis of party system institutionalization for these cases. However, since the third wave of democratization began in 1974, an increasing number of the world's democracies have been in intermediate- and low-income countries, many of which have fluid party systems. A broader effort to classify party systems must incorporate the crucial dimension of institution-alization, yet this dimension remains undertheorized in comparative politics.

This is not to suggest that the number of parties and the ideological distance are irrelevant criteria in comparing, analyzing, and classifying party systems. Rather, in comparing and classifying party systems beyond the advanced industrial democracies, we need to pay attention to the level of institutionalization in addition to Sartori's two dimensions.

A system is a combination of interrelated parts that interact in a patterned way to form a complex whole. A party system, then, is the set of parties that interact in patterned ways. The notion of patterned interactions suggests that some rules and regularities in how parties compete are widely observed, even if these rules and regularities are contested and undergo change. The idea of a system also implies continuity in the components that form the system. If there is a sharp discontinuity in the component parts, a different system has displaced the previous one.

A party system has three boundaries beyond which it becomes questionable to use this term. With extreme party-system volatility, such that the major parties in one election cease to exist in the next, it may be meaningless to speak of a system. Under these circumstances, it is doubtful that the parties interact in a patterned way. Such cases are unusual, but Russia in the 1990s and Peru in the first half of that decade approximated this condition. Second, in cases of extreme personalism, where parties have little control over who gains access to political office and where many politicians are not affiliated to a party, it is doubtful that a system exists. In such regimes, political competition revolves around personalities rather than parties; the latter are of secondary importance for most voters and many candidates. Conaghan (1996) contends that Peru since 1992 is such a case and that is a no-party system. Third, as Sartori (1976) has observed, a system must consist of at least two parts; it is an oxymoron to speak of a one-party system. In cases of a single party, it is more appropriate to speak of a party-state system.

Although my definition of a party system draws upon Sartori's (1976: 43–44), my understanding of the boundaries of this concept differs from his. Sartori uses the notion in a more restricted way. For example, he argued (1976: 185) that Colombia did not have a party system, and his introduction to the Brazilian edition of his book stated that Brazil did not have one either.

Sartori is hinting at an interesting insight because the Colombian and Brazilian systems differed substantially from those in the advanced industrial democracies. But it distorts the case to say that these countries did not have party systems. The Colombian system had two major parties (Liberals and Conservatives) that had dominated electoral competition since the nineteenth century, and patterns of competition between them exhibited considerable regularity. Electoral volatility (the turnover from one party to others, from one election to the next) has been modest for decades. Moreover, Colombian parties have long been well rooted in the electorate, and they have been important political actors (Archer 1995). Similarly, both between 1946 and 1964 and 1966 and 1979, Brazil's parties met the fundamental requirements of the notion of system. There were patterned interactions in the competition among parties; the number of parties and the parties themselves were reasonably constant; the electoral strength of the parties changed over time, but not by dramatic leaps and bounds; and parties won electoral support on the basis of distinctive and patterned social bases. If cases with high continuity in the main parties and moderate electoral volatility do not have party systems, by implication, presumably most third-wave democracies would not have systems because Colombia and Brazil (1945–64) had more institutionalized systems than most third-wave cases. Contrary to Sartori's view, wherever open-party competition exists for even a few years, a system almost always develops as politicians find it useful to create a label that helps establish a symbolic universe for voters and helps organize legislative affairs. Only in exceptional cases of fluidity, personalism, and volatility do the properties that define a system virtually cease to exist.

Rather than follow Sartori's restrictive notion of system and his dichotomous distinction between systems and nonsystems, this analysis focuses on different levels of institutionalization. *Institutionalization* refers to a process by which a practice or organization becomes well established and widely known, if not universally accepted. Actors develop expectations, orientations, and behavior based on the premise that this practice or organization will prevail into the foreseeable future. In politics, institutionalization means that political actors have clear and stable expectations about the behavior of other actors. In Huntington's words, "Institutionalization is the process by which organizations and procedures acquire value and stability" (1968: 12).

An institutionalized party system, then, is one in which actors develop expectations and behavior based on the premise that the fundamental contours and rules of party competition and behavior will prevail into the foreseeable future. In such a system, there is stability in who the main parties are and how they behave. Institutionalization does not completely preclude change, but limits it.

Implicitly, Sartori sees institutionalization (though he uses the term "structural consolidation" instead) as a dichotomy: either a system is structurally consolidated, and relatively few systems are, or it is not a system. Yet nothing in the definition of a system implies such a rigid demarcation of boundaries. At a time when most of the world's democracies have less-institutionalized party systems, seeing them as nonsystems, as not amenable to comparison with the established democracies, would represent a loss. Party-system institutionalization, then, is most usefully conceptualized along a continuum.[3]

The notion of institutionalization should not be teleological, nor is the process linear; there is no necessary progression from weak to greater institutionalization. Party systems can deinstitutionalize—the Italian, Canadian, Peruvian, and

Venezuelan cases in the 1990s serve as examples. Institutionalization need not rest on any particular kind of party. It can occur in systems with comparatively loose parties, as in the United States, or with programmatic, ideological parties, as in some Western European countries. As Kitschelt (1995) has argued, institutionalization can occur through programmatic positions or through clientelism.

Although weak institutionalization is typically associated with a variety of problems, this does not imply that extreme institutionalization is positive. On the contrary, very high levels of institutionalization may result from a stultified party system. The relationship between party-system institutionalization and the quality of democracy, then, is far from linear (Schedler 1995). An institutionalized party system is hardly a panacea.

Dimensions of Party-System Institutionalization

There are four dimensions of party-system institutionalization. First, more-institutionalized party systems enjoy considerable stability (Przeworski 1975); patterns of party competition manifest regularity. A system in which major parties regularly appear and then disappear or become minor parties is not well institutionalized.

Second, in more-institutionalized systems, parties have strong roots in society. Linkages between parties and citizens are stable; otherwise, parties do not structure political preferences over time and there is limited regularity in how people vote. Strong party roots in society help provide the regularity in electoral competition that institutionalization implies. In fluid or less-institutionalized party systems, more citizens have trouble locating what the major parties represent, and fewer identify with parties. Similarly, linkages between organized interests and parties are generally more developed than in fluid systems.

As a consequence of these linkages between parties and their constituencies, parties within more institutionalized systems tend to be consistent in their relative ideological positions. A party that is markedly to the left of another party does not suddenly move to the right of it simply to gain short-term electoral advantage: parties are constrained by their need to maintain a faithful following (Kitschelt 1989: 1–8, 41–74). If major parties change their relative ideological position, it implies weak ties between parties and society and a lack of regularity in the process of how parties compete and how they relate to social actors.

Third, in a more-institutionalized system, political actors accord legitimacy to parties. They see them as a necessary part of democratic politics even if they are critical of specific parties and express skepticism about parties in general. Where citizens believe that parties are a core institution of democratic politics, there is a greater likelihood of system stability.

Finally, in a more-institutionalized system, party organizations matter. Parties are not subordinated to the interests of a few ambitious leaders; they acquire an independent status and value of their own. Institutionalization is limited as long as a party is the personal instrument of a leader or a small coterie. The party becomes autonomous vis-à-vis individuals who initially may have created the party for instrumental purposes. It is a sign of greater system institutionalization if party structures are firmly established, are territorially comprehensive, are well organized, and have resources of their own. In more institutionalized systems, there is a routinization of intraparty procedures, including procedures for selecting and changing the party leadership (Panebianco 1988: 53–65; Janda 1980: 19–28, 98–107).

Peaceful transfer of the leadership from one person or a small coterie to a different group indicates a process of institutionalization. The Mexican PRI, in which the president dominated the party but in which there was turnover in the presidency and frequently in the party leadership every six years, reflects a form of institutionalization; the period during which a particular individual dominated the party was clearly defined. Conversely, cases such as Alberto Fujimori's Cambio 90 in Peru, Fernando Collor's Party of National Reconstruction in Brazil, or Perón's Justicialist Party in Argentina, in which a single leader created and continued to dominate a party, manifest weak institutionalization.

Party-system institutionalization implies a commitment to an organization and to some minimal collective goals (especially winning elections); it requires loyalty beyond allegiance to a single leader. In more-institutionalized systems, few politicians change parties, nor do they publicly evince support for candidates of other parties.

These four dimensions of institutionalization need not go together, but they almost always do. Conceptually, a party system could be fairly institutionalized along one dimension but weakly institutionalized along another, but empirically this is the exception.

Party systems characterized by a lower degree of institutionalization can be termed fluid. This implies less regularity in patterns and rules of party competition, weaker party roots in society, less legitimacy accorded to parties and elections, and weaker party organizations, often dominated by personalistic leaders.

COMPARING LEVELS OF INSTITUTIONALIZATION:
ELECTORAL VOLATILITY

To develop the argument that contemporary democratic party systems differ in profound ways that cannot be captured by Sartori's typology, let us compare some cases of Western Europe, Southern Europe, East Central Europe, and Latin America according to the four criteria of institutionalization proposed earlier.

The data show sharp differences in the degree to which party systems are institutionalized. These differences have important implications for democratic politics.

The first criterion of institutionalization, that patterns of party competition manifest regularity, is easy to measure and compare through an index of electoral volatility. Electoral volatility refers to the aggregate turnover from one party to others from one election to the next (Przeworski 1975; Pederson 1983). It is computed by adding the net change in percentage of votes gained or lost by each party from one election to the next, then dividing by two. For example, in a two-party system, if Party A wins 43 percent in the first election and 53 percent in the second while Party B declines from 57 percent to 47 percent, volatility equals 10 + 10 divided by two, or ten.

Table 2.1 shows patterns of electoral volatility for democratic lower-chamber elections in 1945–96 for several third-wave and established democracies. Only the most recent democratic period is counted in countries in which there was a democratic breakdown. Excluding earlier democratic periods enables us to ascertain whether third-wave cases usually have distinctive party systems.

There are stark differences between the more- and less-institutionalized cases. Volatility is much higher in most of the Latin American and post-Soviet cases than in the established democracies. Party systems range from very stable (the United States, Switzerland, Finland, and Sweden) to extremely volatile (Bolivia, Brazil, Ecuador, Peru, Poland, and Russia). In the United States, on average, if we used election results in one election to predict results of the next, we would err by only 4.0 percent of the aggregate vote. In Peru, following the same procedure, the error would be almost fifteen times greater (58.5 percent). These dramatic differences in the stability of patterns of party competition are related to significant differences in democracy that are explored in Chapter 11.

PARTY ROOTS IN SOCIETY

In more-institutionalized party systems, parties develop strong and stable roots in society. Where parties have strong roots in society, most voters feel connected to a party and regularly vote for its candidates. Organized interest groups frequently support a party and may be organized by party leaders.[4]

Party roots in society and electoral volatility, while analytically separable, are intertwined because strong party roots in society limit electoral volatility. If most citizens support the same party from one election to the next, there are fewer floating voters, hence less likelihood of massive electoral shifts that are reflected in high volatility. Conversely, where parties have weak roots in society, there are more independent voters, hence more voters who are more likely to shift electoral allegiances from one election to the next, thus bringing about greater potential for massive electoral volatility.

TABLE 2-1
Lower-Chamber Electoral Volatility in 26 Countries

Country	Time span	No. of electoral periods	Mean volatility	Country	Time span	No. of electoral periods	Mean volatility
United States	1944–94	25	4.0	Argentina	1973–95	7	18.8
Switzerland	1947–95	12	4.7	Costa Rica	1953–94	10	22.9
Finland	1945–95	14	7.8	Mexico	1988–94	2	22.4
Sweden	1944–94	16	8.5	Chile	1973–93	2	23.4
Uruguay	1971–94	3	10.4	Slovakia	1990–94	2	26.5
Belgium	1946–95	16	11.0	Venezuela	1958–93	7	27.4
Colombia	1970–94	6	11.2	Czech Rep.	1990–96	2	29.2
Norway	1945–93	12	11.2	Poland	1991–93	2	31.4
Italy	1946–96	13	12.0	Brazil[a]	1982–94	4	33.0
Portugal	1974–93	8	15.2	Bolivia	1979–93	4	34.5
Greece	1974–93	6	15.5	Ecuador	1979–96	4	38.6
Spain	1974–93	6	16.3	Russia	1993–95	2	54.0
France	1945–93	14	18.3	Peru	1980–95	3	58.5

SOURCES: Data about Latin America come from Nohlen 1993; *Statistical Yearbook of the Republic of Argentina*, Vol. 10, 1994 (Buenos Aires: INDEC); Argentina 1995, legislative, Mark Jones, personal communication, Argentina 1995, presidential; from many articles in the *Boletín Electoral Latinoamericano* (San José: Instituto Interamericano de Derechos Humanos); Bolivia 1993, René Mayorga, personal communication; Brazil 1994, *Folha de São Paulo*, November 16, 21, 1994; Ecuador 1996, provisional results published on the World Wide Web by Emerinfo at "http://mia.lac.net/opcion96/resultados/exit-dipn.htm"; Paraguay 1993. Diego Abente, personal communication; Peru 1995, official results published on the WWW at "http://ekecorp.net.pe/jne"; and Venezuela 1993, parliamentary elections in Venezuela, on the WWW at "http://www.universal.nl/users/derksen/election." Data for Europe and the United States come from Mackie and Rose (1991). For updates after 1991 and for data on Russia and Poland, see several issues of the *European Journal of Policy Research*. Data for Slovakia and the Czech Republic were provided by Kevin Krause, personal communication. Data on 1995 and 1996 come from the "Parliamentary Elections around the World" page on the WWW (http://www.universal.nl/users/derksen/election).

NOTE: Calculations of volatility have followed five rules: (1) In cases of splits in a party, the faction that wins the larger share of the vote in the next election is generally considered the continuation of the old party. The exception is when the smaller party retains the original name. The other faction is considered new. (2) The reverse applies to mergers. The smaller merging party is considered to have disappeared in the next election. (3) Formal alliances are treated as a combination of the allied parties. Volatility is calculated by comparing their combined share in the last election in which they participated separately with their share in the current election. (4) When changes of name did not arise from mergers or result in splits, the newly named party was considered to be the same as the party with the old name. (5) In countries with two-round voting, only first-round results have been taken into account.
[a] Data for Brazil correspond to seats because complete data in votes were not available for some elections.

Where parties are deeply rooted in society, most voters support the same party over time and in different kinds of elections. Surveys and voting data provide indications of the extent to which voters cast their ballot on a partisan basis (and hence the extent to which parties are rooted in the electorate). Parties are more rooted if most voters say that they voted or intend to vote for candidates of the same party in consecutive elections.

Similarly, data from the local to the national level may indicate congruence or divergence between voting patterns for one position and another. For exam-

TABLE 2-2

Presidential Vote Compared with Lower-Chamber Vote, Concurrent Elections

Country	Time span	No. of elections	Mean difference	Country	Time span	No. of elections	Mean difference
Mexico	1982–94	3	3.2	Venezuela	1973–93	5	12.3
Peru	1980–95	4	9.7	Chile	1989–93	2	15.3
United States	1944–92	13	10.3	Colombia	1974–94	6	16.3
Paraguay	1989–93	2	10.4	Ecuador	1978–96	4	25.9
Argentina	1973–95	4	10.9	Brazil	1994	1	44.1
Costa Rica	1970–94	7	11.0				

SOURCES: See Table 2-1.
NOTE: The absolute values of the differences between shares of the presidential and lower-chamber vote that each party got are added and the sum divided by two.

ple, the difference between presidential and legislative voting provides relevant information in assessing how deeply parties penetrate society. Where parties shape the political preferences of most voters, this difference should be less pronounced, other things being equal.[5] Citizens vote more frequently on the basis of party labels, and therefore they tend to vote for the same label in legislative and presidential elections. Table 2.2 shows the mean difference between the percentage of lower-chamber votes won by parties and their percentage in presidential elections. Table 2.2 is limited to concurrent presidential and lower-chamber elections because the dynamics in nonconcurrent ones predictably differ (Shugart and Carey 1992: 226–58), with a tendency toward a higher aggregate difference between presidential and legislative voting.

Widespread ticket splitting also tends to indicate weak party roots in society. This indicator is useful primarily for presidential or semipresidential systems because some parliamentary systems afford no possibility of splitting the national ticket.[6] In the United States, since 1976, 25 percent of voters have split their ticket at the national level. In contrast, surveys indicated that in Russia, 70 percent of voters planned to split their tickets in the 1993 national elections (White, Rose, and McAllister 1997: 139).[7]

The percentage of respondents who report having a party preference also helps us assess the extent to which parties are deeply rooted in society. The data show a chasm between most of the advanced industrial democracies and most of the third-wave democratizers, excluding Greece and Uruguay, where party identification approaches that of most of Western Europe. In most Western European countries, 60–70 percent of voters identify at least somewhat with a party (H. Schmitt 1989), though this figure has declined in recent decades. According to White, Rose, and McAllister (1997: 135), only 22 percent of respondents in Russia report identifying at least somewhat with a party. Elsewhere,

Rose (1995: 22) gives figures of 80 percent reporting a party preference in England compared to 40 percent for the Czech Republic, 30 percent for Slovakia, 20 percent for Hungary, and only 15 percent for Poland. Rose (1995) talks of demobilized voters in East Central Europe, referring to individuals who have no preferred party and don't trust parties; such voters form the majority in the entire region.

In southern Europe, in 1989, party identification figures ranged from a low 30 percent in Spain to 63 percent in Italy (H. Schmitt 1989: 183–84). In Latin America, according to Latinobarometro data (see Lagos 1996 for details), the eight countries for which data are available (Argentina, Brazil, Chile, Mexico, Paraguay, Peru, Uruguay, and Venezuela) had a considerable range in the share of party identifiers, from 67.1 percent of respondents in Uruguay to under 40 percent in Argentina (37.6 percent), Chile (35.9 percent), Venezuela (33.3 percent), and Brazil (32.5 percent). In a 1995 poll in Lima, Peru, only 20 percent of respondents said they identified with a party (Conaghan 1996: 22). In sum, in virtually all of the advanced industrial democracies, most voters have a party preference, whereas in many third-wave democracies, the great majority do not.

The ability of parties to survive a long time provides one indication that they have probably captured the long-term loyalties of some social categories. Although major parties could in theory survive a long time by consistently winning the support of independent voters, this prospect is unlikely. Consequently, in more institutionalized systems, parties are likely to have longer organizational histories than in cases of lower institutionalization. Table 2.3 shows the percentage of the vote in the most recent lower-chamber elections that was captured by older parties, with 1950 as the somewhat arbitrarily chosen cutoff point to define an older party. The analysis was stringent for assessing whether a party has existed since 1950. A party could change its name, but only if there were clear organizational continuity. When a party that existed in 1950 experienced later schisms, only one (as a rule the larger) of the offspring is counted as having existed in 1950.

Once again, the contrasts are stunning. In the 1994 U.S. elections, parties that were created by 1950 captured 97.2 percent of the vote; Norway (90.0 percent), Sweden (88.7 percent) and Finland (82.3 percent) were close behind. In contrast, few pre–1950 parties in Bolivia, Brazil, Ecuador, and Peru are still electorally important. In Peru, only one party created by 1950, APRA, ran in the 1995 elections, capturing a feeble 4.1 percent of the lower-chamber vote. Table 2.3 excludes the post-Soviet cases because the long period of communist rule made it more difficult for older parties to survive (Cotta 1994). Still, the rapidity with which parties have appeared and disappeared in Russia and Poland is notable. Moser (1995: 10) observes that "of the thirteen electoral blocs participating in the

TABLE 2-3
Percent of Recent Lower-Chamber Vote for Parties Founded by 1950

Country	Parties founded by 1950	Election year	Pct. of vote
United States	Democratic, Republican	1994	97.2
Norway	Liberal, Conservative, Labour, Centre, Christian People's	1993	90.0
Sweden	Social Democrat, Moderate Unity, Centre, Left, People's	1994	88.7
Finland	Social Democrat, Swedish People's, Centre, National Coalition, Left-Wing Alliance	1995	82.3
Paraguay	Colorado-Asociación Nacional Republicana, PRLA	1993	80.2
Switzerland	Christian Democrat, Liberal, Conservative, Radical Democrat, Social Democrat, Swiss People's	1995	76.6
Mexico	PRI, PAN, PPS, PARM	1994	75.1
Colombia	Liberal, Conservative	1994	72.1
Argentina	Radical, Justicialist, PDP, PDM, PAL, PB	1995	69.1
Uruguay	Colorado, Nacional	1994	61.2
Belgium	Christian People's, Liberty and Progress, Francophone, Socialist, Flemish Socialist, Volksunie, Christian Socialist[a]	1995	60.0
Venezuela	AD, Copei	1993	56.7
France	Socialist, Communist, Conservative, Gaullist	1993	52.7
Spain	Socialist, Communist (United Left), Catalan, Republican Left, Basque Nationalist	1996	50.1
Costa Rica	Partido Liberal	1994	44.7
Chile	Radical, Socialist, Christian Democrat	1993	42.1
Bolivia	MNR	1993	36.2
Italy	PDS (former PCI)	1996	21.1
Brazil	PDT, PTB-PSB	1994	12.8
Ecuador	PLRE, PCE	1996	9.6
Greece	Communist Party of Greece	1993	4.5
Peru	APRA	1995	4.1

SOURCES: Nohlen 1993; Mackie and Rose 1991. For updates after 1991 see the *European Journal of Political Research*. Data on 1995 and 1996 are from the "Parliamentary Elections around the World" page on the World Wide Web (http://www.universal.nl/users/derksen/election).

[a] The Christian People's and Christian Social parties emerged from a split in the Catholic party in 1968. The French and Flemish Socialist parties are the product of a split in the Socialist party in 1978. For purposes of this table, they are considered to be continuations of their predecessors rather than new parties.

1993 parliamentary elections only four existed under the same label a year earlier."

Again excluding the post-Soviet cases, Table 2.4 looks at party longevity from a different angle. Whereas Table 2.3 measured the share of seats circa 1996 of relatively old parties, Table 2.4 indicates the ages of parties that won at least 10 percent of the seats in recent legislative elections.[8] In determining the foundational year of parties, I allowed for changes of names if there were clear organizational continuity. Table 2.4 again underscores the ephemeral nature of many parties in Bolivia, Brazil, Ecuador, and Peru, and the enduring nature of many parties in multiparty systems in Western Europe.

The ability of nonpartisan and antiparty candidates to win office serves as another indicator of party rootedness in society. Where citizens are attached to a party, such candidates do not win office. In the consolidated democracies, it is uncommon for large numbers of nonpartisan or antiparty candidates to fare well. In contrast, in new democracies with fluid party systems, political independents can win office. Space for populists is greater, especially in presidential systems, because candidates can appeal directly to the masses in order to become head of state without needing to be elected head of the party. Candidates can capture high executive office such as the presidency and governorships without being rooted in an established party. For example, Brazilian President Fernando Collor de Mello (1990–92) created a party in order to run for president in 1989, and he ran against parties. Seven months after his inauguration, his party won only forty of 503 lower-chamber seats in the October 1990 congressional elections. His party disappeared in the months following his resignation from office in order to avoid impeachment hearings in 1992. Peruvian President Alberto Fujimori (1990–present) also created a party in order to run for the presidency; he, too, campaigned against parties and has subsequently eschewed efforts to build a party. In Peru, political independents dominated the 1995 municipal elections. Having seen from Fujimori that antiparty appeals could win popular support, a new cohort of antiparty politicians has emerged.

Personalism and antiparty politicians are also common in some post-Soviet cases. Russian President Boris Yeltsen is not a member of a party and has undermined parties. Alexander Lebed, who finished third in the 1996 Russian presidential election, ran as an independent, as did Stanislaw Tyminski, who finished second in the 1990 Polish presidential election. Nonpartisan candidates have fared well in the plurality races for both chambers of the Russian parliament. In the 1993 elections, well over half of the single-member-district candidates for the lower chamber were independents without partisan affiliation, and only eighty-three of the 218 deputies elected belonged to a party (Moser 1995: 98). In 1995, more than 1,000 of the 2,700 candidates for the single-member-

TABLE 2-4
Years Since Founding of Parties with 10 Percent of the Lower-Chamber Vote, 1996

Country, election year	Parties	Years since founding	Avg. age	Country, election year	Parties	Years since founding	Avg age
United	Democratic,	168		Costa	Nat'l. Liberation	51	
States,	Republican	140	154	Rica,	Social Christian		47
1996				1994	Union	43	
Colombia,	Liberal,	147		France,	Socialist	86	
1994	Conservative	147	147	1993	Gaullist	51	43
Uruguay,	Colorado	160			National Front	18	
1994	Nacional	160	115		Union for French		
	Broad Front	25			Democracy	18	
Sweden,	Social Democrats	106		Mexico,	PRI	67	
1994	Moderate Unity		101	1994	PAN	57	43
	(Conservative)	97			PRD	6	
Norway,	Conservative	114		Chile,	Socialist	40	
1993	Labour	102	99	1993	Christ. Democrat	58	40
	Center (Farmers')	81			Nat'l. Renovation	30	
Switzer-	Social Democrat	108			UDI	9	
land,	Christian Democrat			Italy,	Democratic Party		
1995	(Catholic)	103		1996	of the Left	75	39
	Radical Democrat	100	97		Forza Italia	3	
	Swiss People's			Ecuador,	PSC	45	
	(Farmers, Traders &			1996	PRE	16	30
	Citizens)	78		Venezuela,	AD	60	
Belgium,	Christian People's			1993	Copei	50	
1995	(Catholic)	149			MAS	28	29
	Liberty & Progress				Causa R	7	
	(Liberal)	149			Convergencia	4	
	Francophone		89	Bolivia,	MNR	55	
	Socialist	106		1993	MIR	25	
	Francophone				ADN	18	
	Liberal	22			Condepa	8	22
	Flemish Socialist	18			Civic Union		
Finland,	Social Democrat	97			Solidarity	7	
1995	Center (Ag. Union)	89		Portugal,	Socialist	20	
	National Coalition	77	78	1994	Popular Social		22
	Left-Wing Alliance				Democrats	20	
	(Dem. Union)	51		Greece,	PSM	19	
Paraguay,	ANR (Colorado)	109		1993	New Democracy	19	19
1993	PLRA	109	74	Brazil,	PMDB	31	
	Nat'l. Encounter	4		1994	PFL	12	
Argentina,	Radical Civic Union	106			PSDB	8	13
1995	Justicialist	51	54		PPR (PDS)	3	
	Frepaso	5		Peru,	Cambio 90	7	
Spain,	PSOE	65		1995	Unión por el Perú	1	4
1996	Communist (UL)	65	49				
	Popular	19					

SOURCES: See Table 2-3 for electoral data

district seats were independents. Independents won seventy-eight of the 225 single-member seats; the largest single party could muster only fifty-eight seats (White, Rose, and McAllister 1997: 203, 224).

In more-institutionalized party systems, such personalism is the exception. In the Latin American countries with more institutionalized systems, presidents are almost always long-term members of major parties. In Western Europe, the same is true of prime ministers.

These indicators show that there are profound differences in the "rootedness" of parties in society. Notwithstanding some erosion of party voting in recent decades, in most of the advanced industrial democracies, parties have strong roots. In most of the advanced industrial democracies, over half of the voters identify with and vote for the same party over time (Dalton et al. 1984). In contrast, in Russia, Poland, and Peru, party roots in society are weak, and only a small minority of voters stick with the same party election after election. Rather than being channeled through parties and other democratic institutions, democratic politics acquires a highly personalized character.

THE LEGITIMACY OF PARTIES AND ELECTIONS

Legitimacy usually refers to attitudes about the political regime (Linz 1978: 17–18; Morlino and Montero 1995: 232–35), but the concept can also refer to democratic institutions. Parties are legitimate to the extent that political actors have a positive attitude toward them or, minimally, consider them necessary parts of a democratic regime. Comparatively positive attitudes toward parties increase the likelihood that the system will be stable. Posed in this way, the concept is not tautological; one can empirically measure both legitimacy and stability, and the two need not go together.

Because parties typically rank among the least-trusted democratic institutions even in long-established democracies, it is important to avoid unrealistic expectations in measuring legitimacy. Even allowing for growing citizen disaffection with parties in institutionalized systems, parties have lower legitimacy in most third-wave democratizers. White, Rose, and McAllister (1997: 51–52) report that in Russia, parties are the least trusted among the sixteen institutions evaluated in a series of public opinion surveys. On a scale of 1 (no trust) to 7 (great trust), only 2 percent of respondents gave parties a 6 or 7, compared to 60 percent who gave them a 1 or 2. Forty-three percent agreed with the statement, "We do not need parliament or elections, but instead a strong leader who can make decisions and put them into effect fast" (White, Rose, and McAllister 1997: 46). Such questions are not typically asked in the established democracies because legislatures and elections are such an accepted part of the political landscape.

Parties also ranked as the institution (among eight) that commanded the least sympathy in Portugal, Spain, Greece, and Italy, but nevertheless "the legitimacy of parties is high in all four countries" (Morlino and Montero 1995: 256). On a sympathy index scale ranging from 1 (least sympathy) to 10 (greatest), parties scored a mean 4.4 in Portugal, 4.2 in Spain, 4.1 in Italy, and 4.9 in Greece in 1985 (Morlino and Montero 1995: 258). Greek parties scored only 10.9 percent below the midway point (5.5) of the scale. On White, Rose, and McAllister's (1997: 52–53) trust index, which ranged from 1 (least trust) to 7, Russian parties scored only 2.3 of 7, 42.5 percent below the midway point (4.0) of the scale.

In a survey in central Europe, pollsters asked several questions that tapped the comparative legitimacy of parties. One question asked citizens whether they approved of the dissolution of parties and parliament. Forty percent responded affirmatively in Poland compared to only 8 percent in Austria. Thirty-one percent of Polish respondents said they would prefer a one-party system as compared with 8 percent in the Czech Republic. Thirty-nine percent in Poland said that they approved of rule by a strong man compared to 22 percent in Austria and only 19 percent in Slovakia (Linz and Stepan 1996: 285, citing Plasser and Ulram 1993: 46–47).

The Latinobarometro (Lagos 1996) asked a question about trust in institutions. Although parties were generally the least-trusted institution, there is nevertheless significant variance across cases. In Uruguay, which has one of the more institutionalized party systems in Latin America, 41.0 percent of respondents expressed a lot of or some trust in parties. In Peru and Brazil, only 21.2 percent and 17.4 percent of respondents, respectively, expressed a lot of or some trust in parties; in Venezuela, where the party system deinstitutionalized and experienced a major crisis in the 1990s, only 16.0 percent expressed a lot of or some trust. The level of trust in parties at the low end of the Latin American range is much lower than in the southern European democracies.

The Latinobarometro also asked respondents whether they believed that democracy could exist without political parties. A high percentage of respondents who believed that parties are necessary for democracy suggests greater legitimacy of parties. A sizable majority of respondents in Uruguay (78.2 percent) and Argentina (70.8 percent)—both of which have moderately institutionalized party systems—agreed that parties are necessary to democracy. At the low end were Brazil (47.4 percent), which has a weakly institutionalized party system, and Paraguay (46.8 percent), where democracy came into being only in 1993.

PARTY ORGANIZATION

With the partial exception of the United States, party organizations have long been relatively solid in countries with more institutionalized party systems. Party organizations are quite robust in the Scandinavian countries and in Germany. Parties in these countries have historically been well financed, had active (though now declining) mass memberships, cultivated sizable and professionalized staffs, and commanded strong loyalty on the part of elected representatives. Parties developed relatively clear, stable procedures for selecting leaders and for organizational structures. Although there were organizational differences between the centrist and conservative parties, on the one hand, and the leftist parties on the other, these differences pale in comparison to those between parties in more- and less-institutionalized systems.

In most third-wave democracies, parties have precarious resources and are weakly professionalized. Many are personalistic vehicles. In Peru and Russia, parties exercise little control over nominations. In Peru, for example, President Fujimori has used focus groups and surveys to determine who runs on the ballot of his party. Fujimori himself, rather than the party, has controlled congressional nominations (Conaghan 1996); this personalistic control of candidate selection is the antithesis of an institutionalized system. Moreover, as is also true in Russia, candidates can gain ballot access without a party and can win elections as independents.

Politicians in some fluid systems are not loyal to their parties; switching from one party to another is commonplace. For example, in the Brazilian legislature of 1991–94, the 503 deputies changed parties 260 times (Samuels forthcoming). Between the Russian parliamentary elections of December 1993 and October 1995, 128 of 450 Duma members switched parties. Similarly, in the weeks following the December 1995 election, 142 Duma members switched parties (White, Rose, and McAllister 1997: 184, 238). Neither citizens nor political elites evince loyalty or sympathy toward parties. Organizational loyalty is greater among politicians in countries with more-institutionalized party systems.

In sum, party systems vary markedly in levels of institutionalization, which varies independently from the number of parties. Whereas analysts who compare party systems on the basis of the number of parties lump together multiparty cases regardless of the level of institutionalization, weakly institutionalized cases differ markedly from solidly entrenched ones. Institutionalization also varies significantly relatively to ideological distance in the party system. Some polarized systems (e.g., France from the 1960s to the 1980s, Italy from the 1940s to the 1980s) are well institutionalized, which may help explain why they did not conform to all of Sartori's (1976) pessimism about polarized multipartism. Other polarized systems (e.g., Brazil in the mid- to late 1980s) are less-institutionalized and function in a different manner.

These differences in institutionalization are associated with profound differences in democratic quality. In a more-institutionalized system, voters are more likely to identify with a party, and parties are more likely to dominate patterns of political recruitment. In fluid systems, the electorate votes more according to personality or clientelism than party; antiparty politicians are more able to win office. Thus populism and antipolitics are more common with weakly institutionalized systems. Personalities rather than party organizations dominate the political scene. Given the propensity toward personalism and the comparative weakness of parties, mechanisms of democratic accountability are usually weaker; consequently, the quality of democratic practice tends to be lower. Weak party roots in society and a high degree of personalism enhance the role of television in campaigns, especially for executive positions. Democracies with fluid party systems tend to have weak mechanisms of accountability,

With weakly institutionalized systems, turnover from one party to others is usually high, which increases the chances of significant change in policy and reduces the likelihood of high continuity. Weak institutionalization also means a higher degree of uncertainty regarding electoral outcomes, and such uncertainty proved inimical to democracy until the 1980s.

In brief, these differences between more- and less-institutionalized systems are so important that they can fruitfully be used as a starting point for analyzing, classifying, and comparing party systems. The dynamics and characteristics of weakly institutionalized systems differ profoundly from those with well-institutionalized ones. The degree of institutionalization is crucial for many questions related to the quality of democratic practice and accountability. The chances of democratic survival are lower with fluid party systems, given the higher degree of personalism, the greater degree of uncertainty, and the weaker mechanisms of accountability.

Despite the importance of variance in party-system institutionalization, this dimension has not been explored for structuring comparisons among party systems. Sartori (1976: 244–48) proposed a suggestive contrast between systems that were "structurally consolidated" and those that were not, and he deliberately excluded the unconsolidated systems from his analysis. Although Sartori anticipated the importance of levels of party-system institutionalization, my approach differs in some respects. Sartori thought of structural consolidation as a dichotomous variable; either a system was structurally consolidated and hence could be included in his typology, or it was not consolidated and was not even a system. But posing this contrast in dichotomous terms is conceptually and empirically misleading because conceptually, institutionalization is a continuous variable. Other scholars (e.g., Bendel 1993) have also hinted at the importance of party system institutionalization, but without developing the point in depth or using this notion to structure comparisons and analysis.

If variation in the level of institutionalization is a crucial component of party systems, then why has this issue been neglected in the literature? Analyses of Western European and U.S. party systems have dominated the theoretical literature. The better work on Western European systems has reached a high degree of sophistication, but it has not paid much attention to this issue because for most of the twentieth century, there was relatively little crossnational variance in institutionalization. In their study of thirteen Western European countries from 1885 to 1985, Bartolini and Mair (1990: 73) found that France had the highest mean electoral volatility during that century, at 15.2 percent, while Austria (5.7 percent) had the lowest. All the Western European cases are relatively institutionalized. The variance in institutionalization does not warrant systematic attention in thinking about how to compare party systems. This situation changes, however, when we turn to the third-wave cases. By expanding the universe of cases around which we theorize from the advanced industrial democracies to newer, less-consolidated democracies, variance in party-system institutionalization—which is limited and of secondary importance if we compare only the Western European cases—becomes extensive and of primary importance.

This general argument about the importance of institutionalization for comparing and analyzing party systems is relevant to Brazil. Indeed, the most important feature of the Brazilian party system, even more than the number of parties and the ideological distance among them, is the low level of institutionalization. The same is true of the party systems in countries as different as Ecuador, Peru, and Russia.

Social Cleavages and Party Systems

One of the most important issues in the study of party systems is why they acquire the features they do. Looking primarily at Western European party systems, an important body of literature has emphasized the role of social cleavages in structuring party systems. In their seminal study, Lipset and Rokkan (1967) argued that the main differences in Western European party systems reflected different structures in social cleavages (see also Rokkan 1970: 72–144). These cleavage structures changed over time, but the systems they gave rise to in the 1920s tended to remain stable through the mid–1960s, when Lipset and Rokkan wrote. Parties won the loyalties of different social groups, and they retained these loyalties. The authors argued that four main cleavages structured party systems: religion, class, core versus periphery, and urban versus rural.

Lipset and Rokkan's work spawned a plethora of studies that examined differences in party systems as expressions of different cleavage structures. Studies subsequent to Lipset and Rokkan used the notion of cleavage in two distinct ways. Following Lipset and Rokkan, some analysts have focused on social cleavages, that is, on the way in which social attributes such as class, religion, education, region, and ethnicity affect party preference and voting behavior

(Bartolini and Mair 1990; Kitschelt 1992; Rose and Urwin 1969). They argue that social cleavages determine the physiognomy of party systems.

Other analysts (Dogan 1967; Inglehart 1977, 1984; Knutsen 1988; Zuckerman 1975) focus on political cleavages, that is, on political factors that shape the party system. These scholars agree that enduring cleavages structure party systems, but they argue that these cleavages can be political rather than sociological in origin. Still others (e.g., H. Daalder 1966; Lijphart 1984: 127–149; Scully 1992) combine the social- and political-cleavages approaches.

The social-cleavage approach has received some stiff challenges since Lipset and Rokkan formulated their arguments. Proponents of the *political*-cleavage approach (e.g., Knutsen 1988) and of issue-dimension approaches (e.g., Lijphart 1984: 127–49) shifted away from an emphasis on sociological factors. These scholars showed that political cleavages not rooted in Lipset and Rokkan's structural variables were becoming more important determinants of partisan preference and voting behavior.

In one of the most important challenges to the social-cleavage approach, Inglehart (1977, 1984) and Kitschelt (1989, 1994) claimed that Lipset and Rokkan's sociological factors, especially class, were gradually being superseded by a new cleavage between postmaterialists (whose political orientation revolves mostly around nonmaterial issues) and materialists. Inglehart argued that an increasing number of citizens vote on the basis of quality of life concerns not closely related to material interests or to their structural position in society. Kitschelt (1989, 1994) noted that new "left-libertarian" organizations were challenging the traditional parties and disrupting established linkages between social cleavages and party loyalty. In a converging analysis, Clark and Lipset (1991) noted the decline of class voting in Western Europe. Sartori (1969) criticized the sociological bias of Lipset and Rokkan, arguing that it needed to be complemented with an awareness of how political factors help create cleavages. Przeworski and Sprague (1986) made a similar argument, showing that where class determines voting behavior, this is a result of political institutions rather than the inherent structuring propensity of class. Zuckerman (1975) called attention to some conceptual problems in the relationship between social cleavages and political behavior, including party sympathy. Dix (1989) questioned the applicability of the social-cleavage approach for understanding Latin American party systems. Dogan (1995), Inglehart (1977, 1984), and Kitschelt (1994) demonstrated that sociological cleavages have a declining capacity to explain the vote. Kirchheimer (1966) and Pizzorno (1981) observed that parties were increasingly catch-all in nature (i.e., without sharply defined social bases) rather than drawing support from sharply defined social strata.

Despite these challenges, the social-cleavage approach still has prominent proponents. In the Western European context, Bartolini and Mair (1990) largely reaffirmed Lipset and Rokkan. The social-cleavage approach is sometimes used in analyzing party systems in Latin America (Soares 1967, 1973, 1982) and in other new democracies (Kitschelt 1992). J. S. Valenzuela (1995) and Yashar (1995) mainly use a social-cleavage approach in their excellent analyses. Rueschemeyer, Stephens, and Stephens (1992) tend to view parties as expressions of one particular social cleavage—class—in their more general theoretical formulations (though not in their analysis of Latin America). By defining conservative parties as representatives of the upper strata, Gibson (1996: 7) implicitly draws somewhat on a class approach to party in his excellent study.

The degree to which social cleavages structure the party system varies by case and over time. Most third-wave cases have features that make the social-cleavage approach less fruitful than it was with Western European party systems until the 1970s. A social-cleavage approach is most powerful when social groups identify strongly with a party. This was more likely to occur in the first wave of democratization for several reasons. First, working-class parties not only integrated labor into the political system but also addressed many salient social issues such as health care. Workers developed attachments to parties that endured for decades. In later democracies, the state and populist leaders were often the prime movers in incorporating labor into the political system. The class parties that emerged in the first-wave cases were rarely reproduced in later cases.

Second, in first-wave democracies, the proportion of the labor force in manufacturing and mining was much higher than it became in most third-wave democracies (Keck 1992). A large, unionized industrial labor force was propitious for the formation of working-class parties. In third-wave cases, in an era of greater globalization of production, more capital-intensive manufacturing, and more service industries, the difficulties of creating a bond that unites workers are greater because intraclass fragmentation is greater (Weyland 1996).

Finally, when working-class and other parties formed in the first wave of democratization, they did not compete with the modern mass media, especially television. Workers toiled long hours, and cultural opportunities for them were more restricted than is the case in many contemporary third-wave democracies. Workers' organizations (including parties) exercised great social influence for workers. In the third-wave cases, television provides an alternative source of information and images.

For these reasons, one would expect the social-cleavage approach to be less useful for third-wave democracies than it was for most Western European cases until the 1970s.[9] To empirically illustrate the shortcomings of the social-cleavage approach in a third-wave democracy, I rely on data from Brazil, but other studies have shown that social cleavages leave a high share of the vote unexplained in many third-wave cases. In Brazil, in some elections, sociological factors have been poor indicators of the vote; social cleavages have not consistently structured the party system to a high degree. For example, in the 1994 presidential elections, the main two contenders were Fernando Henrique Cardoso, supported by a coalition of centrist and conservative parties, and Luis Inácio da Silva (Lula), supported by the left. Cardoso overcame Lula's early lead and ultimately won in a landslide, 54 percent to 27 percent. Despite the markedly different ideological profiles and campaigns of the two candidates, sociological cleavages did not structure the vote to a significant degree.

Table 2.5 shows the results of a nationwide survey conducted three weeks before the election, indicating the breakdown of support for the two candidates by income category, level of education, and size of municipality. These three variables are not exact proxies for the cleavages Lipset and Rokkan identified, but if class or regional cleavages effectively predicted the vote, we would expect significant differentiation of the vote by these three variables.

In fact, the social bases of Cardoso's support differed little from Lula's. There is virtually no difference between the two main candidates in patterns of support by income. Despite the large size (n=10,560) of the sample, a chi square test of Table 2.5 is not statistically significant at the .1 level if we exclude voters who planned to vote in blank or null the ballot, who had no preference, or who didn't know how they would vote. Cardoso drew support evenly across different educational levels, while Lula did marginally better among the most educated than among other groups. Lula fared slightly better than average in large municipalities and slightly worse in small ones, with Cardoso drawing roughly even support across different sizes of municipalities. Education and municipality were statistically significant at a .001 level but were not substantively that important.

In the 1989 presidential elections, social cleavages were a more powerful predictor of the vote but still left a large share of variance unexplained. Three of the five leading presidential contenders had distinct sociological bases while the other two enjoyed relatively even support across most social categories. Moreover, some results ran counter to what one would expect on the basis of a crude cleavage model.

Table 2.6 shows the preferred presidential candidates of different income groups on the basis of a November 1989 nationwide survey conducted shortly after the first round (October 3, 1989) of the presidential elections. The plurality winner in the first round and eventual winner in the runoff, conservative Fernando Collor de Mello, fared much better among the poor than among higher-income groups.[10] If a crude social-cleavage model worked, one would

TABLE 2-5
Vote Intention in the 1994 Presidential Election

	Cardoso	Lula	6 minor candidates	blank/ null[a]	Total	N
By household income[b]						
0–5	42	22	16	19	100	4,677
5–10	45	26	17	12	100	2,102
> 10	48	25	16	11	100	2,467
TOTAL	44	23	16	17	100	10,560
By education						
Up to middle school	43	21	16	20	100	6,737
Through high school	46	26	15	13	100	2,813
Some higher education	41	32	15	11	100	1,010
TOTAL*	44	23	16	17	100	10,560
By size of municipality						
Up to 19,600 voters	46	20	16	18	100	1,933
19,600–160,000 voters	43	23	15	17	100	2,572
> 160,000 voters	42	26	17	16	100	6,055
TOTAL*	44	23	16	17	100	10,560

SOURCE: Nationwide DataFolha survey, September 9, 1994. N=10,560. CESOP archive DAT/BR 94 set.
[a]Combined total for blank vote, null ballot, no answer, and doesn't know.
[b]Number of minimum salaries. The minimum salary at that time was equivalent to US$64.79 per month (*Conjuntura Econômica*, 48, 10 [October 1994], 39).
*Significant at a .001 level, excluding blank/null.
The entire distributions are statistically significant (excluding blank, null, and no answer) at a .001 level for education and size of municipality. The entire distribution for household income is not significant below a .10 level. Chi[2] tests.
Household income: None of the individual distributions is statistically significant vis-à-vis the rest. Chi[2] tests.
Education: The distributions for Cardoso and Lula are statistically significant at a .001 level. The distribution for six minor candidates is significant at a .01 level. Chi[2] tests.
Size of municipality: The distributions for Cardoso and Lula are significant at a .001 level. The distribution for six minor candidates is not significant below a .10 level.

expect a conservative candidate to fare better among the wealthy. Conservative Paulo Maluf and center-left candidate Mário Covas had roughly similar social bases; both did much better among the higher-income categories. Covas's support base also runs counter to what one would expect on the basis of a crude class model; equally damaging to a class model is the fact that two such different candidates had similar social bases. Although candidates' social bases were more sharply distinguishable in 1989 than in 1994, two major candidates, the leftist Lula of the PT and Leonel Brizola of the center-left Democratic Labor Party (PDT) did not have very distinctive social bases. Both candidates had quite even support across different income groups. Moreover, the relationship between political position on a left-to-right scale and income is erratic; the center-left

TABLE 2-6

Vote in the 1989 Presidential Election

	Collor	Brizola	Lula	Covas	Maluf	Others	None[a]	Total	N	Pct.
By household income[b]										
> 20	13.3	13.3	20.0	17.0	19.3	11.1	5.9	100.0	135	3.7
10–20	18.6	17.1	15.9	19.8	12.4	13.2	3.1	100.0	258	7.1
5–10	24.5	15.9	15.7	16.9	13.5	8.8	4.7	100.0	510	14.0
2–5	32.9	15.4	19.6	11.0	6.6	9.6	5.0	100.0	940	25.8
1–2	38.8	17.8	16.3	6.7	5.6	9.9	4.9	100.0	892	24.4
0–1	49.0	13.2	16.5	3.5	3.1	7.6	7.1	100.0	714	19.6
None[c]	35.3	12.4	20.4	9.5	8.5	6.5	7.5	100.0	201	5.5
TOTAL	34.7	15.5	17.4	10.1	7.6	9.3	5.4	100.0	3650	100.0
By education										
Illiterate	54.9	11.5	11.5	2.5	2.7	7.4	9.6	100.0	366	10.0
3rd grade	44.7	12.5	17.3	5.7	6.0	8.3	5.5	100.0	687	18.8
4th–8th grade	34.8	17.6	17.8	8.2	8.1	8.6	5.0	100.0	1692	46.4
9th–11th grade	22.0	14.7	19.8	18.0	8.8	11.9	4.7	100.0	645	17.7
Some univ.	11.2	17.7	17.3	25.0	12.7	12.7	3.5	100.0	260	7.2
TOTAL	34.7	15.5	17.4	10.1	7.6	9.3	5.4	100.0	3650	100.0
By population of municipality										
< 19,999	49.2	11.4	12.7	5.9	6.2	8.5	5.9	100.0	1313	35.9
20,000–99,999	34.2	18.4	17.4	7.0	8.0	10.1	5.0	100.0	892	24.4
100,000–499,999	26.7	13.7	22.3	13.2	8.8	10.4	4.9	100.0	636	17.4
500,000 +	18.0	20.4	21.3	17.7	8.1	8.8	5.3	100.0	809	22.2
TOTAL	34.7	15.5	17.4	10.1	7.6	9.3	5.4	100.0	3650	100.0

SOURCE: National Voter Survey Wave 19, IBOPE, November 1989. Roper Center Archive Number BRIBOPE89-OPP602.

[a] Combined total for blank vote, null ballot, no answer, and doesn't know.

[b] Household income is represented by the number of minimum salaries earned by the household. One minimum salary at that time was equivalent to US$43.60 per month: *Anuário Estatístico do Brasil*, 51 [Rio de Janeiro, Ministério da Economia, Fazenda e Planejamento & Fundação Instituto Brasileiro de Geografia e Estatística, 1991], 883–84; and *Conjuntura Econômica* 43, 12 [December 30, 1989], 89.

[c] No answer/missing.

Household income and education: The entire distribution is statistically significant at a .001 level. The distributions for Collor, Covas, and Maluf vis-à-vis all others are also statistically significant at a .001 level. The distributions for Brizola, Lula, and "others" are not statistically significant below .10. Chi^2 tests.

Population of municipality: The entire distribution is statistically significant at a .001 level. The distributions for Collor, Lula, Brizola, and Covas are also statistically significant at a .001 level. The distributions for Maluf and "others" are not statistically significant below a .10 level. Chi^2 tests.

Covas and the rightist Maluf had similar social bases, faring best among the better off, whereas the two main conservative candidates, Maluf and Collor, had diametrically opposed social bases. Thus the pattern of political support is not what one would predict on the basis of a simplistic cleavage model, in which conservative candidates would fare best among the wealthy and leftist candidates best among the poor.

The data on the preferred candidate according to educational level tell a similar story. If social cleavages explained support for parties along the left-to-right scale, the major conservative candidates should have roughly similar social bases. In fact, however, the two main conservative candidates had diametrically opposed social bases. Collor did best among the least educated and worst among the best educated, while Maluf reversed this pattern. The illiterate preferred Collor to Maluf by a twenty to one margin, while those with some university education preferred Maluf to Collor by a thin margin. Lula and Brizola had relatively undifferentiated bases of support according to educational background. This, too, is inconsistent with a crude cleavage model, in which candidates with a sharp ideological profile should disproportionately win support from certain social sectors. Maluf and Covas fared much better among the educated and worse among the least educated. If social cleavages determined bases of support for parties, candidates of such different ideological profiles would have markedly different social bases. Finally, the two center-left candidates had very different patterns of support. Brizola scored fairly evenly across educational groups, while Covas did much better among the educated.

One of Lipset/Rokkan's cleavages revolved around rural versus urban interests. In the 1989 survey, the best proxy for this cleavage is the size of municipalities: Collor fared much better in small municipalities, Covas did much better in large ones, Brizola and Lula did somewhat better in large ones, and Maluf's support was evenly distributed (Table 2.6). Although size of municipality accounts for more of the variance in patterns of support for the presidential candidates than either class or education, for only two of the five main contenders (Collor and Covas) did it make a large difference.[11] Congressional elections have shown the same tendency toward weak differentiation in the parties' social bases.

If the Brazilian party system formed on the basis of social cleavages, then the geographic bases of parties would remain relatively stable over time. However, as is shown in Chapter 4, in the 1980s and early 1990s, the largest party, the centrist PMDB (Party of the Brazilian Democratic Movement), switched from being a party that fared best in large cities and wealthy states to one that did best in small municipalities and poor states.

Other studies have demonstrated that parties do not have markedly different social bases in some other third-wave democracies. In Uruguay, traditionally there was little difference in the social bases of the two traditional parties (Blancos and Colorados) that dominated the system until the early 1970s. Even in the 1980s, when greater differences emerged in the social bases of the three main parties, socioeconomic status (as judged by interviewers) was a poor predictor of voting behavior (González 1991: 113–22). Based on a survey, Seligson (1987: 171) showed that rural-urban residence, age, and housing conditions had a weak impact on voting behavior in Costa Rica. The civil war of 1948 crystallized strong party attachments that did not closely correspond to social cleavages. Baloyra and Martz (1979: 74) showed that in the late 1970s, "there (were) no strong linkages between class and party in Venezuela."

SALIENT SOCIAL CLEAVAGES
WITHOUT CLEAR PARTY EXPRESSIONS

In sum, the party systems of many third-wave democracies are not consistently structured to a high degree by social cleavages. This is not because of the lack of major social cleavages, but rather because these cleavages do not always determine party preference and voting behavior. The Brazilian case illustrates the broader point that salient social cleavages are not necessarily reflected in the party system. The relationship between social cleavages and the party system is an empirical question; we should not assume that social cleavages structure party systems, but rather examine the extent to which they do.

More so than any Western European country, Brazil (like most Latin American countries) is hierarchically divided by profound class, racial, and regional cleavages. Yet these highly visible cleavages have not had a great impact on the post–1985 party system, making it clear that even highly visible social cleavages do not automatically give rise to party divisions.

Racial cleavages have not significantly shaped Brazil's party systems despite the existence of many different ethnic groups and despite profound racial inequalities. Brazil is a multiethnic, multiracial society, with people of diverse European, African, native American, Asian, and mixed heritages. Despite profound racial inequalities, parties have generally made little or no effort to attract different races or ethnic groups. Some politicians have run as candidates of specific ethnic groups (for example, Japanese Brazilians), but on an individual basis; parties have avoided such identifications. The center-left PDT (Democratic Labor Party) and the leftist PT (Workers' Party) have been partial exceptions by dint of their efforts to cultivate the vote of the Afro-Brazilian movement. That movement, however, has not been a powerful political force, and it has not mobilized the vote on behalf of any particular party. Race has not had a major political impact in voting patterns (Berquó and Alencastro 1992).

The low political saliency of race is a contrast to many other cases. In the United States, for example, the Democratic Party has courted the African-American vote, and African Americans have overwhelmingly voted for Democrats in recent decades. Issues of race have been manipulated by both parties and have played a visible role in party politics.

Few countries have such sharp class inequalities as Brazil. Income distribution is among the worst in the world, and the poor remain desperately poor. It is impossible to understand Brazilian politics outside the context of a society rent by these class inequalities. Yet none of the parties of the post–1945 period could be considered a clear expression of a class cleavage to the same degree that many European parties once were. The Brazilian Communist Party, PCB, (1945–47) and the Workers' Party, PT, (1979–present) might be considered parties predicated on the existence of the class cleavage. The PCB, however, was banned in 1947 and thereafter had limited impact on party dynamics.

Although the PT espouses class rhetoric, its class base has been highly heterogeneous since at least 1985. This fact is suggested by the social bases of support for its presidential candidate in 1989 and 1994, as reported in Tables 2.5 and 2.6 above. The PT's support is quite uniform across different income and educational levels. It has consistently fared better in large urban areas than in the countryside, but with the expansion of the party's electoral base in 1989, it became less of an urban-based party than previously. The PT wins slightly more support from the better-off, better-educated segments of society, not from the poor, as one might expect on the basis of the party's appeals and program.

Class has sometimes been an important sociological determinant of voting behavior in Brazil since 1945 (Lamounier 1980; Soares 1967, 1973, 1982; von Mettenheim 1995). Nevertheless, seeing Brazilian parties as expressions of classes understates the complexity of the linkage between class and party. As Dix (1989: 29) observed, Soares's evidence underscores that before 1964, even in what was one of Brazil's most ideological, class-conscious cities (Rio de Janeiro), the major parties had heterogeneous bases of support. Even among unskilled workers, who formed the category (among seven) least prone to vote for the conservative UDN and most inclined to the center-left PTB, 18 percent identified with the UDN and 42 percent with the PTB (Soares 1967: 487). PTB identifiers were more common among workers, where they formed about 40 percent of the total, than among nonworkers, but even among the highest occupation category (professionals and high administrative personnel), 11 percent identified with the PTB. The interclass basis of party support has been even more pronounced in the post–1985 period.

Brazil's party systems have not primarily rested on class-based parties. Many workers do not vote for "workers' parties," and many nonworkers vote for what are supposedly "workers' parties." In her study of voting intentions in a medium-sized city (Presidente Prudente) in the interior of the state of São Paulo in the 1989 presidential election, Kinzo (1991: 266) found that workers were somewhat more disposed than nonworkers to vote for the Workers' Party, but still, only 12 percent of workers favored the PT in the first round. In the runoff, workers were only marginally more inclined to vote for the PT candidate than the population as a whole; 33 percent of workers compared to 27 percent of the population as a whole stated that they intended to vote for the PT candidate.

Furthermore, few major parties in Brazil have seen themselves as advancing the project of a specific class. They claim to advance the interests of all classes or at least of several classes that are perceived as having contradictory interests in conventional class analysis. The Communist Party from 1945 to 1947 and to a lesser degree the PTB from 1945 to 1964 are partial exceptions; both presented themselves as labor parties. The PT has also presented itself as a labor party, but the evidence on its social base belies this claim.

Classes are not a spontaneous or natural product. As Przeworski (1985: 47–132) has argued, they are formed through the process of political struggle, and the nature of the party system influences class formation. Whether workers develop a shared identity as part of the same class and as such have meaningful common bonds is an open question, varying from one country to another. Institutions, especially unions, the state, and parties, shape whether workers think of themselves as a class (see also Przeworski and Sprague 1986; Sartori 1969). How workers act politically depends more on how parties and unions organize them than on some behaviors and perspectives that workers assume just because they are workers. But then institutions are the key factor, for they shape class identity and behavior. In the absence of a party that sees itself as a voice for the working class and that organizes workers, workers may identify themselves primordially as Catholics, as citizens of a given province or state, as white, or as male (Sartori 1969).

Where class voting is salient, it is more because the parties are disciplined, offer clear choices, and appeal strongly to class than because workers "naturally" support labor or socialist parties (Przeworski and Sprague 1986). Notable in many third-wave cases is how little class voting is salient, precisely because of how class and other political identities have formed. In most third-wave democracies, classes have not always or even usually constituted political actors. Social classes are internally divided, not only according to class fraction (as class analysts would readily recognize), but also by ideology, religion, ethnicity, nationality, region, race, and gender. In Brazil, notwithstanding striking inequalities, classes—especially the subordinate classes—have generally not overcome these divisions and acted, *qua* class, as cohesive actors.

A class model of parties understates the extent to which political institutions—especially corporatist structures and political parties—have shaped class in many third-wave cases. In Brazil, the political incorporation of the urban working class took place between 1930 and 1945 under the leadership of president Getúlio Vargas and under the aegis of corporatist institutions. Until the 1980s, corporatism fragmented the working class, made organized labor dependent on the state and relatively co-optable, and weakened the autonomy and power of the labor movement (Collier and Collier 1991; Erickson 1977; Keck 1989, 1992; Mericle 1977; A. Souza 1978; Weyland 1996a). The corporatist institutions and the absence of a major working-class party until the early 1960s shaped workers' consciousness, leading to relative political quiescence. In sum, a class approach, while helpful in understanding some aspects of the formation of party systems in Brazil, leaves major questions unexplained.

Although it is a mistake to treat parties as representatives of class interests, another theme of this book is that party patterns have profound consequences for classes. In Brazil, party patterns have contributed to the maintenance of a patrimonial style of politics that is favorable to elite interests. Even though this statement might superficially suggest that one can treat parties as expressions of social classes, asserting that the system benefits elites shifts the unit of analysis from individual parties to the system as a whole. It also focuses attention on the consequences of political patterns rather than the representational side. It is problematic to treat particular parties as expressions of class interests on the basis of party ideology or program. Rather, we should look at the social bases of a party to determine which groups it preferentially represents.

Religious cleavages have been a powerful influence in many party systems, but they have not held much sway in Brazil. Religious cleavages were salient in the late nineteenth century, when conservative Catholics battled the secular tendencies of many political elites, including Emperor Dom Pedro II. Although the dominant political elite were not as anti-Catholic as those in many Latin American countries, they did take some measures against the church. Dom Pedro II, Emperor from 1840 to 1889, imposed a series of restrictions on the church. Some Catholic parties emerged in defense of the church's privileges, and sharp church/state conflict broke out in the 1870s. These church/state conflicts showed that there was a religious cleavage in Brazilian society, just as was the case in most other predominantly Catholic countries at the time. But whereas in some countries political and religious figures fueled the flames of this cleavage, in Brazil, after a short interlude they sought accommodation. Although it had the potential to become a major political issue with expression in the party system, the religious question largely faded away. A few Catholic parties emerged, and they were rather like Catholic parties in other Catholic countries of that period: conservative, suspicious of a secular state, hostile to liberalism and socialism, committed to the defense of the church's privileged position. But they were minor parties with ephemeral existences, and the religious cleavage did not gain strong political expression. In contrast to the situation in many Latin American and European countries where liberals and conservatives bitterly divided over religious questions, in Brazil, these two parties experienced little strife over these issues. The absence of religious conflict between liberals and conservatives contributed to an overall elite consensus and stability that contrasted with the situation in most of Spanish America (Carvalho 1980).

After the demise of the Empire in 1889, Republican political leaders officially severed church/state ties in the 1891 constitution. This action was relatively consensual among the political elite, and it did not incur ecclesiastical wrath. Legal disestablishment freed the church from a subservient relationship with the state. The state/church relationship improved during the Old Republic (1889–1930). Religious issues caused few political conflicts and were not an important source of cleavage among the political elite. Until Vargas's fall in 1945, the political elite experienced little division over religious issues.

This situation changed only slightly during the years of populist democracy, 1946–64. At the elite level, religious questions created few divisions. At the mass level, regular churchgoers were almost surely more favorably disposed than others toward the conservative parties, but religious questions were not salient in the party system. A Christian Democratic party was created in 1945, but it never elected more than 4.9 percent of the lower chamber of Congress, and only one senator in eighteen years. The parties on the left of the political spectrum, with the partial exception of the communists, were not anti-Catholic. The Communist Party was banned in 1947 and not legalized again until 1985, so its moderate anti-Catholic proclivities did not create major waves. Religious issues were not salient in the two-party system (1966–79) created by the military regime, though there were many sharp conflicts between progressive clergy and the military government.

Nor have religious conflicts been important in the party system that has emerged since 1980. In most Catholic countries, religion is a more predictable guide of political beliefs and voting behavior than class (Linz 1980; Rose and Urwin 1969; Dogan 1967; Converse 1964). In Brazil, by contrast, voting patterns show little difference between practicing Catholics and other citizens, even when controls for class, education, and region have been introduced. Based on a 1982 survey, Bruneau and Hewitt (1989) found little difference in the political views of self-described practicing Catholics and others.[12] The relative lack of political saliency of religion in party politics reflects not the absence of social divisions over religion, but rather the limited politicization of these social divisions.

In a recent study based on two large 1994 surveys, Pierucci and Prandi (1995) showed that religious practice affects voting behavior in Brazil, but its impact is significant only if we consider specific forms. Religion's impact comes not from the common (in other Western countries) cleavage between Catholics, Protestants, and nonpracticants, but rather from specific forms of religious practice. Voting patterns of Catholics did not differ greatly from those of non-Catholics, but members of Catholic base communities were more likely to vote for the left than other voters were. Religious affiliation per se, without further differentiation, had little impact. Cardoso was the preferred candidate of 43.6 percent of the Catholics and 40.3 percent of Protestants, while Lula had the support of 23.9 percent of Catholics and 18.6 percent of Protestants.

One new religious dimension started to affect party politics in the late 1980s, namely, the preference of most of Brazil's Protestant population—especially the Pentecostals—for conservative candidates (Mariano and Pierucci 1992). Although this population has grown rapidly in recent decades, it still represents only about 10 percent of Brazil's total. Protestant voters have elected a growing number of their kind to Congress, but the movement does not target a specific party. The impact of the religious cleavage in party politics, though perhaps expanding, is still limited.

In sum, Brazilian parties cannot be fully understood through the prism of social cleavages. To be sure, some parties have primarily won their votes in rural areas, while others have been more urban-based, and some have disproportionately won votes among upper- rather than lower-income groups. But the relationship between a party's social base and its programmatic orientation in Brazil has not been linear.

Why do some cleavages that are sociologically important become salient in party systems, while others do not? Politicians and parties have some choice over what issues they focus on and how they focus on them. Electorally successful parties must focus on issues that resonate with voters, but these issues are not necessarily defined by *social* cleavages. Instead political issues proper, value questions, or personalities may mobilize voter sentiment.

Sociologically salient cleavages become politically important in part because parties and politicians focus on them. Parties help define what social cleavages find expression in party systems. Parties, then, should not be seen as exclusively as expressions of societal cleavages, but also as independent variables that help shape those cleavages. In addition to being shaped by social cleavages, parties and politicians have considerable relative autonomy vis-à-vis these cleavages and in turn help to shape them (Sartori 1969). Political elites and parties are responsible for institutionalizing certain cleavages as the defining issues of modern politics. It was because parties organized and fought for given interests that some cleavages, rather than other sources of identity, came to define the main issues of contemporary politics.

In sum, a social-cleavage approach overstates the extent to which the many third-wave party systems are structured by such cleavages. The social-cleavage approach assumes that voters form partisan attachments and vote according to the sociological categories into which they fit. This assumption depends on four premises: (1) that voters' interests depend on their position in society, that is, on class, region, ethnicity, etc.; (2) that voters are conscious of these interests; (3) that they vote accordingly; and (4) that the party systems are highly institution-alized because individuals consistently vote in a way that can be predicted by their social location. All four assumptions are generally problematic and are more questionable in third-wave contexts than was the case in Western Europe until at least the 1970s. Let us consider them in turn.

1. Citizens have some common interests based on class, region, ethnicity, gender, and other structural factors, but the potential bases for differentiation or commonality of interests in society are infinite. Whether voters prioritize interests determined by social cleavages or interests related to more specifically political or cultural issues is not certain. The social-cleavage model assumes that social location determines political position. In many cases, however, political position is shaped more by political issues than by social location.

2. Citizens are aware of differences generated by class, gender, ethnicity, etc., to varying degrees, and they experience them in different ways. Voters may not be highly conscious of the "interests" that social cleavages would seem to determine. Interest is a subjective category, so citizens may not consciously articulate the idea that a particular social cleavage creates common political interests with some social category.

3. Even if voters' interests depended mostly on structural categories such as class, region, and ethnicity, they would not necessarily vote on this basis. Citizens may pay paramount attention to issues that do not depend on their structural position in society. In the debate about party systems in the advanced industrial democracies, this point has become clear in the literature about postmaterialism; Inglehart (1990) and others have argued that an important determinant of citizens' voting behavior is whether or not they have a postmaterial orientation, independent of structural considerations.

Postmaterialism is not the only nonstructural factor in voting behavior, although it has been the most widely debated. In third-wave cases it is unlikely that postmaterialism explains the limits of the social-cleavage approach. Post-materialism surfaces mostly among well-educated and affluent voters, of whom there are far fewer in third-wave democracies.[13] The social-cleavage approach assumes that competition among parties occurs among programmatic grounds: voters choose a party because programatically it will represent their interests.

The social-cleavages literature assumes that such cleavages structure voting patterns and party systems to a high degree. As the earlier discussion of institutionalization indicated, one of the ways in which we need to rethink the theoretical literature on party systems is to reexamine the degree to which and the ways in which they are structured. Virtually all have some structure, but it is a mistake to assume, as the literature on the advanced industrial democracies implicitly does, that they are equally highly structured. Most third-party systems are less structured than those on which the theoretical literature is based. This insight has not been adequately incorporated into the literature.

In third-wave cases, individual personalities, independent of party, may have a sizable impact on electoral campaigns. The party system is less structured than in Western Europe not only through social cleavages, but in general. Voters may vote to a significant degree on the basis of the personal characteristics of candidates rather than following structurally determined interests. *Personalismo* remains important in many Latin American countries; in fact, it has become a more important phenomenon in some countries than it was in the past. Personalism is rarely accorded serious social science treatment, but it is empirically observable and measurable in less-institutionalized party systems.

The reverse side of the weak structuring of party systems by social cleavages is that in many Latin American party systems, catch-all parties with heterogeneous social compositions have dominated. Where party preference is not highly structured by social cleavage, parties attract voters of socially heterogeneous backgrounds.

The limited tradition in Latin America of surveys and studies of electoral behavior before the 1980s makes it difficult to be certain without further research whether the social-cleavage model has always been less powerful than in most of Western Europe, or whether the predictive capacity of social cleavages in determining the vote has declined over time, as has occurred in Western Europe. The first possibility is almost surely correct for most Latin American countries, and the second is right for many countries, including Brazil. Whether the reason for this decline in the structuring of the party systems by social cleavages is similar to or different from the Western European cases awaits further research.[14]

The limited explanatory capacity of the social-cleavage model in understanding most third-wave party systems is related to the earlier discussion about the need to think about varying degrees of institutionalization of party systems. Where party systems are highly structured by social cleavages, there is little space for new parties to emerge. Based on their social background, most voters are loyal to specific parties. Under these conditions, electoral volatility tends to be lower, and party roots in society are strong.

A more institutionalized party system is structured to a high degree, and social cleavages can provide this structuring. Where party systems are closely linked to social cleavages, they tend to be quite institutionalized. Voters' party preferences are closely linked to sociological factors that change at a moderate pace; thus, party system change is moderate. However, the reverse is not necessarily true; a low degree of structuring of the party system along social cleavages does not necessarily imply weak system institutionalization. Party systems can be highly structured by political issues or partisan identities that are autonomous of social cleavages.

Where social cleavages do not explain the structure of the party system, weakly institutionalized party systems are more likely. Social background does not strongly bind voters to parties, so party roots in society tend to be weaker. Because citizens are less attached to parties, they are more likely to vote for candidates of different parties in the same election and across time, making electoral volatility higher.

Why is a social-cleavage approach less useful as an explanation of many third-wave party systems than it was in most of Western Europe during the first seven decades of this century? Part of the answer is sociological: in most third-wave democracies, social fragmentation (i.e., intraclass divisions—see Weyland 1996a) was more profound than in the earlier-industrializing countries of northern Europe and North America. As the literature on populism has made clear (e.g., Weffort 1978; Germani 1974), among the popular classes, a strong class identity did not crystallize in most Latin American countries (Chile was an exception). Rather, a more diffuse identity prevailed, one as being part of "the people." This identity was rooted in, although not fully determined by, structural realities: a smaller working class, a larger poor urban underclass outside the formal sector, and greater contrasts between the modern and traditional sectors of the economy that made it difficult to forge a common identity. This made it difficult for parties to win support on the basis of appeals to class (Dix 1989). Part of the answer is political: in authoritarian or oligarchic political systems with little open competition, politicians did not politicize issues of class, region, or religion by organizing political parties. Such politicization could have threatened entrenched ruling elites, and there was usually little incentive to organize parties in authoritarian or oligarchic political systems.

The Shaping of Party Systems from Above

Most analysts of party systems have emphasized the way they are shaped from below. The social-cleavage approach discussed above sees party systems as expressions of cleavage structures. Another major approach to understanding party-system formation is the spatial model, pioneered by Downs (1957). Through its many modifications (Enelow and Hinich 1990; Robertson 1976), the spatial model has claimed that party systems form according to the distribution of voters' preferences. According to this approach, voters chose the candidate or party closest to their own preferred positions on issues. Like the social-cleavages approach, the spatial model emphasizes how society—in particular, the distribution of preferences among voters—shapes party systems. A top–down perspective is not entirely absent in analyses of the established democracies, but it is less articulated than either the social-cleavage or the spatial approaches.

We can think of a continuum from lesser to greater elite and state shaping of the party system from above. Once again, there are theoretical reasons to expect systematic differences between first- and third-wave cases, with third-wave party systems being more subject to greater shaping from above. Most first-wave cases established histories of long and continuous democracy, so there were fewer opportunities for authoritarian leaders to suppress the old party system and create a new one. During authoritarian periods and democratic transitions states can most profoundly reshape party systems. Civil society was generally more robust at an early stage in the Western European cases than in most third-wave democracies, creating a counterbalance to the state.

When we turn to third-wave cases, the neglect of the political elite's role in shaping party systems appears to be a result of the limited variance in the cases that have been the basis for most theorizing about party systems. This fact is curious, considering the shift away from societal explanations and toward political explanations in other subfields of political science. Nevertheless, there has been insufficient work on how political elites and the state shape party systems from above. (For exceptions, see Chibber and Torcal 1997, Gunther et al. 1986, Katz and Mair 1994, Kitschett 1994, Przeworski and Sprague 1986.) Although demands and preferences from their constituents constrain them, political elites have some autonomy in framing issues and political competition. This is probably the most important way in which political elites shape party systems.

Third-wave party systems are especially subject to elite reshaping from above. They are less institutionalized and hence more prone to disruption by state leaders. If a party system is deeply rooted in society, it is difficult for state leaders to alter it significantly from above. Third-wave democracies are more likely to have experienced democratic breakdowns and transitions, and such moments are particularly given to reshaping party systems from above. The authoritarian regimes that previously governed third-wave democracies had an arsenal of weapons—including repression, banning parties and party leaders, and blatantly favoring some parties—that enabled them to reshape party systems. The state generally exercised greater influence over political development in general, so it is not surprising that it also shaped party-system formation more than in first-wave cases.

States can reshape party systems in several ways. They can abolish or proscribe parties and the party system, sometimes with long-term consequences. Because of a ban or proscription, or because of a long hiatus with no competitive elections, previously significant parties may permanently wither, and fresh opportunities may emerge for new or established parties. In Chile, for example, after seventeen years of military rule (1973–90), the communists failed to return to their former strength, and an important new party, the PPD (Party for Democracy), emerged. The proscription of APRA in Peru in the 1940s and 1950s did not diminish that party's support, but it may well have facilitated the emergence of competitors.

State leaders can create parties from above and can use public resources to build parties and create an uneven playing field. The Mexican PRI is a good example. Created from above, it became the dominant institution in Mexican politics for decades. Some of the major parties of both of Brazil's democratic periods were also created by the outgoing authoritarian regime.

State leaders can impose electoral and party legislation, thereby shaping the menu from which voters can choose. The Pinochet dictatorship in Chile (1973–90) engineered two-member districts in hopes of favoring the right and muffling the left. Democratic elections since 1989 suggest that it succeeded in doing so.

Third-wave party systems are also more susceptible to shaping from above by political elites outside the state than are first-wave systems. Because parties are less rooted in society and organizational routines less institutionalized, politicians in third-wave democracies have more autonomy vis-à-vis constituents than politicians in first-wave democracies. They can use this autonomy to switch parties, foster party mergers, and induce party schisms.

Party switching by individuals and mergers and schisms can fundamentally alter a party system. Rarely are these actions of politicians responses to below. Although the "electoral connection" (Mayhew 1974) may explain a wide range of politicians' behavior, in most third-wave democracies it does not explain politicians' decisions to change parties, nor does it explain party mergers and schisms. These strategic decisions can have lasting effects.

The Brazilian case illustrates the general point that states and political elites shape party systems from above. In Brazil, the shaping of party systems by the state has been crucial, as M. Souza (1976) and Lamounier and Meneguello (1986) have emphasized. The state has been a powerful actor in party-system formation in two ways. First, state leaders have played a major role in organizing parties.

Second, the state has shaped party-system formation by dissolving parties and party systems. On five occasions—1889, 1930, 1937, 1965, and 1979—state leaders dissolved existing party systems. Each time—with the exception of 1937—they then created new party systems. All five state interventions against existing party systems—most profoundly, that of 1965—disrupted processes of party-system institutionalization.

State leaders created the main parties of the Empire (1822–89). The Liberal and Conservative parties were created by powerful governing elites, who used the parties to further their own objectives, and the parties remained instruments of personalistic domination.

The leaders of the military coup of 1889 suppressed the Liberals and Conservatives, fearing that the parties would remain loyal to the monarchy. When the military relinquished power in 1894, these parties never returned to the scene. The parties of the empire had weak roots in society, but they had become more important during the waning decades of monarchical power. The military's dissolution of these parties set back efforts at party building. State leaders then forged the parties of the 1889–1930 regime, known as the Old Republic.

The Old Republic collapsed with a coup in 1930. Fearful that the old regime's organizations represented a threat, in the early 1930s President Getúlio Vargas (1930–45) suppressed many of the parties that had been created during the Old Republic. Seven years later he banned all parties.

After Vargas was deposed in 1945, Brazil had a semidemocratic regime that lasted nearly two decades (1946–64). Two of the three major parties of the period, the populist, center-left PTB (Brazilian Labor Party), and the center-right PSD (Social Democratic Party), were created in 1944–45 by Vargas, who was aware of the winds of democratization that were blowing in much of Latin America. These two were as much a creation from above, to bolster the interests of Vargas and his supporters, as from below (M. Souza 1976). Of course, these parties thrived only because they were able to generate popular appeal.

Vargas's actions first in suppressing parties (1937–44), then in building two parties that governed during most of Brazil's first democratic period, decisively shaped the contours of party politics. Had Vargas made other choices, Brazilian party development would have been different. There was no historical necessity for Vargas to organize two major parties, though under free conditions it was virtually inevitable that one major party would have supported Vargas and his allies. Vargas's idiosyncratic decision had a fundamental impact on the 1945–64 party system. The most important cleavage in party politics between 1944 and 1954 was not social, but rather the divide between pro- and anti-Vargas forces.

In 1965, yet another state intervention decisively recast the party system. Disappointed with the results of the 1965 elections and convinced that the post–1945 party system was dysfunctional, the military dictatorship banned the existing parties and laid down electoral rules that led to the emergence of a two-party system. The party system of the 1946–64 period had become moderately institutionalized by the time of the coup. The suppression of these parties disrupted the process of institutionalization.

Cognizant of a need for legitimacy, the military fostered the creation of two new parties, the pro-regime Arena (Renovative National Alliance) and the moderate opposition party, the Brazilian Democratic Movement, (MDB). The decision of the military regime to reshape the party system and build new parties rather than suppressing them, as the militaries of Argentina, Chile, and Uruguay did, has had a profound impact on party formation since 1965. By 1974, these two parties had started to take root in society and become relevant actors in the political process. In 1979, aware that electoral trends increasingly favored the MDB, the government again abolished the extant parties and imposed a reform of the electoral system, this time permitting the gradual reemergence of a multiparty system. Once again, state intervention decisively reshaped the party system. Most of the current parties have lineages that can be traced back to those of the 1966–79 period; in the case of the two largest parties, the PMDB and the PFL, this lineage is direct.

State leaders also helped organize some of the major parties of the new period of democracy (1985–present). The second-largest congressional party of the post–1985 period, the conservative Party of the Liberal Front (PFL), was created by governors of Brazil's northeastern states; again, governing elites took the lead in creating a party. The heir to Arena, the PDS, was also fundamentally a creation from above.

Because of these multiple state interventions, Brazilian party-system formation has been punctuated by discontinuities that cannot be explained by a sociological interpretation. During the later decades of the Empire (roughly the 1860s to the 1880s), parties started to assume greater significance, though they were still quite limited. Then with the collapse of the Empire, the old parties were dissolved by the military government of 1889–94, leading to their demise. During the democratic period of 1946–64, the party system started to become relatively institutionalized, only to be extinguished by the military regime. If party systems had been the product of long-term structural trends, as cleavage approaches suggest, we would not expect such marked discontinuities. As Lamounier and Meneguello (1986) have emphasized, the state has been the key actor in causing these discontinuities.

The role of the Brazilian state and political elites in shaping and reforging party systems is not unique within Latin America. Even seemingly well-established party systems have been decisively reshaped by state interventions. For example, the Chilean military regime of 1973–90 deliberately set out to change the party system, and it succeeded. The party system has moved from three main blocs (left, center, right) to two as a consequence of the military's machinations. Peruvian President Alberto Fujimori (1990–) tried to recast the party system of his country. His efforts to displace the traditional parties proved successful; by 1995, they had virtually disappeared. In some other countries of the region, party systems have been formed and reshaped by state actors.

State leaders do not always succeed in reshaping the party system as they intend to. In Brazil, for example, the military regime of 1964–85 wanted to diminish party-system fragmentation. During the period of military rule, a restrictive electoral system limited fragmentation, but by the end of the 1980s, fragmentation had easily surpassed that of the 1946–64 democratic period. Although the military regime did not have a lasting effect in restraining fragmentation, it did obliterate for good the main parties of 1945–64.

If states have been important in shaping party systems in several third-wave cases, why has our theoretical understanding of party-system formation been slow to recognize this fact? Most of the influential theoretical works on party-system formation have been written by scholars familiar with West European or U.S. party systems. The United States and parts of Western Europe are exceptional in enjoying long, continuous democracies. States have not intervened to recast party systems, as has occurred in many third-wave countries. The United States and Northern Europe had more robust civil societies, and political life generally was less state-led and more societally determined. In Western Europe, the sociological approach to party-system formation has more compelling foundations than in Latin America because of the earlier emergence of democracy and the less patrimonial form of political development. Even among the advanced industrial democracies, however, there is one case in which the state deliberately recast the party system: France under de Gaulle (Suleiman 1994).

As the following chapters will show, the Brazilian case also underscores the role of political elites outside the state in shaping party systems from above. Political elites since 1985 have engaged in hundreds of cases of party switching. They have promoted many party mergers and splits. These actions have significantly affected the party system, and they cannot be understood from a bottom-up perspective.

Emphasis on the role of states and political elites in party-system formation directs attention to the role of choice and leadership in shaping party politics. Political elites emphasize some issues and muffle others. Especially before the institutionalization of a party system, their choices affect the issues that emerge as salient in different political systems. These choices affect which cleavages become politically relevant.

With occasional exceptions (M. Souza 1976; Lamounier and Meneguello 1986), most scholars writing on party systems in Latin America have not paid sufficient attention to the role of the state. Just as the literature on corporatism (Malloy 1977; Schmitter 1971, 1974; Stepan 1978b) questioned the view that patterns of interest representation should be seen as emanating only from society when in fact they were often structured from above. Now is it time for analysts to recognize the profound impact states and political elites have had on party-system formation in third-wave democracies.

Conclusion

In sum, most of the literature, especially that on social cleavages and spatial patterning, implicitly sees party-system formation as reflecting society; it emphasizes a down–up approach. This approach understates the impact of states and political elites in forming party systems. This influence is especially important when we turn to many new democracies.

Analyses of third-wave parties and party systems have proliferated in the past decade, but they have generally not attempted to challenge the way we theorize about and compare party systems.[15] Such a challenge is in order. Analyzing third-wave party systems enables one to perceive some issues of great importance that do not surface in Western European cases.

PART II

The Brazilian Party Systems
Past and Present

CHAPTER 3

A Legacy of Party Underdevelopment, 1822–1979

Why do party systems form as they do? What explains the difficulties of party-system institutionalization in Brazil? My analysis of these questions draws on three kinds of factors: the actions of state leaders and political elites, the constellation of social actors and therefore the way that societies form and evolve, and institutional rules. In Brazil, all three have worked against party-system institutionalization, though with different weights at different times. This chapter underscores how the first two factors created historical obstacles to institutionalizing a party system, with some attention to institutional rules for the 1946–64 period.

This chapter is included not merely or principally to provide background. Political systems are the product of historical legacies which, although they do not determine present outcomes, condition what is possible. So it is with the Brazilian party system of the post–1979 period: it is shaped by the historical formation of the political system.

Brazil has a long history of weak parties, and this chapter explains why this was so during the long period under discussion here. The argument for the pre–1945 period focuses on the preference of dominant elites for weak parties, the state's dissolution of the existing party systems in 1889, 1930, and 1937, and overwhelming structural and political obstacles to the formation of modern parties. Several features of the political system were inimical to subsequent party building: the political exclusion of the masses, a system in which powerful political elites dominated the local scene and enjoyed ample autonomy vis-à-vis national parties, a patrimonial order in which parties and the state were treated as if they were the private property of dominant elites, and the historic subordination of parties to powerful individuals.

The second part of the chapter examines positive trends and limits in party building during Brazil's first democratic interlude, from 1945 until 1964. On the positive side, modern mass parties emerged for the first time, and they were important actors in the political system, primarily because through parties individuals were competitively elected to key political posts. Electoral participation expanded exponentially, and parties established consistent social bases. Between 1945 and 1960, the party system was becoming more institutionalized.

But the continuities in party politics were also significant. The local and state orientation of national politicians limited the development of a national party system. Individual politicians rather than parties were the main mechanism of representation. A majority of the adult population did not enjoy citizenship rights because the illiterate were not enfranchised. The patrimonial fusion of state, party, and economic interests did not fully erode. Electoral volatility was moderately high, indicating considerable flux in the party system, and parties structured the vote less than in many democracies. The allegiance of political elites to party organizations was often shallow. After 1960, a process of disaggregation afflicted the party system. Intraparty conflicts were exacerbated and ideological polarization increased, ultimately contributing to the breakdown of democracy in 1964. Despite these problems, the party system was more institutionalized than it has been since 1985. This suggests that it is misleading to see Brazil's party weakness of the post–1985 period simply as a product of past party fragility, even though past legacies have contributed to present problems.

The final part of the chapter looks at parties and elections during the first fifteen years of military rule, 1964–79. In contrast to the military dictatorships of the southern cone between 1966 and 1990, the Brazilian authoritarian regime allowed elections, parties, and Congress to function most of the time. During the first decade of military rule, these institutions had limited political significance. After 1974, however, they became a key element in the process of political liberalization and democratization.

Brazil's Parties of Notables, the 1830s to 1945

The most notable feature of Brazilian party development until 1945 is the complete absence of modern parties. Before developing this point, a brief discussion about the difference between modern (or mass) and premodern parties (or parties of notables) is in order. Small elite groups that vie for power strictly on the basis of intraelite struggles differ substantially from modern parties that attempt to build constituencies in society as a means of gaining power. Such elite groups, which were often called parties, had been on the scene for centuries before modern parties emerged. This distinction between parties of notables and modern mass parties says much about the nature of the political system (Sartori 1976: 20; Weber 1946: 102–7; J. S. Valenzuela 1985: 37–41).

Modern mass parties and their precursors differ in two major respects.[1] First, the audience of the premass party is restricted to elite groups. Such parties have no reason to mobilize the masses, who do not participate in institutional politics. Parties of notables are loosely organized elite groups with few linkages to groups in society. These parties are like cliques and remain highly personalized. In contrast, common citizens are a key public for modern parties. Parties try to get their message to the broad mass of citizens and attempt to win their votes. To succeed over time, they must develop stable bases of support in society. Consequently, they must construct linkages with groups in society. Modern parties link elites and the voters who choose them. Second, premodern parties are loosely structured, with little formal organization. Their structures are linked primarily to parliamentary activity. Modern mass parties vary a great deal in how much they are structured and how much formal organization they have, but they need an ongoing organization (Duverger 1954: xxiii–xxxvii; LaPalombara and Weiner 1966).[2]

This distinction between modern and premodern parties is important here, for although Brazil has had premodern parties since the 1830s, modern mass parties emerged only in 1945. Brazil gained independence in 1822. During Brazil's first 123 years (1822–1945) as an independent nation, the country underwent four major changes in party systems, from the two-party format of the Empire (1830s to 1889), to the radically decentralized and usually one-party-per-state regime of the Old Republic (1889–1930), to the great flux of the early Vargas years (1930–37), and finally the no-party state of the Estado Novo (1937–45). Despite these discontinuities in party systems, meaningful changes in the political system, and significant social changes, there were important continuities in the nature of Brazilian parties. Until the 1930s, participation in parties was restricted to a narrow group of elites, and parties had weak roots in society, with essentially no popular participation. Parties were in a symbiotic relationship with the state but subordinate to it. Clientelism and patronage were the dominant fibers of Brazilian parties, and the proclivity of politicians to switch parties to gain access to patronage, still a common feature of Brazilian parties, was already apparent, reflecting limited party allegiance. Until the 1930s, parties were controlled by a small group of elites. The boundaries between party, oligarchy, and state were permeable in a patrimonial political system (Faoro 1975; R. Graham 1990; Lewin 1987; Schwartzman 1982; Uricoechea 1980).

A central tale of the first 123 years of Brazilian political history was the absence of mass parties. None of the pre–1930 organizations in Brazil remotely resembled modern parties, and those of the 1930–37 period also fail to qualify. Both of the defining features of modern mass parties were absent. Brazilian politics was restricted to a narrow elite group, and the franchise remained extremely restricted until the 1930s. Indeed, there was a consensus among political elites that the masses should deliberately be excluded from politics. The other main defining feature of modern parties, permanent organization, was also absent. Even though parties were important stepping stones to power and resources, they themselves were bereft of resources, institutionalized structures, and party professionals.

During the Old Republic, Brazilian party underdevelopment became exceptional. In many countries, by contrast, party development occurred rapidly during this period. By the 1920s, all of the northern European nations had well-developed parties; in fact, the interwar period arguably represented the years when parties were at their zenith as dominant political actors. The decades between 1889 and 1930 witnessed a rapid transition from elite-based politics and parties to modern mass democracies and parties. Well-disciplined and organized working-class parties sprouted and consolidated all over northern Europe and in Canada, Australia, and New Zealand. The bourgeois parties were less disciplined and organized, but they, too, consolidated positions as major political actors. In Latin America, mass parties had established themselves particularly in Argentina, Chile, and Uruguay.

Brazil's lack of modern parties was exceptional for what is now a middle-income country. What explains the late emergence of modern parties in Brazil? The answer hinges around structural and political factors, which together created insurmountable obstacles to building modern parties. The desire of state leaders and political elites to rule through personalistic channels, coupled with structural features of Brazilian society, conspired against mass parties.

The governing elite had no need or desire for stronger parties. With no history of open competition and extremely restricted participation, the elite had no incentives to organize broad-based parties. Throughout the Empire, elections were held regularly, but free competition among parties was unknown. Fraud and coercion were rampant, and the government so controlled elections that it never lost an election after 1840 (R. Graham 1990: 71–98; Uricoechea 1980: 35–60). As was the case in the Empire, after 1894 elections were regularly scheduled and held, but the electoral flimflam of the Old Republic equaled if not surpassed that of the Empire. Without fair elections and with a restricted electorate, competing elites had nothing to gain by organizing parties.

Competitive regimes—even if they are predemocratic—give governing elites incentives to build parties. Before institutionalized competition was the basis for selecting top political leaders, there was little need to organize to create mass parties because competition was less meaningful. The loose elite groups that formed in parliament to defend different points of view and regional interests sufficed. In Brazil, there was nothing resembling free and fair political competition until the 1930s.

Institutionalizing open competition in elections as the means for selecting top-level political leaders implied an acceptance of competition and parties (Hofstadter 1969). This acceptance was slow in coming in Brazil. During the Empire, elections were not endorsed as the means of selecting top leaders. After the implementation of a presidential system in 1889, the chief executives frequently did their best to undermine parties, lest they become an independent source of power that could challenge them. Especially after 1889, parties were seen as a threat that promoted particularistic interests and could divide Brazil. Brazil's political culture, marked by antiparty ideologies, did not provide fertile ground for the emergence of parties (Lamounier 1974).

The extremely restricted nature of political participation reinforced the lack of incentives to build parties. If the suffrage is narrow, elites can function in parties of notables. Broad electoral participation encourages the emergence of mass parties. When common citizens have acquired the franchise, political elites need mass support—otherwise they will lose elections and disappear from the political landscape.

At different paces in different countries, the growth of the electorate meant that politicians who created solid parties had a great advantage. Politicians created mass parties to help mobilize the vote and establish ongoing linkages with voters. The expansion of the electorate obliged politicians to seek votes more actively than they had in the past. As participation expanded, politicians either developed reasonably stable constituencies or failed to make the adjustment to the era of mass politics. The expansion of the suffrage induced changes in party organization and campaign methods as old organizations attempted to adjust to new situations (Hofstadter 1969; Weber 1946; Duverger 1954; J. S. Valenzuela 1985: 37–41).

The causal pattern between the emergence of modern parties and the broadening of political participation was not unidirectional; parties encouraged the expansion of the electorate as a means of strengthening their own positions. Convinced that the new voters would support them, some parties fought to broaden the franchise. Parties encouraged broader participation as much as it fostered party development.

But it was not merely that Brazil's governing elite had weak incentives to build mass parties. Rather, its members had positive incentives to oppose them. Party weakness served the interests of key actors until 1945. The emperor and presidents, political elites, and local bosses were free to transact as they wanted, unburdened by party ties. As R. Graham (1990: 167) puts it, "The lack of a [party] system facilitated communication among the political elite. Government could still be an arrangement among friends. By not dividing themselves too rigidly into distinct parties, they could keep talking across party lines."

The desire of leading political elites to quash parties heightened during the Old Republic. The military dissolved the traditional parties in 1889 because it saw them as threats. Beginning with Campos Sales (1898–1902), civilian presidents consistently undermined efforts to build national parties, fearing that they would compete with the executive in a nation where decentralization had gone to such an extreme that maintaining the country intact was a challenge. Vargas represented another step in the progression of state leaders who undermined parties, first attacking the Republican machines in many states and then banning all parties. In sum, before 1945, state and other governing elites had at best weak incentives to build parties, and often were downright hostile to them, perceiving them as threats.

The second key factor that shapes party-system development is societal formation. In this respect, the most important feature of Brazil before 1945 was the extreme weakness of civil society. There was no capacity from below to push elites into creating modern parties.

An independent citizenry needs a minimum of information and knowledge to function politically. In Brazil this was not usually the case before 1945. The problem was not only one of juridical rights, but also of having minimal life conditions. Where people eked out a survival existence in isolated conditions in the countryside, with no access to communication about politics, effective participation was impossible. High levels of illiteracy and a large, impoverished, and unorganized peasant population worked against the broadening of participation in politics, and therefore worked against the emergence of mass parties.

Before 1945 (and to a diminishing degree even later), Brazil lacked the social and political conditions needed for an independent electorate. Brazil was predominantly a rural society until the second half of the twentieth century, and most peasants were dependent on landowners. Local political bosses reigned supreme, and they purchased or otherwise thwarted the vote of their tenants. There was no effective notion of rights that pertained to all citizens. Under such conditions, not only party building, but institution building in general, was problematic.

The heteronomy of common people was exacerbated by the weakness of popular organization. Politically, the popular sectors were unorganized because industrialization, urbanization, and unionization occurred relatively late. The weakness of the popular sectors limited the extent to which class emerged as a cleavage basis that would stimulate party organization.

Until 1945, parties were little more than appendages of the personal volition of the landed elite and political class. At the local level, landowners and political notables were often one and the same, and they had close connections even when they were not (Lewin 1987). In the less-developed regions of Brazil, this held true until 1964. Such personalistic domination of parties and of political life more generally was a major cause of party weakness before 1945 (Oliveira Vianna 1949; Leal 1949).

THE ENDURING LEGACY OF THE PRE–1945 PERIOD

Several features of Brazil's pre–1945 historical legacy continue to affect party politics until this day. First, Brazil has historically been characterized by the political exclusion of the masses. The first efforts to incorporate a broader segment of society into electoral politics occurred in the 1930s. Popular incorporation occurred gradually in the decades following 1930, but the illiterate gained the franchise only in 1985. Brazilian politics to this day remains more elitist than is the case in the other middle-income countries of Latin America, with the possible exception of Mexico.

A second historical legacy has been the patrimonial fusion of party, state, and individual power. During the Empire, oligarchs of both parties treated political office like personal property, appropriating whatever sinecures they could. This practice continued virtually unabated through the Old Republic. Patrimonialism has declined since 1930, but it remains an ingredient in Brazilian party politics.

Third, despite the centralizing efforts of Vargas (1930–45) and the military regime (1964–85), Brazilian politics retains a federalism and localism that are exceptional in Latin America. The historic roots are clear: during the Empire and the Old Republic, local landlords were also political bosses who effectively resisted state encroachments, even while using the state to their advantage. To a considerable degree, powerful local elites built the political system from below, and they constructed mechanisms to retain autonomy vis-à-vis the central state.

In comparative perspective, the complete absence of national parties by as late as 1930 stands out. Extreme decentralization and poor transportation and communication systems enabled local oligarchs to rule with few obstacles from government or party organizations. Frequently, especially in the hinterland, their use of violence was legendary. The Old Republic thus became the quintessence of oligarchical politics. The phenomenon of untethered rule by local political bosses, which reached its zenith during the Old Republic, was known as *coronelismo* (Leal 1949, Queiroz 1975; Cammack 1982; Faoro 1975: 620–53).

A fourth important legacy is that parties were historically subordinate to powerful individuals. Rural power, clientelism, and patronage continued to be the central determinants of access to political power, and parties were highly personalistic. Most state leaders preferred a fluid, personalistic political system; they rejected the ties that a strong party organization would entail.

Brazil has modernized at a rapid pace since the days of unbridled personalism, but vestiges of this personalism remain in place until this day.

Parties and Liberal Democracy, 1946–64

My discussion of Brazil's first democratic period emphasizes three points. First, modern mass parties emerged for the first time, and they became important actors in the political system. Nineteen forty-five was the beginning of some profound changes in party politics.[3] Second, alongside the changes were equally important continuities that help explain why the party system did not become more institutionalized. Brazil did not fully overcome the heritage of party weakness during this period. Understanding both the changes and their limits and the reasons for the changes and continuities is crucial to grasping why the party system has evolved in a certain manner. Third, notwithstanding some propitious indications of party building, the party system became only moderately institutionalized, and parties remained weaker than in quite a few Latin American countries.

OVERVIEW

Before developing these three points, a brief overview of the 1945–64 party system is necessary. As World War II was drawing to a close, dictator Getúlio Vargas and his opponents saw the writing on the wall: an era of mass politics and electoral competition was approaching. This perception occasioned the first efforts to create mass parties. In Minas Gerais in 1943, the opposition signed the Mineiro Manifest, which called for the establishment of democracy. This was the inaugural act of politicians who two years later formed the União Democrática Nacional (UDN), the National Democratic Union, one of the three large parties of the 1945–64 period. Initially the UDN was a very heterogeneous coalition of anti-Vargas forces. In 1945, Vargas himself began to maneuver to create mass parties. His appointed state governors led the way in creating the Partido Social Democrático (PSD), the Social Democratic Party, in May 1945, and the new party endorsed Vargas's candidate for president, General Eurico Dutra. Simultaneously, Vargas's lieutenants in the labor movement began to organize a new labor-based party, the Partido Trabalhista Brasileiro (PTB), Brazilian Labor Party (Gomes 1988: 288–324). When Vargas was overthrown in October 1945, the era of mass parties in Brazil began.

After Vargas was deposed, presidential elections were held in December 1945, and for the first time ever, party competition became an important feature of access to the most powerful political positions. There were, however, two limitations to party competition during this period. First, after achieving a strong showing in the 1945 presidential election, the Communist Party was banned in 1947, a victim of the Cold War. Its proscription had consequences for the party system as a whole, for as Duverger (1954) argued, parties of the left provided a stimulus for more-organized, cohesive parties. Moreover, the proscription was in its own right antidemocratic. Second, occasional military vetoes and interventions meant that at some key moments, military actions rather than electoral results and constitutional norms decided the course of events. Particularly significant in this regard were a November 1955 preventive coup that deposed the acting president, a military veto of João Goulart's assuming full presidential powers when Jânio Quadros resigned in 1961, and the 1964 coup that overthrew Goulart. Because of these restrictions on competition and participation, the Brazilian political system between 1945 and 1964 cannot be considered a full democracy.

At the national level, the 1945–64 party system had three large parties and a panoply of smaller ones. The largest party in Congress was the PSD, which Hippólito (1985) characterized as centrist, though it has often been considered conservative (Soares 1973) with a predominantly rural base.[4]

Until 1962, the UDN had the second-largest congressional delegation. Of the three major parties, it was the most conservative, and it was somewhat more ideological than the PSD. Although it was also stronger in rural than urban areas, the UDN was somewhat more urban-based than the PSD. Like the PSD, it fared better in the less-developed regions of the country, but it was strong in some of the largest cities of the developed regions, including Rio de Janeiro. Virulently anti-Vargas and anti-PTB, the UDN adhered to liberal democracy in its discourse, but its antipopular elitism led it to adopt postures incompatible with democratic practice. Frequently the party called on the military to prevent populists from taking office. It opposed allowing João Goulart to assume the presidency in 1961, and it called for coups in 1954 and 1964 (Benevides 1981).

The PTB was the most progressive of the three parties, and in 1962 it surpassed the UDN's congressional delegation and became the second-largest party in Congress. Like the PSD, the PTB was a creation of Vargas and the state apparatus, especially the ministry of labor, capitalizing on the support Vargas won from organized labor during the Estado Novo. Political pundits averred that Vargas had created the PSD with his right hand and the PTB with his left. It was an urban-based party (Soares 1973), and it fared especially well in working-class areas (Simão 1956). A populist party, it was dominated by Vargas until his suicide in 1954. After the Communist Party was proscribed, most of the left supported the PTB (Benevides 1989; Delgado 1989).

In addition to these three parties, a plethora of other agglomerations proliferated, but the three main parties dominated presidential and national legislative
elections. After 1950, the party system became quite fragmented, i.e., a large
number of parties obtained seats and no party was dominant. The effective
number of parties in the Chamber of Deputies increased from 2.77 in 1945 to
4.10 in 1950, 4.59 in 1954, 4.50 in 1958, and 4.55 in 1962. The effective number of
parties in the Senate, based on election results (rather than Senate composition),
increased from 2.24 in 1945 to 2.72 in 1947, 5.25 in 1950, 3.61 in 1954, 3.22 in 1958,
and 4.26 in 1962.

The PSD suffered a decline between 1945 and 1964, falling from 52.8
percent of the seats in the Chamber in 1946 to 28.8 percent in 1962. It also
experienced large declines in the Senate and for the presidency. The UDN
also declined in lower Chamber seats, from 26.9 percent of the seats in 1946
to 22.2 percent in 1962.   However, it offset these drops with strong results
for president and governors in 1960 and 1962, respectively. The PTB grew
rapidly. Its share of seats in the Chamber of Deputies rose in every election,
increasing from 7.7 percent of the seats in 1946 to 28.4 percent in 1962, when
it came within two seats of equaling the PSD's total. The centrist Christian
Democratic Party (PDC) and a bevy of smaller parties also expanded their
share of the vote. Overall, conservative and centrist parties declined while
populist/reformist parties grew (Soares 1973; Santos 1986: 72–78; O. Carvalho
1958).

ELEMENTS OF CHANGE IN PARTY POLITICS

After 1945, Brazil developed mass parties that differed markedly from those
of the pre–1945 period. Brazil's parties since 1945 have been modern in the sense
defined above; they needed to win votes and appeal to the masses rather than
being restricted to elite groups; they had more formal organization than the
pre–1945 parties even though their organizations were still weak in comparative
perspective; they organized on a nationwide basis rather than being restricted
to a few large cities. Parties became important means of access to power, and
electoral participation was much broader than it had been before 1945. Moreover, during 1946–64, Brazil developed a moderately institutionalized party
system.

I explained the late emergence of modern parties in terms of the frequent
crushing of parties by state leaders, the lack of incentives for party building by
powerful elites, and the weakness of Brazilian civil society. During the 1946–64
period, these features of the Brazilian political system changed somewhat—but
not completely.

Especially prior to 1930, the masses were excluded from politics, so elites had
little incentive to create modern party organizations to cultivate popular sup-

port. This situation began to change in 1945. More than six million citizens voted, better than a threefold increase in relation to the previous record set in the 1930 presidential elections. The electoral law excluded the illiterate—still a majority of the adult population—but the age of mass politics and modern parties had begun (Soares 1973: 40–68; Ramos 1961: 68–88). After 1945, in order to win office, Brazilian parties had to cultivate popular sympathies.

Between 1945 and 1964, electoral participation expanded rapidly. From 1945 to 1960 the number of voters in presidential elections increased by more than 100 percent in absolute terms, and in relative terms from 13.4 percent to 19.1 percent of the total population.

Popular participation gave elites the need to win popular allegiance, and parties are the main means of institutionalizing popular loyalties. The days of oligarchical politics in which legitimacy could rest solely on elite bases had ended. From 1946 on, politics would either have to include the popular sectors or forcefully exclude them.

The change in popular participation was also qualitative. There was a decrease in fraud and coercion, and more voters were able to cast their ballots without fear of reprisal. Labor unions, neighborhood associations, and by the early 1960s peasant unions began to assert themselves. Brazilian civil society became more developed. Whereas before 1945 there was little independent popular citizenship, after 1945 the popular classes increasingly became a political subject. Brazil underwent massive structural changes that gradually loosened the personalistic, preparty domination of politics.

Brazil became an increasingly urban country, and landlords gradually lost the unfettered dominance they had exercised until 1930. In view of the personalistic mechanisms of political control that pervaded the countryside, urbanization had important political consequences. In the cities, personalistic domination was weaker than in the countryside (Blondel 1957: 101–30). Urban denizens were less physically isolated, less dependent on their *patrão* (because they could change jobs more easily), and had more exposure to education and political organizations and ideas. Even in some rural areas, peasants organized after 1955, undermining personalized traditional clientelism and *coronelismo* (J. S. Martins 1981). Corporatism and clientelism continued to tether popular participation, but fewer people were directly controlled by powerful political bosses. Even where local bosses still reigned supreme, their domination became kinder and gentler.

CONTINUITIES

Three continuities deserve particular mention: a relatively constrained popular presence in politics until the early 1960s, the power of local political elites and state governors who rejected centralized and disciplined national parties, and widespread use of public resources to build political support and further political careers. All three continuities have shaped Brazilian party politics since 1945.

The corporatist mechanisms of interest articulation created during the Estado Novo were institutionalized in the new political order (M. Souza 1976: 105–36; Schmitter 1971). The early phases of working-class incorporation into political life occurred under the aegis of corporatist mechanisms during the first (1930–45) Vargas period (Collier and Collier 1991). These mechanisms were reinforced rather than dismantled after Vargas's overthrow. They continued to shackle working-class organization until the early 1960s, when more pluralistic, independent patterns began to emerge, only to be decapitated by the 1964 coup.

Corporatist controls reduced labor's ability to act autonomously. The state licensed, funded, and regulated unions in a variety of ways, all of which made them dependent on the state. The limited size and heterogeneity of the working class militated against powerful popular organizations, and corporatism reinforced these barriers.

Parties had less incentive to serve as the conduits of popular demands because the popular classes were comparatively weak politically and fragmented by corporatist institutions. The weakness of popular political organization favored clientelistic exchanges. Politicians had little incentive to promote mass entitlement programs given weak collective popular action on their behalf. The weakening of unions by corporatist controls and by the fragmentation of the popular sectors made the emergence of a strong working-class party less likely.

In rural areas, mechanisms of control over the popular-class vote, including personal bonds that linked landowner and peasant, vote buying, coercion, and occasional fraud, continued to vitiate elections (Blondel 1957: 73–100). Throughout this period, Brazil continued to be primarily a rural society. Until the mid-1950s, there were no efforts to organize workers in the countryside. Such efforts became significant after the late 1950s, but they were limited to a few states (J. S. Martins 1981: 21–102).

The upshot was a weak popular presence in politics until the early 1960s, when popular organization and mobilization began to achieve a crescendo. The popular classes remained weakly organized compared to Argentina, Chile, Uruguay, and some other Latin American countries. This had repercussions for party building: There was a weaker sociological base for labor parties in Brazil than in Argentina, Chile, or Uruguay.

A second important continuity that still affects the post–1979 party system is the ongoing power of traditional political elites (Hagopian 1996). In small and medium *municípios*, local political notables exercised considerable influence over the vote throughout the populist period. Traditional political elites reduced the extent to which parties would constrain them by creating loose, highly decentralized, and relatively undisciplined organizations. They deliberately limited party control over political life—and over their own capacity to attend to regional clienteles. Local politics remained a paramount concern for most politicians. The local orientation of politicians thwarted building powerful national parties. Several studies of the 1945–64 regime have underscored the autonomy of state-level organizations vis-à-vis the national party, as well as the autonomy of individual politicians from both the state and national party organizations (Peterson 1962: 188–207; Lima Júnior 1983; Hippólito 1985: 119–33; Oliveira 1973; Benevides 1981: 160–71).

In addition to engineering rules that favored decentralization, traditional political elites protected their autonomy vis-à-vis party leaders through an open-list proportional-representation system for the lower chamber of the National Congress and for state assemblies. With the open-list system, deputies were elected on the basis of votes for them, not for the party. This system created incentives for intraparty competition and helped give individual politicians autonomy. Formal rules of the game institutionalized the preference of Brazilian politicians for loose parties in which they could more easily attend to local interests because they were not tied down by party obligations.

Another institutional rule that shaped the party system and tended to limit its institutionalization was the overrepresentation of small states, which were mostly poor and in the northeast and north. There, politics retained a more patrimonial character; individual political bosses rather than parties were the kingpins of political life. Whereas political rules had not been a major factor in the weakness of Brazil's pre–1945 parties, they assumed some importance thereafter.

The third important continuity in party politics is the centrality of patronage for the careers of most politicians. Politicians relied on bringing home resources and favors to their constituents—above all, to local elites. As is argued in Chapter 8, this legacy, too, has persisted into the present.

ASSESSING PARTY-SYSTEM INSTITUTIONALIZATION, 1945–64

The 1945–64 period witnessed complex trends in terms of party-system institutionalization. On the one hand, parties became more important conduits to power and were more organized than they had been before 1945. The party system was more institutionalized than it has been since 1985, and parties developed some roots in society. Analysts who have focused exclusively on the weakness of Brazilian parties during this period have missed this part of the picture. On the other hand, party organizations were weak, personalism in politics was pronounced, the party system exhibited high volatility in presidential and senatorial elections, the allegiance of political elites to parties was sometimes tenuous, and ticket splitting was widespread.

To consider these issues systematically, let us return to the criteria of institutionalization discussed in Chapter 2. The first was the degree of stability in interparty competition. This can be assessed through an index of electoral volatility, which shows the share of votes or seats that change hands from one party to another, from one election to the next. Electoral volatility is calculated by taking the absolute value of each party's percentage change in votes or seats from one election to the next, adding these values for all the parties, and dividing by two. If Parties A, B, and C win 44 percent, 34 percent, and 22 percent, respectively, in Election T1, and 38 percent, 43 percent, and 19 percent, respectively, in Election T2, the absolute values of the differences (6 percent + 9 percent + 3 percent) total 18 percent, and electoral volatility is 9 percent.

When we calculate electoral volatility for Brazilian presidential elections, a great deal depends on whether we focus on parties or coalitions as the unit of analysis. If we choose parties, presidential electoral volatility was extremely high: 48.8 percent from 1945 to 1950, 48.7 percent from 1950 to 1955, and 18.1 percent for 1955–60, for a mean of 38.5 percent. This would place Brazil among the cases of low volatility for the current Latin American democracies.[5]

Even if we use coalitions as the unit of analysis, electoral volatility for presidential elections was high: 16.8 percent for 1945–50, 34.6 percent for 1950–55, and 18.1 percent for 1955–60, for a mean of 23.2 percent. This figure is considerably higher than that found in the more institutionalized party systems of Latin America (Costa Rica, Chile, Colombia, Uruguay, Venezuela). In the lower chamber, volatility in seats was 24.8 percent between 1945 and 1950, 8.1 percent between 1950 and 1954, 7.3 percent between 1954 and 1958, and 14.9 percent between 1958 and 1962. With the exception of the 1945–50 figure, these numbers reflect a reasonably stable party system for the lower chamber. The mean for the four electoral periods, 13.8 percent, would place Brazil among the lower range of contemporary Latin American democracies, and is much lower than the mean for the post-1982 period.

Senate electoral volatility measured in seats is a less reliable indicator because the plurality electoral rules could lead to a relatively small shift in votes producing a substantially larger one in seats. Moreover, the relatively low number of seats disputed, ranging from 21 in 1958 to 45 in 1962, increases the likelihood of substantial disproportionality between votes and seats. Volatility was 17.9 percent for 1945–47, 41.9 percent for 1947–50, 27.0 percent for 1950–54, 16.7 percent for 1954–58, and 24.7 percent for 1958–62, for a mean of 25.6 percent. Even allowing for the disproportionality of the electoral system for the Senate, these results point toward a low level of institutionalization. But the results here are less conclusive than those for the presidency and Chamber of Deputies. Considering presidential, Chamber, and Senate elections together, the party system exhibited moderately high volatility, though not as high as it has in the post–1985 period, nor as high as Bolivia, Peru, and Ecuador have experienced since the early 1980s.

The second criterion of party-system institutionalization is that parties have relatively strong roots in society and therefore structure voting patterns to a high degree. Citizens are more apt to identify with a party and vote for its candidates for most positions and in most elections.

The difference between presidential and legislative voting provides information for assessing how deeply parties penetrate society and structure the vote. Where parties shape political preferences, this difference should be less pronounced. Citizens more frequently vote on the basis of party labels, and therefore they tend to vote for the same label in legislative and presidential elections.

Because of the nonavailability of data in legislative votes, the president's share of the vote had to be compared with the distribution of lower Chamber seats. After 1950, elections were nonconcurrent, so election results from different years had to be compared. Nonconcurrence would usually increase the discrepancy between a party's share of votes for the presidential election and its share of Chamber seats. Coalitions rather than parties were used as the main unit of analysis; that is, I compared the presidential candidates' share of the vote with the same coalition's share of congressional seats. Doing so has the compelling advantage of using the unit that was most relevant at the presidential level.

The absolute values of the difference between each coalition's share of the presidential vote and its share of lower-chamber seats were added for all the coalitions, and divided by two.[6] The difference between the presidential and lower-chamber votes was 11.7 percent in 1945. The difference between the presidential vote and parties' share of lower-chamber seats was 27.2 percent in 1950; there was a 27.9 percent difference between the 1955 presidential and 1954 congressional elections, a 31.4 percent difference between the 1955 presidential and 1958 congressional contests, 34.8 percent for the 1960 presidential against the 1958 congressional races, and 30.9 percent between the 1960 presidential and congressional polls.

Between 1945 and 1964, there was on average a 25 percent discrepancy between the vote for president and lower-chamber seats. This would place Brazil much higher than most Latin American countries in the post–1980 period (Mainwaring and Scully 1995: 9–11). These aggregates understate—possibly by a considerable margin—the individual-level incidence of citizens who vote one way in the presidential election and another in the balloting for Congress. If citizen A votes for party X's presidential candidate and for a candidate of party Y for the lower chamber, while citizen B votes for party Y's presidential candidate and for party X for deputy, these two actions cancel each other in terms of the presidential vote/legislative seat differential—yet both cases depart from party voting.

This information, although not conclusive, suggests that parties were not particularly strong in structuring the vote. Populist appeals and leaders were often more important than party labels (Weffort 1978). Antiparty politicians sometimes won key executive positions, including the presidency.

Personalism continued to characterize political life, especially for executive positions. This phenomenon was evident from the dissociation between party strength in Congress and the popular vote for executive candidates. In presidential and gubernatorial elections, party affiliation did not structure the vote highly. The president and state governors had most of the policy-making power, and their election depended more on their own electoral appeal than on party organizations. In two of the four presidential elections during the period (1950 and 1960), the winning candidate came from a coalition of parties that had only about one-quarter of the seats in the Chamber of Deputies, indicating a significant dissociation between presidential candidates' ability to win votes and the strength of their parties.

The survey data available from the 1945–64 period adds to the overall picture of relatively weak parties and a moderately weakly institutionalized party system. IBOPE surveys in March 1964 reported that 64 percent of the electorate had a party preference in eight major cities (Lavareda 1991: 135). Lavareda concludes that party identification was relatively high and that the party system was quite consolidated. But this conclusion is not warranted because of the lack of congruity between party identification and voting patterns. For example, the PSD, which was Brazil's largest congressional party in 1962, had only 11 percent of the preferences among those who expressed a party leaning (and 7 percent of the total) in March 1964. This means that some combination of three possibilities obtained:

1. The focus on large urban areas in IBOPE's survey skewed results against the PSD because the PSD fared better electorally in small *municípios*. Still, this observation does not fully explain the PSD's low survey preferences.

2. Voters' preferences changed dramatically between the 1962 congressional elections and March 1964.

3. Party identification was not a good predictor of voting behavior.

All three possibilities—and any combination thereof—raise doubts about Lavareda's conclusions regarding institutionalization. In the first case, the nonrepresentative character of the sample for the nation as a whole skews results. In the second case, voters' preferences were changing so rapidly as to make party identification of secondary import; party identification is meaningful only if it

TABLE 3-1

Difference Between Presidential and Vice-Presidential Vote, 1950–60

Party	A Presidential (Pct.)	B Vice-Presidential (Pct.)	A + B (Pct.)
1950			
PTB/PSB	48.7	35.1	138.7
UDN/PDC/PDL	29.7	33.4	88.9
PSD/PTB	21.5	23.8	90.3
PST		7.6	0.0
1955			
UDN/PDC/PDL	30.2	41.8	72.2
PSD/PTB	35.7	44.3	80.6
PSP	25.8	13.9	185.6
PRP	8.3		
1960			
UDN/PDC/PDL	48.3	39.3	122.9
PSD/PTB	32.9	41.3	79.7
PSP	18.8		
MTR		19.4	0.0

SOURCE: Compiled from data in Lavareda 1991: 175–78.

is usually stable over time and orients the vote. In the third case, a preference for a party would have little significance.

Other information suggests that party preferences did not consistently structure voting behavior. A 1960 poll in the city of São Paulo indicated that among PTB sympathizers, only 39 percent intended to vote for the presidential candidate (Henrique Lott) the party supported, compared to 44 percent who supported the other two candidates and 17 percent who were undecided. In Porto Alegre, only 50 percent of the party's sympathizers intended to vote for Lott, compared to 37 percent for the other candidates and 13 percent undecided (Lavareda 1991: 149). These low figures raise doubts about how much party sympathies structured the vote and, by extension, how institutionalized the system was. If party allegiances were strong, party sympathizers would support the candidate chosen by their party.

The high incidence of ticket splitting (permitted under the electoral code) between presidential and vice-presidential candidates further underscores that many citizens did not vote along party lines. Table 3-1 summarizes the aggregate differences between presidential and vice-presidential voting patterns between 1950 and 1960. (In 1945, there was no election for vice president.) These differences are substantial. For example, the PTB/PSB coalition won 49 percent of the presidential vote in 1950, but only 35 percent of the vice-presidential vote. In 1960, when Jânio Quadros won the presidency by a landslide, his running mate lost to PTB candidate João Goulart.

Survey data show frequent ticket splitting between the president and vice president in 1960. In that year, IBOPE conducted surveys in ten major cities, asking citizens for whom they intended to vote for president and vice president. Only in two of the ten cities did a plurality of supporters of Jânio Quadros state that they intended to vote for his running mate, Milton Campos. In Porto Alegre and Recife, under 10 percent of Quadros's supporters intended to vote for Campos, and in four others, from 13 percent to 23 percent planned to support Campos. This underscores a huge disjunction between voting for presidential and vice-presidential candidates and, by extension, weak party voting and party structuring of the electorate (data from Lavareda 1991: 151).

So far, the discussion has focused on linkages between parties and individual citizens. Linkages between parties and organized groups are also relevant. In Brazil, such connections were tenuous. The labor movement and the PTB enjoyed a symbiotic connection (Erickson 1977), but the PTB did not serve as the partisan expression of the labor movement, in contrast to the situation of many European labor parties. Labor and other groups generally circumvented partisan and legislative channels and interacted directly with state agencies (Schmitter 1971).

The third criterion of party-system institutionalization was that parties and elections enjoy legitimacy; they should be perceived as the proper means of constituting governments. Here we are hampered by the paucity of academic surveys. Nevertheless, other information shows that the legitimacy of parties and elections was questioned by powerful political actors. The frequent military interventions culminating in the 1964 coup, the fulminations of political leaders (including President Quadros) against parties and Congress, the practice of UDN leaders of questioning the legitimacy of election results, the participation of UDN leaders in conspiring against the governments of Vargas and Goulart, the cavalier attitude that part of the left had about liberal democracy, and the breadth of the conspiracy against Goulart all underscore this point.

The final criterion of party-system institutionalization was that party organizations matter. Here, the bulk of the evidence indicates that parties were weak. Until 1954, much partisan conflict revolved around the pro- and anti-Vargas cleavage. Politicians often changed parties, indicating a low degree of loyalty on the side of the politicians and diffuse identities among the parties. F. H. Cardoso's data (1975b: 68–71) showed that among the twenty-eight São Paulo federal deputies elected in 1974 who had belonged to a pre–1964 party, eleven had belonged to at least two parties and four had belonged to three. Among the forty-one state deputies elected in 1974 who had belonged to a pre–1964 party, twelve had belonged to two parties, two to three parties, and one to five parties. These figures probably understate the incidence of pre–1964 party switching because the sample of pre–1964 politicians still in office in 1974 was not representative of the entire population of such politicians. Many older politicians of the 1946–64 period who had been involved in politics for a longer time and therefore had more time to switch parties would have retired by 1974 and hence were not included in Cardoso's survey. It is not clear whether this pattern was generalizable to other states, but such frequent party switching reveals weak commitments of the political elite to party organizations.

Despite differences among them, all three major parties of the 1945–64 period shared some characteristics. They were ideologically heterogeneous, had weak national organizations and limited resources, and were decentralized (Peterson 1962). They relied extensively on state patronage to win votes, and they were loosely organized clientelistic machines (O. Carvalho 1958). Party allegiance was limited, and many politicians changed from one party to another. Party discipline in Congress was limited, as Santos (1986: 92–109) showed for the 1961–64 period. Decisions about candidacies and electoral coalitions were made by the state organizations with essentially no oversight by the national organizations (Peterson 1962). The parties were generally dominated by a small group of charismatic leaders; this was especially true of the PTB, dominated by Vargas and Goulart, and the fourth-largest party of the period, the PSP (Progressive Social Party), led by Ademar de Barros. In many *municípios* of the interior, politics remained a clash of clans rather than a clash of competing organizations based on different ideas or programs (J. M. Carvalho 1966).

Three factors limited party-system institutionalization during the 1945–64 period. First was the weak development of civil society. The political incorporation of the popular sectors remained far from complete, and not only because of the exclusion of the illiterate. In the expansive rural regions, local elites still exercised personalistic domination. In urban areas, corporatism and clientelism limited the popular presence in politics. Brazil's pattern of formation of political actors until the late 1950s limited incentives for party elites to develop strong linkages to civil society. Second was the preference of political elites for decentralized, comparatively undisciplined parties. Third was the institutionalization of this preference in electoral and party legislation.

PARTIES AND THE BREAKDOWN OF DEMOCRACY

Between 1945 and 1960 the party system was becoming institutionalized as the profile of the parties became clearer. However, beginning with the election of Jânio Quadros as president in 1960, the party system began a process of disaggregation that simultaneously reflected and contributed to growing polarization in the political system (Santos 1986; M. Souza 1976; Ramos 1961), which culminated in the breakdown of democracy in 1964.

Internal conflicts within all three of the major parties were exacerbated after Quadros's election, contributing to the political crisis. Initially euphoric with Quadros's victory, the UDN became less enamored with the president when he ran roughshod over the party. When Goulart assumed office, parts of the UDN assumed an intransigent position, and by 1964 most of the party leadership actively supported a coup. The PSD divided over Quadros, and while Goulart was in office the PSD/PTB alliance broke down. Much of the PSD moved to the intransigent opposition, but factions of the party continued to support Goulart (Hippólito 1985: 213–47). The PTB, reflecting (and also contributing to) increasing polarization in society, adopted increasingly radical positions. The combination of growing polarization, high fragmentation, and internal party conflict made it difficult for Congress to function effectively, leading to what Santos (1986: 37–58) described as a paralysis of decision making.

Concerned about Goulart's leftist proclivities, the military nearly blocked him from assuming the presidency and insisted that presidential powers be curbed. Congress consented, and passed a constitutional amendment that instituted a semipresidential system in September 1961. Frustrated by the limits that this system imposed, Goulart pressed for and got a plebiscite that restored full presidential powers in January 1963.

In late 1963, President Goulart responded to the combination of economic recession, ascending inflation, and political isolation by moving to the left, a strategy that backfired. On March 31, 1964, the military deposed the Goulart government and began a period of twenty-one years of authoritarian rule. Several factors contributed to the breakdown of democracy. After a prolonged period of rapid growth, the economy went into a tailspin in the early 1960s. On the left, responding to the utopian hopes the Cuban revolution inspired, student and progressive church groups, labor unions, and peasant organizations became radicalized. On the right, the military, some business interests, and conservative Catholics became fearful that revolution or social breakdown might occur. These actors joined the coup coalition.

In the early 1960s, the party system became more polarized as the dominant faction of the PTB moved to the left and the dominant faction of the UDN to the right. By the time Goulart assumed the presidency, the party system had moved to polarized pluralism in Sartori's (1976) terminology. This combination of fragmentation and polarization often spells trouble for fledgling democracies, and it did in Brazil. As in Chile in 1973 but in contrast to Argentina in 1976, one of the major parties—the UDN—and some minor ones actively conspired against the democratic government (Benevides 1981: 118–31). Many PSD leaders welcomed the coup, and some joined the anti-Goulart cabal, although the party leadership did not.

In the 1960s, the major congressional parties became so divided that supra-party blocs rather than party loyalties became the basis for congressional negotiations. The Nationalist Parliamentary Front embraced more nationalistic and progressive positions, while Democratic Parliamentary Action defended more conservative postures. These features allowed authoritarian actors to charge that the parties were corrupt, oligarchical, and nonrepresentative, and such criticisms fueled the fire that led to the breakdown of democracy.

The major parties never overcame their dependence on and subordination to the state. Parties had limited relevance in designing and implementing policies, and they were dependent on patronage and clientele networks (J. M. Carvalho 1966; Hagopian 1996; M. Souza 1976). Through patronage, governors could effectively control party organizations.

The weakness of Brazilian parties made possible a personalism in politics that had deleterious consequences when two erratic personalities—Quadros and Goulart—assumed the presidency in the 1960s. Quadros was elected in a land-slide in 1960, but resigned office after seven months, hoping that Congress would grant him semidictatorial powers. A maverick antiparty politician, Quadros could not have been elected in a country where parties were stronger. Goulart, who replaced Quadros, became frustrated with widespread congressional opposition in late 1963, and his ambivalence about respecting the constitution, coupled with poor leadership, helped bring about his own downfall (Stepan 1971, 1978a; Santos 1986; Skidmore 1967).

The process of building a party system was destroyed by the leaders of the 1964 coup. Of the five times that state leaders in Brazil destroyed party systems, this was the most consequential. The parties of the 1946–64 period had developed roots that were shallow enough to be pulled up, but were still significant.

Parties and Military Rule, 1964–79

The military coup of March 31, 1964, ended "Brazil's experiment in democracy" (Skidmore 1967). Compared to the recent military dictatorships in the Southern Cone, one of the distinctive features of military rule in Brazil was that parties, elections, and Congress continued to function, albeit under severe constraints at times. When it took power, the military immediately purged Congress and took actions against renowned progressive politicians (and some centrist politicians as well). However, it allowed the pre–1964 parties to exist until October 1965, when it dissolved them in response to some key defeats in the context of partially controlled elections. At that time the military government allowed—indeed encouraged—two new parties to form and compete

(Kinzo 1988; Jenks 1979: 88–105). Legal parties functioned throughout the entire military period. Congress was closed on a few occasions, including a long stretch from December 1968 to October 1969, but otherwise it functioned.

There is nothing unusual about authoritarian regimes that sponsor elections (Hermet et al. 1978). Many famous Latin American dictators, including Somoza and Stroessner, regularly held elections, allowed rubber-stamp legislatures to function, and tolerated parties as long as they were not serious opposition forces. But compared to the military dictatorships in Argentina (especially 1976–83), Chile (1973–90), and Uruguay (1973–84), the existence of parties, legislatures, and elections was a distinctive feature of Brazilian military rule. In the Southern Cone, the military was implacably hostile to parties. This sentiment was attenuated in the Brazilian armed forces.

In the Southern Cone, where politicians have deep organizational commitments, congressional representatives would not have been willing to join new parties sponsored by the military government. In Argentina, Uruguay, and especially Chile, the military could not have induced enough civilian politicians to support authoritarian rule to maintain a Congress and sponsor elections. In Chile, for example, it would have been unfathomable for a Communist or Socialist deputy to join a new party created by the military. In Brazil, by contrast, the government sponsored the creation of two new parties: the National Renovating Alliance (Arena, Aliança Renovadora Nacional), the progovernment party, and the Democratic Brazilian Movement (MDB, Movimento Democrático Brasileiro), the official opposition party. The military attracted enough support from elected civilian politicians to gain some legitimacy, organize support at the local level, and deflect some international criticism of human-rights abuses.

Because many pre–1964 politicians supported the coup and the authoritarian government, the military stood to gain by allowing these allies to organize support for them. Many politicians also supported the coups in Chile and Uruguay, but because party identities were stronger, the parties were less controllable and co-optable. Strong party identities and attachments among political elites and the electorate closed off the space for reconstructing a party system. In any case, because the sense of crisis was deeper in Argentina, Chile, and Uruguay, the potential gains of allowing parties to function were diminished. In this way the nature of the precoup parties shaped the political context in which the military functioned and influenced the nature of military rule.

Elections were held according to a more or less regular timetable in Brazil, although they were vitiated by pressures and manipulations. Candidates faced restrictions on how they campaigned, and many MDB politicians were stripped of their offices and political rights. Elections were restricted to senators, federal and state deputies, and most local officials; the most important offices were no longer elected. The president was chosen from within the military, and governors were essentially selected by the central government, though their selection was formally ratified by state legislatures. Mayors of state capitals and some other cities were appointed by the state governors.

For the first decade of military rule, party politics were relatively unimportant. The MDB suffered frequent purges and was not allowed to present effective opposition. Constitutional changes promoted the hypertrophy of executive power (Alves 1985: 31–100). Congress was closed for ten months in 1968–69. The MDB had little access to the media, and was consistently defeated in elections that were a far cry from being fair and free. The situation got so bad that the party discussed dissolving itself in the early 1970s (Kinzo 1988: 110–28).

But parties, elections, and Congress ultimately proved to have highly consequential implications for military rule and for the gradual and protracted transition to democracy. The existence of these institutional arenas characteristic of liberal democracy prevented the military from effecting a radical break from the past in terms of legitimizing discourse. The military never directly attacked liberal democracy as an ideal; rather, it focused its attacks on perversions of liberal democracy. Its partial adherence to democratic discourse prevented the military from fully institutionalizing an authoritarian regime (Kinzo 1988; Lamounier 1989; Linz 1973).

President Ernerso Geisel (1974–79) started to promote a "slow and gradual" liberalization in 1974. He allowed the 1974 elections to be conducted in a more open atmosphere. The MDB scored a success, winning sixteen of twenty-two Senate seats, surprising even the party's own leaders (Cardoso and Lamounier 1975). Riding on the crest of this victory, the MDB began an organizational push; in 1974, it had directorates in only 28 percent of the nation's *municípios*, but one year later, it was organized in nearly 80 percent of them (Kinzo 1988: 30). It began to channel more of the opposition's demands and hopes.

After 1974, elections became a vital part of the dynamic between government and opposition (Kinzo 1988; Lamounier 1989). Their results were crucial to the prolonged transition from military rule to democracy; in no other recent transition to democracy except the Mexican did the electoral arena have similar importance (Lamounier 1989). More typically, serious elections were held only after and because the military had decided to leave power.

The 1974 election results led to a series of government machinations aimed at bolstering the government party. Yet in the urbanized parts of the country, which accounted for an increasing percentage of the population, the MDB continued to trounce Arena. The erosion of Arena's electoral base is evinced in Table 3-2. After routing the MDB in the popular vote for Senate races in 1966

TABLE 3-2
National Results for Legislative Elections, 1966–78
(Percent of Popular Vote)

Years	Arena	MDB	Blank/Null	Total Votes
Senate				
1966	44.7%	34.2%	21.2%	17,259,598
1970[a]	43.7	28.6	27.7	46,986,492
1974	34.7	50.0	14.1	28,981,110
1978	35.0	46.4	18.6	37,775,212
Chamber of Deputies				
1966	50.5	28.4	21.0	17,285,556
1970[a]	48.4	21.3	30.3	22,435,521
1974	40.9	37.8	21.3	28,981,015
1978	40.0	39.3	20.7	37,629,180

SOURCE: Kinzo 1988: 63.
[a]In 1970 there was a renewal of two-thirds of the Senate, and each citizen cast two votes. Thus the total number of votes is twice the number of voters.

and 1970, Arena was defeated in 1974 and 1978. Its better than two-to-one advantage in lower-chamber elections in 1970 dwindled to a razor-thin margin by 1978 (Kinzo 1988: 63).

After 1974, elections were akin to plebiscites: people voted for or against the military government, and more and more voted against it. The geographic bases of support for the two parties exacerbated the government's problems. The MDB fared especially well in large cities, whereas Arena did best in smaller *municípios*. The cities were growing rapidly, so this meant a medium-term horizon of an eroding electoral base for Arena.

Arena fared worst in the most developed regions of the country—precisely those states that had most benefited from the inegalitarian developmental model. By 1978, in the southeast the MDB outpolled Arena in lower-chamber elections by 47.9 percent to 29.7 percent, while in the poverty-stricken northeast, Arena still racked up a convincing 57.8 percent to 22.1 percent margin (Kinzo 1988: 65). How far could the government pursue ambitious economic modernization while relying on the most traditional and backward regions for political support?

In the major cities, a class pattern to the vote emerged. By 1974 in São Paulo, the poorest neighborhoods—though not necessarily the poorest people—voted overwhelmingly for the MDB (Lamounier 1975, 1980). The MDB became known as the party of the poor, against the government, while Arena became identified as the party of the rich, for the government (Caldeira 1980: 88–95; Lamounier 1975: 33–42; 1980: 38–41).

Under Geisel, political liberalization already reflected what Alves (1985) has termed a "dialectic" between the regime and opposition, but the contours of liberalization were still limited. Although the regime was pushed to make unintended concessions, it still controlled most of the significant decisions. Still, the government realized that things could not go on in this fashion forever. If it wanted to continue the process of political liberalization, the government needed to allow elections to become more meaningful—but as things stood, it would lose openly competitive elections. In response to this situation, in April 1977 the government closed Congress for a few weeks and imposed changes in electoral laws to favor Arena. One-third of the Senate would now be elected indirectly in a system that assured Arena control of these seats. Access to the media was curtailed.

Finally, the new electoral rules increased the minimum number of federal deputies per state to eight and set a maximum of sixty deputies per state. These changes exacerbated malapportionment, overrepresenting the less-populated, mostly poor states, which toed the government line, and underrepresenting the largest ones, especially São Paulo, thereby diminishing the representation of opposition states. The new rules allowed Arena to stem its losses in the 1978 elections. After the sharp decline from 1970 to 1974, Arena stabilized its share of the vote in 1978. But major changes in the party system were soon to occur.

CHAPTER 4

Elections, Parties, and Society, 1979–96

The primary argument of Part 2 of this book is that the Brazilian party system is weakly institutionalized. This chapter presents much of the empirical evidence for this argument.

The first sections of the chapter present background information on parties and elections in the post–1979 period. After this overview, I argue that Brazil's party system is weakly institutionalized. The first criterion of a more-institutionalized system is that patterns of party competition are relatively stable. The period under consideration witnessed tremendous electoral volatility, reflecting the inability of the parties to win enduring allegiances. Governing parties were particularly prone to abrupt electoral demise.

The second criterion of a more institutionalized party system is that parties develop deep roots in society. Most individuals identify with a party and vote on the basis of their party sympathies. In Brazil, however, party voting is the exception, and it has declined considerably since 1974–82. Rather than vote on the basis of parties, after 1985 most citizens voted for individual candidates, or in response to personal ties to political patrons or to issues. Party affiliation is especially insignificant in elections for executive posts, where personality is particularly important. Politicians from small parties can capture powerful executive posts, including the presidency. Survey data also show that party affiliation is not a major criterion when citizens cast their ballots.

If parties have solid roots in society, there is a high degree of continuity in their social bases, and therefore in patterns of electoral geography. Between 1982 and 1990, however, Brazil was marked by striking instability in electoral geography. Moreover, the percentage of citizens who express a party preference in surveys is low, and it has declined considerably since the late 1970s. Linkages between parties and organized interests are tenuous.

The third criterion of an institutionalized party system is that parties and elections enjoy legitimacy. In Brazil, there is ample evidence that parties have poor public standing. Survey evidence makes clear that elections enjoy less legitimacy in Brazil than in the southern cone countries.

The final sections of the chapter discuss two other features of the party system. After 1985, the party system became extremely fragmented, that is, the vote was dispersed among a large number of parties. Since the 1988 municipal elections, Brazil has had one of the most fragmented party systems in the world. As is shown in Chapter 9, extreme multipartism has compounded the difficulties of democratic governance.

Finally, party competition from the mid–1980s to the early 1990s was characterized by a large ideological distance from leftist to rightist parties. The dynamic of political competition between 1985 and 1992 was frequently flavored by significant ideological dissensus. Since 1992, there has been a trend toward consensus and diminishing ideological distance.

The 1979 Party Reform and the Abertura

The year 1979 marked a watershed in the movement toward the gradual restoration of democracy. General João Figueiredo, the last of the string of five military chief executives, assumed the presidential sash in March. His presidency was characterized by a gradual easing of repression in most parts of the country, as well as by a concomitant increase in the importance of parties and elections. Repression against parties and politicians was less frequent than during the Médici and Geisel governments.

The robust economic expansion of 1967–74 had slowed and was further threatened by the oil shock of 1979. Table 4-1 provides some basic economic data for the 1979–96 period.

Following the strategy established by his predecessor, Figueiredo hoped to control the political situation even as he continued the liberalization project. In this context, parties and elections acquired more significance than they had under previous military presidents. If it could win elections, the government would be able to liberalize while remaining in control. But in view of Arena's past electoral performance and demographic trends, regime elites did not believe that they could win decisively with the existing electoral rules. They thought that the government party could win a plurality against a divided opposition, so they changed the electoral rules. In November 1979 the government dissolved both parties and imposed new electoral legislation designed to maintain Arena largely intact (but with a new name, the PDS, Democratic Social Party) while dividing the opposition into several parties (Keck 1992: 40–60;

TABLE 4-1
Brazilian Economic Indicators, 1979–96

Year	Change in GDP (pct.)	Inflation (pct.)	External debt (US$ billions)	Debt as pct. of exports of goods & services
1979	6.4	77[a]	50	—
1980	8.0	95	54	321
1981	−1.9	91	72	313
1982	0.9	98	83	417
1983	−2.4	179	98	416
1984	5.7	209	105	363
1985	7.9	239	107	379
1986	7.6	59	111	460
1987	3.6	395	121	431
1988	−0.1	993	114	315
1989	3.3	1,862	115	307
1990	−4.4	1,585	122	347
1991	0.9	476	120	342
1992	−0.9	1,149	136	348
1993	4.2	2,489	146	340
1994	5.8	929	148	303
1995	3.9	22	159	302
1996	3.1	9	178	318
1997	3.5	4	188	—

SOURCES: For all data except 1979 inflation: UN Economic Commission for Latin America and the Caribbean, *Economic Survey of Latin America*; id., *Preliminary Overview of the Economy of Latin America and the Caribbean.*
[a]For 1979 inflation, Alves 1985: 165.
NOTE: There are minor discrepancies from year to year among ECLAC sources. The figures for 1997 are preliminary, as is the 1996 figure for debt as a percentage of exports.

Kinzo 1980, 1988: 204–17). Aided by the April 1977 electoral package and other electoral laws, the PDS hoped to fare reasonably well.

The government expected that the new electoral law would encourage fragmentation of the opposition, but still be stringent enough to block the emergence of strong parties on the left. The new legislation mandated that all parties contain the word "party" in their name. This measure was aimed at disrupting the growing pro-MDB sentiment by forcing it to change its name in the hope that doing so would erode the linkages it had created to society.

Reform of electoral and party legislation, including changing the rules that had made it virtually impossible for more than two parties to exist, had long been a demand of the opposition, but it was carried out by the government to its own advantage. The government's hope that Arena would essentially remain intact while the opposition divided was borne out in the short run. Before the reform, 231 of the 420 federal deputies were in Arena; afterward, though the numbers shifted slightly from one month to the next, Arena had about 215 (Kinzo 1988: 209). The number of opposition deputies increased from 189 to 205, but the opposition was no longer united, and the government expected it would be able to co-opt some of the parties.

Five opposition parties emerged out of the splintering of the old MDB (Kinzo 1980). The direct heir to the MDB, the PMDB (Party of the Brazilian Democratic Movement) was the largest, with 115 deputies in January 1982, and also the most heterogeneous. It included everything from clandestine leftist organizations (including the two communist parties) to conservatives, but the social-democratic current was arguably the strongest. The PMDB remained by far the largest opposition party throughout the rest of the military period.

A centrist party that grew out of the conservative faction of the MDB and the liberal faction of Arena, the Popular Party (PP) was the second-largest opposition party with sixty-nine deputies in January 1982. In early 1982, the PP dissolved itself and merged with the PMDB in response to changes in electoral laws.

The remaining opposition parties were much smaller and had viable organizations in only a few states. The PDT (Democratic Labor Party) was a center-left party, social-democratic in orientation but populist and personalistic in style. Only ten deputies were members of the party in early 1982, but Leonel Brizola's come-from-behind gubernatorial victory in the 1982 elections in the state of Rio de Janeiro put the party on the map. From 1982 on the PDT was a serious contender in two major states (Rio de Janeiro and Rio Grande do Sul), and later in the 1980s it established a presence in other states.

The PT (Workers' Party) anchored the left of the party spectrum. Labor leaders, progressive church groups, leaders of social movements, intellectuals, and parts of the socialist left helped create the PT (Keck 1992; Meneguello 1989). These actors eschewed the PMDB's broad-front strategy, arguing that it subordinated popular interests and that it was important to create a partisan vehicle that would support popular struggles. Although the PT had only five deputies in 1982, the military government considered it a threat because of its leftist orientation and its connections to combative unions and social movements. The party's discourse emphasized radical social change, popular participation and mobilization, and internal democracy. Initially, its electoral strength was concentrated in São Paulo, and only in the late 1980s did it become more than a regional party.

Finally, the PTB (Brazilian Labor Party) was ideologically akin to the PP, attracting centrist opposition figures. A minor party with only four deputies in early 1982, it competed with the PDT for the legacy of the pre–1965 PTB. The new PTB grew out of the most clientelistic factions of its pre–1965 namesake.

With the exception of the PP, all the parties that were created in 1979–80 continued to be significant until the merger of the PDS and the center-right Christian Democratic Party (PDC) in 1993. Together they accounted for all of the 479 deputies elected in 1982, 349 of the 487 (71.7 percent) elected in 1986, 270 of the 503 (53.7 percent) elected in 1990, and 221 of the 513 (43.0 percent) elected in 1994. They were joined by four new significant parties later in the 1980s: the conservative Party of the Liberal Front (PFL), the center-left Brazilian Social Democratic Party (PSDB), the center-right PDC, and the rightist Party of National Reconstruction (PRN). In the 1990s, the PPR (Reformist Progressive Party) (1993–95) and the PPB (Brazilian Progressive Party), created out of the mergers of older parties, became important labels on the right of the political spectrum. (See page xvii for a list of the major post–1979 parties.)

After 1980, party competition dominated opposition activity. This trend marked a change from 1974 to 1980, when other forms of opposition activity such as social movements sometimes overshadowed parties as a means of channeling opposition. After the electoral reforms of 1979 and the emergence of the new parties, most grassroots leaders came to see electoral politics as important. Many activists became involved primarily in party politics and withdrew from engagement in social movements (Alvarez 1990; Mainwaring 1987, 1989).

A New Party System

In the Southern Cone, after the last experience of authoritarian rule, the party systems more or less resembled those of the preauthoritarian era, and the same parties resurfaced as dominant. In all three countries, there were important changes in the party system, but the initial postauthoritarian system bore some semblance to the previous one.

In Brazil, by contrast, notwithstanding continuities in the predominant style of the catch-all parties, none of the major preauthoritarian parties survived. Six post–1979 parties could partly trace their lineage to pre–1965 parties: the PCB/PPS (Brazilian Communist Party, which changed its name to the Popular Socialist Party in 1992), the PC do B (Communist Party of Brazil), the PSB (Socialist Party of Brazil), the PDT (Democratic Labor Party), the PTB (Brazilian Labor Party), and the PDC (Christian Democratic Party). Of the six, only the PDT became a sizable party in the post–1979 period, and it won only 5 percent (1982), 5 percent (1986), 9 percent (1990), and 7 percent (1994) of the lower-chamber seats in the first four elections under the new party system. Moreover, to see either the PDT or the PTB as the direct progeny of the old PTB would misstate the case.

For most of the electorate, the pre–1964 party system was an unfamiliar reference point by 1985, and the major postauthoritarian parties had weak roots going back to the preauthoritarian period. Nor is there a strong continuity in political "tendencies" or in the pre–1965 and post–1979 party systems, despite continuities in political style and organization of the catch-all parties.

The disappearance of the pre–1964 parties in Brazil is striking. Remmer (1985) studied eleven cases of redemocratization in Latin America. Nowhere were the discontinuities between the pre- and postauthoritarian party configurations as pronounced as they were in Brazil (which she did not examine). Usually, eighteen years of essentially democratic government would be sufficient to ensure that some parties would establish strong roots in society. In Argentina, Chile, and Uruguay, the major precoup parties survived years of brutal repression, and once elections were convoked, they returned and were still the biggest parties. Several parties underwent internal transformations, but they all reappeared. In Peru, two old parties (Acción Popular and APRA) were the most powerful contenders in the first elections after military rule.

Three factors help explain why the precoup parties resurfaced in Brazil's neighbors but not in Brazil (see also Remmer 1985). First, as Kinzo (1990) has argued, the existence of new parties that acquired some legitimacy, significance, and organizational capabilities for thirteen years (1966–79) under military rule helped obliterate the identities of the previous ones. In 1979, when Arena and the MDB were dissolved, they had existed for nearly as long as the parties of the 1945–64 period. If parties and elections had merely been manipulable façades designed to provide a veneer of legitimacy, as is the case in many authoritarian regimes (Hermet et al. 1978), their existence under military rule would not have created loyalties capable of disrupting precoup party allegiance. But as Lamounier (1980), Reis (1978), and von Mettenheim (1995) have shown, people established loyalties to these parties.

Second, the precoup parties in Brazil had moderately weak identities and roots in society, and political elites' attachments to them were sometimes shallow. Were it not for this, Arena and the MDB would not have gained sufficient respectability to obliterate the old identities.

The effects of the precoup weakness of parties and their comparative importance during military rule were mutually reinforcing. Because loyalties to the pre–1965 parties were not deeper, the military government could dissolve them and create new ones that eventually became meaningful. And because these new parties acquired significance, they greatly diminished the already tenuous loyalties to the precoup parties.

Finally, the longevity of authoritarian rule and the rapidity of demographic change favored wholesale modifications in Brazil's party system. Brazil's military government lasted longer than those of its neighbors, so citizens' and elites' attachments to the previous parties had more time to fade. Because of rapid demographic changes, by 1982, when the first elections with the new parties were held, over 60 percent of the voters had never voted for the pre–1964 parties. The electorate expanded from 22,387,000 to 58,617,000 (Lamounier 1989: 57) between 1966 and 1982. The great majority of these new voters had no or weak attachments to the pre–1965 parties.

From the 1981 Electoral Package to the End of Military Rule

By 1981, the government was nervous about its prospects for the 1982 elections, the first since 1965 that involved state governorships. Support for the military government dwindled as the economy deteriorated. It became apparent that the opposition was likely to overwhelm the PDS; the government's earlier calculations about the 1979 electoral reform had gone awry. Therefore, in November 1981, in another manipulation of electoral legislation, the government changed the rules of the game. The "November package" imposed three changes that enhanced the government's prospects for the very important gubernatorial posts. First, the new law banned electoral coalitions for senator and governor, so that parties would have to run on their own. This measure blocked the opposition parties from joining forces against the PDS (Fleischer 1984). Second, the new legislation made straight party voting mandatory. This measure introduced a powerful incentive for voting for a large party. Governors were (and are) powerful figures, and in plurality elections, voting for a minor party meant wasting a vote for the most important elected position in the polity. Consequently, the measure stood to benefit the PDS, which was still the largest party. The government expected a reverse coattails effect, that is, that local candidates where the PDS was strongest would bring in votes for the party's gubernatorial candidates. Finally, the new law required parties to present a full slate of candidates in any *município*; otherwise they would be barred from the ballot there. In small towns, some opposition parties were not able to field a full slate. The PDS was able to present more full slates than any other party,[1] so it enjoyed an advantage. To ensure the viability of the smaller opposition parties—the only means of fragmenting the opposition—the government decided that the stringent threshold for obtaining representation in Congress would not be observed following the 1982 elections.

Because the new electoral rules favored the two biggest parties in any state, the PMDB and PP merged into one heterogeneous party. Angered by the government machinations, leaders of both parties believed that winning the 1982 elections was crucial in order to advance their own political designs and the liberalization process. They calculated that without joining forces, they would be able to win in only a few states. After the PMDB/PP merger and with some other shuffling of party affiliations, the PMDB had 195 congressional representatives in August 1982, compared to 260 for the PDS, sixteen for the PTB, ten for the PDT, and six for the PT (Kinzo 1990: 108).

The elections for state governor in 1982 extended the arena of party competition into some of the most important positions within the political system. Given the emasculation of legislative power, the concentration of power in executive hands, and the devolution of greater power to governors from the presidency after 1979, the governors controlled vast resources. They appointed the mayors of the capitals and "national security" cities, as well as the directors of state-owned (as opposed to federally owned) public enterprises and heads of hundreds of public agencies. They also controlled the distribution of substantial material resources.

Perhaps the most important stake in the 1982 elections was one that few voters were aware of: control of the electoral college that would vote for Figueiredo's successor in January 1985. The presidential succession would be decided by an electoral college composed of the National Congress and six representatives from the governing party in each state. These representatives were to be elected in the November 1982 contest.

The election results were mixed, as Tables 4-2 to 4-5 suggest. The opposition won control of ten state governments, including those of most of the developed states. The PMDB and PDT won the governorships of the three most populous and powerful states, São Paulo (PMDB), Rio de Janeiro (PDT), and Minas Gerais (PMDB). The states won by the opposition accounted for 56 percent of Brazil's population and 75 percent of its GDP. The opposition also outpolled the PDS in popular votes for governor. The four opposition parties together won a narrow majority of seats (244 of 479) in the Chamber of Deputies and a sizable margin in the popular vote for the Chamber.

Nevertheless, the government could also claim some victories. The PDS won nearly half the seats (235 of 479) and retained the largest delegation in the Chamber of Deputies. With forty-six of sixty-nine seats, it maintained absolute control of the Senate (thanks partially to some indirectly elected posts), and it won twelve of twenty-two gubernatorial contests, including some major states (Rio Grande do Sul, Pernambuco, Bahia). The 1982 election results appeared to have ensured the government of a victory in the 1985 electoral college for president, in which case it would have remained in power until 1991.

Even though it fared reasonably well on the electoral front, in other respects the military government was falling apart. Between 1980 and 1984, per capita income fell approximately 15 percent, and in 1983, the inflation rate jumped to 239 percent. Meanwhile, the foreign debt increased from $6.6 billion in 1971 to nearly $100 billion by 1984, and by 1982 the debt crisis was under way. It became apparent that some of the 1970s growth had come at the price of an increasing external debt.

Between 1982 and 1985, the military government disintegrated as a result of the economic crisis, poor leadership, and corruption. In the context of the erosion of the legitimacy and of increased tension between the PDS and the government, a massive mobilization on behalf of a constitutional amendment that would have restored direct popular presidential elections took place in the first four months of 1984. Regime cohesion crumbled, and increasing numbers of PDS politicians supported the call for direct presidential elections. That proposal ultimately failed by a narrow margin to win the two-thirds support of

TABLE 4-2
Lower-Chamber Seats Won by Party, 1982–94

Party	1982		1986		1990		1994	
	No.	Pct.	No.	Pct.	No.	Pct.	No.	Pct.
PDS/PPR[a]	235	49.1	32	6.6	42	8.3	52	10.1
PMDB	200	41.8	261	53.6	108	21.5	107	20.9
PDT	23	4.8	24	4.9	47	9.3	34	6.8
PTB	13	2.7	17	3.5	38	7.6	31	6.0
PT	8	1.7	16	3.3	35	7.0	49	9.6
PFL	—	—	116	23.8	84	16.7	89	17.3
PL	—	—	6	1.2	15	3.0	13	2.5
PDC[a]	—	—	6	1.2	22	4.4	—	—
PC do B	—	—	5	1.0	5	1.0	10	1.9
PCB/PPS[b]	—	—	3	0.6	3	0.6	2	0.4
PSB	—	—	1	0.2	11	2.2	15	2.9
PRN	—	—	—	—	40	8.0	1	0.2
PSDB	—	—	—	—	37	7.4	62	12.1
PSC	—	—	—	—	6	1.2	3	0.6
PRS	—	—	—	—	4	0.8	—	—
PST/PP[c]	—	—	—	—	2	0.4	36	7.0
PTR[c]	—	—	—	—	2	0.4	—	—
PSD	—	—	—	—	1	0.2	3	0.6
PMN	—	—	—	—	1	0.2	4	0.8
PRP	—	—	—	—	—	—	1	0.2
PV	—	—	—	—	—	—	1	0.2
TOTAL SEATS	479	100.0	487	100.0	503	100.0	513	100.0

SOURCES: Lamounier 1990, 186–89; Wesson and Fleischer, 119; *Folha de São Paulo*, October 29, 1990, November 16, 21, 1994.
[a]The PDS and PDC merged to form the PPR in 1993.
[b]The PCB changed its name to the PPS in 1992.
[c]The PST and PTR merged to form the PP in 1993.

Congress that was required for a constitutional amendment, but the massive mobilizations strengthened the hand of the opposition and of potential PDS defectors. Many PDS politicians, including eight of nine PDS governors of the northeastern states and seventy of 235 federal deputies, left their party and created the Liberal Front. By July 1984, the defectors had decided to support the likely PMDB candidate for president, Tancredo Neves, a well-known centrist politician from Minas Gerais who had been a minister under Vargas and Goulart, a federal deputy, Senator (1978–82), and governor (1983–84).

TABLE 4-3
Senate Seats Won by Party, 1982–94

Party	1982 No.	1982 Pct.	1986 No.	1986 Pct.	1990 No.	1990 Pct.	1994 No.	1994 Pct.
PDS/PPR[a]	15	60.0	2	4.1	2	7.4	2	3.7
PMDB	9	36.0	38	77.6	8	29.6	14	25.9
PDT	1	4.0	1	2.0	1	3.7	4	7.4
PTB	0	2.7	0	—	4	14.8	3	5.6
PFL	—	—	7	14.3	8	29.6	11	20.4
PL	—	—	0	—	—	—	1	1.9
PDC[a]	—	—	0	—	0	—	—	—
PSB	—	—	0	—	0	—	1	1.9
PMB	—	—	1	2.0	—	—	—	—
PSDB	—	—	—	—	1	3.7	9	16.7
PRN	—	—	—	—	2	7.4	—	—
PT	—	—	—	—	1	3.7	4	7.4
PST/PP[b]	—	—	—	—	0	—	4	7.4
PMN	—	—	—	—	0	—	—	—
No party	—	—	—	—	0	—	—	—
PCB/PPS[c]	—	—	—	—	—	—	1	1.9
TOTAL SEATS	25	100.0	49	100.0	27	100.0	54	100.0

SOURCES: Lamounier 1990, 187–89; *Folha de São Paulo*, October 29, 1990, November 16, 21, 1994; International Foundation for Electoral Systems, *Newsletter*, 1, 4 (1990), 5; Nicolau 1996a: 39.

NOTE: Senate terms are eight years long. In alternate elections, two-thirds and one-third of the Senate seats are disputed. In 1982, one seat per state was contested, and the new state of Rondônia elected three senators. In 1986, two seats were disputed in twenty-three states, and the Federal District elected three senators. In 1990, one seat per state was disputed. In 1994, two seats per state were disputed.
[a]The PDS and PDC merged to form the PPR in 1993.
[b]The PST and PTR merged to form the PP in 1993.
[c]The PCB changed its name to the PPS in 1992.

Neves skillfully broadened his coalition, assured the military that no radical changes would occur, and won acceptance within the armed forces. Arguing that ousting the military had to be the foremost objective, he persuaded almost all of the opposition to agree to focus on an electoral-college victory. He cut deals with ex-PDS elites, promising them prominent positions in the new government in return for delivering electoral college votes (Mainwaring 1986; Hagopian 1992, 1996). Among other concessions was one that at the time seemed innocuous: Senator José Sarney, who had been the president of the PDS but had defected to the Liberal Front, would get the vice-presidential slot.

TABLE 4-4
Senate Seats Held by Party, 1982–94

Party	1982 No.	1982 Pct.	1986 No.[a]	1986 Pct.	1990 No.	1990 Pct.	1994 No.	1994 Pct.
PDS/PPR[b]	46	66.7	5	6.9	3	3.7	6	7.4
PMDB	21	30.4	45	62.5	27	33.3	22	27.2
PDT	1	0.5	2	2.8	5	6.2	6	7.4
PTB	1	0.5	1	1.4	8	9.9	5	6.2
PFL	—	—	15	20.8	15	18.5	18	22.2
PL	—	—	1	1.4	—	—	1	1.2
PDC[b]	—	—	1	1.4	4	4.9	—	—
PSB	—	—	1	1.4	1	1.2	1	1.2
PMB	—	—	1	1.4	—	—	—	—
PSDB	—	—	—	—	10	12.3	11	13.6
PRN	—	—	—	—	3	3.7	—	—
PT	—	—	—	—	1	1.2	5	6.2
PST/PP[c]	—	—	—	—	1	1.2	5	6.2
PMN	—	—	—	—	1	1.2	—	—
No party	—	—	—	—	2	2.5	—	—
PCB/PPS[d]	—	—	—	—	—	—	1	1.2
TOTAL SEATS	69	100.0	72	100.0	81	100.0	81	100.0

SOURCES: Lamounier 1990, 187–89; *Folha de São Paulo*, October 29, 1990, November 16, 21, 1994; International Foundation for Electoral Systems, *Newsletter*, 1, 4 (1990), 5; Nicolau 1996a: 39.

NOTE: Senate terms are eight years long. In alternate elections, two-thirds and one-third of the Senate seats are disputed. "Total held" refers to the composition of the Senate after the respective elections; it combines the seats of the newly elected senators with those who did not run that year. In 1982, one seat per state was contested, and the new state of Rondônia elected three senators. In 1986, two seats were disputed in twenty-three states, and the Federal District elected three senators. In 1990, one seat per state was disputed. In 1994, two seats per state were disputed.

[a]Omits the 1988 election of three senators from the newly created state of Tocantins. Senate size increased from 72 to 75.
[b]The PDS and PDC merged to form the PPR in 1993.
[c]The PST and PTR merged to form the PP in 1993.
[d]The PCB changed its name to the PPS in 1992.

In January 1985, the PFL helped elect Neves president and Sarney vice president. The final tally in the electoral college was 480 to 180, making Neves the first civilian elected president since 1960. Thus, military rule ended when an unlikely alliance of the former opposition and old-regime politicians joined forces.

The Impact of Military Rule on Party Building

The military dictatorship had ambiguous effects on party building, two of them deleterious. First, by abolishing the old parties and allowing the creation

TABLE 4-5
Governorships Won by Party, 1982–94

Party	1982 No.	1982 Pct.	1986 No.	1986 Pct.	1990 No.	1990 Pct.	1994 No.	1994 Pct.
PDS/PPR[a]	12	54.5	—	—	1	3.7	3	11.1
PMDB	9	40.9	22	95.7	6	22.2	9	33.3
PDT	1	4.5	—	—	3	11.1	2	7.4
PFL	—	—	1	4.3	9	33.3	2	7.4
PTB	—	—	—	—	2	7.4	1	3.7
PT	—	—	—	—	—	—	2	7.4
PTR[b]	—	—	—	—	2	7.4	—	—
PRS	—	—	—	—	1	3.7	—	—
PSDB	—	—	—	—	1	3.7	6	22.2
PDC[a]	—	—	—	—	1	3.7	—	—
PSL	—	—	—	—	1	3.7	—	—
PSB	—	—	—	—	—	—	2	7.4
TOTAL	22	100.0	23	100.0	27	100.0	27	100.0

SOURCES: Lamounier 1990, 187–89; *Folha de São Paulo*, October 29, 1990, November 16, 1994; Power 1991: 86; *Jornal do Brasil*, November 17, 1994.

NOTE: In 1982, in addition to the twelve PDS governors elected by popular vote, the newly created state of Rondônia had an appointed PDS governor. In 1988, the PDC candidate won the gubernatorial election in the newly created state of Tocantins.

[a]The PDS and PDC merged to form the PPR in 1993.
[c]The PTR merged with the PST to form the PP in 1993.

of new ones in 1965 and 1979, it disrupted the sedimentation of party identities, which is a key factor in the institutionalization of party systems (Converse 1969). Second, the period of military rule reinforced the formation of parties (Arena/PDS) and politicians whose main function was obtaining patronage for their constituencies (Power, forthcoming).

Conversely, the military era also brought about some promising changes in party development. The period between 1974 and 1982 witnessed the growing penetration of parties in political life. At first in the largest cities of the most developed regions, then later in smaller towns there and the large cities of the underdeveloped regions, the MDB won the sympathies of a large part of the population. By the late 1970s, intellectuals and artists, students, and leaders of unions and social movements were engaged in attempts to build more effective parties. This was the first time in Brazilian history that so many social actors had taken on the task of party building.

During the years of plebiscite-like elections, when citizens were largely voting for or against the military government, party identification increased. Between

1974 and 1982, fully three-quarters to four-fifths of São Paulo voters identified with one of the parties. As Lamounier (1980: 31–64) showed, casting a ballot for the MDB vote was a vote for the *party* that opposed military rule, not for charismatic leaders or clientelistic politicians, and not an issue-oriented vote (see also Reis 1978; von Mettenheim 1995). In the early 1980s, the PMDB appeared to have the potential to become a large mass party with a predominantly social-democratic orientation.

The PT was an innovative party with deeply committed activists, considerable grassroots participation, and tight discipline. More than any party in the past, it was built from the grassroots up rather than from political elites down. With the possible exception of the Communist Party (1945–47), previous Brazilian parties had been internally created (i.e., by political elites within Congress), in Duverger's lexicon. By contrast, the PT was externally created, that is, by social organizations outside the legislature. In brief, despite the legacy of party fragility and the new problems created by the military government, there were real opportunities for party building when Sarney assumed office in 1985.

Party Competition in the New Democracy

Unfortunately, those opportunities were squandered in the first decade of the new democratic period.[2] Rather than promoting party building, democracy in the first decade led to an enervation of parties. Rather than take advantage of the positive trends in party building of the second decade of military rule, Presidents Sarney and Collor helped undermine parties. Given the opportunity to revise electoral and party legislation, political elites adopted institutional rules that were inimical to party building. From the perspective of party building, the first seven or eight years of democracy could hardly have been worse (M. Souza 1989).

Tancredo Neves was scheduled to take office on March 15, 1985, but became very ill and died without taking office. In his stead, Vice President José Sarney assumed the presidential sash. Sarney had been a prominent supporter of military rule until 1984.

One of the first measures of the postmilitary period was a constitutional amendment, approved in May 1985, that revamped the electoral system. The new electoral law abolished the requirement that citizens vote a straight party ticket, which had been imposed in 1981. It allowed representatives to change parties at will, permitted interparty alliances in elections, and eliminated the national threshold for attaining representation in Congress. Parties now needed only to reach the electoral quotient in a given state, that is, the number of votes divided by the number of seats. These changes encouraged a proliferation of parties in virtually all of the states as well as at the national level.

The new constitutional amendment eliminated or reformed some authoritarian aspects of the electoral system. It abolished the electoral college and instituted direct elections for president. It did away with having one-third of the Senate elected by the state legislatures. It reinstituted elections for mayors of state capitals and of cities that previously had been classified as "national security" *municípios*, and established a November 15, 1985, date for these elections. Under military rule, these mayors had been appointed by the state governors. For the first time since 1881, illiterates were granted the right to vote, a measure that enfranchised some 25 percent of the adult population at one fell swoop. Finally, in June 1985, Congress passed a measure that allowed for the legalization of the communist parties for the first time since 1947.

The November 1985 municipal elections were the first to be held under these new electoral laws. Balloting was held only in those cities that had not had municipal elections in 1982, that is, state capitals and "national security" *municípios*. The results showed a virtual collapse of support for the PDS, which won in only one capital city and mustered only 3.8 percent of the total vote for the twenty-five capitals. The elections also evinced a move toward multipartism. In nineteen of twenty-five capitals, including all of the biggest ones, at least three parties won a minimum of 5 percent of the vote. Five parties won at least 5 percent of the aggregate vote for the twenty-five capitals: the PMDB (33.0 percent), PTB (14.4 percent), PDT (14.0 percent), PT (11.2 percent), and PFL (8.8 percent) (Lamounier 1990: 188). The results also showed some centrifugal ideological tendencies, with a marked increase in PT and PDT strength.

The 1986 gubernatorial and congressional elections were an exception to the rapid progression toward a fragmented party system with significant ideological distance. They were the first general elections in the new democratic period, and hence were a key test for the parties: they would determine who would govern at the state level. Most important, the national legislature that was elected was going to write a new constitution.

The elections were conducted in the penumbra of the Cruzado Plan, the economic plan introduced in February 1986 to stem inflation. The plan froze prices and the exchange rate, decreed an 8–16 percent wage increase for workers, and replaced the old currency (cruzeiro) with a new one (cruzado). In the short term—which was long enough to exploit the plan for political ends—real wages and production rose rapidly and inflation dropped drastically. In 1986, inflation fell to 59 percent and the economy grew 8 percent. President Sarney manipulated the plan for electoral purposes, taking advantage of its temporary popularity while ignoring the warnings from his own economic team that serious problems had emerged.

The government, the PMDB, and the PFL covered up the problems until just after the elections, and the PMDB was the big beneficiary. It scored an overwhelming victory, winning twenty-two of twenty-three gubernatorial contests. It also won an absolute majority in both chambers of Congress, capturing 261 of 487 seats in the lower house and thirty-eight of the forty-nine Senate seats that were up for grabs that year.[3]

The PFL fared reasonably well, capturing the remaining governor's position and easily establishing itself as the second-biggest party. Together, the PMDB and PFL captured nearly 80 percent of the seats, and the PDS was the only other party that managed as much as 5 percent. The PDT and PT fared poorly in relation to their 1985 performance, winning only twenty-four and sixteen seats in the Chamber of Deputies, respectively. The PDT elected one senator and no governors, and the PT did not elect any senators or governors (see Tables 4-2 to 4-4).

Unfortunately for the PMDB, this landslide resulted from manipulations of economic policy that looked good for a few months, but proved disastrous after that. The PMDB's 1986 victory resulted in part from its practice of recruiting ex-PDS/Arena cohorts. Beginning with the 1982 PMDB victories, PDS politicians flocked to the PMDB, principally to take advantage of the new opportunities for patronage. This conservative ingression accelerated after the disintegration of the PDS in 1984. Because of party switching among congresspeople, the PMDB's delegation increased from 224 members in February 1985 to 246 in July 1986. During this same period, the PDS's congressional delegation shrank from 196 to eighty-one, and the PFL's jumped from eighty-two to 149.

The influx of ex-Arena/PDS cohorts into the PMDB changed the latter's nature. The Congress that was seated in early 1987 had 306 PMDB representatives, 213 of whom had different party affiliations (Arena or MDB) before the 1979 electoral reform. Over one-third of this group—seventy-two to be exact—had belonged to Arena (Fleischer 1988). These changes from the PDS to its previous archenemy made PMDB majorities in the new Congress misleading. Of the 559 members of the new legislature, only 166 legislators had belonged to the MDB in 1979, compared to 217 who had belonged to Arena (Fleischer 1988). In many states, ex-Arena/PDS leaders broadened the party's electoral appeal but diluted its internal cohesion.

Shortly after the election, the Cruzado Plan came unhinged, giving rise to an escalation of inflation beginning in 1987. The cost of living rose 365 percent in 1987, 933 percent in 1988, and 1,722 percent in 1989, while per capita growth hovered slightly above zero. With the unraveling of the Cruzado Plan, the Sarney government started to become unglued. Legitimacy, credibility, and governability eroded as social problems escalated. The PFL-PMDB alliance that had brought Sarney to the presidency fell apart.

The constitutional assembly of 1987–88 marked a period of institutional atrophy, with unprecedented movement from one party to another (see Chapter 5). After twenty months of debate, on October 3, 1988, the assembly promulgated a lengthy, detailed and controverted charter. Several constitutional issues proved divisive for the PMDB and the PFL, and the former suffered a veritable hemorrhage. Deeply divided over policy issues and its relationship to the Sarney government, and discredited by that association, the party lost 130 of its 261 deputies and twenty-three of its forty-five senators in defections to other parties, in three and one-half years. During this period the party system constructed under military rule and modified gradually between 1979 and 1987 tottered.

The new constitution introduced further changes in electoral legislation. The most important was the requirement of an absolute majority in elections for president, state governor, and mayors of cities with at least 200,000 registered voters. The constitution lowered the voting age from eighteen to sixteen, thereby expanding the electorate. (Voting is not compulsory for those sixteen and seventeen, in contrast to the situation for those eighteen and older).

Convinced that their party had become irremediably vitiated, in June 1988 disgruntled PMDB leaders formed the Brazilian Social Democratic Party, PSDB. It was a heterogeneous party, but less so than the PMDB because it included few conservatives, few politicians who had supported Arena/PDS, and few who supported Sarney. Most members considered themselves social democrats. In contrast to the PMDB, which neither supported nor broke with Sarney, the PSDB opposed the government. Most progressive PMDB leaders left the party, disgruntled with its transformation into a clientelistic machine.

The demise of the PMDB and to a lesser extent the PFL has been indicative of a more general failure of parties to capitalize on the good will they built during the transition from military rule to democracy. By allowing a massive ingression of former Arena and PDS politicians into the party, the PMDB facilitated its resounding victory in the 1986 elections. In doing so, however, it became extremely heterogeneous ideologically, with major factions that ranged from the far left to the far right.

Party development depends first and foremost on favorable structural and institutional conditions, but it also depends on leadership. In the New Republic, the PMDB leadership bears some of the blame for what has happened to the party. PMDB leaders made choices that discredited the party and democratic practice (M. Souza 1989). They opted to allow countless ex-Arena and PDS supporters into the party; they opted for extremely heterogeneous electoral coalitions in 1986; they supported Sarney when they could have criticized the government; they supported the manipulation of the Cruzado Plan; they were voracious in their appetite for state positions and resources.

The 1988 municipal elections took place in a climate of economic disarray and political frustration. The economy was in bad straits, and the Sarney government was discredited. Disgruntled that the PMDB and PFL had gone along with arrant manipulation of economic policy for electoral gain in 1986, the electorate rejected these parties, and the PT and PDT benefited. In contrast to what happened in 1986, the 1988 elections indicated that a highly fragmented party system without anything approaching a dominant party was emerging.

The 1989 presidential elections were marked by the climate of economic deterioration, near hyperinflation, and an erosion of political legitimacy and credibility. The new rules for presidential elections encouraged a proliferation of candidates, and the discrediting of the parties in power opened the doors to new contenders. Under the aegis of first-place finisher Fernando Collor de Mello, who captured 28.5 percent of the vote, a new conservative party, the PRN (Party of National Reconstruction) burst onto the scene (see Table 4-6). Collor ran a populist, somewhat demagogic campaign, emphasizing his commitment to fighting wealthy public-sector employees and corruption, shrinking and rationalizing the state, combating inflation, bettering the lot of the poor, and putting Brazil back on the path to development. The scion of a traditional political family, Collor nonetheless used his youth and his opposition to Sarney as governor of the small state of Alagoas (1987–90) to project an image of a political outsider. The fact that he could win the presidency despite not having a party organization underscored the bankruptcy of the governing parties. Before the campaign, he was not widely known outside his own state. His campaign was antiparty and antipolitician.

The PT rallied to second place behind Luis Inácio (Lula) da Silva's 16.1 percent of the popular vote, allowing him a narrow victory over PDT candidate Leonel Brizola (15.5 percent), to make it into the runoff. Lula benefited from anti-Sarney sentiment, as the PT put in its best showing ever. The parties associated with the Sarney government, the PMDB and PFL, suffered staggering setbacks. PMDB candidate Ulysses Guimarães won a feeble 4.7 percent of the valid vote, and PFL candidate Aureliano Chaves did not even muster 1 percent. Seventy-two million people voted, compared to 12.6 million in the previous presidential election, in 1960.

In the contentious runoff, Collor defeated Lula by a 53 percent to 47 percent margin. Collor fared better among the poorest strata, where surveys indicated he had a 51–41 percent advantage over Lula, and worst among those who earned more than ten minimum salaries, where Lula enjoyed a 52–40 percent margin, but the correlation between income and intended vote was modest. Collor enjoyed his greatest popularity (55–38 percent) among those who had not

TABLE 4-6
Results of Presidential Elections, 1989 and 1994

Party	1989, First round			1994		
	Candidate	Votes	Pct.	Candidate	Votes	Pct.
PRN	F. Collor de Mello[a]	20,611,011	30.5	C. Gomes	387,927	0.6
PT	L. Inácio da Silva[b]	11,622,673	17.2	L. Inácio da Silva[c]	17,126,291	27.0
PDT	L. Brizola	11,168,228	16.5	L. Brizola[d]	2,016,386	3.2
PSDB	M. Covas	7,790,392	11.5	F. H. Cardoso[e]	34,377,198	54.3
PDS/PPR	P. Maluf	5,986,575	8.9	E. Amin	1,740,210	2.8
PL	G. Afif Domingos	3,272,462	4.8			
PMDB	U. Guimarães	3,204,932	4.7	O. Quércia[f]	2,773,793	4.4
PCB	R. Freire	769,123	1.1			
PFL	A. Chaves	600,838	0.9			
PSD	R. Caiado	488,846	0.8			
PTB	A. Camargo	379,286	0.6			
PRONA	Enéas Carneiro	360,561	0.5	Enéas Carneiro	4,672,026	7.4
PSP	Marronzinho	238,425	0.4			
PP	P. Gontijo	198,719	0.3			
PCN	Zamir	187,155	0.3			
PN	Lívia	179,922	0.3			
PLP	Mattar	162,350	0.2			
PV	Gabeira	125,842	0.2			
PMN	Brant	109,909	0.2			
PPB	Pedreira	86,114	0.1			
PDC do B	Horta	83,286	0.1			
PSC	—	—	—	Hernani Fortuni	238,623	0.4
TOTAL VALID VOTES		67,626,649	100.0		63,332,154	100.0
Blank		1,176,413			7,193,917	
Null		3,477,847			7,445,605	
Total votes		72,280,909			77,971,676	
Abstentions		9,793,809			16,810,734	
Eligible voters		82,074,718			94,782,410	

SOURCE: Tribunal Superior Eleitoral

[a]The PST and PTR officially supported Collor.
[b]The PSB and PC do B officially supported Luiz Inácio da Silva in 1989.
[c]The PSD, PPS, PV, and PC do B officially supported Luiz Inácio da Silva in 1994.
[d]The PMN officially supported Brizola in 1994.
[e]The PFL and PTB officially supported Cardoso.
[f]The PSD officially supported Quércia.

completed primary school and faced his biggest deficit (32–57 percent) among those who had some higher education. Here the correlation was stronger but still not overwhelming (Singer 1990: 137–138; see also Kinzo 1991; Moisés 1993). Lula generally fared better in the more developed states, but lost in his own state of São Paulo, the wealthiest of all.

The October 1990 congressional and gubernatorial elections took place in the context of the early difficulties of the Collor administration and the ongoing search to restore economic order. The gubernatorial elections polarized into pro- and anti-Collor camps. In the first round, Collor's allies fared reasonably well, but in the second round, the opposition to Collor won all the larger states.

In the congressional elections, the PMDB and PFL remained the two largest parties. The PMDB recovered from the disastrous presidential campaign of the previous year, winning 108 of 503 seats in the Chamber, but it suffered major losses in relation to the 1986 congressional elections. Capturing eighty-four seats in the Chamber, the PFL also rebounded from the trauma of the presidential defeat, but it too incurred losses relative to the 1986 congressional elections.

No other party managed as many as 10 percent of the seats in the Chamber. The parties that finished in third (PDT—forty-seven), fourth (PDS—forty-two), fifth (PRN—forty), sixth (PTB—thirty-eight), seventh (PSDB—thirty-seven), and eighth (PT—thirty-five) places were bunched closely together. The PSDB was a big loser. Having attracted the support of sixty deputies between 1988 and 1990, the party saw its delegation in the Chamber of Deputies reduced to thirty-seven. The party had captured the imagination of many intellectuals and elites but failed to win a commensurable mass following. The PT won thirty-five seats, more than doubling its 1986 total, but this was a disappointment after the promising campaign of the previous year. Nineteen parties won seats in the Chamber—a number matched in few democracies. In the Senate elections, the PMDB (eight seats) and PFL (eight seats) combined captured more than half of the twenty-seven seats being contested.

By the time of the second round of the gubernatorial races, Collor's economic plan was showing signs of political vulnerability. Inflation was resurging, and production and employment were falling. These problems had an impact at the polls, and virtually all of Collor's candidates were defeated (Lamounier 1991).

In 1991, the Collor government began a downward spiral that did not cease until the president's resignation in December 1992. By mid-1992, the possibility of impeachment loomed large. In late September 1992, the Chamber of Deputies voted by an overwhelming margin to impeach Collor.

Vice President Itamar Franco became interim president in September 1992 and assumed the presidency in December, when Collor resigned rather than face a Senate trial. Franco was an intemperate, erratic president, with little vocation for the leadership of one of the world's largest nations. In 1993, the economy began to grow again, but not enough to offset the declines in per capita income since 1981. Moreover, until July 1994, inflation accelerated, reaching a record 2,489 percent in 1993.

In 1994, elections were held for the presidency, state governors, two-thirds of the senators, the entire Chamber of Deputies, and state legislatures. In the presidential campaign, the PT's Lula established an early commanding lead that collapsed after the sudden drop in inflation in July with the full implementation of a new stabilization plan. Monthly inflation fell from 47 percent in June (about 10,000 percent annualized) to 5 percent in July, 3 percent in August, 2 percent in September, and 3 percent in October.[4] The economy continued the strong recovery that had begun in 1993. The great beneficiary of the stabilization plan was PSDB candidate Fernando Henrique Cardoso, who as finance minister during the Franco government had designed the plan shortly before resigning to run for president. In a matter of weeks, Cardoso surpassed Lula in the polls on his way to a convincing first-round victory, garnering 54.3 percent of the vote compared to 27.0 percent for Lula.

The PMDB won nine of twenty-seven gubernatorial contests and the PSDB won six, including those in São Paulo, Rio de Janeiro, and Ceará. The remaining twelve state houses were split among six parties. In the congressional elections, the PMDB remained the largest party, winning 107 of 513 Chamber seats. For the third consecutive election the PFL came in second, with eighty-nine seats, followed by the PSDB (sixty-two), PPR (fifty-two), PT (forty-nine), the newly founded Progressive Party (PP) (thirty-six), PDT (thirty-four), PTB (thirty-one), and ten smaller parties. In the Senate, the largest three parties followed the same order as in the Chamber: the PMDB (twenty-two of eighty-one seats), the PFL (eighteen), and the PSDB (eleven). The fact that the same parties have been the biggest for several elections suggests that the system may be moving toward slightly greater stability after a period of great flux.

In Cardoso's first three and one-half years, the government achieved several important objectives that had eluded his predecessors: low inflation, some growth, income redistribution, less corruption, and massive foreign investment. Cardoso also made modest progress in state reform. International optimism about Brazil burgeoned, in contrast to the experience of the late 1980s. On the strength of his accomplishments, Cardoso won congressional support for a constitutional amendment allowing the reelection of presidents, governors, and mayors.

Electoral Volatility

Chapter 2 laid out four features of more institutionalized party systems. The first was comparative stability in patterns of party competition. In Brazil, by contrast, flux, volatility, and instability have been the rule. Nothing resembling a consolidation of voting patterns and party strength has occurred. After being the dominant party during the 1966–82 period, the PDS collapsed in 1984–85, primarily because of the Figueiredo administration's mismanagement of economic and political affairs. The PMDB then became the dominant party thanks to its opposition to military rule, but its identification with the Sarney government led to an erosion of support after the demise of the Cruzado Plan in late 1986. The PFL also lost support after 1986. The flip side of the decline of the PDS, PFL, and PMDB was the ascension of the PT, the PDT, the PSDB, and the PRN. A dizzying array of new labels proliferated.

From 1982 to 1986, volatility in lower-chamber votes was 48.6 percent, and from 1986 to 1990 it was 45.2 percent. The 1986–90 figure is artificially elevated because of the PMDB's massive vote, inflated by the Cruzado Plan. Even if the PMDB had merely retained its 1982 share of the vote, however, volatility would still have exceeded 30 percent. Among the major Latin American countries, from 1980 to the early 1990s, only Peru had higher electoral volatility for the lower chamber (Mainwaring and Scully 1995). From 1990 to 1994, volatility declined to 21.1 percent, if we count the PPR as the successor party to the PDS. This is still high, even compared to quite a few Latin American countries.

Although it is an uneven comparison because his data are in votes, Pedersen's (1983: 39) calculations for thirteen Western European democracies for the 1948–77 period provide some indication of how extreme Brazil's electoral fluctuations were in the 1980s. The country with the highest average volatility was France, with an index of 16.8 percent—well under half the Brazilian index. The period average for the 103 election periods in the thirteen nations was 8.1 percent, about one-fifth the Brazilian mean for the 1982–86 and 1986–90 electoral periods. The average volatility in the Weimar Republic (18.8 percent), a notable case of electoral instability, was less than half the volatility in Brazil for these two electoral periods (Shively 1972: 1221).

Senate electoral volatility in seats has been even higher, though the nonproportionality of the electoral system for Senate elections makes returns more susceptible to higher volatility, when measured in seats. After winning 60.0 percent of the seats in 1982, the PDS fell to 4.1 percent in 1986 and 7.4 percent in 1990. The PMDB jumped from 36.0 percent in 1982 to 77.6 percent in 1986, then fell to 29.6 percent in 1990. The overall volatility was 57.9 percent for 1982–86 and 50.0 percent for 1986–90.

Presidential electoral volatility between 1989 and 1994 was exceptionally high: 59.9 percent if we do not consider the effect of party alliances, and 57.1 percent if we take them into account. At the presidential level, this places Brazil's as the most volatile party system among the large and medium-sized Latin American countries, although, of course, one electoral period does not constitute a trend.

Reflective of weak party roots in society, Brazil's high electoral volatility was reinforced by two factors. Changes in electoral legislation help account for the dramatic shift from bipartism to extreme multipartism and help explain the electoral volatility of 1982–86. Brazil went from an electoral system that severely penalized all but the top two parties in each state (1982) to one that facilitated a large number of parties after 1985. These changes encouraged a dispersion of the vote, lowered entry barriers, and reduced the advantages of the largest two parties. The changes in electoral rules help explain the post–1985 dispersion of the vote relative to 1982. But they do not explain the magnitude of the changes from one election to the next after 1985, because the subsequent changes in electoral rules have had little impact on the effective number of parties.

The economic crisis also contributed to electoral volatility by derogating the image of governing parties (Remmer 1991). It weakened the parties that were once dominant: the PDS until 1984 and the PMDB from 1985 to 1989. The demise of the PDS and the PMDB (even though the latter remained the largest party) accounts for a considerable part of the electoral volatility of the 1980s.

Despite extreme electoral volatility, there was continuity in some electoral trends in five of the elections of the post–1979 period (1982, 1985, 1988, 1989, and 1990), while 1986 was an anomaly that broke the pattern. There was a significant and progressive decline of the duopoly of the PDS and PMDB, with the former party suffering a severe erosion. The converse of this declining hegemony of the PDS and PMDB was the rise of other parties, with the PT, PDT, PSDB, PTB, PRN, PFL, and PPR being particularly significant.

Party Voting

The second criterion of party-system institutionalization is that parties have solid roots in society. This issue can be assessed in several ways, including the incidence of party voting.

If parties have strong roots in society, they guide the way most citizens vote. Rather than cast their ballots according to issues or personalities, most citizens generally continue to vote for the same party. Conversely, if parties have weak roots in society, most citizens vote on the basis of other factors, ranging from issue voting to personal loyalties.

Beginning with the 1985 municipal elections, the electorate did not vote as much on the basis of party as it had between 1974 and 1982.[5] In the 1985 mayoral elections in São Paulo, the winning candidate, Jânio Quadros of the PTB, came from a party that was organizationally weak and had only 3 percent of the electorate's support at the beginning of the campaign. The number of PTB sympathizers increased throughout the campaign, from 3 percent to 8 percent, but this was because the candidate's popularity led to increasing support for the party, not vice versa. According to DataFolha survey data, in April 1985, as the campaign was about to start, the PMDB had the support of 46 percent of the electorate. Identification with the PMDB peaked at 54 percent in June. As the campaign unfolded, this figure fell to 34 percent by September and 24 percent in December, one month after the election. Thus the candidate of a party with which 3 percent of the electorate identified beat one from a party with which 46 percent identified. Quadros ran as an antiparty candidate in Brazil's largest, most urban, and wealthiest city, where one might expect personalism to be less rampant and parties more significant.

Countless other examples show limited party voting, particularly the 1989 presidential election. With the exceptions of the PMDB and PT candidates, the presidential aspirants did not emphasize their parties, and the results confirmed the weak impact of party loyalties for presidential voting. The candidates of the PMDB and PFL, which had by far the largest congressional delegations, captured only 4.7 percent and 0.9 percent of the valid vote, respectively. These parties had won 53.6 percent and 23.8 percent of the lower-chamber seats, 77.6 percent and 14.3 percent of the Senate seats, and 95.7 percent and 4.3 percent of the state governors' offices, respectively, only three years earlier. The two finalists came from parties that had sixteen and twenty-six, respectively, of the 570 congressional representatives. Collor had to create a party in 1989 so that he could run for president. He ran an antiparty campaign, and his history of party switching (Arena–PDS–PMDB–PRN) revealed a man true to his antiparty discourse.

Even though in presidential systems there is almost inevitably some disjunction between a party's congressional and presidential votes,[6] the magnitude of this gap in Brazil was extraordinary in 1986, 1989, and 1990. The presidential versus legislative vote differential, explained in Chapter 2, was staggering for the 1986–89 period. Parties that won 82.7 percent of the lower-chamber seats in 1986 accounted for only 6.2 percent of the presidential vote in 1989, for a differential of 76.5 percent. Even leaving aside individuals whose defections from one party to another canceled each other, three out of four voters chose different parties in 1986 and 1989. Parties that won 58.5 percent of the lower-chamber seats in 1990 managed only 6.2 percent of the presidential vote the year before, for a differential of 52.3 percent. This is by far the highest differential in presidential vote versus legislative seats of any major Latin American country (see Mainwaring and Scully 1995 for comparative data).

The differential in presidential vote versus Senate seats was even more pronounced: 88.4 percent comparing the 1986 Senate results with the 1989 presidency, and 67.9 percent comparing the 1989 presidential vote with the 1990

Senate seats. Three parties (PMDB, PFL, PMB) that won 93.9 percent of the Senate seats in 1986 won only 5.6 percent of the presidential vote three years later. Four parties (PDT, PRN, PT, PSDB) that won 2.0 percent of the Senate seats in 1986 won 75.9 percent of the valid presidential vote in 1989.

In 1994, parties were more important actors in the presidential campaign, largely because the elections were concurrent with legislative races. With concurrent elections, more politicians have an incentive to get the vote out, and presidential coattails mean that candidates for other offices are more likely to push their party's candidate actively. This makes the 1994 differential in the presidential vote versus congressional seats somewhat nonanalogous with those of 1986, 1989, and 1990. Still, the leading contenders in 1994 were from major parties (the PSDB and PT), which was not true in 1989. The differential in the presidential vote versus lower-chamber seats declined to 31.5 percent—still a high figure, but markedly below the level in 1986, 1989, and 1990. The differential in the presidential vote versus Senate seats fell to 36.0 percent, high, but down sharply. Nevertheless, it is clear that Cardoso won the election not so much because of his party, but primarily because of the drastic decline in inflation after July 1 (Meneguello 1995).

Cardoso enjoyed the support of two significant parties, the PSDB and the PFL, as well as the PTB, but he easily outpolled all three parties combined—they won 31.9 percent of the valid popular vote for the lower chamber. Lula also far surpassed the PT's lower-chamber vote (13.2 percent), and third-place finisher Enéas Carneiro ran on a ticket (PRONA) that has never elected a single member of Congress. Conversely, the largest congressional parties once again failed to field strong presidential candidates. The candidate of the largest party in Congress (PMDB) won a meager 4.4 percent of the valid vote. The PFL, the second largest, decided not to field its own candidate because party leaders knew they did not have a viable one. The PPR, the third-largest party in Congress, captured only 2.8 percent of the presidential vote.

Weak party voting is also suggested by voting patterns for the lower chamber. Voters can cast their ballot for a party or for a specific candidate in lower-chamber elections (see Chapter 6 for details on the electoral system). For the major catch-all parties, the percentage of votes cast for the label is low, generally below 10 percent, although with some variation across parties and elections (Samuels 1996).

High electoral volatility shows weak party voting (although the opposite is not necessarily true, that is, low electoral volatility does not necessarily indicate high party voting). Where party voting is pronounced, citizens generally vote for the same party election after election, providing stability to aggregate electoral returns.

Survey information also points to weak party voting. An IBOPE poll of 600 people (300 each in Greater Rio de Janeiro and Greater São Paulo), conducted

November 2–8, 1987, asked people about what qualities they sought in a presidential candidate. Only 33 percent said they would not vote for a candidate from a different party than their own. Most respondents do not consider party a priority in choosing their president.

In IDESP's surveys, the percentage of respondents who say they chose a candidate on the basis of party declined from 43 percent in 1982 to 24 percent in 1986 and 18 percent in 1988 (Muszynski and Mendes 1990: 64). For every ten people who said they voted on the basis of party in 1982, only four did by 1988. IBOPE surveys asked a similar question during the 1989 presidential campaign. Only 4 percent of respondents said that they voted completely and 7 percent mostly on the basis of party, compared to 38 percent who said that they mostly and 28 percent who completely chose on the basis of the individual. Eighteen percent said they gave equal weight to the candidate and the party, and 5 percent said they did not know or did not respond (Olsen 1989: 12).

A 1994 IBOPE survey asked, "When you choose candidates for various positions, do you make an effort to vote for candidates of the same party, or do you vote taking into consideration only the candidate, regardless of his/her party?" Twenty-four percent of respondents chose the former response, 67 percent the latter, and 9 percent said they did not know or gave no answer.[7]

The low incidence of party voting explains some survey data that are perplexing from the viewpoint of ideological and party consistency. A March 16–23, 1988, IBOPE survey conducted in the city of São Paulo asked respondents for whom they would vote for mayor if the election were held then: 47.7 percent of PT sympathizers[8] said they would definitely vote for Sílvio Santos, a famous conservative television magnate who was flirting with running. Santos's popularity among supporters of the conservative parties that were considering launching him was the same. Because the PT is the most ideological and disciplined of the larger parties, the high level of (preliminary) support for a populist conservative was striking, even though his popularity would have declined substantially when the PT began its campaign.

Party voting is declining in most democracies as television becomes more significant in elections and as a new generation of more-educated voters casts ballots according to issues (Dalton et al. 1984; Nie et al. 1979: 47–73). But as the variety of indicators used here show, the Brazilian case is exceptional; party voting is weak, especially for the very important executive positions.

Party Identification

Party identification is analytically different from party voting, although if the former concept is meaningful, it should help predict party voting. Party identification refers to a process by which a voter sees him- or herself as sympathetic

TABLE 4-7
Party Identification, 1989–94
(Percent)

Party	1989	1990	1991	1992	1993	1994
PMDB	9.8	10.2	16.3	19.2	18.0	17.6
PT	15.6	9.2	12.4	16.8	14.4	13.4
PDS/PPR	3.6	4.7	4.4	6.9	4.6	2.1
PDT	4.3	3.9	4.4	3.6	4.6	2.7
PFL	3.1	3.6	4.6	4.4	5.2	4.0
PTB	0.5	0.8	0.6	1.1	1.2	—
PSDB	1.3	2.0	1.7	3.5	2.5	5,1
PRN	7.9	7.6	2.1	0.3	0.2	—
Other parties	1.9	1.8	2.1	1.4	1.5	3.1
TOTAL PARTY IDENTIFIERS	48.0	43.8	48.6	57.2	52.2	48.0
No preference/ no answer	51.7	55.0	51.2	37.9	44.0	51.8

SOURCE: Meneguello 1994, 159, based on DataFolha national surveys.
NOTE: Data are in response to an open-ended question. Presumably totals do not equal 100.0 percent because of rounding.

to some party. The original idea of party identification was that most citizens are not politically well informed, do not have stable attitudes on political issues, and do not make careful assessments of issues and candidates in every election. But, the argument went, most voters have relatively stable attachments to parties. Party identification acts as a short cut by reducing the amount of information citizens need to process in order to vote. Rather than sort out their own positions and the parties' stances on a wide range of issues, citizens develop a preference for a party and generally stick with it (Converse 1964, 1969; Campbell et al. 1960). Levels of party identification therefore provide information for assessing how deeply parties are rooted in society.

Although aspects of the party-identification model have been questioned, most observers agree that party identification is a useful concept that helps us analyze linkages between citizens and parties (Cain and Ferejohn 1981; Heath and McDonald 1988). Of the many possible uses of data on party identification, the one of present interest is how many citizens have a party preference. Where parties have strong roots in society, citizens identify with the parties and support them over time.

In August 1994, about 42 percent of the Brazilian electorate expressed a party preference according to DataFolha data, based on national surveys. Table 4-7

Elections, Parties, and Society

TABLE 4-8
Party Identification in the City of São Paulo, 1974–93
(Pct.)

Party	1974	1978	1982	1985	1986	1988	1989	1991	1993
Arena/PDS/PPR	26	15	17	2	5	6	6	10	7
MDB/PMDB	55	61	33	34	27	13	11	14	17
PT	—	—	13	14	16	16	31	16	20
PTB	—	—	11	4	6	1	1	2	0
PSDB	—	—	—	—	—	3	2	7	4
Others	—	—	1	9	11	4	5	7	3
No preference	19	24	25	37	35	57	43	43	50
Cases	840	578	1,003	690	2,561	—	—	—	—

SOURCE: Muszynski 1988, 4a, based on CEBRAP and UDESP DataFolha surveys; Muszynski and Mendes 1990, 64; Meneguello 1994, 172.
NOTE: Some column totals do not equal 100 percent because of rounding.

shows the evolution of party identification at the national level from 1989 to 1994. Table 4-8 shows the evolution of party identification in the city of São Paulo between 1974 and 1994, evincing a sharp drop over time.

IDESP is a well-known research institute that conducts detailed surveys. According to its data, those expressing a party preference declined from 81 percent in 1974 to 63 percent by 1985, 40 percent in 1988, and rising to 48 percent in 1994 (Meneguello 1994: 172). A survey in Presidente Prudente, a medium-sized city in the state of São Paulo, revealed an even sharper drop in party identification: from 80 percent of voters in 1976 to 23 percent in 1989 (Kinzo 1991: 262). By contrast, in the early 1980s, in the advanced industrial democracies, party identification ranged from 90 percent in Canada to 54 percent in Denmark (Dalton et al. 1984: 300–1, 196).

Although they are low, the Brazilian figures may overstate party identification, not because of flaws in the surveys but rather because in a volatile party system, the notion of party identification loses some of the meaning it had in the U.S. context.[9] As developed in the United States, party identification referred to (a) a relatively stable orientation of citizens toward parties and (b) an orientation that guided voting behavior. These conditions have not obtained in Brazil after 1985.

In Brazil, preferences for different parties have sometimes risen and fallen on an almost monthly basis, depending on the vicissitudes of certain candidates and in response to elections. For example, when the mayoral campaign was starting in mid-1985, 54 percent of São Paulo voters declared themselves sympathizers of the PMDB. At that time, the party was still enjoying the crest of popularity it reaped because of its central part in bringing about the end of military rule. But when candidate Fernando Henrique Cardoso faltered, the percentage of PMDB sympathizers fell to 34 percent by September, and, weeks after his defeat, to 24 percent in December. In a period of only six months, 30 percent of the electorate of São Paulo and 56 percent of PMDB sympathizers had defected from pro-PMDB identification.

Another example of the rapid short-term oscillations in party identification occurred during the 1989 presidential campaign. A nationwide IBOPE poll in November of that year (n=5,000) indicated that only 5.5 percent of respondents identified with the PMDB, which only a year earlier competed with the PT for being the party with the most sympathizers. Thirteen percent said they identified with the PRN, Collor's campaign vehicle, which had essentially been created that year. These figures represented short-term responses to the 1989 campaign, not enduring loyalties to parties.

These short-term fluctuations indicate that only a minority of Brazilian citizens have stable party preferences. To a greater degree than in the United States, immediate political events drive party preference, rather than party preference shaping voting behavior. When this is the case, the assumption that party identification is relatively stable no longer pertains.

Arguments about party identification also rest upon the assumption that it shapes voting behavior. But at least for executive positions, party preferences do not drive the voting behavior of most citizens. Many people who declare party sympathy do not vote on that basis.

One indicator of this disjuncture between party identification and vote in Brazil comes from a 1987 IBOPE survey in the city of São Paulo, with 1,600 respondents. This survey allowed for retrospective reflection on the 1985 mayoral election. The interviewers asked for information about the respondents' party leanings (stimulated), then asked for whom the individual had voted in 1985. The results (Table 4-9) reveal that a significant share of PMDB and PT voters crossed party lines. Among PMDB sympathizers, PMDB candidate Fernando Henrique Cardoso had a narrow 36.3 percent to 24.0 percent margin over PFL-PTB-PDS candidate Jânio Quadros (the ex-president). A plurality of PT sympathizers voted for Cardoso or Quadros. Aware that their candidate had scant chances of winning, PT supporters may have crossed party lines to vote strategically. Still, the fact that many PT sympathizers would vote for the conservative populist Quadros suggests a weak attachment to PT ideals. Moreover, strategic voting for a viable candidate does not account for defections of PMDB supporters because Cardoso was considered the frontrunner.

Survey data showed weak correlations for PMDB and PFL sympathizers between party identification and vote in the 1989 presidential elections (see also

TABLE 4-9
Party Identification and Voter Behavior,
São Paulo Mayoral Election, 1985

Candidate/Vote	Party preference[a]				
	PMDB	PT	PDS/PFL	Other party	No party preference
Eduardo Suplicy (PT)	4.4%[b]	33.5%	4.4%	10.9%	6.4%
Fernando Henrique Cardoso (PMDB)	36.3	16.5	14.5	15.7	22.1
Jânio Quadros (PTB/PFL/PDS)	24.0	18.2	43.4	43.7	30.7
Other candidate	0.5	2.4	2.2	2.5	1.3
Did not vote	22.9	20.3	22.9	18.4	17.4
Does not remember	10.2	6.7	11.3	5.3	13.9
Blank/null vote	1.7	2.3	1.2	3.6	7.6
No answer	—	—	—	—	0.6
Number (N=1,600)	412	378	127	90	593

SOURCE: IBOPE survey, city of São Paulo, October 23–November 11, 1987.
[a]Stimulated
[b]Percentage of party supporters who voted for a particular candidate.

Kinzo 1991: 263). In November 1989, IBOPE conducted a national survey in the aftermath of the first-round presidential election. Among PMDB sympathizers, only 29.9 percent voted for Ulysses Guimarães, the party's candidate, compared to 36.3 percent who voted for Collor. Among PFL sympathizers, 45.3 percent voted for Collor, 12.6 percent for Lula, and only 2.1 percent for the party's candidate. Party sympathy was a powerful predictor of voting behavior among PDT, PT, PDS, PSDB, and PRN sympathizers; 87 percent, 69 percent, 57 percent, 85 percent, and 86 percent of party sympathizers, respectively, said they voted for their party's candidate. Table 4-10 gives a further breakdown.

Excluding minor parties for which no breakdown is available, but which account for only seventeen of 3,650 respondents, among the 1,962 respondents who said they had a party preference, 1,328 (67.7 percent) voted for that party's candidate. However, sympathizers of the two largest congressional parties massively deserted ship. The fact that declared party preference changed so markedly indicates that even the figure of 1,328 respondents who voted for the candidate of their declared party cannot be taken as party voters; a party voter remains loyal to the same party over a period of time. Further, in a September 1994 survey, only 19 percent of PMDB sympathizers, 45 percent of PDT sympathizers, and 18 percent of PPR sympathizers said they intended to vote for their party's presidential candidate.[10]

TABLE 4-10

Party Identification and Voter Behavior, 1989 Presidential Election, First Round

Candidate/Vote	Party preference										Total
	PMDB	PDT	PT	PDS	PFL	PSDB	PRN	Other	None	No opinion/ No answer	
Did not vote	2.5%[a]	1.3%	3.3%	0.7%	6.3%	2.9%	2.1%	4.9%	2.7%	3.7%	2.7%
Chaves (PFL)	—	—	0.2	—	2.1	—	—	—	0.8	1.6	0.5
Collor (PRN)	36.3	2.9	3.7	19.9	45.3	3.8	85.7	18.5	38.2	53.5	34.7
Afif (PL)	4.0	—	1.0	1.4	14.7	1.9	2.9	22.2	3.6	2.1	3.3
Brizola (PDT)	4.5	87.3	9.1	11.3	6.3	1.9	2.5	12.3	11.9	7.0	15.5
Luiz Inácio da Silva (PT)	10.4	4.9	68.8	4.3	12.6	1.0	0.4	4.9	11.1	8.0	17.4
Covas (PSDB)	8.5	1.9	6.4	3.5	5.3	84.6	2.3	9.9	11.8	8.0	10.1
Maluf (PDS)	2.0	0.3	3.3	56.7	1.1	1.0	2.1	8.6	9.4	8.0	7.6
Guimarães (PMDB)	29.9	0.3	1.4	0.7	2.1	1.9	1.5	1.2	2.8	2.7	3.5
Other	1.5	0.6	1.6	—	2.1	1.0	0.2	16.0	2.4	1.6	1.9
Blank/Null	—	—	0.5	1.4	1.1	1.0	—	—	3.2	1.1	1.5
No answer[b]	0.5	0.3	0.7	—	1.1	—	0.2	1.2	1.9	2.7	1.2
Number	(201)	(308)	(574)	(141)	(95)	(104)	(475)	(81)	(1,484)	(187)	(3,650)
Pct. of total	5.5	8.4	15.7	3.9	2.6	2.8	13.0	2.2	40.7	5.1	100.0

SOURCE: IBOPE, National Voter Survey, Wave 19, November 1989. N=3,650.

[a]Percentage of party supporters who voted for a particular candidate.

[b]Includes no opinion, does not remember.

Given the rapid shifts in party identification in response to the elections at hand, expressing a preference for a party at one particular moment, especially during a highly politicized presidential campaign, did not imply that a voter had developed an enduring allegiance to it. Symptomatic of these rapid fluctuations in party identification is the response pattern manifested in the survey of Table 4-10. Thirteen percent of the respondents voiced a preference for the PRN, making it the second-most-preferred party although it had not existed a year earlier. Only 5.5 percent voiced sympathy for the PMDB. Many of the PRN sympathizers were such because of their recent vote for Collor rather than vice versa.

In congressional elections, one might expect more voters to be loyal to their preferred party because television is less crucial and political networks are more important. Nevertheless, data from a March 1987 survey provide evidence of ample cross-party voting for Senate candidates in the November 1986 elections. Voters gave their spontaneous party preference and also mentioned whom they had chosen for the two Senate positions. The fact that the survey asked about spontaneous party preference (i.e., without listing parties) meant that the number of party identifiers was lower than it would have been with a stimulated party identification (when the interviewer mentions a party by name). Only 47.7 percent of the population expressed a party preference. This method should have left a core of voters more strongly identified with a certain party; it should therefore provide a high estimate of party voting. Nevertheless, PDS sympathizers chose a PDS candidate only 41 percent and 37 percent of the time (for the two Senate positions, respectively); PDT sympathizers, 59 percent and 53 percent; PMDB, 75 percent and 71 percent; PT, 47 percent and 44 percent; and PFL, 64 percent and 57 percent.[11]

Voters who declare a party preference often have shallow predilections. This is suggested by responses to an IBOPE survey that asked, "For each one of the following parties that I mention, please tell me if you always trust it, usually trust it, usually don't trust it, or never trust it."[12] When asked about their attitudes toward their own party, 43.2 percent of PMDB sympathizers (n=49) either responded negatively (usually or always mistrusting the party) or did not offer an opinion. Similar anomalies are found among some other parties. Evaluation of their own party by party sympathizers is not especially positive, so party identification is not likely to be very deep.

Party identification decreased after 1985. As Lamounier and Muszynski (1986) and Muszynski (1988) have argued, the decline relative to the pre–1979 period is not surprising. With a two-party system, it was easier for the electorate, most of which has very limited political information, to retain the names and identities of the parties. The plebiscitary character of elections—for or against the military government—during the two-party period facilitated higher levels of party identification. Between 1974 and 1980, political options were simple: one voted for or against the dictatorship.

More noteworthy is the erosion in party identification after 1985, a process that suggests disaffection with the major parties. Party identification has been declining in many Western democracies in recent decades (Dalton et al. 1984), and from this perspective it might appear that there is nothing unusual about the decline in Brazil. However, in the advanced industrial democracies, declining party identification has coincided with increasing issue voting and with the rise of well-educated, independent voters with no fixed party attachments. In Brazil, by contrast, declining party identification reflects not a questioning of old, well-established institutions, but rather the failure of new ones to develop roots in society.

Declining party identification and electoral volatility have gone hand in hand. The former has reinforced electoral instability because where citizens do not have stable attachments to parties, they are more likely to change from one party to another (Shively 1972; Converse 1969).

Discontinuity in Social Bases of Parties: Electoral Geography

If parties have solid roots in society, there is a high degree of continuity in their social bases and therefore in patterns of electoral geography. There should be consistency in how well a party fares in the various regions and states, in large urban areas as opposed to towns and rural areas, etc. This is an easy test: even party systems that are not well institutionalized can meet it. For example, as Soares (1967, 1973) has shown, the Brazilian party system of 1945–64 exhibited considerable continuity and structuring in this sense (see also Simão 1956; Ferreira 1964; Lavareda 1991). It does not necessarily indicate a high level of party-system institutionalization if there is continuity in electoral geography, but if such continuity is limited, the party system is weakly institutionalized.

To assess continuity in electoral geography, I undertook two kinds of tests. For four parties I calculated correlations of the vote by state for national elections between 1978 and 1994. For 1978, 1982, 1986, 1990, and 1994, I used the lower-chamber vote.[13] I also included the presidential elections of 1989 and 1994. I excluded the Federal District, which did not elect deputies in 1978, and Tocantins, which was created in 1988. I computed results for the (P)MDB, the PT beginning in 1982, and Arena/PDS/PPR. Because the 1984 schism from the PDS that led to the formation of the PFL took the better part of the former party, I also looked at the combined results of the PDS/PPR and PFL beginning in 1986. For the PMDB and PDS, I included the 1978 elections in order to assess how these parties' electoral bases changed over a longer period. However, the trends are the same if one begins with the 1982 elections.

The raw data reveal some extraordinary shifts in parties' performances in different states. The (P)MDB declined from 75 percent of the vote in Rio de Janeiro in 1978 to 7 percent in 1990, from 39 percent to 2 percent in the Federal District from 1986 to 1990, and from 67 percent to 0 percent in Rondônia between 1986 and 1990. Only a fraction of these declines is explained by the party's declining fortunes at the national level. Arena/PDS/PPR suffered a sharp demise at the national level, from 50 percent in 1978 to 43 percent in 1982, 7 percent in 1986, 9 percent in 1989 (presidential), and 8 percent in 1990. Even given this overall pattern, several state-level declines are remarkable. For example, the PDS declined from 60 percent to 0 percent in Alagoas, from 79 percent to 0 percent in Amapá, from 60 percent to 0 percent in Rondônia, and from 100 percent to 0 percent in Roraima between 1982 and 1986.

Table 4-11 shows the ecological correlations with states as the unit of analysis, that is, the correlation of a party's statewide vote between any two elections. A correlation of 1.0 (the highest possible) for 1978–82 would mean that a party's 1978 vote in a given state would perfectly predict its 1982 vote in that state, relative to national patterns. A correlation of 0 would mean that the party's 1982 vote in a state varied completely randomly relative to the 1978 vote, once again compared to national patterns.

Some of the correlations are high. For example, with a correlation of .754, the PMDB vote in a state in 1982 correlated strongly with its 1986 vote in that state. Over time, however, the cumulative weakness of the correlations is notable. The MDB's 1978 vote percentage in a state does not correlate strongly (.152) with its 1990 percentage. The PDS's geographic base changed profoundly, most dramatically between 1982 and 1986, when there is actually a slight negative correlation (–.011) after a powerful positive correlation (.727) between 1978 and 1982. The PT, in contrast, shows modest continuity in its geographic base by state over time. But because the PT, unlike the PMDB and PDS, never conquered a major share of the electorate in congressional elections, its stable social base is less significant than the dramatic change of the other two parties. The stability of a small party does not offset the lack of stability of big parties because the former has a smaller weight in the party system.

For the (P)MDB, there is no single astonishing shift, but the biggest two changes occurred in 1978–82 and 1986–89. Arena/PDS underwent a dramatic shift in 1982–86. The PT experienced a significant change from 1986 to 1989.

The correlations between these parties' votes, disaggregated by state, and the states' per capita income are found in Table 4.12. The idea was to verify whether

TABLE 4-11
Vote Correlation by State, 1978–94

| | Arena/PDS/PPR | | | | | |
	1982	1986	1989p	1990	1994p	1994
1978	0.744	−0.033	0.054	0.055	−0.091	−0.162
1982		−0.072	0.246	−0.019	−0.053	−0.230
1986			0.281	0.680	0.453	0.593
1989					0.196	0.543
1990					0.309	0.628
1994p						−0.110

| | (P)MDB | | | | | |
	1982	1986	1989p	1990	1994p	1994
1978	0.248	0.240	−0.054	0.127	−0.030	0.056
1982		0.662	−0.223	0.547	0.139	0.389
1986			−0.180	0.582	0.083	0.388
1989					0.359	0.178
1990					0.364	0.702
1994p						0.416

| | Arena/PDS/PPR + PFL | | | |
	1989p	1990	1994p	1994
1986	0.277	0.540	0.161	0.671
1989		−0.054	0.167	0.255
1990			0.279	0.523
1994p				0.241

| | PT | | | | |
	1986	1986p	1990	1994p	1994
1982	0.452	−0.015	0.418	−0.056	0.475
1986		0.121	0.530	0.288	0.582
1989			0.163	0.443	0.264
1990				0.263	0.679
1994p					0.513

NOTE: p designates a presidential election. All other correlations are based on lower-chamber elections.

a party fared better in the more-developed states or the poorer ones. The data again show remarkable changes in the (P)MDB's and Arena/PDS/PPR's social base. In 1978, the MDB fared much better in the wealthy states than the poor ones. By 1986, the powerful positive correlation between per capita income and PMDB vote had disappeared, and by 1989–90 it had become slightly negative.

TABLE 4-12
Party Vote by State Correlated with GDP Per Capita

	1978	1982	1986	1989p	1990	1994	1994p
(P)MDB	0.533	0.419	–0.021	–0.229	0.019	–0.189	–0.228
Arena/PDS/PPR	–0.533	–0.526	–0.013	–0.040	–0.040	–0.061	0.308
Arena/PDS/PPR + PFL			–0.456	–0.056	–0.150	–0.302	0.308
PT		0.503	0.503	0.181	0.711	0.709	0.254

NOTES
GDP data by state correspond to 1985.
p designates a presidential election. All other correlations are based on lower-chamber elections.

Arena/PDS/PPR changed sharply where it fared best. In 1978 and 1982, the party did much better in the poorer states. This negative correlation with per capita income by state dropped sharply in 1986 and disappeared in 1990.

Formerly strongest in the major cities and in the most-developed regions of the country, the PMDB is now weakest there, and is strongest in the interior and the less-developed parts of the country. An August-September 1987 IBOPE nationwide poll of 5,000 people, for example, showed that there were more PMDB party identifiers in the underdeveloped Center-West (32.3 percent) and Northeast (33.3 percent) than in the South (25.1 percent) and Southeast (20.7 percent). PMDB sympathizers were most prevalent (29.0 percent) in the smallest *municípios* (those with under 20,000 inhabitants), and least common (22.1 percent) in the biggest, those with over 100,000 inhabitants.

These telling signs of discontinuity in electoral patterns and of weak party rootedness in society are reinforced by other evidence. Sadek (1988) showed that a similar discontinuity has occurred at the *município* level in the state of São Paulo. Whereas the MDB in the 1970s did better in large, urban, industrial *municípios*, the PMDB in 1986 had its best results in those of the opposite characteristics. This means that the kind of discontinuity in electoral geography across states also holds across *municípios*, at least for the state of São Paulo.

In a similar fashion, Meneguello and Alves (1986) calculated correlation coefficients between district-level vote patterns in the city of São Paulo for the 1974 and 1978 Senate elections, the 1982 gubernatorial election, and the 1985 mayoral election. The city was divided into fifty-six administrative units that can be categorized according to their standard of living. Researchers grouped these administrative units into eight socioeconomic categories based on income and other variables, Category I being the wealthiest and VIII the poorest. Their analysis (113) demonstrated there were strong positive correlations between pro-PDS districts in 1982 and pro-PMDB (the PDS's archenemy) districts in 1985. The wealthier districts tended to vote for the government more than the poor districts, regardless of who was in office. Opposition to whomever was governing, not party loyalty, was more significant. Conversely, there were strong positive correlations between the opposition vote in 1982, when the PMDB, PT, and PTB were opposition parties, and in 1985, when the PFL/PTB alliance and the PT were the main opposition contenders (114). These significant discontinuities in electoral patterns at the local, state, and national levels point to weak party penetration in society.

Discontinuities in Party Organizations

The ability of parties to survive a long time provides an indication that they have captured the long-term loyalties of some social groups, and therefore that they are deeply rooted in society. If parties establish strong roots, they should be able to endure. Leaders may change the party's name, but the connections they establish with citizens and organized interests will ensure the party's capacity to survive. It was precisely this kind of rootedness in society, leading to allegiances of citizens and organized interests to parties, that led Lipset and Rokkan (1967) to speak of the "freezing" of party systems. Therefore, the longevity of parties provides an indication of their rootedness in society.

On this variable, the Brazilian party system ranks as one of the least institutionalized among the medium-size and large Latin American countries, as Tables 2-2 and 2-3 showed. Of the six largest parties in the Brazilian party system as of 1998, the oldest (PMDB) was created in 1966, but as the evidence on its changing geographic base made apparent, it is a very different party than it was until 1982. Two other parties (the PT and the PDT) were created in 1979; the PFL was founded in 1984; the PSDB in 1988; and the PPB in 1995. Four parties were important for ephemeral periods: the Popular Party, created in 1979 and dissolved in 1981; the PRN, created in 1989 but insignificant after Collor's impeachment in 1992; the PDS, which merged with the PDC in 1993; and the PPR, which merged with the PTB and PP in 1995.

Parties and Organized Interests

Thus far, I have looked at linkages between parties and individual citizens. Parties' linkages to the major interest groups and social movements are another facet of the relationship between parties and society. This subject could be analyzed at length, but here I deal with it briefly.

Given the importance the organized working class had in party-system formation in Western European countries, the relationship between unions and parties is especially important. In Brazil, party activists have been key figures in most unions, but in the catch-all parties, linkages to unions are weak. Until the legalization of the communist parties in 1985, the PMDB harbored that important part of the Brazilian left. But when the communist parties were legalized, they left the PMDB and took their union connections with them. Some union leaders supported the PMDB until 1987, but its collapse as a credible advocate for reform occasioned their departures.

By the mid-1980s, the PT had become the dominant party force in the union movement (Keck 1992: Chap. 7), but it would be misleading to portray it as *the* party of organized labor in Brazil. Labor leaders helped create the PT, but Catholic Church activists and members of the old left were also influential (Keck 1992: 61–85).

Despite the increasing prominence of the PT, the union movement has remained divided in party terms. Labor has been organized into several competing central organizations, each of which has represented divergent partisan sympathies. The so-called Sole Labor Confederation (Central Única dos Trabalhadores, CUT) is closely allied with the PT. The labor opposition to the CUT has been organized under different auspices beginning with the loosely organized CONCLAT, created in 1981. By 1985, the CUT had become the most powerful central labor organization, and the opposition decided to create the General Labor Confederation (CGT). The CGT was later eclipsed by another central organization known as Força Sindical (Union Power).

The battles within the labor movement have not been narrowly partisan, but have rather expressed different conceptions of what workers should strive for. Força Sindical leaders believe that capitalism is the way to go, that privatization can benefit workers and society, and that the interests of capitalists and workers are not intrinsically opposed in the medium term. They have generally supported stabilization plans, arguing that inflation had highly corrosive effects, above all for workers. CUT leaders have voiced a more radical and traditional view of labor-capital relations, seeing workers' interests as fundamentally opposed to capitalists'.

The rhetoric of the PT and the CUT evinces a fundamental difference between the Brazilian labor-party linkage than that found in countries where one party has dominated the partisan representation of the labor movement. In Brazil, both the PT and the CUT have emphasized the autonomy of the latter vis-à-vis the former. In rhetoric, PT and CUT leaders have argued that the party should be more subordinate to the movement than vice versa. Força Sindical leaders have criticized the CUT for being too closely linked to the PT, but the unions have been more autonomous with respect to the party than in many countries.

The relationship between social movements and parties is even more patchwork than that between unions and parties. A wide array of social movements burgeoned in Brazil beginning the mid-1970s, but many of them have been organized strictly at the local level. There have been strong affinities between many grassroots movements—especially those linked to the Catholic Church—and the PT, but the party's insistence on respecting the autonomy of the movements is telling. Although the PT is the party of choice of most grassroots leaders, many support other parties. The feminist, environmental, and human-rights movements have been divided between those who have a party preference and those who do not, and among the former group, between those who favor the PT and those who prefer other parties.

Business interests generally eschew close connections to parties (Makler 1994). They prefer to put their eggs in several baskets, and they almost always support individual candidates and politicians rather than parties. In a survey of 132 banking sector leaders, Makler (1994) found that only seventeen (12.9 percent) were members of parties. Among those seventeen, party preferences were divided: three PDS, two PMDB, one each PFL, PDT, and PL, and nine others. Even more revealing was the distribution of responses to the question, "What political party is best for Brazil's economic future?" Only twenty-seven bankers (20.5 percent) answered that any party was best for the country's future, indicating that parties have not captured the sympathies of this important group. Those who voiced a preference for some party were inclined to see the PL most favorably (ten people), followed by the PSDB (five), PMDB (four), PDS (four), PFL (two), PDT (one), and PT (one).[14]

Given the nature of Brazilian parties, the option of business leaders to support individual politicians rather than party organizations is not surprising. Most parties are too heterogeneous and undisciplined to be the principal agents of representation. Parties are rarely the principal loci of decision making. By supporting individual candidates, business groups create connections to individual politicians, thereby gaining privileged access. In the post–1985 period, organized elite interests have sought influence within Congress, indicating that it is not irrelevant. But they have gone through individual politicians rather than parties.

The Legitimacy of Parties and Elections

The third criterion of a more institutionalized party system is that parties and elections have legitimacy. Survey data provide useful information in this regard, and in Brazil they evince a lack of credibility of parties.

An IBOPE survey of 500 respondents (100 each in São Paulo, Rio de Janeiro, Belo Horizonte, Recife, and Curitiba) carried out in June 1988, asked the question, "For each of the parties I mention, tell me if you completely trust (*confiar*) it, usually trust it, usually don't trust it, never trust it, don't have an opinion, or don't know." The responses indicated deep discrediting of parties.

Only 26.5 percent usually or always trusted the PMDB, which nevertheless had the third-highest ranking behind the PT's 42.7 percent and the PDT's 27.6 percent. Only 16.6 percent trusted the PFL, 13.4 percent the PDS, and 15.7 percent the PCB.

Another IBOPE survey, this one of 500 individuals in the city of São Paulo, conducted March 16–23, 1988, posed a similar question: "For each party I mention, tell me if you have a favorable opinion, a negative opinion, or no opinion." The most striking result is the high percentage of those who had no opinion on most parties, ranging from 39.2 percent for the PMDB to 65.2 percent for the PDT (which was a minor party in São Paulo). Only 12.4 percent viewed the PDT favorably, 13.2 percent the PFL, 15.0 percent the PDS, 18.2 percent the PTB, 25.2 percent the PMDB, and 39.2 percent the PT.

Other survey questions also indicate disenchantment with parties. In one poll, only 38.8 percent of respondents agreed completely or mostly with the statement, "The main parties have proposals for the country's problems," compared to 52.5 percent who disagreed completely or mostly. The level of trust in the parties' ability to address the nation's problems declined significantly among middle- and high-income groups, who are generally better informed. Among the better off (25.8 percent of the sample), only 29.3 percent mostly or completely agreed with the statement, compared with 70.6 percent who completely or mostly disagreed. Only 50.6 percent of respondents fully agreed with the statement, "Without political parties, there is no democracy." Agreement with the statement, "The parties only want the vote of people, not their opinion," was overwhelming; 75.4 percent agreed completely, 12.7 percent mostly agreed, 5.1 percent mostly disagreed, and a paltry 3.7 percent completely disagreed. Only 9.6 percent of respondents fully agreed that "The parties inform the people of their policies for the country's problems," while 18.7 percent more or less agreed, 14.0 percent more or less disagreed, and 53.3 percent completely disagreed. A mere 25.1 percent of respondents mostly or completely disagreed with the statement, "Today I don't know what the main proposals of the parties are."

A national survey conducted during the 1989 presidential campaign asked citizens whom parties represent and whom they should represent. The responses reflected widespread cynicism. Thirty-two percent said the parties represented the whole population or voters, 49 percent said they represented politicians, and 19 percent gave other responses or did not answer (Moisés 1993: 594).

In a September 1989 survey, 52.8 percent of respondents stated that social groups or movements should control candidate selection, compared to 32.0 percent who said parties should; 3.1 percent gave other responses, and 12.1 percent didn't know or gave no response (Moisés 1993: 595). In most countries, including Brazil, candidate selection is one of the parties' major functions.

Therefore it is significant that such a high percentage of respondents think that parties should not control candidate selection.

In a survey in Presidente Prudente, Kinzo (1991: 273) asked an interesting battery of questions that reconfirmed the limited legitimacy of parties and elections. Only 43 percent agreed that "In any situation, a democratic government is preferable to a nondemocratic government." Sixty-seven percent agreed that "The people do not know how to vote," and 50 percent agreed that "Only the best educated people should vote." Sixty-nine percent agreed that "The important thing is that a government can accomplish a lot, not that it is elected." And 52 percent agreed that "Parties don't do any good; they hurt more than they help the country."

Surveys have consistently shown that parties and politicians are the least-trusted institution of Brazilian society. The 1995 *Latinobarómetro* of eight Latin American countries asked respondents how much they trusted different institutions (Lagos 1996). Parties ranked last in most countries, but trust in parties was lowest in Venezuela (16 percent responded that they trusted parties some or a lot) and Brazil (17 percent). Trust in parties was substantially higher in Uruguay (41 percent), Mexico (40 percent), Chile (33 percent), and Argentina (27 percent) (Basáñez et al. 1995: 91). Brazilians were more likely than citizens of the other countries to agree that "Democracy can function without parties." Forty-seven percent of Brazilian respondents agreed, compared to 43 percent in Mexico, 41 percent in Peru, 40 percent in Venezuela, 37 percent in Chile, 32 percent in Paraguay, 20 percent in Argentina, and 15 percent in Uruguay (Basáñez et al. 1995: 106).

Muszynski and Mendes (1990: 64) also underscored the low legitimacy of parties. The percentage of São Paulo respondents who agreed with the statement, "Political parties are useless," was relatively stable in surveys taken in 1974 (23 percent), 1982 (23 percent), and 1986 (25 percent), but in 1988 it jumped to 39 percent—an indictment of the way parties functioned after the rebirth of democracy. In all democracies, citizens manifest some ambivalent attitudes about parties, but the discrediting of parties in Brazil is particularly high.

These answers reveal a perception that parties are self-serving and do not represent the interests of the Brazilian people. Parties have failed to create positive public images and enduring allegiances. Public credibility dramatically eroded after the failure of the Cruzado Plan.

To a greater degree than respondents in Brazil's Southern Cone neighbors, democracy as a form of government is not unequivocally accepted. In the 1995 *Latino Barómetro*, only 48 percent of Brazilian respondents agreed that "Democracy is preferable to any other form of government." This was the lowest figure among the eight countries, trailing Uruguay (86 percent), Argentina (82 percent), Venezuela (64 percent), Paraguay and Peru (58 percent), Mexico (57 percent), and Chile (54 percent) (Basáñez et al. 1995: 75).

Moreover, in a 1988 survey, 40 percent of São Paulo respondents agreed that "It would be better if the military returned." Sixty-eight percent agreed that "The people don't know how to vote," and 47 percent that "Only the best educated should vote" (Muszynski and Mendes 1990: 71).[15] Forty-eight percent of Argentines, 29 percent of Chileans, and 52 percent of Uruguayans agreed that the people do not know how to vote; as to whether only the best educated should vote, 22 percent of Argentines, 20 percent of Chileans, and 12 percent of Uruguayans agreed. In Argentina (15 percent) and Uruguay (6 percent), far fewer respondents agreed that "It would be better if the military returned."

In a July 1989 national survey conducted by IBOPE (n=3,753), 92.1 percent of respondents agreed that "what Brazil needs is a great leader," reflecting the flip side of the cynicism regarding democratic institutions. Lamounier (1994) has referred to this hope in the great leader as "plebiscitarian presidentialism," and O'Donnell (1994) has called it "delegative democracy." Finally, the percentage of those agreeing that "It is more important that political leaders (*o governante*) be capable than elected" grew from 53 percent in 1974 to 65 percent in 1978 and 74 percent in 1988 (Muszynski and Mendes 1990: 64). The trend after 1985 was toward less legitimacy of parties and elections.

Extreme Multipartism

The number and relative size of parties shapes the character of democratic politics. It affects how governments govern because the need for and nature of coalitions depend on the number and size of parties, and as a consequence they affect government and opposition strategies. They may also affect the degree of ideological polarization; in general, a higher number of parties is associated with greater polarization (Cox 1990; G. B. Powell 1982: 99).

The effective number of parties in Brazil has changed rapidly since the move away from strict bipartism in 1979. The party system changed from rigid bipartism (1966–79) to incipient multipartism (1980–81), back to bipartism in most states and at the national level (1982–84), to moderate multipartism with a dominant party (1984–87), and to extreme multipartism with no dominant party (1988–present). This shift is reflected in changes in the effective number of parties. It was moderate in 1982 (2.39 in the lower chamber and 1.86 in the Senate) and 1986 (2.83 in the Chamber of Deputies and 2.27 in the Senate), but by 1990 it was one of the highest in the world, with 8.65 effective parties in the Chamber of Deputies. Despite plurality-single-member-district electoral rules, the Senate had 5.54 effective parties after the 1990 elections. In 1994, the effective number of parties in the lower chamber declined slightly to 8.13. Still, eighteen parties won lower-chamber seats, and the largest party conquered only 20.9 percent of the seats. In the Senate, the effective number of parties increased slightly to 6.08.

The anomaly in this pattern of extreme multipartisan was the 1986 elections, when two circumstances favored the PMDB and limited party-system fragmentation. These elections were the first in the new democratic period, and the PMDB benefited by having led the party opposition to military rule. In addition, political manipulation of economic policy led to a short-term boom that favored the PMDB, followed by a bust after the election that discredited the party.

The pulverization of the party system can also be seen by data on the relative size of the largest parties. In 1990 and 1994, the largest party (PMDB) won only 21.5 percent and 20.9 percent, respectively, of the lower-chamber seats, an exceptionally low figure by comparative standards and lower than ever before in Brazilian history. Similarly, the shares of the largest two (38.2 percent in both 1990 and 1994) or three parties (47.5 percent and 50.3 percent, respectively) are extraordinarily low. In 1990, the share of lower-chamber seats of the four largest parties (55.8 percent) barely exceeded that of the largest party in 1986 (53.6 percent), and the share of the seven largest parties (78.8 percent) only slightly surpassed that of the two largest in 1986 (77.4 percent).

Extreme multipartism is facilitated by the electoral system, which makes it easy for many parties to attain representation and reduces the disincentives against forming or voting for minor parties. A high district magnitude facilitates the representation of many parties. For elections for federal and state deputies and local representatives (*vereadores*), there is a system of proportional representation. For federal deputies, the entire state constitutes the electoral district, and each state has from eight to seventy federal deputies (sixty until 1994). Few countries in the world have such large district magnitudes as the bigger Brazilian states. (The Netherlands and Israel both have only one district in the nation and have higher district magnitudes with 150 and 120 representatives, respectively.) Even the lowest district magnitude (eight for federal deputies) is high enough to allow for considerable dispersion of the vote. In 1994, 513 deputies were elected in the twenty-six states and the Federal District, for an average district magnitude of 19.0. In addition to the Netherlands and Israel, Austria (20.3) and Italy until 1993 (twenty) are among the few established democracies with higher average district magnitudes (Taagepera and Shugart 1989: 137–138).

Some proportional systems impose a minimum percentage (threshold) that a party must attain in order to win a seat. With a high (e.g., 5 percent) threshold, parties face a double barrier: they must reach the 5 percent minimum, and they must convince citizens to risk "wasting" their vote on a small party. In Brazil, between 1985 and 1995, there was no national threshold. The state threshold (namely, the electoral quotient or the number of votes divided by the number of seats) is low, so parties can attain representation with a small percentage of the vote. In the state of São Paulo, a party can win a seat in the Chamber of Deputies with 1.43 percent of the vote. If that party or coalition did not exist in other states, it could win a seat in the lower chamber with less than 0.4 percent of the national vote.

An unusual feature of Brazil's proportional representation system allows coalitions in proportional elections. This arrangement substantially lowers barriers to the representation of small parties, as is illustrated in the following example. Parties A, B, and C form a coalition for proportional elections. The coalition wins 20 percent of the vote and four of twenty seats. Sixty percent of the coalitions' votes came from A with the remaining 40 percent divided evenly between B and C. Because B and C won 4 percent each of the total vote, they would not have reached the electoral quotient (5 percent of the statewide vote) if they had run alone, hence they would not have been eligible to win any seats. But running in tandem with A, their chances of capturing a seat would be reasonably good, depending (see Chapter 6) on the intracoalition distribution of preference votes. Some parties of a coalition of three parties might face a threshold substantially lower than one-third that of a single party.[16]

These incentives to extreme multipartism were reinforced by electoral rules for executive positions until 1994. The two-round-majority format for presidential, gubernatorial, and mayoral elections in large cities gives party elites incentives to run their own candidates because a candidate need only be the second-place finisher in the first round to have a shot at winning. Voters are presumably more inclined toward "sincere" voting and less toward "strategic" voting for the same reason.

Between 1985 and 1994, the noncoincidence of legislative and presidential elections added to the incentives for extreme multipartism. As Shugart and Carey (1992) and Jones (1995) have shown, in other Latin American countries, concurrent elections have generated a tendency toward a two- or two-and-one-half-party system, even when coupled with proportional representation for legislative elections. The shift in Brazil from nonconcurrent to concurrent elections in 1994 might therefore encourage a moderation of extreme multipartism.[17]

Brazilian federalism facilitates the representation of a large number of parties because key resources are distributed at the local or state level. Politicians need not belong to a large national party in order to gain access to such resources (Samuels 1998).

Congressional rules at times encouraged the formation of small parties. In the late 1980s, any party with at least one representative was entitled to certain congressional privileges such as office space, telephone and graphic expenses, and an automobile. Some candidates switched to minor parties after election in order to obtain access to such privileges.

In combination, these electoral arrangements facilitate extreme multipartism by making it easy for small parties to win representation and by not erecting disincentives for citizens to cast their ballots for small parties. These electoral arrangements make it possible for many parties to have representatives in the National Congress, and most state legislatures also have many parties. In recent years, nearly twenty parties have had representatives in Congress, a number matched in few democracies.

Ideological Distance

In a party system, ideological distance refers to the size of the spread of opinion among the relevant parties on a left-to-right scale. Ideological distance is an important dimension of party systems. Several analysts have associated larger distances with less governmental and regime stability (G. B. Powell 1982: 92–96; Sartori 1976: 131–73; Sani and Sartori 1983). Greater ideological distance can make it more difficult to govern, increases the stakes of gaining or losing power, and can reduce the sense of security that is important in nascent democracies.

Sani and Sartori (1983) devised three measures of ideological distance.[18] They used mass-level survey data to determine how polarized ten Western European and the the U.S. party systems were. Using mass survey data to reproduce the Sani and Sartori measures for Brazil is fraught with problems; it is questionable whether most poorly educated voters understand the left-right scale well enough to place themselves with accuracy. Instead, I used elite survey data because the reliability of answers more than compensated for the diminished comparability. The elite data are not fully comparable with mass data because elites generally manifest greater intraparty coherence in their ideological self-location than mass constituents. This predictably would have the effect of creating a larger ideological distance among party elites than among the mass public.

Sani and Sartori called one of their measures "distance." Citizens placed themselves along a left-to-right scale, 1 being the farthest left and 10 the farthest right. Sani and Sartori then calculated the mean self-placement for all of the relevant parties, subtracted the mean of the farthest left from that of the farthest right party, and divided by nine (the largest possible value of this subtraction process). Using this method for Brazil in 1990, the "relevant" (in Sartori's sense) Brazilian parties had the mean self-placements indicated in Table 4-13.

The farthest-left party was the PT, with a mean self-placement of 1.00, and the farthest-right party was the PDS, with a mean of 6.93. The distance between PDS congresspeople and their PT counterparts was .66 (= 6.93 – 1.00 divided by nine). This is a greater distance than Sani and Sartori found for any of the eleven advanced industrial democracies they covered, which ranged from .01 (United States) to .64 (Italy and Finland). In her 1989 survey of 685 state deputies, Kinzo

TABLE 4-13
Left-Right Location of Brazilian Parties, 1990
(by Members of the National Congress)

Party	No.[a]	Mean Ideological Self-Placement	No.[b]	Mean Overall Ideological Placement
PMDB	74	4.42	216	4.88
PFL	39	6.05	217	7.74
PDS	15	6.93	212	8.47
PSDB	32	3.75	207	3.95
PRN	7	5.71	205	7.42
PDT	17	2.71	209	3.11
PTB	6	5.17	208	6.92
PT	5	1.00	210	1.50
PL	9	5.11	209	7.23
PDC	8	6.13	204	7.42

SOURCE: Timothy J. Power, 1990 survey of Brazilian National Congress.
NOTE: Farthest left on the ideological scale = 1; farthest right = 10.
[a]Number of legislators of a particular party who placed their own party on the left-right scale.
[b]Total number of legislators who placed that party on the left-right scale.

(1993: 77–79) also obtained information on this subject. The mean ideological self-placements ranged from 1.8 (PT) to 5.3 (PFL), for a distance score of .39.

In Brazil, in the 1980s political elites placed themselves considerably to the left of where the media and other politicians located them (Rodrigues 1987; Power 1993; Kinzo 1993: 78). This phenomenon was especially pronounced on the right. The overall effect was to understate the distance between the farthest-left and -right parties. On the other hand, using elite rather than mass data on self-placement tends to indicate greater ideological distance because elites locate themselves in a more consistent fashion.

The second measure of ideological distance is ordinal similarity, the extent to which members or sympathizers of two parties differ ordinally across the left-to-right spectrum. Ordinal similarity "is equal to the proportion of pairs of partisans (of any two groups) that are 'tied' or in the 'wrong' order" (Sani and Sartori 1983: 321). High ordinal similarity (the maximum value is 1) between two parties means that a large share of their voters locate themselves in the same ideological space, or that they are located in a relative space contrary to their parties' positions—for example, Voter X of Party A is to the left of Voter Y from Party B, even though Party A is to the right of Party B. Low ordinal similarity

TABLE 4-14
Ideological Self-Location of Brazilian Deputies by Party, 1987

Party	No. of Deputies	Radical Left	Center Left	Center	Center Right	Radical Right
PT/PCB/PC do B/PSB	21	67%	33%	—	—	—
PDT	22	—	95	—	5%	—
PMDB	224	2	74	22%	2	—
PTB	15	—	33	54	13	—
PL/PDC	9	—	22	78	—	—
PFL	100	—	18	72	10	—
PDS	29	—	10	69	21	—
TOTAL	420	5	52	37	6	—

SOURCE: Rodrigues 1987, 103.

(the minimum is zero) means that the voters or elites of a party occupy a completely different ideological space from those of another.

To calculate ordinal similarity, Sani and Sartori grouped citizens into five categories: left (corresponding to those who had classified themselves as 1 or 2 on the left-to-right scale), center-left (3 and 4), center (5 and 6), center-right (7 and 8), and right (9 and 10). For Brazil, I used Rodrigues's 1987 survey (1987: 103), which asked federal deputies to classify themselves as radical left, center-left, center, center-right, or radical right.[19] Table 4-14 shows the distribution of the parties according to Rodrigues's data.

To calculate the ordinal similarity between the PDS and the PT/PCB/PC do B/PSB cluster, we take each case in which a group of PDS politicians appears in the same column as, or farther to the left than, politicians of the leftist parties and multiply their respective shares of the overall frequency distribution. Thirty-one percent of the deputies of the leftist parties and 10 percent of PDS deputies declared themselves center-leftists; otherwise, all of the deputies of the leftist parties located themselves to the left of all of the PDS deputies. Multiplying 31 percent by 10 percent produces the ordinal similarity between these groups: 0.03. This figure approximates the lowest possible value (zero). For the eleven cases that Sani and Sartori (1983: 324) studied, values ranged from .02 (Italy) to .56 (United States), with a median score of .25.

The final measure of party-system distance is overlap, which refers to the extent to which the electorates (or legislators) of different parties identify themselves in the same space of the ideological spectrum. Comparing two parties, one takes the sum of the absolute values of the differences between the figures in each column, divides this sum by the theoretical maximum (which is

200, because each row adds up to 100), and subtracts this figure from 1. Comparing the leftist parties and the PDS in Table 4-14, we have an overlap of 0.10. Using Power's data on self-placement, the PT/PDS overlap in 1990 was zero, and using overall placement of parties by the deputies (rather than deputies' own self-placement), it was 0.01. Again, these figures approximate (and in one case reach) the lowest possible values. The eleven cases that Sani and Sartori analyzed ranged from .11 (Finland) to .86 (United States), with a median of .46.

The data indicate considerable ideological distance in the Brazilian party system at the elite level in the late 1980s and early 1990s. After the emergence of the PT as an important actor in the party system, the ideological distance between the left and the right was substantial. Brazilian parties are often characterized as pragmatic, personalistic, and nonideological, but these old adages are no longer entirely true. The leftist parties are deeply committed to ideological principles.

Although the Sani/Sartori measures are useful, they have one flaw: they measure only the distance between the farthest left and right parties without considering their size. If the farthest left or right party is small and ideologically isolated, even if there is considerable distance from the left to the right, the overall dynamic of the system need not reflect significant ideological distance. In Brazil, the left is the outlier responsible for scores that suggest a large ideological distance, and it is comparatively small. The distance among the rest of the parties is substantially smaller, and the left has moderated its views and practices since the early 1990s.

Between 1985 and 1992, ideological conflict among the political elite surfaced when major debates about the proper direction of the country took place and during electoral campaigns. Profound disagreements about the nature of Brazil's problems and the proper policies to deal with this crisis were apparent in the 1987–88 constitutional assembly. There were several broad areas of intense disagreement, with heated debates over protection of national industries, openness to foreign investment and trade, agrarian reform, the magnitude of state interventionism, social and labor rights, and the system of government (Kinzo 1990: 117–32). The left advocated greater control over foreign investment and greater protection for Brazilian industry, while the right argued on behalf of greater openness to the world economy. The left believed that agrarian reform was a major priority, while the right saw it as undermining the stability needed for development. The left was statist and the right advocated free markets on some issues. The left argued on behalf of a major expansion of social and labor rights, while the right generally argued against it.

A large ideological distance was equally apparent in the 1989 presidential campaign. Ideological disagreements were ubiquitous. Collor, Maluf, and Afif delivered a liberal anti-statist discourse, while Lula was the most statist of the major candidates.

A significant though diminished ideological distance was also manifest in the 1994 presidential campaign. Cardoso situated himself as a centrist candidate, favoring some positions normally seen as conservative (for example, selective privatization and economic stability), while at the same time emphasizing the need to address social inequalities. Lula situated himself toward the left of the political spectrum, though less so than in his previous campaigns, and he criticized the neoliberal approach to economic adjustment and growth.

A 1990 IDESP survey of 450 Brazilian elites from various walks of life also evinced ideological dissensus, especially on the crucial issue of the state's role in the economy. For example, 37 percent of the elites completely agreed with the statement, "The public sector should only act in classic areas such as security, education, and justice (the legal system)." Twenty-six percent agreed with strong reservations, and 36 percent completely disagreed (Lamounier 1990: 24). A 1991 IDESP survey (Lamounier and Souza 1991) of the National Congress also manifested ideological dissensus on the role of the state, foreign capital, and agrarian reform.

At the mass level, ideological conflict has been moderate. Many voters are comparatively unaware politically and do not vote according to ideological issues (Reis 1983; 1988). The fact that only one of two citizens identifies with a party—and even then, often a tentative one—and that many cannot locate themselves on a left-right scale indicates that most people are not ideological. Avelar (1989: 113) presented survey data indicating that in eight Brazilian cities, between 60 percent and 80 percent of respondents said that they did not know what the left-right distinction meant.

Even as it sometimes made democratic governance more difficult, the diversity of political ideologies among Brazilian parties also presented advantages. The existence of a viable leftist alternative changed the dynamics of party competition. The development of the PT into a national party in the late 1980s gave citizens the choice of voting for a leftist party that was an actor to reckon with (Keck 1992; Meneguello 1989). This breadth of options is in most respects salutary, especially in a context in which various alternatives were tried and failed.

Conclusion

In post–1985 Brazil, the party system has been weakly institutionalized. High electoral volatility indicated limited stability in patterns of party competition. Weak party roots in society were manifested in low levels of party identification, limited party voting, sharp discontinuities in patterns of party support, and in citizens' statements that party does not determine their vote. Many survey responses show limited legitimacy of parties and elections. In all of these ways, the Brazilian party system reflects the distinctive dynamics of third-wave democracies.

Weak Parties and Autonomous Politicians: Party Organization in the Catch-All Parties

Chapter 4 discussed three of the four dimensions of party-system institutionalization. The final dimension, party organization, is the subject of this chapter. In more-institutionalized party systems, party organizations are important; parties are not subordinate to powerful leaders; politicians are loyal to their parties. This chapter analyzes several aspects of party organization of the catch-all parties, focusing on the relationship between politicians and parties. The analysis underscores the weakness of these parties *qua* organizations and the autonomy individual politicians enjoy vis-à-vis their parties.

A first facet of this overarching theme is party discipline, that is, whether legislators vote as a united bloc on controverted legislative matters. The Brazilian catch-all parties are comparatively undisciplined in Congress and rarely try to oblige politicians to follow the leadership. Discipline was especially relaxed during the constitutional congress, particularly in the PMDB. Discipline increased somewhat thereafter, but it still lags behind levels in most democracies.

Also indicative of the autonomy of individual politicians and the loose character of the parties is the limited loyalty of politicians toward their parties. Since 1985, many politicians have changed parties in order to accommodate their interests and changing political tides.

Political campaigns are run by and financed by individual politicians rather than parties, and campaigns focus on individual candidates rather than parties. Among candidates for major executive positions, television has partially displaced party organizations. Candidates run their own campaigns, with little emphasis on the party, and they run by themselves, with little help (financial or otherwise) from the party. Candidates for proportional positions emphasize their own qualities rather than their party affiliation. They, too, run and finance their own campaigns.

The national parties are weak. The national party organs of the catch-all parties have fairly broad powers on paper, but in practice are bereft of resources and personnel, play virtually no role in campaigns, have a weak presence in congress, rarely meet, and are weakly professionalized. Among the middle-income countries of Latin America, Brazil is unique for the weakness of national organizations. The flip side of this weakness is that the catch-all parties are very decentralized. To a degree unparalleled in Latin America, Brazilian parties and politicians function according to a federal logic. The combination of lack of discipline, weakness of national parties, decentralization, and federalism have made for ideologically heterogeneous parties.

Finally, Brazilian catch-all parties are organizationally fragile. They have meager resources and sponsor few activities. All of this adds up to a portrait of party weakness that complements the analysis in Chapter 4.

This chapter emphasizes similarities in organization and internal dynamics among the catch-all parties. Notwithstanding some ideological differences among them, the catch-all parties are relatively similar in terms of party organization and internal dynamics. Their conception of what a party should be and how it should operate does not vary greatly from one party to the next. Conversely, the catch-all parties differ radically from the PT, the PC do B, and the PPS in terms of party organization and internal dynamics; on a number of dimensions the PDT stands in an intermediate position.

Why Party Organization and Internal Dynamics Matter

Party organization and internal dynamics have received little attention in analyses of Latin American parties, and have more generally been somewhat neglected in comparative politics in recent decades. Although a reasonably large corpus of works has emerged on Latin American parties since the 1980s, little of this literature has focused on party organization, internal dynamics, or the relationship between parties and politicians.[1] The abundant recent scholarship, including that on Brazil, has focused mostly on parties and elections, on the history of individual parties, and on changes in party systems. Party organization and internal dynamics have been neglected.

Most of the literature on individual parties has focused on how they have responded to and shaped major events in the political systems, rather than providing a detailed look at the inner mechanisms of their processes. How do they actually function? We know little about such fundamental themes as how parties choose candidates, whether they are centralized or decentralized, whether they are disciplined or not, etc.

Even now that we are two decades into the third wave in Latin America, there have been few major studies of party organization. The neglect of this theme must be understood both in relation to intellectual trends and to changes in how parties function. In recent decades, studies of voter behavior have burgeoned, enhancing our understanding of important subjects. Unfortunately, this trend contributed to the demise of party organization as a subject of inquiry. In these studies, the relevant unit was the individual voter or the party system, and party organization was secondary.

That tendency was reinforced by the growing importance of television, which has displaced party organization for some effects, thereby contributing to the trend to relegate this subject to the back burner. Television made it possible for candidates to present themselves to the people without the intermediation of party organizations. In earlier periods, parties organized local meetings for candidates, distributed political propaganda, and provided information to members. These activities receded with the advent of television. In some Latin American countries, political consultants have displaced party professionals in directing campaigns.

With the ascendance of the vote-maximizing view of parties came a tendency to downplay the party organization. The subject was not particularly important because the crucial issue was winning votes. Rational-choice theorists generally assumed that efforts at vote-getting determine party organization. Parties would organize internally so as to maximize their ability to win votes (Katz 1980: 13; Schlesinger 1991).

In recent years Kitschelt (1989, 1994), Panebianco (1988), and Katz and Mair (1994) have again called attention to party organization. The way parties are organized and function internally affects their linkages to the state and civil society, and hence the way they represent different groups in society. Organization indicates much about what kinds of parties dominate a political system and ultimately about the system itself. Organizational rules, identities, and practices determine access to internal power as well as affect party linkages to the state and to groups in society.

By recognizing the impact of organization on linkages between parties, civil society, and the state, we avoid the dichotomy between Duverger's emphasis on organization and Epstein's (1967) on functions. Party organization and functions, that is, the way parties operate in the political system, are interrelated. The ways in which parties organize shape how they relate to civil society and the state, and as a result can affect patterns of governability (González 1991; Coppedge 1994) and representation. In Brazil, for example, the looseness of party organization has contributed to the difficulties presidents often face in winning stable bases of support; has fostered an individualistic pattern of representation in

TABLE 5-1
Party Discipline in the National Congress, 1988–94

Party	1/28–6/24/88	6/25–9/2/88	1989–94
PC do B	99.8	99.8	n.d.
PT	98.5	97.8	98.0
PCB	97.1	100.0	n.d.
PSB	95.3	94.7	n.d.
PDT	83.6	90.4	98.0
PDC	79.6	76.6	n.d.
PFL	76.6	76.5	89.2
PDS	77.4	79.9	87.9
PL	73.5	67.6	n.d.
PTB	72.2	68.4	85.4
PMDB	65.7	64.7	86.8
PSDB	—	82.6	86.5
TOTAL	71.9	73.1	n.d.

SOURCE: For 1989–94, an approximate figure for the lower chamber was derived from Limongi and Figueiredo 1995, 506. For the constitutional congress, Mainwaring and Pérez-Liñán 1997.

which individual politicians rather than parties are the key agents of representation; and has made it more difficult for parties to establish deep roots in society.

Undisciplined Parties and Autonomous Politicians

The discussion of party discipline focuses on a simple phenomenon: whether legislators of the same party vote together in controverted congressional matters. Many legislative issues are relatively consensual across party lines; they are not relevant to the assessing of party discipline. Even if we leave out consensual issues, most parties in most Western democracies are disciplined.

One of the defining features of Brazil's catch-all parties is their limited discipline (Table 5-1). The assessment of party discipline relies on data from Limongi and Figueiredo (1995) for 1989–94, and from Mainwaring and Pérez Liñán (1997), who analyzed roll-call voting during the constitutional congress of 1987–88. For 1989–94, Figueiredo and Limongi analyzed the 221 roll-call votes in the Chamber of Deputies in which at least 10 percent of those who voted opposed the winning side.

Despite different methods of calculation, one can obtain a reasonable approximation of one method through a simple conversion of the other. To make the scores more compatible, Figueiredo and Limongi's scores were converted by adding 100 and dividing by two. The main difference between the two sets of scores should then be a result of the different criteria for including votes (a minimum of 10 percent opposing the winning side in one case and 25 percent in the other). The higher threshold Mainwaring and Pérez Liñán used would in most cases slightly depress discipline scores relative to Figueiredo and Limongi.

The PT and the minor leftist parties demonstrate near-perfect discipline, but the catch-all organizations are less disciplined than parties in most democracies. In the advanced industrial democracies, except for the United States, the norm is ironclad discipline. The United States is an outlier; discipline scores are lower than in the other advanced industrial democracies; U.S. scores are generally higher than in Brazil during the constitutional assembly, but slightly lower than during the 1989–94 period. In Venezuela, parties were so disciplined from the 1950s through the 1980s that there were few roll-call votes; the party leaders cast their votes for the entire party (Coppedge 1994). Jones (1997) reports that there are few roll-call votes in Argentina, but that parties are highly disciplined. In Uruguay, which by reputation has comparatively undisciplined and factional-ized parties, roll calls occur most often when the Congress acts to maintain or override a presidential veto. Between 1985 and January 1995, there were forty-one roll calls to override presidential vetoes in which at least 25 percent opposed the winning side. For these forty-one roll calls, the mean unity scores were 99.0 for the leftist Broad Front, 93.1 for the centrist Colorados, and 92.2 for the centrist Blancos (Moraes and Morgenstern 1995).

During the constitutional congress, Brazil's catch-all parties were much less disciplined than U.S. parties in terms of absolute loyalty, and somewhat less disciplined in relative loyalty (Mainwaring and Pérez Liñán 1997). Given that U.S. parties are comparatively undisciplined, this result says a lot. State dissi-dences and defections of individual politicians have been tolerated by the parties, which generally do not impose centralized discipline. Although there is a paucity of directly comparable cross-national information on party discipline, it is clear that Brazil's catch-all parties lack discipline.

Although Brazilian discipline scores are low for the post–1988 period, they increased after the constitutional congress. Party leaders since 1988 have formed a "college of leaders" in the National Congress. This body had considerable power in defining the legislature's agenda, controlling deputies' assignment to and removals from congressional committees, and designating the heads of committees. These powers gave party leaders leverage over rank-and-file mem-bers (Novaes 1994: 133–44; Figueiredo and Limongi 1995, 1996). Party leaders dictate the congressional agenda.

In the constitutional congress, parties ceased to be the major mechanism for organizing legislative support and opposition. The PMDB was particularly divided. Rather than parties, supraparty fronts dominated the constitutional congress. The PDS, PTB, most of the PFL, about half of the PMDB, and some minor parties formed the conservative "Centrão" ("Big Center," a misnomer in view of the group's ideological proclivities), while the PT, PDT, the other half of the PMDB, and some minor parties formed the "Bloco Progressista" (Progressive Bloc). This formation of supraparty blocks was particularly noteworthy in the constitutional convention of 1987–88, but it was not entirely new. In the period between 1961 and 1964, the fundamental cleavages in Congress revolved around such blocs rather than parties.

In the catch-all parties, the party outside Congress has little authority over the deliberations of congressional representatives. On paper the national executive committees or national directorates can impose decisions on congressional representatives. In all of the main parties, members statutorily agree to abide by the program, and elected representatives supposedly must follow discipline whenever an absolute majority (i.e., more than 50 percent of the entire body, including those who are absent or abstain) of the national executive committee and the legislative party agree to impose discipline (the Brazilian term is *fechar questão*). Party statutes allow the leadership to expel members who violate programmatic commitments. In practice, however, the leadership of the catch-all parties rarely tries to impose sanctions against nonconforming members. Congressional representatives eschew disciplinary measures as authoritarian, and leaders avoid them because of their potential to drive away members. Congressional representatives vote according to their own viewpoints and in the interests of their clientele. Party deliberations outside Congress have little impact on the way congressional representatives vote.

The flip side of the autonomy enjoyed by individual members of Congress is the weakness of the party leaders, who have difficulty imposing discipline. The leader has only modest power over his/her fellow party members. What power the leaders have derives more from congressional rules than intraparty rules. Party leaders have modest control over internal congressional affairs but have weak influence over noncongressional matters.

Politicians can vote against positions adopted by the national party with little fear of sanction. The situation in some European countries, in which representatives have limited autonomy vis-à-vis their parties and can even lose their mandates for failing to follow the party line, is anathema among the catch-all Brazilian parties. Platforms have little significance because the representatives have no obligation to follow them. Although party legislation grants the parties the means of expelling recalcitrant representatives and of imposing discipline in congressional votes, such measures are rare. Party programs are seldom binding on politicians.

Party organs meet infrequently to discuss major political questions. Novaes (1994: 124–30) showed that between 1991 and April 1993, PSDB federal deputies held about 1.5 party meetings per month. PMDB and PDS deputies met less than once a month, and PFL deputies met less than every other month. The PDT, with almost two meetings a month, and the PT, with about 2.7 per month, assembled the deputies most frequently.

In Brazil, weak discipline is part of a system in which individual politicians have considerable leeway, party organizations are weak, and parties, except on the left, are not particularly valued. Weak discipline is the first piece of evidence in the overall argument of this chapter.

Party Switching

Politicians in most democracies are loyal to their parties. In Brazil, since 1984 politicians of the catch-all parties have frequently changed parties, thereby evincing limited loyalty. Politicians have operated more as individual entrepreneurs or members of a state organization than as loyal cogs in a nationwide machine. Perhaps no other feature so radically distinguishes Brazilian catch-all parties from those in the other more developed countries of Latin America as the weak loyalty of politicians. This is a second piece of evidence suggesting the autonomy of individual politicians and the weak institutionalization of party organizations.

The frequency of party switching for the 1987–90 legislature is seen in Table 5-2, which compares the number of congressional representatives per party for March 1987, September 1988, January 1990, and October 1990. There were no congressional elections during this period except for eleven seats for the newly created state of Tocantins. Except for those seats, all other changes in the size of congressional delegations resulted from individuals who switched parties.

At least eighty-two representatives changed parties between February 1987 and September 1988, at least fifty-seven between September 1988 and January 1990, and at least fifty-eight more between January and October 1990. Even if we take only these four data points, there were at least 197 cases of party switching among the 559 representatives elected in November 1986. The PMDB hemorrhage was particularly strong; 152 of the 305 representatives had left the party by October 1990. The PFL had a net loss of thirty-one of 134 seats. The biggest gainers were two parties that did not exist in 1986: the PSDB and the PRN. These aggregate data underestimate the actual number of people who switched parties. If Representative A moved from Party X to Party Y and Representative B moved from Party Y to Party X, these migrations would not appear in the aggregate data. If representative C moved first to one party and then another in the same subperiod, it would appear as only one change.

TABLE 5-2
Party Switching, 1987–90

	February 1987	September 1988	January 1990	October 1990
		Number of Representatives		
PMDB	305	235	200	153
PFL	134	125	108	103
PDS	37	34	32	35
PDT	26	28	35	43
PTB	19	29	26	32
PT	16	16	16	17
PL	7	7	19	13
PDC	6	13	17	22
PCB	3	3	3	3
PC do B	3	5	6	6
PSB	1	6	8	10
PSDB	—	48	61	72
PRN	—	—	24	34
Other	2	10	11	24
No party	—	—	4	—
Missing data	—	—	—	3
TOTAL	559	559	570	570

SOURCE: Kinzo 1990, 108; *Folha de São Paulo*, January 14, October 29, 1990.

Many cases of party switching were incongruous from the ideological point of view, with politicians moving from one party to its archenemy. In 1987, seventy-two congressional representatives of the PMDB had previously belonged to the party's *bête noir* (Arena/PDS) under the military government (Fleischer 1988). This migration from the PDS to the PMDB was reproduced at the state and local levels. In 1985, 200 of the approximately 800 PDS local organizations (*diretórios*) switched overnight to the PMDB (Hagopian 1996). After 1982, when the opposition won state elections in nine states, many Arena/PDS politicians flocked to the PMDB. The differences in ideologies, practices, and social bases among the catch-all parties are sufficiently diffuse that most politicians can accommodate themselves within several parties.

Samuels (1996) has shown that party migration continued unabated during the 1991–94 legislature. There were 260 cases of party switches among the 503 deputies elected in 1990. Table 5-3 regroups Samuels's data to examine patterns of party switching. The first and second columns show the ideological family (i.e., the dominant ideological position) and party from which a legislator

TABLE 5-3

Party Switching and Ideological Family, Federal Deputies, 1991–94

Deputy's original ideological family and party	Ideological family of party to which deputy switched					No. of deputies who left the party	No. of deputies who left/ original no. of deputies (pct.)	No. of party switches beyond contiguous family	Pct. of party switches beyond contiguous family
	Left	Center-left	Center	Center-right	Right				
Left									
PT	3	—	—	—	—	3	8.6	0	0.0
PSB	*1*	1	—	—	—	2	18.2	0	0.0
Center-left									
PDT	4	*6*	1	2	4	17	36.2	6	35.3
PSDB	1	—	2	—	2	5	13.2	2	40.0
Center									
PMDB	—	7	—	11	14	32	29.6	14	43.8
Center-right									
PP	—	1	—	*2*	7	10	—[a]	1	10.0
PTB	—	1	—	*4*	26	31	81.6	1	3.2
PDC	—	1	—	*5*	4	11	50.0	1	9.1
PSC	—	—	1	*1*	5	7	116.7	0	0.0
Right									
PFL	—	3	2	9	*23*	37	44.0	5	21.7
[b]	—	1	2	13	*12*	28	280.0	3	10.7
PRN	—	1	7	8	*32*	48	120.0	8	16.7
PL	1	1	2	—	*7*	11	73.3	4	36.4
PDS	—	1	1	2	*14*	18	42.9	2	11.1
TOTALS	10	24	18	57	151	260	51.7	47	18.1

SOURCE: Calculated from Samuels 1996.
NOTE: The figures for switches to another party of the same ideological family are in italics.
[a]The PP did not exist at the start of the legislature, so it is impossible to calculate a figure.
[b]Small rightist parties.

defected, and the next five columns show the ideological family of the party to which he/she moved. For example, three legislators left the PT and all went to leftist parties. I regarded the PT, PSB, PPS, PSTU, and PV as leftist; the PDT and PSDB as center-left; the PMDB as center; the Progressive Party (PP), PTB, PSC, and PDC as center-right; and the PFL, PRN, PL, PDS, and some minor parties as right.

Column 8 shows the total number of defections by deputies a party suffered during the legislative session. This is not the same as the number of deputies who switched parties, because many deputies switched more than once. Column 9 shows the number of defections divided by the initial number of deputies. The PDT, PTB, PSC, and all of the rightist parties were especially prone to defections. Fully 174 of the 260 party switches involved movement from one center-right or rightist party to another. The center, center-left, and especially the left had higher loyalty levels. Among the fifty-four deputies elected from leftist parties in 1990, there were only five defections during the 1991–95 legislature.

Of the 260 cases, forty-seven, or just over 18 percent, involved jumping to a noncontiguous "ideological family." By noncontiguous, I mean that the politician switched to a party that was neither in his/her initial ideological family nor immediately to the right or left of that family. If a legislator's initial party were the PMDB, he/she would need to move to a leftist or rightist party to count the migration as one to a noncontinguous ideological family. Such cases of party switching are exceptional because they represent a move to a party with a markedly different policy outlook. Among the parties that suffered at least ten defections, the PDT (35.3 percent of defections) and PMDB (43.8 percent) were most likely to experience egressions toward noncontiguous ideological families.

The substantial number of party migrations to noncontiguous ideological families underscores a point made later in the chapter: the ideological heterogeneity of the national catch-all parties. In no other large Latin American country is there so much switching to parties with markedly different profiles. On the other hand, the fact that 82 percent of the cases of switching involved moves within the same ideological family or to a contiguous one also underscores that party labels are far from devoid of meaning, even in a context of weak parties.

The ease of switching parties accentuates individual autonomy vis-à-vis the parties in other arenas. It is difficult for the leadership to impose discipline when a representative can easily change to another team.

The period since 1984 has witnessed an unprecedented incidence of party switching among Brazilian politicians. Many politicians of the catch-all labels have seen parties as vehicles for getting on the ballot, not as organizations to which they owed an allegiance. Even politicians with programmatic commitments did not necessarily have strong attachments to their parties. Politicians join and switch parties not so much on the basis of national ideological positions, but rather of their own political ambitions and their loyalties to powerful politicians within their state. Asked why he had joined the conservative PPB, one former leftist politician responded that "in the interior, party labels don't mean anything. What matters are the people who form the ticket: their competence, honesty, and dignity."[2]

The propensity of Brazilian representatives of the catch-all parties to switch parties is unknown in the other more developed nations of Latin America, although there are some similarities in Ecuador and Russia.[3] In Chile, Venezuela, Uruguay, Argentina, Costa Rica, and Mexico, loyalties are relatively strong, and most successful politicians stick with their party.

What explains this frequent switching? More detailed work needs to be done on this subject, but some reasons are clear. Politicians believe they will benefit by changing parties, either because their own career prospects are better or their political/ideological proposals have a better chance of being accepted in those parties. The cost of switching is often low given the absence of legal sanctions and the electorate's toleration of politicians who change affiliations.[4]

As is argued in Chapter 6, many politicians depend on getting access to resources, and such access is easier if they join the party or coalition in office. Whoever is in power holds resources; hence it is desirable to join ranks with them. There is a lengthy history of politicians supporting the government to ensure access to resources and to positions in the state apparatus (Leal 1949; Hagopian 1996). For example, seventy-eight of the 101 mayors who were elected on the MDB ticket in the state of São Paulo in 1978 switched to Arena or the PDS to take advantage of Governor Paulo Maluf's largesse (Castro 1987). Sixteen of the fifty-three state deputies elected on the MDB ticket in 1978 also joined Maluf's party. If they wanted access to state resources, mayors and deputies needed join Maluf's party. This phenomenon was also pellucid in the defections from the PDS to the PFL and the PMDB between 1982 and 1986. After excoriating the PMDB for years, PDS politicians flocked to the party so they could gain access to the new wielders of patronage. Thousands of politicians flocked from the PDS to the PMDB when the latter came to power in the mid-1980s.

Politicians may change parties to get a better committee assignment in Congress (Novaes 1994: 135). Either for career or programmatic reasons, politicians may not be happy with the current leadership and believe that internal change is unlikely. Between 1984 and 1992 it sometimes seemed easier to join a different party or create a new one than win control of their current agglomeration. This pattern explains the biggest group of defectors from the PMDB, leading to the creation of the PSDB in 1988. Some politicians get disgruntled when they do not win a nomination to an executive post (president, vice-president, governor, vice-governor, or mayor). Consequently, they move to another party where they are assured of nomination, or they create their own party, as Collor did in 1989. Powerful leaders can usually convince some political allies to change parties with them. Finally, candidates for governor and president need to assemble broad coalitions to win elections. To do so, they sometimes encourage members of other parties to join theirs. On a few occasions, politicians have even been paid to switch parties. In September 1993, the PSD (Social Democratic Party) went from a half dozen to twenty deputies, reputedly by buying affiliations.[5]

Individualistic Campaigns

This section examines the extent to which campaigns are controlled by parties as opposed to individual politicians. This question reveals information about the relationship between parties and politicians at a key moment in the careers of the latter, and it has implications for the postelectoral period. Where campaigns are controlled by party organizations, parties have a mechanism for inducing discipline. If a candidate fails to accept the party line or is excessively critical of the leadership, the party can channel resources elsewhere, diminishing the candidate's chances of getting elected. Conversely, where campaigns are run and financed by individual candidates, elected representatives are less beholden to their organizations. Under these conditions, politicians are less likely to toe the line and are more apt to act as individual entrepreneurs.

When they campaign, politicians choose some combination of cultivating a personal vote, i.e., running on their own image, positions, and clientele networks, and promoting a collective (party) label. Brazilian campaigns of candidates of the catch-all parties are predominantly individualistic. They are run by and centered around individual politicians more than parties. This is a third indicator that underscores the weak institutionalization of party organizations in Brazil.

The individualistic nature of most campaigns is suggested by responses to Power's survey question on how politicians get elected (Table 5-4). Politicians of the catch-all parties overwhelmingly believe that personal effort, not party label, is decisive for getting elected. In the main catch-all parties, only 9 percent (PFL) to 22 percent (PMDB) of the respondents said that the party label was more important than their own organization and political activities. Politicians of leftist parties, by contrast, see the party as more important. Among the members of leftist parties, 69 percent of the respondents said that the party label was more important than their own organization and political activities.

Table 5-5 provides further information on politicians' perceptions of what helps get them elected. Again, legislators of the catch-all parties believe that their own campaign effort is more important than the organization. They considered campaign statements and promises, the candidates' campaign, and personal charisma more important than party organization and the support of grassroots groups. Politicians of leftist parties gave more weight than those of catch-all parties to the two items related to the party itself than to the candidates and their campaign.

This emphasis on individual qualities in campaigns has not always been as pronounced as it was after 1985. As Lamounier (1980), Reis (1978), and von Metten-

TABLE 5-4

Politicians' Perceptions of Party vs. Individual Campaign Effort

"Some politicians are elected on the basis of a party label; that is, the strength of the party organization or the profile it has in public opinion. Other are elected because of their own capacity for organization or their own political activities. In your case, which is more important?"

	Party more important	Individual effort more important	Invalid	N
PMDB	22.2%	76.2%	1.6%	63
PFL	9.1	90.9	—	44
PDS	—	92.9	7.1	14
PSDB	12.5	87.5	—	32
PDT	26.7	73.3	—	15
Left[a]	69.2	30.8	—	13
Other	9.1	90.9	—	36
TOTAL*	17.5	81.6	0.9	217

SOURCE: Timothy Power, 1990 survey of the Brazilian National Congress.
*Complete distribution is significant at .001 level. Chi^2 test.
[a]The left includes the PT, PC do B, PCB, and PSB.

heim (1995) have shown, between 1974 and 1982 party labels were important for most voters. During these years, even though campaigns were individually run, most opposition politicians emphasized their party affiliation, especially in the large urban areas that were redoubts of (P)MDB strength. After 1985, however, politicians of the catch-all parties not only ran their campaigns in individualistic fashion, they also emphasized their own attributes more than their party affiliation. The campaign of 1986 was a partial exception; some PMDB politicians rode the crest of ephemeral popularity of the Cruzado Plan and underscored their partisan affiliation.

The flip side of this individualism is limited party control over campaigns. The catch-all parties are generally oblivious to the ideological predilections of individuals who want to use the label. They accept a broad range of candidates without making ideological or organizational demands. Politicians need the support of a party to appear on the ballot, but this legal exigency is not terribly confining. Party statutes that insist upon adherence to some ideological principles and organizational fealty hold little weight in practice.

Legislative and presidential candidates of the catch-all parties both tend toward individualistic campaigns, but there are differences between legislative and executive campaigns. For the former, competition prevails among candidates of the same party competing for proportional positions (federal and state deputy and *município* councilors). Intraparty competition is often sharper than

TABLE 5-5

Politicians' Perceptions of What Gets Them Elected

"In your opinion, why did voters choose you in the last election? Please indicate the weight of the following factors, using a scale from 1 (least important) to 10 (most important)."

	PMDB		PFL		Left[a]		PDT	
	Mean	No.	Mean	No.	Mean	No.	Mean	No.
Your statements and promises	7.2	71	7.5	41	5.9	11	7.3	16
Party organization	5.9	73	4.3	40	8.3	12	6.2	16
Support of grassroots groups	5.8	71	6.3	42	9.3	15	6.3	17
Your electoral campaign	8.3	75	8.0	43	7.3	14	8.2	16
Family tradition/historic loyalty	5.8	74	5.4	42	3.8	13	5.1	16
Personal charisma	7.2	71	7.5	42	5.7	13	7.8	17

SOURCE: Timothy Power, 1990 survey of the Brazilian National Congress.
[a]The left includes the PT, PC do B, PCB, and PSB.

interparty competition. Parties do not dictate how campaigns should be run, nor do they control the candidates' programmatic commitments. One occasionally finds campaign literature promoting candidates of two competing parties that do not form an electoral coalition. At times, party leaders and candidates for governor recruit politicians from other parties.

For proportional positions, getting elected depends primarily upon candidates' personal efforts and connections. Candidates can sometimes make electoral inroads more easily against their own colleagues than against candidates of other parties. If a voter has a party preference, he/she may be less likely to switch to another party than to a different candidate from his/her preferred party. This phenomenon is largely a result of the electoral system, described in Chapter 8, which combines proportional representation (PR) and an open list. Candidates for state and federal deputy and for municipal councils compete against members of their own parties. Candidates thus have an incentive to run on their own appeal more than the party's. A proportional system with an open list functions like a simultaneous primary and general election. It is a general election in that party votes determine the number of seats, but it is like a primary in that the electorate selects which candidates will represent them.

Among the catch-all parties, campaigns for executive positions are also candidate-centered and -run. Candidates bring their own campaign teams with them. The party neither dictates how campaigns should be run, nor provides much help in running or financing campaigns.

In campaigns for executive positions, television is important. In Brazil, to a greater extent than in other Latin American countries, the massive growth of television has encouraged individualism in campaigns for executive posts. Candidates for governor and president and for mayor in large cities need to communicate effectively on television. Collor's election in 1989 underscored the power of television politicians and the potential for bypassing party channels and becoming a viable candidate despite weak organization. As then-Senator Fernando Henrique Cardoso (PMDB-SP) put it in a 1988 interview, in furthering a political career, "A TV channel is worth more than a party."[6]

The importance of TV in Brazilian political campaigns for executive positions stands out for several reasons. Most citizens do not have stable party preferences, so the percentage of floating voters is high; most citizens decide their vote not on the basis of party, but rather of other factors. The personal image voters form of candidates for executive positions is decisive. Limited political awareness, low levels of education, and limited access to other sources of information mean that television is the most important source of political information for most citizens. Most Brazilian families own televisions, and the industry is large and sophisticated. In most democracies, television has encouraged greater emphasis on individual qualities of candidates. But its impact is greater in Brazil, where parties were never such powerful actors as they are in the advanced industrial democracies or in several Latin American countries. Television is less of a factor in campaigns for proportional positions because these candidates get little TV exposure, but parties are similarly absent in directing the campaigns.

Among the advanced industrial democracies, the United States is known for individually run campaigns, but even the U.S. campaigns are in one respect less individualistic than the Brazilian. In the United States, the parties have become important actors in financing (Adamany 1984). In Brazil, conversely, in addition to running their own campaigns, candidates were almost entirely responsible for their own financing schemes until the implementation of party finance reform in 1995.

The most distinctive absence of Brazilian catch-all parties during campaigns is in financing. As the former treasurer of the PMDB in the state of São Paulo explained, "The party does almost nothing in campaign finances. We hire technical people for television propaganda, and candidates are allowed to use the party's printed materials at cost. The party pays for public rallies (*comícios*) that are held for the party as a whole. Otherwise, you're on your own. . . . If you want to do something fancy for the television, you pay. The money spent by candidates is raised by the candidates."[7]

Campaigns in Brazil are expensive, and campaign funds are raised almost entirely by individual candidates. Politicians raise money from individuals, interest groups, and firms to conduct their campaigns. Many also rely on state resources to finance their campaigns (see Chapter 6). When individuals and interest groups make financial donations, they generally channel them to individual politicians rather than parties; then they can exercise greater influence over the politician. The leftist parties are exceptions to this rule; donors occasionally provide money to the party rather than to individual candidates.

Candidates spend widely varying amounts and in different ways. Many spend large sums renting and purchasing automobiles and airplanes for transportation, hiring campaign consultants and workers, renting offices and telephones, printing campaign materials, distributing T-shirts and other goods at campaign stops, and attempting (sometimes illicitly) to win the sympathies of mayors and other local figures.[8] For many candidates for federal or state deputy, having the support of local politicians, especially mayors, is invaluable. Because of the large number of candidates for deputy, and because of deputies' low profile with the electorate, candidates need to make inroads among the local population. They are not permitted to purchase television or radio time, and purchasing newspaper space is of limited utility given the low readership. The support of mayors enables candidates to be well received and get publicity in local arenas.

Precise information on campaign expenses is impossible to obtain. Virtually all candidates violated the restrictive legal norms until a campaign finance reform law in 1993 permitted greater freedom for firms and individuals to contribute to campaigns. Firms had not been allowed to contribute to campaigns, but they had done so anyhow.[9] Even with the new campaign finance law, most politicians believe that widespread cheating occurs. The new law allows firms to contribute generously to campaigns (up to 5 percent of their annual sales).

Politicians cite high campaign expenditures. Federal Deputy Euclides Scalco (PMDB-PR), at the time a member of the PMDB's national executive committee, said that in 1986, "at least 50 percent of the congresspeople purchased their victories. In Paraná, one deputy admitted that he spent five million dollars to get elected."[10] State Deputy Waldemar Chubaci (PMDB-São Paulo), who was the PMDB's treasurer for the state, estimated that on average, successful candidates for state deputy in São Paulo spent $200,000 in 1986 and that successful candidates for federal deputy spent $600,000.[11]

Even allowing for the fact that São Paulo is the wealthiest state and probably has the most expensive campaigns in Brazil, these figures are high. They would make São Paulo elections among the most expensive in the world. A leading news weekly, *Istoé Senhor*, estimated that candidates for the Chamber of Deputies spent $200,000 to $5 million on campaigns in 1990 and candidates for the Senate spent $10 million.[12] One campaign coordinator for a candidate (Ayres da Cunha of the PSDB) for federal deputy in São Paulo said they would spend at least $15 million in 1994.[13] In 1994, *Veja* estimated that a successful campaign for federal deputy would cost an average of $1 million.[14] Candidates' official statements usually showed expenses below these amounts, but analysts are uniformly skeptical about the lower levels declared. To provide a comparative indicator, in 1988 the winning candidates for the U.S. House of Representatives spent an average of $393,000.[15]

Even more staggering are the expenditures in gubernatorial and presidential campaigns. *Istoé Senhor* estimated that closely contested gubernatorial campaigns would cost the principal candidates $25 million in 1990.[16] It also estimated that the two second-round presidential candidates in 1989 spent $100 million between them.[17] *Veja* estimated that Collor's campaign chest alone amounted to $120 million.[18] Spending in the 1994 presidential campaign was less profligate. Cardoso reported spending about $35 million, but this official report, according to *Veja*, considerably underestimated actual expenditures.[19] According to candidates' official statements, the second most-expensive campaign was Quércia's ($10 million), followed by Brizola's ($3 million) and Lula's ($3 million).[20] The expense of campaigns acts as a further fillip to individualism because candidates' financial resources are sometimes vast, while those of the parties were extremely limited until 1995. According to official data, the PPB candidate for mayor in São Paulo in 1996 expected to spend around $10 million, and his PSDB competitor rivaled that amount at $9.5 million.[21]

The major exception to individual campaign financing is free television time, which is allocated to the parties according to the size of their lower-chamber delegation. (In 1994, one-third of the free TV time was distributed equally to all parties, and the remainder was distributed based on the number of lower-chamber seats.) TV time for proportional candidates is limited, although in 1994 it was substantially greater than in previous elections, and it largely promotes individuals rather than parties. Free TV time makes the figures on campaign expenditures all the more remarkable; if candidates could purchase TV time, they would have an incentive to spend more lavishly. For 45–60 days before an election, there is free campaign time every day on every channel. In 1994, there were two hours per day, one from 7:00 to 8:00 A.M. and another from 8:30 to 9:30 P.M. Neither parties nor individual candidates are allowed to purchase additional time. Because of the imperative of having personal appeal and the limited importance party labels hold for most citizens, when candidates appear on television, they emphasize their own qualities more than party issues.

Compared to most other Latin American countries, Brazil has been a pioneer in the use of surveys and political consultants. Individual candidates rather than parties are responsible for hiring consultants and conducting surveys.

To sum up, campaigns are conducted and financed by individuals rather than parties. In addition, campaigns generally do not center around parties, but rather around individual candidates. Aspirants to executive positions generally need to build broad party alliances; otherwise, they are unlikely to win. Moreover, governing effectively requires multiparty support except in the unusual cases in which a single party wins an absolute majority of both houses of the federal Congress, or of the legislative assemblies in the states. The need for candidates for president and governor to win broad multiparty appeal usually leads them to downplay their party connections. If they tie their campaign too closely to a single party, presidential and gubernatorial candidates may limit their appeal beyond that particular party. Consequently, these candidates usually run individualistic, supraparty campaigns.[22]

Weak National Parties

Another characteristic of the catch-all parties is the weakness of the national organizations. The parties have three main national organs: the national convention, the national directorate, and the national executive committee. Party statutes grant these national organizations meaningful power over state and local party organizations, as well as over elected representatives. For example, in all major parties, by statute the national leadership can expel members and cancel the mandates of representatives who do not follow party guidelines. Higher levels of the party can intervene in lower levels to maintain integrity, to reorganize finances, to ensure discipline, to prevent the local or state organization from establishing an electoral coalition with other parties, and to preserve statutory norms, ethics, and political orientation. The national directorates typically have the authority to dissolve state directorates. The national parties have the statutory right to establish electoral alliances at the national and state levels. Recourse to these measures would suffice to create more disciplined and centralized parties.

The national convention, the largest body of the three, consists mostly of delegates chosen at state party conventions. It also include the members of the national directorate and congressional representatives. Formally, the national convention is the party's ultimate authority. It supposedly establishes guidelines for action, decides on electoral coalitions, and approves the presidential candidate's platform. Perhaps most important, it determines the presidential and vice-presidential candidates. The power to determine presidential nominations is important, and would seem to make the national convention an important event, even if that were its only function.[23]

Although it is vested with some significant formal powers, in practice the national convention is too unwieldy and meets too infrequently to exercise much authority. The national conventions have consistently ratified choices already made for presidential and vice-presidential candidates; the conventions themselves therefore are not that significant. In most cases, it is apparent in advance of the convention who controls most of the delegates, so top leaders put that name forward. It is conceivable that a national convention could really decide (rather than merely ratify) the presidential candidate, but this does not occur in the normal course of events.

State organizations sometimes fail to support their party's presidential candidate. In 1989, for example, many state and local organizations abandoned the presidential candidates of the PMDB and PFL, and in 1994, many again abandoned the PMDB's presidential candidate. National conventions formally have several other seemingly important functions such as establishing the party program and deciding on electoral coalitions, but in practice they do not exercise these powers. On infrequent occasions, dissident groups attempt to convoke a national convention to further their own positions within the party, but such maneuvers are rarely effective.

The second national party organ in Brazilian catch-all parties is the national directorate, which in most parties is elected by the national convention. The party's leader in the Chamber of Deputies and Senate may automatically be a member of the national directorate. The size of the directorate varies by party; in the PMDB it had 148 members plus ex-presidents of the national party in 1996, while in the PSDB it had 177. The national directorate supposedly directed the national activities, coordinated presidential campaigns, coordinated finances, created and supervised national organs, was responsible for carrying out the program and statutes, and established guidelines for party activities in Congress. In practice, however, the national directorates of the catch-all parties rarely meet and have little real power.

The national directorate typically elects the national executive committee, which in 1996 usually had around fifteen members in the major parties. The executive committees are small enough and have enough statutory power to make important decisions, but in practice they meet infrequently and avoid major decisions. The PMDB National Executive Committee enjoyed some prominence in the struggle against military rule, but with the return of civilian rule and the disintegration of party cohesion, it became irrelevant. It ceased meeting with any regularity and, fraught with internal conflicts, became paralyzed through inactivity. Members of the national executive committee commented on its enervation. Criticizing party president Ulysses Guimarães, Deputy Francisco Pinto, a member of the National Executive Committee, said that "we don't decide anything; we merely approve deliberations already made in informal meetings."[24] Deputy Euclides Scalco, also a member of the Executive

Committee, noted that this body never discussed or resolved major issues.[25] Ulysses Guimarães's close associate, Senator Mauro Benevides, himself a member of the National Executive Committee, observed that holding too many party meetings was dangerous because it accentuated internal differences. He said that he and Guimarães preferred to avoid having the National Executive Committee debate major policy questions. They believed that the PMDB's internal divisions would become exacerbated if party organs debated polemical policy questions.[26]

In the PFL, an unusual situation indicative of the weakness of the national party leadership occurred during the constitutional congress. Party President Marco Maciel, a senator from Pernambuco, was the leader of a minority group that favored breaking with the Sarney government and projecting a clear profile as an opposition party. However, Maciel and the National Executive Committee were marginal within the party, and a more conservative, *adesista* line prevailed.[27]

To the extent that party organizations at any level are significant, state and local organizations reign supreme. Until 1997, the national organizations were arguably weaker than in the United States, which has long been noted for the weakness of national party organizations. In Brazil, they function principally to choose presidential candidates, and for this particular purpose, they have more authority than the national party organizations in the United States, where the widespread institution of primaries has reduced the ability of party organizations to control candidate selection. On the other hand, national organizations in the United States, especially the Republican National Committee, play a prominent role in fund raising. By contrast, in Brazil, campaign finance is almost entirely controlled by individual candidates.

How secondary party organization can be to presidential campaigns was illustrated by Collor's victory in the 1989 campaign. He had virtually no party organization, while the two largest parties (PMDB and PFL) never got their campaigns off the ground, despite having more substantial organizations. However comparatively weak U.S. national party organizations may be, it is unlikely that a candidate could become president with a flimsy organization.

The national organizations generally had no independent national headquarters until the early 1990s; party headquarters were installed in an office in the National Congress until that time. Until 1996, national parties had virtually no budget and no staff. By contrast, individual politicians usually have reasonably large staffs; federal deputies, for example, usually have seven or eight staff members in Brasília, and many more in their own states during campaign periods. The contrast to the U.S. parties is again instructive; American national parties have vastly more resources.

Probably the national parties will become more professionalized as a result of the substantial increase in public funding after 1995 (see below). Even if this happens, it is noteworthy how long it took Brazil's national parties to become moderately professionalized and acquire meaningful authority.

One issue that has not been explored in the literature is why, given that national parties have significant statutory powers, they are reluctant or unable to exercise them. It is unusual for the catch-all parties to expel or even sanction members, to veto state-level alliances, or to intervene in state party organs.[28] Part of the explanation is that as the system evolved after 1985, national party leaders have been in a weak position to impose sanctions because of the frequency of party switching. Thus the costs of imposing the statutory mechanism that would enhance the power of the national leadership at the expense of state leaders and individual politicians are high. Similarly, the risks for state party leaders and national legislators of asserting autonomy are low.

Decentralization

Party decentralization has a lengthy history in Brazil, though with some increase in centralization during the military dictatorship followed by decentralization since then. In the catch-all parties, the national organizations interfere relatively little with state organizations and leave almost all major decisions up to the latter. Decentralization is apparent in how national party organizations are formed, in the battles over local politics, and in electoral alliances.

In the catch-all parties, national organizations are formed through a series of elections originating in local organizations. As mandated by the 1971 Organic Law of Political Parties (Law 5682 of July 21, 1971), which remained in effect until 1995, there are three levels of party organization: local, state, and national. Except in large cities, local units usually are organized at the *município* level. Although there is no exact translation for *município*, the closest equivalent in the United States is county.[29] Every state is subdivided into *municípios*, of which there were over 5,400 by 1997 (the number has constantly grown since 1985). *Municípios* constitute the lowest level of government except in cities with over one million inhabitants, which are further subdivided into districts. In the large cities, local party units are organized at the district level.

These local units are important in establishing control of party organizations. Local conventions directly (for local positions) or indirectly determine who runs for what positions and who controls the party. Until 1995, candidate selection was regulated by federal law (specifically, the 1971 Organic Law of Political Parties), so the process was essentially the same in all the catch-all parties. (The PT developed its own mechanisms for candidate selection and had a ratification process that conformed to the exigencies of the law.) Participants at local conventions formally determine the slate for councillors and for mayor. The selection of the candidate for mayor is important because mayors have influence over local patronage opportunities. Local conventions choose the local director-ate, which in turn elects the local executive committee and party president. The post of local president can also be important, as this individual controls some patronage positions that can enhance politicians' political prospects. Partici-pants in local conventions also vote for delegates to the state convention, and these delegates control vital aspects of party life.

For the majority of individuals whose political life is centered largely around a particular *município*, the most important event of the local conventions is the selection of the local executive committee and directorate. These organs deter-mine—at least formally—the candidacies for mayor and councillors. But for politicians who move in a broader orbit, the selection of the delegates for the state convention is also important. They determine candidate selection for governor and vice governor, senator, and federal and state deputies, and they elect the delegates who select candidates for president and vice president.

Local conventions choose delegates for the state convention.[30] The state convention includes, in addition to delegates chosen in local conventions, all members who are federal senators or federal or state deputies and incumbent members of the state party directorate. Delegates to the state conventions elect the state directorate, which in turn elects the state executive committee and the state president. These delegates formally determine candidacies for governor, vice governor, federal senators and deputies, and state deputies, and they also choose delegates for the national conventions. Finally, the national conventions select the candidates for president and vice president, as well as the national directorate, which elects the national executive committee and the national party president. Delegates often merely ratify agreements made among party bosses, but even when this is the case, the bargaining power of bosses depends on how many delegates they control. Thus the national party organs are directly (in the case of the national convention) or indirectly (with the national directorate and executive committee) chosen by state parties.

The 1995 Law of Political Parties removed the process of candidate selection from public law and gave it to the parties themselves. However, the mechanisms that were put into place by public law have remained mostly intact and are enshrined in party statutes. The decentralized process by which state and national party leaders are chosen has remained intact in all of the major parties.

In the 1946–64 period, some national organizations were strictly a federation of state organizations. The PSD National Directorate, which was the main formal national leadership institution, comprised the presidents (or a delegate

TABLE 5-6

Electoral Alliances by State: Gubernatorial Elections 1994
(Number of States in Which One Party Supported Another)

Party providing support	Party of gubernatorial candidate												
	PT	PSB	PV	PDT	PMN	PSDB	PP	PMDB	PL	PTB	PFL	PPR	TOTAL[a]
PSTU	12	0	1	0	0	0	0	0	0	0	0	0	13
PC do B	14	1	0	4	0	2	0	2	1	0	0	0	24
PT	—	3	0	4	0	1	0	0	0	0	0	0	8
PSB	10	—	0	3	0	1	0	2	1	0	0	1	18
PPS	9	3	0	3	1	3	0	1	1	0	0	0	21
PV	7	2	—	2	0	1	0	2	0	0	0	1	15
PDT	1	1	0	—	1	2	2	3	0	0	0	1	11
PMN	1	2	0	7	—	1	1	2	1	—	—	1	16
PSDB	0	0	0	3	0	—	1	9	0	0	1	1	15
PP	0	0	0	5	0	1	—	4	0	2	4	7	23
PMDB	0	0	0	1	0	1	1	—	0	1	1	1	6
PL	0	0	0	1	1	4	0	8	—	2	4	0	20
PTB	0	0	0	5	0	4	1	3	0	—	4	4	21
PFL	0	0	0	4	0	4	1	2	0	3	—	5	19
PPR	0	0	0	1	0	0	3	3	0	1	2	—	10
TOTAL[b]	54	12	1	43	3	25	10	41	4	9	16	22	240

SOURCE: Nicolau 1994: 17
[a]Total number of states in which the party supported another party's gubernatorial candidates
[b]Total number of times that a party's gubernatorial candidates were endorsed by other parties.

of the president) of state organizations. Regardless of population, each state had one member on the national directorate (Hippólito 1985: 120–24).[31]

National organizations adopt a laissez-faire attitude regarding how state party organizations function. State and local organizations determine with what parties to construct electoral and parliamentary alliances. As several analysts have shown, electoral alliances in the 1945–64 period did not predominantly follow a national logic based on ideological affinities among parties, but rather a state logic based on electoral calculations (Lima Júnior 1983: 61–82; M. Souza 1976: 154–61). At times, state organizations did not even support the party's presidential candidate, opting instead to support a competitor openly.

This pattern, which reflects the autonomy of state party organizations, has continued since 1985. Table 5-6 shows the alliances by state in elections for governor in 1994. The table is arranged in rough ideological order, from parties on the left to those on the right; thus it begins with the PT and progresses to the

PPR. The first entry means that the PSTU officially supported the PT guberna-torial candidate in an electoral alliance in twelve states. These supporting parties are also presented in approximate ideological order, again beginning with the left.

The conservative parties frequently supported gubernatorial candidates rang-ing as far left as the PDT. The PDT, the Green Party (PV), the PSB, and the PC do B all supported rightist parties in at least one state. PMDB, PSDB, and PDT candidates received support ranging from the farthest right to the farthest left parties. Such broad-ranging coalitions are possible only in a context in which state parties have autonomy in deciding with whom to run. As in many other respects, the PT was a partial exception: it was less inclined than other similar-sized parties to be a supporting member of a coalition. With the exception of one state in which it supported a PSDB candidate, it backed parties only at the center-left (PDT) or left (PSB) of the spectrum.

These data on the propensity to form electoral alliances with a diverse range of other parties reinforce the earlier observations about the malleability of the catch-all parties. Only if party identities are loose are they willing to form alliances with so many different competitors.

Although many features of Brazilian politics have changed since 1964, the importance of state and local politics in determining how politicians and parties act has remained constant (Hagopian 1996; Sarles 1982; Nicolau 1996a). In the catch-all parties that still dominate electoral competition, politicians respond first and foremost to local and state interests, somewhat as they do in the United States (Mayhew 1974).

In the catch-all parties, affiliations of individual politicians are usually deter-mined more by state and local than by national considerations. Politicians join and leave a given party because of who is in it and what it represents at the state level as much as at the national level. For example, many PDS politicians of Bahia first flocked to the PFL in 1984–85, then to the PMDB in 1986. Neither migration had much to do with their affinity to the national profile of the PFL or the PMDB; the PMDB leaders were historical adversaries. Rather, the migrations were occasioned by the fact that their *bête noire* in Bahian politics, Antônio Carlos Magalhães, initially dominated the PDS and then moved to the PFL in January 1986. This does not mean that politicians choose a party oblivious to its national profile, but rather that, among the parties whose national profile is compatible with their own positions, they chose the one that at the state or local level will most facilitate their political careers.

The importance of state and local issues was further borne out by questions in the Mainwaring (1988) and Power (1990) surveys of the Brazilian National Congress (see Table 5-7). One question was designed to test directly how

TABLE 5-7

Politicians' Loyalty to State vs. Party

"When there is a conflict between the needs of your constituency and the positions of your party, how do you vote most of the time?"

	With the party	According to needs of region	Split evenly between party and region	N
PMDB	34.0%	52.8%	13.2%	53
PFL	13.6	77.3	9.1	22
PDS, PTB, PL, PTR, PDC	22.2	66.7	11.1	9
Total catch-all parties	27.4	60.7	11.9	84
PT, PDT, PC do B	81.8	18.2	—	11
No party				1
Missing data/no answer				11
TOTAL				107

SOURCE: Mainwaring 1988 survey of the Brazilian National Congress.

deputies and senators perceive their allegiances to their states or districts (*regiões*) as opposed to their parties.[32] The answers suggest how localism and federalism weaken national unity, especially among the large catch-all parties. Only 34 percent of PMDB politicians and 14 percent of PFL politicians said that they voted along party lines most of the time when there is a conflict between party interests and regional or state interests. The difference between the leftist and the catch-all parties shows that the leftist parties constitute an exception to the general patterns of party organization and internal dynamics. Nine of eleven (82 percent) of the representatives of the left and center-left parties said they usually voted along party lines, compared to 27 percent of politicians of catch-all parties who said that they usually did.

One might hope that decentralization would make for more democratic internal processes. However, this claim is dubious in general and does not apply to the Brazilian catch-all parties. Brazilian parties are decentralized, but like most parties in most democracies, they are somewhat oligarchical; at most, a handful of leaders generally dominate the state-level parties. These individuals must be responsive to demands from below, but except for the PT, internal democracy is no more the norm in Brazilian parties than in most.

Party Heterogeneity

The combination of weak organizational controls over individual politicians and decentralization has allowed for heterogeneous catch-all parties at the national level. The ideological complexion of a given party varies considerably from state to state. Moreover, the same party sometimes harbors individuals of quite different political perspectives.

The most exceptional case of heterogeneity was the PMDB between 1985 and 1988, when it became one of the ideologically most diffuse parties in the world. From the time of its inception, the MDB was ideologically heterogeneous, so much so that many MDB politicians insisted that it was not a party but a front (Kinzo 1988). It included everything from revolutionaries or communists to some center-right opposition individuals. Many revolutionaries (especially after 1974) and members of the PCB were part of the PMDB until 1985 because of legal proscriptions, persecution, and strategic considerations (they favored a broad electoral front). At the same time, center-right groups that opposed military rule also supported the (P)MDB. Between 1979 and 1981, the party was acquiring more ideological cohesion as most of the MDB's conservative wing joined the short-lived PP. However, with the PP/PMDB fusion in 1981–82 and the defections from the PDS to the PMDB between 1982 and 1986, the party acquired a strong center-right faction.

By 1987, the PMDB included factions ranging from the far left to the far right. Seventy-two of the 305 PMDB congressional representatives had earlier been members of Arena or the PDS. A significant number were elected in 1986 with the support of the Rural Democratic Union, an organization of landowners that reputedly had links to the paramilitary right. Some of the country's most conservative politicians had joined the PMDB, yet some radical leftist groups continued to be a part of it. The MR-8, a revolutionary group that in the 1970s had supported guerrilla actions, remained part of the PMDB, and several communists who later joined the PC do B were elected on the PMDB ticket in 1986. Several deputies who later joined the Brazilian Socialist Party were also elected on the PMDB ticket in 1986. After 1988, with the defections from the PMDB to the PSDB, the two communist parties, and the PSB, heterogeneity decreased as the party's left wing shrank. However, in some states (most notably Rio Grande do Sul), prominent center-left politicians remained in the PMDB. Even such notably heterogeneous parties as the Democrats and Republicans in the United States, the Blancos and Colorados in Uruguay, the Liberal Party in Japan, and the Congress Party in India probably never have been as ideologically heterogeneous as the PMDB was in the second half of the 1980s.

The heterogeneity of the parties during the constitutional convention is clear in data Rodrigues (1987: 103) assembled on the ideological self-location of deputies (see Table 4-13). PMDB politicians covered virtually the entire ideological range, and the PFL, PDS, and PTB were also very heterogeneous. It seems likely that Rodrigues's data understated ideological heterogeneity because Brazilian politicians tended to locate themselves more to the left than their col-

leagues located them. The self-locations therefore indicate a narrower ideological spread than would have surfaced had conservative politicians identified
themselves as such. Moreover, the wording of Rodrigues's question probably
biased the responses away from the extremes and toward the center; the terms
"radical left" and "radical right" had a pejorative connotation to many people.
No respondents considered themselves part of the "radical right."

Although no other party had factions that covered the entire ideological
spread, the other major catch-all parties were also ideologically diverse. The PFL
and PDS, for example, ranged from the center to the far right (in Rodrigues's
survey, PFL and PDS legislators identified themselves as ranging from the
center-left to the center-right). This ideological diversity further enhances the
tendency toward weak discipline and individualism; it becomes more difficult
to impose discipline as ideological divisions become broader.

Because of the significant interstate differences within parties, in a given state
a particular party may not match its national ideological profile. Moreover, a
party that is to the right of a second at the national level may be to its left in some
states. Thus caution is necessary in making inferences about the political positions of individuals and state parties on the basis of the ideological profiles of
the national parties.

Limited Extraelectoral Activities and Resources

Some time ago, Sorauf (1963: 2) wrote, "Much more than other democratic
parties, those of the United States are essentially electing organizations." In
contrast to parties of the other advanced industrial democracies, Sorauf was
correct. However, the Brazilian catch-all parties are more exclusively oriented
toward elections than American parties and less focused on extraelectoral
activities. This is another part of the syndrome of weak party organizations.

Organizationally, the catch-all parties in Brazil are fragile. With the exception
of the leftist parties, Brazilian parties outside Congress are largely inactive except
for campaign periods. This is true at the national, state, and local levels. Illustra-
tive of the nature of local organization in the interior were the remarks of the
ex-president (1981–88) of the PMDB of a small but wealthy *município* in the state
of São Paulo. When asked how often the party met, he responded, "Rarely. In
the seven years I was president, except for obligatory meetings—that is, party
conventions to choose candidates and delegates—we didn't meet three times.
We met to discuss the PP/PMDB fusion (in 1981–82), and after that there may
have been one or two meetings. . . . People don't want to go to party meetings.
So if you set up a meeting, nobody goes."[33] One staff worker put it bluntly if
perhaps somewhat hyperbolically: "During intraelection periods, the party
ceases to exist."[34] Other interviews made apparent that this was the norm.

Even in Congress, the catch-all parties are not well organized. Asked about relationships among the PMDB representatives from his state, Federal Deputy Tito Costa (PMDB-SP) replied, "Above all there is a dispute for personal space and power, to see who can stand out the most. There is some solidarity among people who are part of the same faction of the party, but even here solidarity is limited. . . . Within the PMDB, there is almost no solidarity. The problem isn't just among the federal deputies from São Paulo; it exists with the Chamber [of Deputies] as a whole. The standard here is everyone for himself/herself."[35] Many other politicians made similar statements.

Outside Congress, parties have an anemic existence when electoral campaigns are not going on. They sponsor few activities, and they have small professional staffs and meager resources.

When parties are loosely organized and sponsor few activities, they can generally get by with minimal financial resources, and this is the case in Brazil. Brazilian parties are generally reluctant to divulge much information about their finances, and they do not even have complete information about them. Nevertheless, the penury of Brazilian parties until 1995 was striking.

Money comes from three principal sources. The 1965 Organic Law of Political Parties instituted public funding for parties, but until 1995, public funding was minimal. In 1987, total public funding for all parties was 5,999,998 cruzados, approximately $100,000.[36] For countries that have public financing of parties, this is meager. In England, where public financing for parties is limited, the Labor Party alone received £317,000 in 1983 (Bogdanor 1984: 130). Twenty percent of the public funding in Brazil is distributed evenly to the parties, and the lion's share, 80 percent, is proportional to the number of representatives.

Between 1987 and 1995, public funding for parties increased substantially, and in 1996 public funding shot up as a result of the 1995 Law of Political Parties, which stipulated that 35 centavos (about 37 U.S. cents) for every eligible voter would go to this purpose. This resulted in a total of about $36 million for twenty-six registered parties, compared to less than $3 million in 1995.[37]

Presumably, the substantial infusion of new funds will enable parties to become more professionalized within a few years. What the parties will do with these new resources remains to be seen. According to three interview sources in January 1997, parties have had trouble figuring out how to spend their new resources.[38] For the PMDB's Pedroso Horta Foundation, the infusion of new money unleashed a serious conflict between advocates of greater professionalization and those accustomed to a barebones operation; the latter won out.

The second source of funding is deductions from the salaries of congressional representatives. These deductions vary according to the party. The PT demands 30 percent of the salaries of congressional representatives, and it suggests a 5 percent donation from party members. The 1996 statutes of the PSDB called for a 5 percent donation from national legislators, and 3 percent from state and municipal legislators, presidents and vice presidents, governors and vice governors, mayors and vice mayors, and from those with positions in public administration. Most other parties had statutes similar to those of the PSDB, but with some differences in details; PFL statutes do not mention specific amounts.

In recent years, parties have made more of an effort to collect these donations than was the case in the 1980s. In 1987, PMDB statutes called for a 3 percent donation, but according to the party treasurer, in December 1987, the donations were slightly more than $30 each, or about 0.5 percent of the salary. Many elected officials made no contribution.[39]

Consistent with decentralization, a significant share of the funding that the national parties obtain is redistributed to state party organizations. PMDB statutes indicate that 20 percent of the public funding goes to the Pedroso Horta Foundation (which itself has state-level organizations that receive 75 percent of the foundation's total funding), 15 percent to the national party, and 65 percent to state parties. Of the funds obtained from the donations of legislators, 40 percent goes to the national party and 60 percent to state parties. PSDB statutes leave the national party with a larger share of resources, but still distribute at least 20 percent of the party's resources to its foundation and at least 40 percent to state parties.

In election years, there is a third source of funding for parties: candidates are generally required to make contributions to their parties.

In contrast to the situation in most advanced industrial democracies, most trade unions, interest groups, companies, and individuals make limited financial contributions to Brazilian parties. Interest groups have overwhelmingly preferred to donate funds to individual politicians rather than parties, although some unions and labor confederations have allegedly (and illegally) contributed financially to the PT. There is no tradition akin to the U.S. political action committees that donate substantial funds to parties or to multiple candidates of a wing of a party.

Adding the income from public funding and representatives' contributions, the PMDB's national organization's income in 1987 would have been around $170,000, of which approximately two-thirds went to state organizations, and only about $57,000 remained at the national level. This accounts for the bulk of party income, and the PMDB was the best-financed party at that time. In contrast, in 1980, U.S. national Republican-Party organs totaled $169.5 million, nearly 3,000 times the income of the national PMDB organization, and the U.S. national Democratic-Party organs totaled $23 million (Adamany 1984: 165). Keck (1992: 111) wrote that legislators' contributions constituted about two-thirds of PT income even when the party had only eight federal deputies.

With such paltry resources, parties necessarily maintain limited activities. Professionalization is minimal. Parties have few employees and party professionals. The 1987 President of the PMDB in the state of Bahia said that when he assumed the position, the state party had only two paid employees.[40] Parties have started to become more professionalized, but the pace has been modest. The use of computers for party purposes is limited.

To some degree, the lack of party funding reflects the fact that Brazil is a middle-income country with limited resources. However, individual campaigns are well financed in Brazil. Money is available in politics, but it is available for individuals more than parties. The finances of Brazilian parties reflected the overall proclivity toward a system in which party organizations were weak and individual politicians had considerable autonomy.

Party Organization in the Leftist Parties

Brazilian parties can be grouped into two broad types: catch-all and leftist. The former includes all main parties except the PT, although the PDT and PSB were between the PT and the catch-all parties on some organizational issues. Despite differences among them, the catch-all parties conform reasonably to the characterizations provided throughout this chapter.

In organizational (as well as ideological) terms, the PT, PPS, and PC do B diverge from this model. These three leftist parties are highly disciplined in Congress, enjoy strong loyalty from politicians, and have strong linkages to unions and social movements. In other respects, they differ organizationally from one another. For example, the PT's (at least rhetorical) commitment to grassroots party democracy contrasts sharply with the centralized and authoritarian nature of the PC do B.

To illustrate these differences between the catch-all parties and the left, I will focus on the PT, with occasional comments on the other leftist parties. The first dimension to call attention to is a difference in discipline among elected representatives. As Table 5-1 showed, the leftist parties are very disciplined.

The PT, PCB/PPS, and PC do B leaders exercise greater control over representatives in Congress. In the PT, decisions made by party members can by statute have a binding effect on congressional representatives (Meneguello 1989: 65–102; Keck 1992), although this statutory provision is rarely followed. Grassroots extracongressional power waned over the years as the party grew and became more professionalized (Novaes 1993; Rodrigues 1990: 7–33), but the congressional party has remained extremely disciplined. The PDT, too, has an extracongressional voice to help impose discipline, in the figure of party president Leonel Brizola, who has a decisive weight in deliberations inside Congress. Thus there exist two different models in which the party outside Congress has influence over congressional representatives: the grassroots activists (PT) and the charismatic leader (PDT).

To facilitate grassroots democracy and participation, the PT devised party nuclei, which none of the catch-all parties have. The nuclei are intended to stimulate participation by the rank and file and provide a mechanism by which activists can have input into major decisions. Article 72 of the party statutes established that congressional representatives should make important decisions only after consulting the grassroots and that key legislative initiatives must be submitted for membership approval. These mechanisms of broad participation and control over candidate selection and congressional representatives weakened over the years as the PT became more professionalized and bureaucratized, but such mechanisms are still stronger than in the catch-all parties.

The PT, the PC do B, and the PPS differ markedly from the catch-all parties in attempting to cultivate deep commitments among activists and develop organizations that work all the time, not just at elections. PT activists are encouraged to participate in popular movements and organizations, and many do. The party has frequently manifested ambivalence toward electoral politics; at times it has been willing to sacrifice votes to maintain principles.

The PT has several mechanisms to create a disciplined congressional party. The leadership often calls for a party-line vote (*fechar questão*), which obligates members to vote in a disciplined way. Candidates must agree to abide by a system under which individual legislators vote the party line when the grassroots so determine. They must agree to support the PT platform and work for a range of popular causes, and the party is finicky about candidate selection. The party has primary elections to determine candidates for key executive posts, and all members are eligible to participate in the primaries. Because of controls over candidates and individual politicians, these primaries have not encouraged individualism and antiparty practices, as has been the case in the United States. The party plays a central role in determining the nature of campaigns, and grassroots party groups actively participate in the campaigns (although the party's growing professionalization has reduced the reliance on volunteer activists in campaigns).

The PT enforces the statutes that require representatives to adhere to the party line. When three of its eight federal deputies went against the grassroots decision to abstain from the electoral college that voted for president in 1985, they were expelled and lost their mandates. The national press and other opposition parties excoriated the PT for this decision, but it underscored the firm insistence that representatives follow the party.

PT politicians are markedly more loyal to their party and less likely to defect to other organizations (see Tables 5-2 and 5-3). The PT (sixteen), PCB (three) and PC do B (three) elected a total of twenty-two representatives in November 1986, and none of them switched to another party. These parties had few new ingressions; three PC do B members were elected on the PMDB ticket in 1986, and one legislator joined the PT in 1990.

To underscore the differences in loyalty, I devised an index of party defection, defined as the share of the party's legislators who defected to another party during a legislative session. For the 1987–90 legislature, the index for the leftist parties was zero, meaning that they suffered no defections among the twenty-two legislators who took office in February 1987. In contrast, the defection index for the PMDB was 49.8 percent (152 defections of 305 legislators), and the PFL's index was 23.1 percent (thirty-one defections of 134 legislators). The total for the catch-all parties was 36.3 percent (185 defections of 510 legislators). In the 1991–94 legislature, party loyalty was again much higher on the left, as Table 5-3 showed.

The PT's organization plays a more prominent role in directing campaigns than does that of catch-all parties. PT candidates also emphasize the party more (Samuels 1996) and place more weight on collective reputation than politicians of the catch-all parties. In contrast, the latter parties are organizationally weak, lack volunteers, and rely on patronage to take the place of volunteers. They are essentially electoral machines.

The contrasting conceptions between the leftist and the catch-all parties of what a party should be are apparent in Table 5-8, which shows responses to questions related to party discipline from the 1988 and 1990 surveys of the Brazilian National Congress. Table 5-8 does not include information on the PDT because the main concern was to show the contrast between the leftist parties and the catch-all organizations.

In sum, the PT is more cohesive, more disciplined, and commands greater loyalty than the catch-all parties. It is also more committed to internal democracy and grassroots participation than the others. More broadly, the leftist parties and to a lesser extent the PSB differ markedly from the catch-all parties. Very different organizations and conceptions of what a political party should be are at stake. The PT follows Duverger's model of an organized, disciplined party, while the catch-all parties are loosely organized.

Parties as Rational Actors?

Most rational-choice theorists agree that rationalistic assumptions are more useful for explaining individual behavior than collective organizations (such as parties). In fact, a major theme in rational-choice theory is that individual rationality can lead to collectively suboptimal outcomes (e.g., Arrow 1951; Olson 1965). However, a small but prominent group of theorists have ascribed rationality to parties, seeing them as vote- (or some other utility-) maximizers. This

TABLE 5-8
Attitudes of Brazilian Legislators on Party Discipline
(Percent Agreeing with Statement)

	Catch-all parties	PT, PC do B, PCB, PSB
Prefers closed-list proportional representation (1990)[a]	24.6% (n=207)	62.5% (n=16)[*]
Favors party fidelity (1990)[b]	53.2% (n=203)	73.3% (n=15)
Favors expelling party member (1990)[c]	51.4% (n=208)	92.9% (n=14)[**]
Favors canceling mandate (1990)[d]	54.1% (n=207)	62.5% (n=16)
Party positions are very important (1988)[e]	48.9% (n=92)	100.0% (n=5)[***]

SOURCE: For 1988, Mainwaring survey of the Brazilian National Congress; for 1990, Timothy Power survey of the Brazilian National Congress.

[a] "If Brazil maintains a system of proportional representation, would you prefer that the order of candidates be determined by the party or would you prefer an open list (as currently exists)?"

[b] "Do you think it is proper for a party to close ranks *(fechar questão)* and impose party fidelity?"

[c] "A political party should expel a politician who votes against the party position." The tabulation collapses the categories of those who fully agreed and those who largely agreed.

[d] "A politician should lose her mandate if she switches parties after the elections." The tabulation collapses the categories of those who fully agreed and those who largely agreed.

[e] "Party positions are very important in your behavior as a legislator." Respondents had two other alternative answers: "not too important" and "more or less important."

[*] The difference between the left and the catch-all parties is statistically significant at a .002 level (Fisher's exact T-test, 2-sided).

[**] The difference between the left and the catch-all parties is statistically significant at a .003 level (Chi^2 test).

[***] The difference between the left and the catch-all parties is statistically significant at a .06 level.

approach was adumbrated by Schumpeter (1950) and developed by Downs (1957), both of whom argued that parties acted rationally to maximize prospects of winning elections. For Downs, parties are rational actors whose activities are oriented exclusively toward winning elections. Following rational-choice perspectives, other analysts also saw parties as utility maximizers, even while modifying some of Downs's claims (Riker 1962; Robertson 1976; Schlesinger 1991).[41] Moreover, a tradition in organization theory has seen organizations as rational actors.

Later chapters argue that the Brazilian case demonstrates the utility of rational-choice theory for understanding the logic of individual politicians, but it also shows the problems arising from perceiving parties as utility maximizers. Treating a party as a rational actor implicitly assumes the existence of a unitary, purposeful actor capable of consciously pursuing a dominant goal such as vote maximization or office seeking. In Brazil, the assumption of a unitary purposeful actor is problematic because the catch-all parties are factionalized. Even the PT, which is highly disciplined in the congressional arena, has experienced continuous internal factionalism. Brazilian catch-all parties are internally factionalized, comparatively undisciplined, and comparatively decentralized; they are not single, cohesive actors.

In Brazil, party activity does not depend in the first instance upon how parties will maximize votes, but rather upon who holds internal power. Over the long run, factions and leaders that consistently direct their parties to what are perceived as defeats are likely to fare poorly in intraparty struggles. But this is true only in the long term. In the short run, nothing ensures that the factions or leaders with greatest mass appeal will control the party. Consequently, the analysis of how individual politicians and different factions obtain power within the party is important. This means that party organization and internal dynamics are crucial. Rather than being determined by and derivative of vote-getting efforts, internal processes determine how parties seek votes, as well as how they relate to civil society and the state (Kitschelt 1989; Panebianco 1988).

Brazilian politicians of the catch-all parties are not only concerned about their party's position relative to the electoral competition; they are equally concerned about their faction's and their own positions within the party. The prevalence of individual or faction logic over collective (especially national) logic undermines the extent to which parties behave as utility maximizers. An individual or a faction may fear that changing to position X (held by their competition within the party) will weaken their position. Even if position X would enhance the party's vote-maximizing potential, it may not be a desirable option for the leaders who control the party. Individuals and factions adopt strategies to maximize their own interests, but that does not necessarily maximize the party's vote-getting potential. For this reason, internal processes (above all, those that determine who gets to run for what) directly determine the way the party presents itself in campaigns. The more significant factions of major parties are concerned with winning votes, but there is no guarantee that the factions, individuals, positions, and campaign strategies that would most effectively maximize votes (or any other utility) will prevail (Panebianco 1988). Under these circumstances of individualistic behavior by politicians and strong intraparty competition, attributing rationality to the organization is problematic.

Given the individualism within the parties and the conflicts between different leaders and factions, even if all individuals within a party acted rationally, the party would not necessarily act as a rational, vote-maximizing actor. Party leaders and factions may be committed to furthering a certain project, and abandoning that project would adversely affect them. Even if a change in positions would yield more votes for the party, it would be contrary to the interests of those factions or leaders (Kitschelt 1989; Panebianco 1988).

To many Brazilians, the catch-all parties are self-interested, self-serving, and concerned about winning votes but not addressing citizens' needs. However much validity these perceptions may seem to have in the public's eyes, intraparty competition and factionalism limit the extent to which a party can assume a logic of its own that supersedes the calculations of individuals within it. For this reason, in thinking about actors' objectives in the Brazilian catch-all parties, it is more important to focus on individual politicians and factions than party organizations. Critical aspects of the ways parties function cannot be derived from collective vote-maximizing logic.

Consider three examples from the largest party of the post–1985 period, the PMDB. In 1987–88, the leadership resisted efforts of the center-left and left factions to adopt an opposition stance vis-à-vis the Sarney government. The electoral costs of being identified with an inefficient, unpopular, and corrupt government were pellucid. However, the party president, Ulysses Guimarães, believed that the party needed to support the government given the apparent fragility of the transition to democracy. Guimarães also had a personal stake in thwarting the leftist intraparty challenge: he wanted to retain control of the party. His coterie followed his predilections. Conservatives in the party went along out of self-interest—they preferred the government's turn to the right, and they gained access to vital positions and public resources by supporting the government. Thus different factions thwarted the possibility of pushing the party to positions more in tune with public opinion. For example, even though public opinion in 1987–88 preferred a four-year term for President Sarney, much of the PMDB (including Guimarães) acquiesced to Sarney's desire for a fifth year.

A second example: In 1989, the party ran Guimarães as its presidential candidate. From the outset, it was apparent that he had poor prospects. The consummate political insider, Guimarães had little charisma or television appeal, and he was temporarily discredited because of his alliance with Sarney. The party could have fielded a more compelling candidate, yet Guimarães had the internal support to secure the nomination. Internal party struggles, not vote maximizing or office seeking, determined what transpired. Individual rationality—Guimarães's desire to be the candidate and his control of enough of the party machinery to win the nomination—triumphed at the expense of collective-utility maximization.

Much the same occurred in the 1994 presidential campaign, when the party ran Orestes Quércia. Five years earlier, Quércia might have been a solid contender, but by 1994 his public image had become tarnished as a result of well-documented corruption scandals. The party knew that Quércia had scant chances of overcoming his tainted image, but Quércia had sufficient control of the machinery to thwart any challenges to his nomination. Again, the interests of individual politicians—Quércia and his coterie—rather than vote maximization dictated the outcome.

Under these circumstances, it is misleading to posit that vote maximizing determines the logic of the party organization. The reverse is generally true: collective strategies for winning votes are subordinated to the logic of individual or factional interests. In sum, rational-choice theorists who see parties as cohesive, rational actors assume a unity in how parties pursue their goals that is illusory for Brazil. In emphasizing the way politicians' individualism and internal struggles impede the catch-all parties from being unitary rational actors, I converge with more general observations by Kitschelt (1989) and Panebianco (1988).

Attributing a single objective to the Brazilian catch-all parties is problematic because of the low collective orientation of politicians. Most politicians of these parties necessarily worry first and foremost about their own careers. The extent to which one can speak meaningfully of any collective goal, much less a single consensual one, diminishes.

The Brazilian case also shows that to the limited extent that parties have collective objectives, these objectives depend on the kind of party. Most analysts who see parties as rational actors (e.g., Downs 1957; Schlesinger 1991) assume that parties have a single objective: winning votes (or elections).[42] In contrast, systems institutionalists argue that parties generally have a variety of other objectives, and they need to maximize several utilities, not only votes (Strom 1990). For the Brazilian catch-all parties, the Downsian assumption that winning elections overshadows other collective objectives is reasonable. To the limited extent that the catch-all parties have had collective objectives rather than being the sum of the objectives of individual politicians, the dominant goal has been power, i.e., winning votes and elections. In this limited sense, the catch-all parties behave consistently with the rational-choice assumption of a single dominant objective.

However, understanding the PT through this prism is difficult. In that party, other objectives have sometimes overshadowed vote maximizing. The party has been internally divided over whether it should be willing to sacrifice programmatic principles in order to attract votes. Different leaders and factions disagree over which of these secondary objectives are most important and about how persistently the secondary objectives should be pursued. It is not some consensual, clear, single objective that inspires party action, but rather competing views of how the party should function.

The PT's behavior is consistent with expectations of systems institutionalists, who claim that organizations have a range of objectives not easily encompassed by the single set of ordered preferences assumed by many rational-choice theorists. In this perspective, organizations have internal dynamics, procedures, and norms that may be difficult to change, even if changing them would enhance the organization's ability to maximize certain goals (Panebianco 1988; Kitschelt 1989; Gouldner 1959; March and Olsen 1989; Selznick 1957; W. Powell and Dimaggio 1991). This perspective challenges the notion that institutional behavior is necessarily functional, adaptive, efficient, or utility maximizing.

In sum, the appropriateness of assuming a single dominant objective depends on what kind of party we are analyzing. The Brazilian catch-all parties appear to have a dominant objective to the limited extent that we can speak of clear collective objectives. The PT, however, has multifarious, less clearly ordered objectives.

A final problem with the assumption that parties are utility maximizers is that they develop organizational ties to groups in civil society, which limit the ways in which they attempt to win votes. Because of organizational ties and commitments, parties usually cannot change positions radically in order to enhance their vote-maximizing capabilities. To put the argument in Downsian spatial terms, they usually cannot "leap over" their major opponents to occupy a radically different space in party competition. Parties depend on developing enduring sympathies. Attempting to leap over their opponents, while perhaps "rational" if it were not for the importance of organizational ties, would almost surely backfire. Such a move would be seen as opportunistic and could erode rather than enhance a party's ability to win votes.

In Brazil, the observation about how ties to organized groups limit parties' ability to maximize votes particularly applies primarily to the PT. The catch-all parties have weak ties to organized interests, and they are often forged through patronage—which implies an instrumental loyalty that can be transferred. However, even the catch-all parties have some ties in civil society, and these linkages constrain the extent to which they can make rapid switches in positions and constituencies so as to maximize votes.

Parties have histories and identities that limit the ways in which they respond to certain problems, and hence ultimately limit their "rationality" in terms of vote maximization. For example, even if a rational calculation were to establish that Party A should enter into an electoral coalition with Party B, if the two parties are historic foes, the historic animosities may lead party leaders to eschew the coalition. A strategy may be electorally sound but politically unpalatable.

As Kitschelt (1989: 41–74) has argued, party leaders are not only responsive to the demands of the electorate at large, they also must be responsive to activists; otherwise, they may lose their position of prominence in the party. In Brazil, this has been particularly true of the PT. Frequently the desire to respond to militants and activists has dictated a strategy different from that of vote maximizing. This desire to respond to activists cannot be dismissed as "nonrational." Parties may need votes, but they also depend on the goodwill, hard work, and enthusiasm of people who work for the party. The PT has historically solicited strong commitments from active supporters, but even the catch-all parties rely on party cadres. Winning a few more votes but alienating droves of activists can hardly be considered a good tradeoff. Consequently, party leaders may consciously and rationally opt for strategies that do not maximize votes.

The ways parties are organized and internal party processes determine how they attempt to win votes, how they act at particular moments, and why they sometimes fail to adopt strategies that might fare better electorally. Organization breeds constraints. The ways parties are organized constrain how they search for votes. Organization and internal processes, far from being a mere derivative of vote maximizing, shape and limit how parties attempt to win votes. In sum, even if Brazilian politicians act as rational actors, political parties do not act as rational vote maximizers. Rational goal-maximizing behavior is more characteristic of politicians than parties.

Conclusions

Analysis of party organization underscores the strong contrasts among Latin American parties and helps overcome the old tendency to generalize about the nature of parties throughout the region as a whole. For example, as Coppedge (1994) has shown, Venezuelan parties are highly disciplined and centralized. The central organization makes the major choices regarding candidate selection. Discipline is so strong that congressional roll-call votes are not taken; rather, the leaders state how their party is voting, and votes are tabulated by party rather than individual. Until the crisis of 1992, politicians were committed to their parties; otherwise, their political careers would never get off the ground. All of this represents a contrast to the Brazilian case, where the catch-all parties are decentralized and moderately disciplined, and where politicians often change parties. In most respects, Venezuelan and Brazilian parties are more different than are American and British parties. Yet in contrast to the abundant literature underscoring the differences between American and British parties, scholarly analysts have neglected organizational differences among Latin American parties.

Examination of organization underscores the weakness of the Brazilian catch-all parties. Brazilian parties are unusual in the extent to which they are electoral vehicles; they exercise weak control over individual politicians; they are not highly disciplined; they play a secondary role in most political campaigns; they have comparatively little control over who becomes a member, what politicians do, and who gets elected. Brazilian parties are loose organizations, designed to permit politicians to operate in a free-wheeling fashion. The catch-all parties lack cohesion; local disputes among political bosses, rather than ideological or political questions, frequently determine party affiliation. This forms a contrast not only with respect to the highly organized parties of most Western European democracies, but also to the catch-all parties of many Latin American nations. In brief, Brazilian party organizations are not strongly institutionalized. This completes the analysis of the four criteria of party system institutionalization discussed in Chapter 2.

In his classic book on democracy, Schumpeter (1950: 269–302) argued that politicians are political entrepreneurs who create parties to further their own interests (above all, getting elected). Schumpeter's view oversimplifies complex realities for many parties, but in the case of Brazilian catch-all parties in the post–1985 period, his portrait has approximated reality. In an interview, one federal deputy went so far as to say that "We don't have political parties in this country."[43] Nowhere was the weakness of national parties as apparent as in internal processes.

Three consequences stem from the weakness of Brazilian party organizations. First, the loose character of parties has contributed to their weakness as actors in the political system. Parties with few resources, limited discipline, and weak loyalties are not likely to establish deep roots in society. Second, because parties exercise comparatively little control over political elites, these elites, rather than the parties, are the principal agents of representation. Brazilian politicians generally function with a high degree of autonomy, and to the extent that they owe allegiance, it is more frequently to state-based factions than to the national party. Third, because national parties are not highly disciplined, presidents cannot always count on parties to organize legislative support.

CHAPTER 6

Patronage, Clientelism, and Patrimonialism

The biggest party in Brazil is the PCB, Brazilian Clientelistic Party. If we can't get rid of this party, we'll never be able to solve the problems of the country.

— Governor Tarcísio Burity (PMDB-Paraíba)[1]

On May 13, 1987, readers of one of Brazil's biggest and most reputable newspapers, the *Folha de São Paulo*, woke up to a story that won journalist Jânio de Freitas a major international prize for reporting. "Bidding for the North-South Railroad was a Farce," read the headline, and the story that followed unveiled one of the most notorious instances of venality in post–1985 Brazil.

The North-South Railroad was President Sarney's pharaonic project to link the plains of central Brazil (near Brasília) to his home state of Maranhão. Minister of Transportation José Reinaldo Tavares first proposed the plan in March 1986 as a way of integrating the expansive central and northern regions more effectively into the Brazilian economy. The project quickly generated opposition. Three federal agencies—the Program of Integrated Development of the Araguaia-Tocantins (PRODIAT), the planning department of the Ministry of Transportation (GEIPOT, Brazilian Enterprise of Planning in Transportation), and the highly reputed Institute of Applied Economic Research (IPEA) of the Ministry of Planning—concluded on the basis of detailed studies that the project was unsound and extravagant.

At a time when the Brazilian economy was a shambles, the estimated initial cost of the railroad was $3.2 billion, $950 million more than GEIPOT had estimated the railroad should cost and $1.5 billion more than the average international cost for a railroad of that length. Respected entities in civil society, including the Brazilian Press Association (ABI), the Order of Brazilian Lawyers (OAB), the Society of Engineers of Minas Gerais, the Federation of Associations of Railroad Engineers, and the Pastoral Land Commission publicly opposed the railroad. The president of the Federal Railroad System pronounced himself against the project and was subsequently fired.

Despite such opposition, the government announced in February 1987 that public bidding would determine which construction firms would build different parts of the railroad. The government rehabilitated an essentially defunct public enterprise, VALEC, to oversee the project. The winners of the bidding were to be determined on May 12, but Jânio de Freitas discovered that the bidding had been rigged and published the results in a cipher in the *Folha de São Paulo* on May 8. When the announced winners exactly matched what Freitas had foreseen, he published his denunciation. It was obvious that the nineteen construction firms had rigged the bidding, abetted by VALEC and some public officials.

Three weeks later, a commission of nine senators began investigations into whether there had been fraud and whether the railroad was a viable project. Despite convincing evidence that underscored both corruption and the economic nonviability of the project, on October 15 the commission voted down a report that concluded that there had been corruption and that the railroad should not be built. Six days later, it approved a report written by a different member of the commission, certifying that there was no evidence of corruption and that the government should go ahead. As far as the government was concerned, the investigation was over and the project was going forward.

How can a project costing a bankrupt nation billions of dollars go ahead despite a broad perception that it was unsound and corrupt? How did the Senate commission conclude that there had not been collusion when the evidence suggested the opposite? To understand these issues, we need to look at the politics of clientelism, patronage, and patrimonialism.

This chapter focuses on the widespread use of patronage to build political careers and govern. Without some attention to the politics of patronage and clientelism, no portrait of Brazilian parties would be complete. Clientelism and patronage are important ingredients in Brazilian party politics. The political use of public resources serves three purposes in Brazil. First, politicans use patronage to win internal control of parties. By using public jobs and resources to construct clientele networks, politicans can dominate their party organizations.

Second, politicians of the catch-all parties use public resources and clientelistic practices to win votes. In contemporary Brazil, patronage is not very effective as an electoral resource for party organizations, partially because the costs of massive patronage are so high that governments lose more votes through poor policy performance than they win through co-opting. For individual politicians, however, reliance on patronage and clientele networks often is effective, and in any case it remains so important in determining internal party control that politicians have a strong incentive to build clientele networks through patronage.

Third, government leaders rely on patronage and clientelism to build support for governing. Because of the limits to party loyalty and discipline, government leaders cannot rely exclusively on parties to build support. They also rely on patronage and clientele networks to forge their political alliances. However, such reliance is no longer consistently effective for governing.

Between 1979 and 1994, reliance on clientelism and patronage to build political support contributed to the economic and political crisis in Brazil. Clientelism, patrimonialism, and their oft-associated progeny—corruption and nepotism—exacerbated problems of democratic legitimacy. This is created on the basis of perceptions that government furthers the public interest, while clientelism responds to particularistic interests. Pervasive clientelism also bolstered the elitist character of the political system by leading to individualistic exchanges of favors rather than promoting broad entitlement. By undermining universalistic, procedural, and meritocratic rationality, clientelism, patrimonialism, and corruption weakened Brazil's public sector and contributed to the economic crisis of the 1980s. Finally, clientelism transformed social programs intended to benefit the poor into patrimonial sinecures of politicians.

Defining Basic Terms

This chapter is organized around three concepts: patronage, clientelism, and patrimonialism. The term patronage is used as it is employed in daily parlance, to refer to the use or distribution of state resources on a nonmeritocratic basis for political gain. As Sorauf (1961: 309) put it, "Patronage is best thought of as an incentive system—a political currency with which to 'purchase' political activity and political responses." It includes both jobs and public-sector resources.

Traditional patronage primarily meant jobs, while contemporary patronage primarily involves public services and works projects, state contracts and concessions, and state investments. Jobs are still central to patronage politics in contemporary Brazil, but the battle to obtain public investments and contracts has become as important. With the enormous expansion of the state apparatus came a commensurate change in the nature of patronage. State development projects have become an important part of contemporary patronage politics (Tarrow 1967: 300–42).

Following most political scientists who have written about the subject, "clientelism" is restricted here to patron–client relations that have four defining features: an unequal character, uneven reciprocity, a noninstitutionalized nature, and a face-to-face character (Scott 1972; Archer 1990; Graziano 1975). Clientelistic relations take place between individuals of different status and power. One partner in the relationship is more powerful than the other, and the weaker partner is generally more dependent on the relationship than the powerful one, who controls access to benefits the weaker partner desires. Clientelism is usually a strategy designed by elites to maintain many features of a system of domination (Flynn 1974), but it can also emerge as a result of grassroots efforts to exploit the limited opportunities available in a semiclosed political system. Clientelism excludes exchanges among individuals of more or less equal status. It includes, however, intraelite exchanges between actors of different power, such as between a governor and a state deputy or between a president and a federal deputy.

Clientelistic relations involve reciprocal exchange; both sides offer something and gain in return. Because they are asymmetrical, clientelistic relationships involve domination, and there may be a threat of coercion. Nevertheless, they are not primarily coercive relationships in which the more powerful side forcefully extracts something from the weaker partner. The relationship involves unequal reciprocity in that the powerful partner generally gains more than the weaker one, but both sides accrue some benefits.

Clientelistic relationships are not based on codified rules or universal criteria. Instead, the exchange is personalized and individualized, based on bargaining (implicit or explicit) between the two sides. Rather than follow a set of general procedures that govern the distribution of public goods to poor communities, public goods are granted as though they were personal favors to clienteles in return for supporting their political patron. Political criteria (allegiance to a person or party) and personal connections prevail over other possible modes of selection of beneficiaries (universal entitlement, random selection, meritocracy, efficiency, etc.).

Brazil's catch-all parties rely heavily on patronage and clientelism. Several such parties have been formed by government leaders through the use of patronage and clientele networks, and their existence depends in good measure upon the use of patronage to secure support in society. These parties are typically controlled by government leaders who use them to promote their own interests.

Even though these parties depend on state patronage, they may not overtly be statist. Indeed, they may even adopt antistatist rhetoric, as some clientelistic parties in Brazil do. They rely on state patronage and clientelism regardless of their discourse regarding the state.

Clientelism in Brazil is not a static phenomenon.[2] To capture the changing nature of clientelism, it is useful to distinguish between traditional and modern varieties. Traditional clientelism rested on an agrarian polity in which the extension of citizenship was narrow. Acting in consort with government authorities, local landlords were the bosses of the political system. These landlords relied on clientele networks to obtain what they needed from the political authorities, but they themselves had unfettered domination in their territories. They acted as *padrinhos* for their tenants, and they did not need to exchange significant material resources in order to maintain their local clientele. Clientelism involved exchanges of favors among individuals who had considerable face-to-face contact. Although modern clientelism is also based on personal ties between patrons and clients, it frequently involves intermediaries. It rests on a largely urban polity with universal adult citizenship. The personal control over individuals that existed in traditional rural society is prevalent only in remote regions. Clientelistic exchanges with the urban popular classes are less affective, less deferential, and less based on personal obedience to an employer.

In modern clientelism, professional politicians and political brokers secure a wide range of public goods for citizens. In contrast to what the literature suggests is the case for modern clientelism,[3] in Brazil clientele networks since 1985 have not primarily been party oriented or controlled; rather they have been individually dominated. Nominations for positions in the bureaucracy are distributed to individual politicians rather than discussed as a party matter. Citizens and organized interests seek out politicians to secure favors, but even if they are loyal to a politician (which is not always the case),[4] that politician is not necessarily loyal to a party.

Finally, modern clientelism offers more choice to the clients than traditional clientelism did. The traditional variety was based on personal bonds whose affective significance may have overshadowed any rational calculus of cost and benefits. The modern variety occurs within the context of a political marketplace, especially in democratic settings. Community leaders, mayors, and poor people can switch loyalties. A multitude of patrons compete for popular votes, thereby giving the clients a range of options they previously lacked. Enduring personal loyalty is the exception rather than the norm, and it usually must be rewarded in ongoing ways because the clients can negotiate with a multitude of patrons (Gay 1994).

Traditional forms of clientelism have not been entirely superseded in Brazil. In the hinterland, traditional clientelism based on personal ties between powerful individuals and their subordinates is still common.

Patrimonialism refers to a situation in which political rulers treat the state as if it were their own property (Weber 1978: 1010–38). In patrimonial polities, politicians do not distinguish clearly between what is their own and what is public, the *res publica*. Rather than allocate public resources according to universalistic criteria, politicians do so on the basis of personal connections, bestowing favors on their friends, family, and *parentela*. They use public monies as though they came from their personal bank accounts; they require that supposedly public servants work to further their personal political projects; they hire their relatives and friends for public jobs, regardless of their qualifications and job performance; they award public contracts to friends and relatives. There is a weak sense of public consciousness and of the *res publica*. Patrimonialism has a long tradition in Brazil (Torres 1933; O'Donnell 1986: 121–55; Schmitter 1971: 47–78; Schwartzman 1982; Oliveira Vianna 1949; R. Graham 1990; Lewin 1987; Uricoechea 1980).

Of the three concepts discussed in this section, patronage is the broadest; some uses of patronage are neither clientelistic nor patrimonial. Obtaining patronage for constituencies or local governments is a legitimate practice. Clientelism usually involves patronage, though some traditional clientelistic exchanges involved landowners' private resources and therefore did not rely on patronage as defined here (i.e., using public goods). Many political manipulations of public resources in the post–1979 period involved nonaffective intraelite relationships, so they cannot be properly termed clientelistic. Although they are different phenomena, clientelism and patrimonialism have some commonalities. Both enable politicians to manipulate political resources for their own benefit. For this reason, I sometimes treat their effects together. Patronage and clientelism are also closely linked because patronage is the primary glue that holds modern clientele networks together.

Neither clientelism nor patrimonialism is coterminous with corruption. Indeed, some forms of clientelism constitute legitimate political practices. However, clientelism and especially patrimonialism easily give rise to corruption. Corruption is not the primary focus of this chapter, but it looms as a major phenomenon in post–1979 Brazil, related to clientelism and patrimonialism (Dimenstein 1988; Geddes and Ribeiro Neto 1992).

The Uses of Patronage and Clientelism

Clientelism and the widespread use of patronage for political purposes are common political phenomena, but they are more prevalent in some political systems than others. They are still central aspects of party politics in Brazil, notwithstanding growing challenges and opposition. Being plugged into a clientele network is the key to getting many public-sector jobs, resources, and concessions. Success or failure in many undertakings depends less on one's talent and organizational skills than on connections to politicians.

Patronage, clientelism, and patrimonialism have long been important fibers of Brazilian party politics. At least until 1930, and in remote rural regions into the 1970s, clientelistic networks superseded parties as bases of political organization (Oliveira Vianna 1949). Until the 1930s, party loyalties, to the extent they existed, were largely shaped by disputes among different political clans.

Between 1945 and 1964 this situation changed somewhat as ideological divisions became prominent; at the national level (though not necessarily at the local level), the parties differed in terms of ideology and social base (Soares 1973). Since 1979, the party system has again had a significant ideological basis. But widespread clientelism and reliance on patronage continue to persist despite the more ideological character of the party system.

Some analysts (Lemarchand and Legg 1972; J. Powell 1970) have argued that clientelism is a transitional phenomenon that will erode with modernization. In the long run this may be true, but the prevalence and durability of clientelism in some political systems, including the Brazilian, is remarkable. Even though clientelism may undergo striking changes, it can be adapted and endure as a feature of politics (Cammack 1982; Chubb 1981; Hagopian 1996). It can even survive in the face of sharp ideological cleavages (A. Valenzuela 1977) and major regime transformations (Oi 1989).

Rather than treat clientelism as a values-based phenomenon, as much of the literature does, this chapter approaches the persistence of clientelism from the theoretical lens of how different actors benefit from it. It assumes that (1) if actors did not benefit, clientelism would become a residual phenomenon and (2) there must be distinctive incentives in the Brazilian political system in order to explain the pervasiveness of clientelism.

For the poor, clientelism offers a way to get some tangible benefits out of a system that generally favors the wealthy, in a context in which broad entitlement has been the exception. As has been the case elsewhere, poverty has been a fecund breeding ground for clientelism (Scott 1969). Poor people need mechanisms that help them cope, and through clientelistic exchanges they can gain access to such mechanisms. Individual citizens and popular groups can win resources and favors through clientelistic channels, and outside of such channels their access to such resources and favors is limited (Oi 1989). Moreover, resources extracted through clientelistic channels are appropriated directly by the individuals or groups for their own benefit (Chubb 1982). Clientelistic exchanges avoid Olson's (1965) collective-action problem; there are no free riders, and those who participate receive benefits for their own use.

The disposition toward individual rather than collective solutions has been reinforced by the historical weakness of popular organizations and mass-based parties. With weak popular organizations, collective forms of class action were less effective than in some other countries, and efforts to engage in collective struggles aimed at broad entitlement seemed futile. The poor have been dubious about the possibility of radical social change that would change their lot while remaining sanguine that through individual effort and connections one could rise up the social ladder (Caldeira 1984). Where broad collective solutions are blocked, a person either seeks individual paths of ascension, principally by taking advantage of clientele networks, or accepts his/her lot. In turn, the institutionalization of clientelistic practices has reinforced the weakness of popular organizations because individuals and popular groups opt for clientelistic arrangements rather than broad-based movements and parties.

Political contacts are often crucial for securing public jobs (L. Graham 1968: 125–39). Getting a job as a janitor in a public building, as a garbage collector, a teacher, a school or hospital director, a police commissioner (*delegado*), a social-security bureaucrat, or a manager of a state enterprise frequently depends on political contacts. According to law, most employees should enter the public service through civil-service examinations (*concursos*), but gaping holes in these regulations make them a farce in many state agencies. In 1985, Minister of Administration Aluísio Alves estimated that in federal public direct administration, 125,000 people had been hired through public service examinations, and 1,700,000 people had been hired according to political criteria.[5] On another occasion, Alves estimated that in the indirect public administration there were 1,300,000 federal employees, of whom 125,000 had entered via civil service exam, 350,000 through some other form of selection process, and the rest through a *pistolão*—a person with connections and power.[6] Alves also estimated that 400,000 people had passed the civil service but had not been hired, making clear that the reason for circumventing the exam was not lack of qualified people.[7]

Although most public-sector jobs pay poorly, they provide greater job security than private-sector employment, usually bringing lifetime job tenure after five years of service (the Cardoso government has pushed for a constitutional amendment that would repeal this provision). They generally provide secure and good benefits, including access to the public health system, a good pension, and paid vacations. In the 1980s, when private-sector employment in the formal market became increasingly difficult to obtain, the advantages of public jobs grew. No wonder, then, that the 1883 affirmation of statesman Joaquim Nabuco still rings true for many: "Public employment is everyone's vocation."

Politicians are responsible for many public-sector appointments, and political loyalty is generally a major criterion in obtaining public jobs and promotions. In early 1985, one journalist estimated that the president had 100,000 positions at his personal disposal.[8] Even poorly paying positions with low skill levels are sometimes fiercely disputed because of their political influence. A notorious case in the 1980s involved Funrural, an agency within the ministry of welfare that is part of the social-security system in the countryside. Local agents process requests, such as granting state aid for newborns and for funerals and signing disability or retirement papers, thus enabling people to qualify for social-security benefits. The agent is one of the most important intermediaries between the state and local citizens, and is in a position to help win votes for a deputy or senator (Avelino 1991). In 1987, José Lourenço, the PFL leader in the Chamber of Deputies, threatened to cease supporting the Sarney government if he were not allowed to make the appointment to a lowly Funrural position in a remote *município* of the state of Bahia.

But it is not only jobs that are determined by political criteria. Political contacts also help to get public services and investments, contracts, and favors from the state. Getting ahead without the support of a politician is difficult in many walks of life. Many people depend on the state and politicians for personal favors. Getting an opening in a public school, receiving retirement benefits, obtaining a concession to open a gasoline station, and getting a permit for a radio or television station often require a politician's intermediation. A teacher who wants to change schools, a doctor who wishes to work in a different public hospital, a person who wants a fellowship or a medical excuse to finance a trip abroad, a bureaucrat who wants to be transferred from one city to another—all often depend on a favor from a politician. Getting a bank loan, winning a contract with a state firm, and getting access to milk stamps often require a politician's support. Access to day-care centers and schools, public housing, medical services, retirement benefits, and scholarships similarly can depend on political favors. Even food programs for pregnant women and poor children and vaccines are used for political purposes. In return for the services and favors they provide, politicians hope to win the allegiance, votes, and financial contributions of those whom they help.

Because access to so many jobs, goods, and services depends on political contacts, citizens rely on favors by *padrinhos*. Thus, the old Brazilian saying, "If you don't have a *padrinho*, you'll die a pagan."[9] In the established Western democracies, receiving retirement benefits, getting on public benefits programs, and going to a certain public school are citizens' rights. In Brazil, these benefits are formally rights, but in practice they often depend upon political intermediaries and favors. Obtaining one's "rights" may involve bureaucratic procedures that an individual can formally do on his/her own, but that because of the parlous state of the public bureaucracy require the favor of an intermediary. Consequently, personal connections are important (DaMatta 1985: 25–54; 1987). In most public agencies, Hernando de Soto's (1989) portrait of the patrimonial bureaucracy prevails over Weber's rational bureaucratic behavior.

As Chubb (1981) and Médard (1982) observed, political systems based on clientelism invert the conventional Marxist wisdom that politics is ultimately determined by economics: political connections determine economic results. In some sectors of the Brazilian economy, especially in the Northeast, having political contacts is as important as knowing how to run a firm efficiently. Political contacts can be decisive for obtaining bank loans, contracts with the state, and state subsidies. Until the early 1990s, the state was paramount as regulator and producer, and through political connections entrepreneurs could often obtain favorable interventions or be allowed to subvert legal norms.

As with Italy, dependence on politicians and the state is particularly marked in the poor regions of the country. Because good private-sector jobs are scarce in these regions, public positions are more desirable. The weakness of unions and other popular groups makes people depend on individual solutions through political intermediaries rather than collective solutions (Caldeira 1984). Because private resources are limited, dependence on state investment is greater.

In contrast to many political systems where contemporary clientelism is a dominant currency, partisanship in the narrow sense is weak in Brazil. There is a politicization of the bureaucracy, but more according to personal than partisan loyalty. This is a contrast to Colombia (Archer 1990) and Italy (Chubb 1982, Graziano 1978, Tarrow 1977), where a specific party attachment was a *sine qua non* for obtaining state favors.

State interventionism helped nourish clientelism: There are more rewards to distribute and more patronage benefits. Because of the state's importance as producer, buyer, provider of services, licenser, and regulator, a wide range of actors depend on the state. Success in many endeavors depends on connections to politicians. Dependence on politicians and the state is a necessary condition for contemporary clientelism: where actors are not tied to state favors and resources, they have no need to depend on political connections, and they can organize in autonomous fashion.

In sum, clients everywhere can benefit from clientelism. But the incentives from below toward clientelism are particularly pronounced in Brazil given widespread poverty, weak popular organization, and state interventionism.

One of the paradoxes of widespread *empreguismo* (creating public-sector jobs for political purposes) is that it expands the constituency for further clientelism. A large contingent of people—an estimated 4,395,000 as of 1985—depend for their livelihood on maintaining the patrimonial-bureaucratic state. As Olson's (1965) theory of collective action predicts, this contingent has a powerful interest in undermining attempts at state reform. With the exception of the president and some state governors, most actors stand to gain little personally through state shrinking because the costs of action are individual, individual contributions to collective action are generally noninfluential, and the benefits of successful state shrinking are collective and nonfungible. Politicians are aware of the political importance of state employees, and many build their careers around protecting them. This explains why politicians have often supported measures that provide blanket job tenure to all public employees, including those who entered the public sector through nepotism or illegally. Thus early in 1986 President Sarney issued a decree law guaranteeing job security for 130,000 public employees who had been hired on a temporary basis without passing a civil service exam.[10] Similarly, Article 19 of the "Transitory Constitutional Dispositions" of the 1988 Constitution gave tenure to all public employees (local, state, and federal) with at least five years in public service, even if they had been hired improperly.

Individuals engage in clientelistic exchanges to obtain resources from the state. But why do politicians of the catch-all parties rely on patronage and clientelism? The next three subsections look at this issue, arguing that patronage and clientelism are used to win control of the party machine, to win votes, and to build support for governing—three powerful political currencies. Emphasis is placed on the incentive system that makes patronage and clientelism a rational response for both clienteles and politicians (Chubb 1982, Grindle 1977).[11]

PATRONAGE AND CONTROL OF THE PARTY MACHINERY

Despite the penury of the catch-all parties, control of the party machine ensures control over all state-level nominations (state deputy, federal deputy, senator, governor, and vice governor) and many appointments. Patronage is important in determining internal organizational control in the catch-all parties at the local and state level.

Participation in local party conventions is open to all members who comprise two broad groups: individuals who actively participate in the parties, and the clientele these individuals organize to attend local conventions. Because members formally control internal processes and positions, different factions and leaders use patronage to entice people into joining the party and attending conventions.

Politicians do what they can to control local conventions. Above all, this entails mobilizing constituents to go to the convention. Among the leftist parties, this process takes place through a combination of ideological/policy and selective incentives. In the catch-all parties, politicians generally use patronage to control local conventions. They offer jobs, provide vouchers for free public-milk programs, secure bank loans, get people on a list for public housing, ensure that someone's children will get a place in the school of their choice, promote public officials, and pay people to join the party and go to the convention. To community activists who deliver enough new party members, they offer jobs and make promises of public works and services. Government-owned vehicles transport loyal phalanxes to and from party conventions. People are paid in devious ways from state resources in order to deliver party affiliations. Obtaining sufficient party affiliations may win an individual a promotion within the bureaucracy.

The incentives to induce poor people to become party members and attend conventions explain the prevalence of poor people among party members in Brazil, although the upper-middle- and upper-income earners were more likely than others to be party members. A 1988 government household survey indicated that of the 2,093,872 party members in Brazil only 191,221 earned 10 or more minimum salaries (IBGE 1990: Vol. 2, 16).[12]

The politicians in power use state resources to get poor people to attend conventions. Such use of public resources is widespread throughout Brazil—particularly in the Northeast and the North, where dependence on the state is greater and where levels of political information and consciousness are more precarious than in southern Brazil.

When local party leaders control local government, they may pressure public officials to become party members, insinuating that their continued employment depends on support for their faction of the party. This practice is illegal, but in a country where impunity for political corruption has been the rule, the law has not always prevailed.

In most neighborhoods and cities, party conventions are frequented by the poor, who are generally organized by an activist who gets something—power, privilege, access to some state resources, a job—out of the deal. Many of those who attend conventions have little understanding of what is going on except that they must vote for a particular candidate. Going to a convention is a way of getting patronage for themselves or their communities.

Cabos eleitorais (perhaps best translated as political brokers, but literally, a *cabo* was a lower-ranking military official who oversaw rank-and-file soldiers in the traditional provincial militaries) help deliver votes, party members, and delegates for politicians. The *cabos eleitorais* are key figures in the clientele networks. They can be poor or wealthy, professionals or blue-collar workers, educated or not, professional politicians or not. In rural regions, local Funrural (social-security) agents are excellent *cabos eleitorais* because they control access to retirement and other state benefits. Community activists of all stripes and colors serve as *cabos eleitorais*. In small towns, the willingness of mayors and councillors to sponsor campaign rallies and to invite politicians for ceremonies celebrating new public projects influences how people vote for deputy. In return for their support, *cabos eleitorais* expect some favor from a politician: a job, a subsidized loan from a state bank, public works for their local community (Greenfield 1977).

In addition to being used to entice common people to join parties and attend conventions, patronage is widely used to win the support of party delegates. Whoever has the most delegates essentially controls the party.

Delegates usually have an informal obligation to support a particular person, but some have looser commitments. In the period between the selection of delegates for the state convention and the holding of the convention, the delegates negotiate with those who want to control the party. Public officials use state resources and jobs as a means of winning over delegates.[13]

Using patronage to win control of party organizations is widespread; it is the norm rather than the exception. Use of state resources to win local conventions and delegates has had a decisive impact in determining who controls the catch-all parties. Gaining control of parties entails controlling membership and delegates, and state resources have generally been decisive in this process, except among the leftist parties. This system of winning internal control of parties through public resources places the people who control patronage—above all governors—at considerable advantage. The opposition within the party may do its best to mobilize people and win delegates, but defeating the incumbents is not easy, given their capacity to provide material incentives to encourage people to turn out. The party ends up becoming an appendage of those who control the state. Governors can almost always control their own party if they are willing to resort to patronage to do so.

Indicative of how effective the use of patronage can be in securing control of the parties is the fact that after the May 1988 party conventions, all twenty-two PMDB governors had control of the party in their states. This control resulted from the governors' ability to distribute patronage, not from their overwhelming popularity among the electorate.

The effectiveness of state patronage in controlling the catch-all parties sets Brazil apart from Argentina, Chile, Uruguay, or Venezuela. In Brazil, governors can dominate party organizations if they are willing to use patronage to construct clientele networks. In these other countries, parties are less dependent on patronage and are less susceptible to control by the state.

PATRONAGE, CLIENTELE NETWORKS, AND ELECTIONS

Patronage is also an important force in elections. Patronage and clientelism are not as effective in securing votes in general elections as they are in ensuring internal party control. Nevertheless, politicians of the catch-all parties still rely on clientelism and public resources to boost their electoral campaigns.

Politicians in democracies with personalistic electoral systems, as is the case in Brazil, need to develop a personal constituency; they cannot rely exclusively, or even mostly, on the party label (Carey and Shugart 1995). Under such circumstances, politicians have two main ways of cultivating a personal reputation: through policy/legislative/ideological work and appeals, and through constituency service. These two are not at odds with each other in principle, but in practice, politicians must make choices about how to allocate their time. In this sense, there is a tradeoff between spending time on policy, legislative, or ideological issues and on constituency service. Most Brazilian deputies rely principally on delivering goods to *municípios* and neighborhoods as a way of developing a distinctive profile. Given low voter interest in policy issues and legislative work, only a minority of deputies can win an election primarily on such a basis.

Despite the substantial number of people who vote according to television images, party sympathies, or ideological issues, many citizens still vote on the basis of what their friends, local community activists, their political *padrinhos*, and local political notables suggest—that is, clientele networks. These are especially important for candidates for state and federal deputy because, as surveys make apparent, relatively few citizens have solid choices for these positions.[14] This makes voters more reliant on the opinions of local political notables. Because they have almost no television time, cannot otherwise personally communicate to a majority of voters, and only rarely are well known for their legislative work, candidates for deputy rely on local networks to get the word out to support them (Avelino 1991; Banck 1994). Candidates for governor and senator also rely on clientele networks, but because they can appeal to the electorate through television, they are less dependent on them.

Patronage cements the clientele networks that politicians mobilize at election time. Electoral legislation prohibits the use of state resources in electoral campaigns, but this legislation is consistently ignored. Politicians supporting the parties in power (at the national, state, or local level) use state resources abundantly in elections. Public vehicles tour the cities and the countryside, distributing electoral propaganda and transporting candidates and campaign assistants. Funds from state enterprises and agencies are used to finance campaigns. State firms print campaign propaganda. Employees of state agencies spend their days campaigning for the politician who secured their jobs for them. State agencies offer medical assistance, milk tickets, scholarships, retirement benefits, jobs, admission to schools, etc., to secure the allegiance of poor constituents. Given the dependence of the poor on the state apparatus, especially in the poverty-stricken areas of the country, such resources help get some candidates elected.

One of the most pernicious uses of the state in electoral campaigns involves the effort to attract the support of businessmen. Many candidates depend upon large campaign chests, so private business is a favorite target for raising funds. Businessmen usually expect some form of reciprocity. For example, large construction firms often support campaigns with the understanding that they will later be awarded public contracts.[15]

Political appointees are often involved in illicit campaign financing. When he resigned in October 1987 as minister of welfare, Rafael de Almeida Magalhães noted how common this practice is. "Using public positions to establish campaign funds is considered acceptable. . . . In public service, anything goes (*tudo pode ser pedido*), as if it were an exchange of favors within a special group of people."[16]

Governments everywhere try to influence elections, but in Latin America until the neoliberal reforms of the 1990s, they did so commonly through patronage rather than attempting to achieve good macroeconomic results in election years. As a result, in presidential election years, public expenditures increased (Ames 1987: 9–33). Among the more-developed countries of Latin America, Brazil and Mexico stand out in the use of patronage in elections. It resembles the U.S. spoils system before the civil-service reforms, but the Brazilian state is larger and has a more pervasive impact on social and political life than the American state had in the nineteenth century.

For executive posts, patronage and clientelism are less effective at garnering votes today than they were in the past. The 1980s made this clear as the parties that relied on such traditional devices suffered embarrassing defeats. The PDS relied on patronage to win elections, but after 1984 the party collapsed. The PFL has fared only slightly better. The PMDB was electorally successful in opposition, but when it formed a government and continued to rely on patronage, its electoral support eroded. The 1989 presidential election, in which the contenders with the greatest access to patronage (the PMDB and PFL) were resounding failures and those that opposed the Sarney government (the PT, PDT, and PRN) were successes, demonstrated the bankruptcy of patronage as a way of winning presidential elections. Patronage, however, is still effective at garnering votes in the less-developed regions of the country, in smaller towns, and for positions in which television is a less decisive influence.

Even though at a collective level (i.e., for party organizations) patronage is no longer a reliable way to win elections, at an individual level (i.e., for particular candidates) it still is valuable. This has much to do with the electoral system, which provides incentives for strong intraparty competition. Extensive clientele networks give candidates an advantage over those who lack such networks (Ames 1995b; Avelino 1991).

Individual politicians have incentives to use clientelistic networks because the cost is collective while the benefits are individual. The only elected official who is likely to be directly blamed for the macroeconomic problems brought on by squandering state resources for political gain is the president. Thus there is a collective action dilemma: what is good for individual politicians determines the logic of the system. But this logic has deleterious results for the system as a whole. The most insidious incentive to patrimonial practices for individual politicians is that through exchanges of favors with state agencies and private businesses, they can become wealthy and help their friends and families become more powerful.

In sum, even though parties may not fare well when they rely on patronage and clientele networks, individual politicians have incentives to continue to rely on these traditional means of winning votes. And party politics in Brazil functions more according to the logic of individual politicians than of party organizations. Even though parties do not fare well when they rely on patronage to win votes, the clientelistic logic of individual politicians prevails.

GOVERNING THROUGH PATRONAGE

This section focuses on the use of patronage to build support for office holders, looking at the influence of the federal executive (presidents and ministers) over state and local executives (governors and mayors), of the state executive (governor and state secretaries) over mayors and state deputies, and of the federal executive (presidents and ministers) over federal deputies. Among the more-developed countries of Latin America, Brazil and Mexico stand out for the extent to which government leaders use patronage to forge political support. Because loyalty and discipline among the catch-all parties are limited, and because the presidential system fails to offer incentives for party cohesion, government leaders cannot rely exclusively on parties to build support. Consequently, they also use patronage for that purpose. By offering public jobs and resources to those willing to support them and withholding state resources from adversaries, executive office holders (especially presidents and governors) try to forge political alliances.

Because of limited party discipline and loyalty and because their own party rarely has a majority in Congress, presidents need to assemble governing coalitions that go beyond their own parties. Patronage and clientelism are valuable resources for forging political support because they enable presidents to obtain the backing of politicians outside their own parties or coalitions. Presidents cultivate the support of governors and (to a lesser extent) mayors of major cities because they are powerful political figures who shape public opinion, have loyal political acolytes of their own, and can drum up legislative support. Governors and mayors, conversely, depend on the federal government because they need resources. Especially until 1988, governors and mayors were dependent on the federal government for nonautomatic transfers of funds that were usually determined by political criteria.

The military regime intentionally fostered the dependence of state and local governments on the federal government (Abrúcio 1998). These governments got a smaller fraction of total public funds than they had in the past. The federal government's share of tax revenue increased from 48.7 percent in 1964 to 56.9 percent in 1984, while the states' and *municípios'* shares decreased from 44.8 percent and 6.5 percent to 38.6 percent and 4.5 percent, respectively (Socolik

1986: 71–72). This centralization of tax revenues at the federal level was reversed after 1982, through a constitutional amendment.

Under military rule, most federal fiscal transfers were discretionary and were funneled from ministries to state and local governments through contracts known as *convênios*, which were (and remain) highly political in nature. As one expert in public finance wrote, the *convênios* "are characterized by the informality of procedures. There are no written rules to govern how much support can be given, nor are there any criteria for deciding whom to support" (Rezende 1982: 493). Because they are not governed by procedural norms, the *convênios* are a fertile breeding ground for clientelism (World Bank 1988).

Between 1964 and 1980, the dependence of *municípios* on these discretionary contracts with the federal government almost quintupled (Brasileiro 1981). During the 1980s, most *municípios* obtained 60–70 percent of their resources from transfers from the federal and state governments. In 1985, 63 percent of such revenue came from transfers from the federal government. The *municípios'* share of total government resources rose from 11.9 percent in 1964 to 16.7 percent in 1984 because of the large increase in transfers from the federal and state governments (Socolik 1986: 71), but the reliance on discretionary transfers meant increasing political dependence.

A similar though less dramatic process occurred with state governments. On average, their own revenue as a share of total expenditures fell from 83 percent in 1965 to 67 percent in 1978. In the North and Northeast, the states were generating less than half their total expenditures by the late 1970s (Rezende 1982: 491). Like local governments, they were forced to rely on *convênios* with the federal government and on foreign loans. In real terms, discretionary federal transfers to state and local governments increased more than sixfold between 1965 and 1983 (Afonso 1985: 457). Without federal resources, state and local governments were strapped for funds.

The foreign debt that many state and local governments contracted reinforced their political dependence on the federal government. By 1994, state and local governments had accumulated nearly $100 billion in foreign debt (out of the Brazilian total of $148 billion). The federal government had to approve new foreign loans and the rolling over of old ones to state and local governments. Such power gives the federal government political leverage in dealing with the subnational governments.

The 1988 constitution redistributed tax revenues to state and local governments, reducing the dependence of local and state governments on the federal government and strengthening the hand of state governors. This shift in resources reinforced a process that was unleashed with the election of state governors in 1982. As Abrúcio (1998) points out, after 1982, state governors were chosen by the electorate rather than the president. This shift gave more power to governors at the expense of presidents. After 1988, the fiscal revenue of states increased while their fiscal responsibilities did not, generating a situation in which governors have ample discretionary powers over the budget (Dain 1995; Abrúcio 1998).

Despite the enhanced political autonomy of governors in the post–1985 period, governors and mayors continue to seek funds from the federal government and to rely on it in countless matters. Among the most important such issues in the 1990s was the negotiation of the foreign debt of state and local governments; mayors and governors depended on federal-government rollovers of the debt. In addition, under the Cardoso administration, governors came under pressure to manage state banks in a responsible fashion; they had been run inefficiently, largely as a consequence of political manipulations. The federal government assumed the right to close these banks if they were run improperly; this assertion of authority tilted the balance of power in the relationship between governors and the president back to the latter.

Aware that a good administration requires resources from the federal government, governors and mayors are often willing to support the president in order to obtain money for projects, loans, or pardons on the state's external debt. Presidents and ministers use this dependence of mayors and governors upon the central government to build constituencies. The federal executive has considerable (though less after 1988) discretionary power in how it uses public resources. It usually chooses which states, *municípios*, and projects to support on the basis of political criteria, generally using public resources to favor political allies and undermine foes.

Gross inequities in public funding result from the discretionary powers of the president and the ministers in allocating public resources. For example, in 1987, the Ministry of Housing funneled generous resources to governors who supported Sarney while starving the governors who were critical of the president. It directed 274 *cruzados* per inhabitant to the state of Amazonas, seventy-three to Goiás, forty-four to Pará, and ten to Minas Gerais. The governors of all four states supported Sarney. In contrast, the ministry channeled no resources whatsoever to the state of São Paulo, whose governor maintained an ambiguous posture vis-à-vis Sarney, and only 0.6 cruzados per inhabitant to the state of Rio de Janeiro, whose governor was among the most critical of Sarney.[17]

In 1987 the state government of Maranhão received more funds (21.3 percent of the total) from the Ministry of Planning than any other state, notwithstanding its small population. Governor Epitácio Cafeteira (PMDB) was a personal friend of Sarney. In terms of funds transferred directly from the ministry to local governments, Minas Gerais (26.8 percent of the total), the home state of the

Minister of Planning and a state whose governor (Newton Cardoso) avidly supported Sarney's quest for a five-year mandate, and Maranhão (17.8 percent of the total) were the big winners.[18] The states of Alagoas and Pernambuco, whose governors opposed Sarney, received only 0.16 percent and 0.12 percent of the funds transferred to subnational governments from the Ministry of Planning, and the state government of Rio de Janeiro received nothing.[19]

Most of Sarney's ministers by 1987 favored "friendly" governors and punished the president's adversaries, and ministers who did not follow suit came under fire. Federal funds for the states of Rio de Janeiro, Bahia, Pernambuco, and Alagoas dried up because of the governors' refusal to support Sarney unconditionally. These state governments were incapable of making public investments because they had no resources. Projects for which funds had been committed were paralyzed when the money was not forthcoming. Another form of bringing governors into line is pardoning or rolling over debts of their states to the federal government and its agencies and assuming foreign debts of such governments.

Presidents and ministers use their broad discretionary powers to favor some mayors and discriminate against others. In 1987, Sarney's home municipality of Pinheiro, Maranhão, which had a population of 82,432 in 1991 (IBGE 1991b, Vol. 9, 37), received more money from the planning ministry than any other *município* in the state. Through the generous flow of resources, President Sarney strengthened his personal domination of local politics.[20] Conversely, because the mayor of São Luís, the capital of Maranhão, opposed Sarney, the city received only 5 million cruzados in 1987 compared to 773 million cruzados for Belo Horizonte, 230 million of Goiánia, and 184 million for Natal, cities in which the mayors were pro-Sarney.[21]

To retain their political bases and obtain legislative support, governors use patronage. Although governors tap into many networks, mayors and state deputies are among their most important allies. Both can help deliver votes, and governors need to work with state deputies in the legislature. Mayors and state deputies of the catch-all parties rely on resources distributed through state secretaries and heads of state agencies, both of which are appointed by governors. Mayors and state deputies need these resources to deliver goods to their clientele.

Governors wield power over state deputies of the governing parties (Abrúcio 1998). The governor can provide resources for a rival politician whose electoral base is in the same region, enabling this rival to challenge the deputy's electoral support. Also, governors usually have considerable control over the party. Through this control, they can undermine the careers of unfriendly deputies, at least those in their own party or alliance (Abrúcio 1998; Hagopian 1996).

An example of the power of governors over state deputies and mayors occurred in the administration of Governor Paulo Maluf (1979–83) in the state of São Paulo. The MDB won an impressive victory there in 1978, capturing fifty-three seats in the state legislature compared to twenty-six for Arena. Elected indirectly with rules that were designed to ensure that Arena would control the state governorships, Maluf wanted a majority in the state legislature, so he used sticks and carrots to convince MDB representatives to switch parties to Arena/PDS. The (P)MDB representatives who switched to Maluf's party had easy access to state resources, enabling them to deliver goods to their own regions of the state. Those who remained in the opposition had limited access to such resources to show their constituencies. The tactics were successful: the governor induced sixteen MDB legislators to join Arena in a phenomenon known as *adesismo* (literally, adhesionism, i.e., the practice of adhering), thereby securing a majority in the legislature. With twice as many popular votes as the government party, the (P)MDB ended up with a minority in the state legislature. Maluf also got seventy-eight of 101 mayors elected on the MDB ticket in 1976 to switch to Arena.[22] The mayors who remained in the opposition were forced to govern with meager resources.

Presidents and ministers use patronage to build legislative support, to strengthen the positions of friendly federal deputies, and to undermine opponents. In order to gain congressional backing, presidents need the support of deputies. In turn, many federal deputies perceive their primary jobs as obtaining resources for their electoral regions, and they rely on presidents and ministers to get the resources. These deputies depend on their ability to deliver goods to the regions they represent, and they win votes fundamentally on this basis. As Federal Deputy Lúcio Alcántara (PFL-Ceará) observes, "A political career in Brazil is closely connected to success in bringing home material benefits. . . . Especially in the poorest regions, communities judge their deputies on what they bring home."[23] Federal Deputy Amaral Netto (PDS-Rio de Janeiro) asserted that "A deputy is a *despachante de luxo*. His reason for being in Brasília is to bring home resources. Otherwise, he's not doing his job."[24] Federal Deputy Joaquim Haickel (PMDB-Maranhão) expressed the point bluntly: "The primary function of a deputy is getting resources; legislating comes second."[25]

My survey of Congress asked how important obtaining resources for their home regions is to deputies and senators. Of the 107 respondents, 58.4 percent responded that it is quite important, 29.4 percent said it is more or less important, and only 11.2 percent said it is not too important (0.9 percent gave no answer). Politicians of the catch-all parties were more likely to say that obtaining resources was important. These responses probably underestimate overall orientation toward obtaining resources because the press was hostile to this practice, often failing to distinguish between obtaining resources for one's region, on the one hand, and patrimonialism and corruption, on the other. Politicians consequently had incentives to understate the importance of patronage to their own careers.

The dependence of deputies on material resources is especially pronounced in the Northeast, and also for those who win most of their votes in small towns and rural regions. In large cities, more people vote along ideological lines, so more politicians can be successful on the basis of their ideological profiles. Although senators are less dependent on clientele networks, they, too, spend much of their time attempting to obtain resources for their states. Senator Saldanha Derzi (PMDB-MS) said that "Both deputies and senators have an obligation to seek funds to solve the problems of their regions. Those who fail to do so are remiss."[26]

Many deputies see themselves as political brokers who mediate the linkage between the federal government and their local constituencies. Mayors, councillors, community leaders, leaders of social movements, and business leaders depend on deputies to get federal resources. In turn, deputies, especially those who win most of their votes in small and medium-sized towns, depend on the electoral support of mayors, community activists, and local political notables. The deputies of the catch-all parties win this support largely on the basis of their ability to deliver resources to the *município*. In order to get federal resources, they need connections to ministers and heads of federal agencies. If a deputy doesn't support the president, most heads of agencies and ministers see to it that he/she doesn't have access to resources.

Presidents, ministers, and heads of government agencies and firms use the dependence of deputies on obtaining resources to pressure them into supporting the president. Sarney's battles in the constitutional congress to obtain a five-year mandate for himself and to secure a victory for a presidential system of government illustrate the way a president can use state resources to build political support. When the ninety-three-person congressional committee charged with elaborating a draft of the constitution voted in favor of a parliamentary system and a four-year mandate for Sarney, it appeared that the president would lose. But Sarney made it apparent to the governors that they would not obtain federal resources or appointments if they failed to support his quest. The "friendly" governors in turn pressured the federal deputies of their states to support the president. Governor Newton Cardoso (PMDB-Minas Gerais) glibly expressed his confidence that such pressure would succeed: "If you give them (legislators) money and jobs, they will support the government again."[27]

The federal government also directly pressured deputies and senators into voting for a five-year mandate. Sarney made it known that legislators who supported him would be generously rewarded with public posts. Powerful positions such as the president of the Federal Savings Bank, the director of the Agency for the Development of the Northeast, the minister of agrarian reform, the president of the National Institute of Agrarian Colonization and Reform were publicly reserved for appointees of political allies willing to fight for Sarney's five-year mandate.

The government also offered scores of millions of dollars of public works projects to deputies, senators, and governors who supported the president. The ministers distributed resources to legislators who supported Sarney and ignored those who opposed him. Minister of Communications Antônio Carlos Magalhães admitted the government's willingness to grant licenses for TV and radio stations to compliant politicians.[28] Having a TV or radio station is an invaluable asset to politicians because of the media's ability to shape the public agenda, promote certain politicians, and attack political adversaries. Before providing resources, the minister of planning requested that deputies sign a statement endorsing a five-year mandate.[29]

Retaliations against government opponents took place. Sarney's personal spokesperson said that voting against a five-year mandate "will be considered a declaration of war," and that congresspeople who did so would lose their positions in the bureaucracy.[30] Sarney's ministers delivered on this promise, firing high-ranking public officials either because they themselves supported a four-year mandate or because they were appointed by a legislator who did.

Arguing that they deserved more nominations and public resources, politicians who favored a five-year mandate pressured the president into taking further measures against his opposition. Federal Deputy Roberto Cardoso Alves (PMDB-São Paulo), later appointed minister by Sarney, captured the spirit when he stated that "It is by giving that we receive," to suggest that the government grant more nominations in exchange for political support. Cardoso Alves feared that the president would otherwise lose his bid for a five-year mandate. Minister Ronaldo Costa Couto publicly advertised that "If there is an open position, our first choice will be to favor politicians who support the president."[31] In Mato Grosso, deputies who favored a five-year mandate requested that the Sarney administration undermine the governor, their political adversary, who supported a four-year term.[32]

Sarney's campaign proved successful. The president convinced scores of politicians to vote against party leaders; both the PFL and PMDB leaders favored a four-year mandate, and the leadership of the latter preferred a parliamentary system of government. Roberto Cardoso Alves observed that "This surprising victory [of presidentialism] was only possible because through giving one receives." Government supporter Federal Deputy Amaral Netto (PDS-Rio de Janeiro) made a similar observation. "Everything here is an exchange of favors. The day that this Congress votes on the basis of convictions, the roof will fall in [*a cúpula vai cair*]."

Executives in all democratic regimes sometimes seek extraparty support, often on the basis of distributing patronage. In this sense, there may appear to be nothing unusual about the practices the Sarney government undertook. What is uncommon is the extent to which patronage rather than party commitments determines how politicians of the catch-all parties act in Brazil. Many politicians support those in power regardless of their party, in order to facilitate access to patronage.

Yet using patronage and clientele networks to govern is less effective than in the past. With the return to democratic government, several changes have weakened the ability of presidents to govern through patronage and co-optation. Ideological issues are salient in Brazilian politics at the elite level. It may have been possible for the military government to buy off moderate MDB legislators and mayors; it is quite another to buy the PT's support. The 1988 constitution restored the fiscal powers of local and state governments, making mayors and governors less dependent on the federal government. As a result, they are more able to govern effectively despite central-government opposition. Competitive elections are now the major currency in politics, and politicians can win office on the basis of their political positions and personal qualities, especially for executive posts.

Events of the 1980s demonstrated that presidents could no longer assure themselves of building political support through patronage and clientelism. Presidents Sarney and Collor discovered the limits to patronage and clientele networks. Sarney was able to co-opt enough people as long as he could retaliate against political adversaries, but when he became a lame-duck president, his supporters deserted him. Collor was not able to forge enough support to stave off impeachment, and he faced broad opposition in his efforts to undertake sweeping neoliberal reforms (see Chapter 10).

Politicians, Clientelism, and Policy Making

For Brazilian catch-all parties and most of their congressional representatives, being in power means above all making appointments in the bureaucracy. That perception cuts across ideological lines, even though it is stronger among conservative representatives. Federal Deputy Francisco Rossi (PTB-São Paulo) said, "If they win elections, politicians have the right to appoint people [to public positions]. What is power? It is occupying positions. It doesn't make sense to win an election and not occupy the positions."[33] Minister Antônio Carlos Magalhães put it more bluntly: "A government that doesn't fire people and hire people isn't a government."[34]

Most politicians of the catch-all parties perceive power in terms of their own access to state resources rather than policy making (Figueiredo and Limongi 1994; Ames 1995a, 1995b). Politicians make appointments to the bureaucracy, and these bureaucrats have considerable power in decision making. In general, Brazilian politicians do not perceive other ways that parties can or should participate in power. They accept a situation in which parties have little input into policy formulation. Individuals they name to the bureaucracy affect policy making, but the party as a collective entity has minimal involvement.

Because appointing people to the bureaucracy is so important, many politicians take a dim view of executives who eschew allowing the political class to control nominations in the bureaucracy. Governor Franco Montoro's (1983–87) efforts to avoid a clientelistic partitioning of the state apparatus in São Paulo caused friction in the relationship between the government and his own party, the PMDB. Clientelistic PMDB politicians were disgruntled with Montoro for his refusal to promote wholesale change in the bureaucracy, averring that PDS supporters in the bureaucracy would undermine the party's efforts to implement policy. This rhetoric thinly veiled a desire to tap into the patronage opportunities the state government of São Paulo offers.

Some politicians who had opposed the military government argued that after 1985 too many conservatives had remained in the bureaucracy. They argued for even broader use of political criteria for nominations than actually occurred. When asked about the pervasive clientelism in the post–1985 period, Federal Deputy Francisco Pinto (PMDB-Bahia) replied, "You shouldn't confuse clientelism [*fisiologismo*] with occupying political space. The new regime should have gotten rid of more bureaucrats from the dictatorship. The same folks from the dictatorship are still in power. . . . When Lenin made the revolution, he didn't allow the czar's allies to remain in powerful positions. You can only carry out your ideas with people who are compatible with them."[35]

Potentially, having politicians determine who gets selected for bureaucratic positions could strengthen the parties' participation in decision making. However, attempting to "democratize" the bureaucracy by making extensive nominations based primarily on political criteria entails risks to the functioning of the state apparatus. Moreover, in Brazil most nominations are made by individual politicians rather than through the party leadership. In the 1980s, the individual character of the nominations resulted in balkanization and private appropriation of the state apparatus rather than strengthening parties' function in decision making. Democratic control of the bureaucracy was limited because the nominations have not been effected via institutional channels (i.e., the parties and Congress), but rather principally through individual politicians.

Even within the context of a world situation in which party government is in decline, Brazilian catch-all parties exercise little influence in the decision-making process. Politicians seek ministers and their staff not to discuss policy, but to find resources for their regions. Pérsio Arida, who occupied high-level economic-policy-making positions in the Sarney and Cardoso governments, said that not once did politicians seek him to discuss programmatic issues. "The party [the PMDB] did not involve itself in the formulation of economic policies. . . . Politicians *did* come to me with clientelistic requests. They wanted something for their region. All the time. The governors wanted to roll over the debts of their states. No politicians came to discuss macroeconomic policy, except to benefit themselves."[36]

In interviews, policy makers reported that politicians were not interested in discussing policy even when their party was in government. The reverse is also true: policy makers do not involve the parties in decision making. PMDB economists were responsible for the Cruzado Plan, a stabilization plan initiated on February 28, 1986. The plan was drawn up in an aura of absolute secrecy lest news of it provoke speculation and capital flight. The PMDB itself was not informed of the plan until President Sarney announced it on national television. When it drew overwhelming positive popular response, the PMDB announced its support and successfully capitalized on the plan in the November 1986 elections. But the party itself was never involved in discussing or supporting it. Until the implementation of the Real Plan in 1994, this pattern was followed consistently.

Politicians openly acknowledge that most of their colleagues are not interested in policy. Asked about the role of state deputies in policy making, for example, State Deputy Luis Máximo (PMDB-SP) affirmed that "Only a few of us try to influence institutional political problems. Most are focused more on local politics. The practice of discussing politics has been abandoned within the PMDB."[37] In a similar vein, ex-Finance Minister Delfim Netto (then a Federal Deputy, PDS-São Paulo) said in an interview that most representatives were neither interested in nor knowledgeable about policy issues.[38]

The limited policy interest of the catch-all parties is also manifest in the lack of attention to party programs. Even from a minimalist perspective, the disregard of Brazilian parties for party programs is notable. None of the main catch-all parties issued programs for the constitutional assembly, precisely the kind of event that usually occasions programs and internal programmatic debates.

The Expansion of Patronage and Clientelism in the 1980s

In Brazil, clientelism and patronage have not been unique to authoritarian or democratic governments. However, the reliance of government leaders on patronage and clientelism expanded after 1979. To develop this point, it is useful to begin with some observations on the use of patronage between 1964 and 1979.

The military government officially abjured clientelism, perceiving it as an integral part of the corrupt populist politics of the past. Most high-ranking leaders of the military government were convinced that clientelism and patronage were deleterious, and they were committed to principles of efficiency. Decision making was more closed and technocratic than had been the case during the populist period. The ministries and agencies that were perceived as economically crucial, including the major public enterprises and the economic ministries, were insulated from clientelistic pressures. The major public enterprises enjoyed considerable autonomy from clientelistic pressures. Many public firms were run almost like private corporations (L. Martins 1985; Trebat 1983).

However, clientelism did not face a sudden death (Cammack 1982; Hagopian 1996; Medeiros 1983; Sarles 1982; Weyland 1996a). At the state and local levels, the distribution of public resources according to political criteria was the norm. Such criteria also remained important in making nominations for all but the highest positions in the bureaucracy. At the federal level, the government essentially divided the public sector into two domains: more technocratic and more patronage-oriented.[39] In many state agencies, clientelism and patronage were admissible, and politicians retained power throughout the entire military period. Positions in this domain of the state were open game for clientelistic politics, generally to favor Arena. The government bolstered Arena's electoral performance by providing politicians with generous access to patronage.

Nevertheless, the government generally reduced politicians' influence in decision making, and at the national level bureaucratic politics displaced party politics (F. H. Cardoso 1975a; Leff 1968: 109–31; Medeiros 1983; Hagopian 1996). To a greater extent than in the democratic governments that preceded and followed the military regime, technocrats controlled public enterprises and the ministries. This dominance of technocrats can be seen in recruitment patterns for ministerial positions, which are important in policy formulation and implementation. Data were tabulated only for the civil ministries, i.e., the military ministries were excluded: minister of the army (but not military officers or ex-officers serving as civil ministers, e.g., minister of housing). Under military rule fewer politicians and more technocrats became ministers. Between 1964 and 1985, nonpolitical ministers outnumbered political ministers by a three-to-one margin (sixty-seven to twenty-three). Conversely, in the periods before and after the military government, politicians outnumbered other cabinet nominations by almost a two and one-half-to-one margin (eighty-eight to thirty-nine, with no data on five ministers for 1946–64 and twenty-nine to twelve for 1985–88).[40]

In interviews, ex-cabinet members of the military government, high-ranking bureaucrats, politicians who supported the military government, and opposition politicians agreed that the domain of clientelism was reduced, and that politicians and parties had limited influence over high-level appointments in public administration between 1968 and 1979. Jutahy Magalhães, who was a state deputy, federal deputy, vice governor, and senator under the military government (Arena-PDS-PMDB-Bahia) observed that politicians didn't have much say about high-level appointments during the military government. "Nominations were almost personal, restricted to a small group of leaders of the government. The president, the governors, and the ministers appointed people [to leadership and intermediate positions in state agencies and enterprises]. The parties were not consulted, were not listened to, perhaps with the exception of the Castello Branco period."[41]

Even though clientelism at the federal level receded between 1964 and 1979, paradoxically the military promoted three changes during this same period that laid the basis for an expansion of clientelism during the 1980s. First, the public sector expanded a great deal between 1964 and 1979, thereby augmenting the pool of state jobs and resources that could potentially be used for building clienteles (Trebat 1983; Baer 1989; Evans 1979). Perhaps even more important was the state's augmented regulatory powers. State agencies acquired greater control over a wide array of prices (rents, many food prices, salary increases, many industrial goods, etc.), and a panoply of state agencies subsidized investment, production, and exports. Through various incentives, restrictions, and controls, the state intervened in most markets. Some scholars (e.g. Baer 1989) referred to the Brazilian model as state capitalism.

Second, notwithstanding the increasing professionalization of many parts of the bureaucracy under military rule, some measures undermined bureaucratic institutionalization and ultimately contributed to the expansion of clientelism after 1979. The military government was committed to restructuring the federal bureaucracy to enhance its efficacy. Its major effort at administrative reform was Decree Law 200 of 1967. Intended to grant greater flexibility to the bureaucracy and to reduce red tape, this measure enabled public firms, autarchies, and ministries to hire people outside the ranks of the bureaucracy at higher salaries than would have been permitted otherwise. The idea was to attract outstanding administrators and executives to public enterprises and other parts of the bureaucracy. One of the side effects, however, was the bypassing of bureaucratic criteria for hiring and promotions. In this fashion, Decree Law 200 opened the doors for political criteria in hiring, promoting, and paying personnel. Public examinations became less frequent as a means of entering public administration and public enterprises.

Amendments to the Consolidated Labor Laws (CLT) in the first three years of military rule also facilitated hiring without a civil-service examination. The amended labor laws recognized two ways of entry into the public administration: via examination, in which case the individual was guaranteed job stability, or for short contracts for a specified time, in which case an examination was not required. This latter category, while intended to give greater flexibility to the bureaucracy, gave rise to political criteria in hiring practices because candidates did not take an examination in order to be hired. Often people were hired on this temporary basis but later granted permanent job stability on the basis of a decree. In a similar vein, Constitutional Amendment No. 1, decreed by the military government at the apogee of state repression in 1969, allowed the president to create public positions via decree laws.

The military government thus simultaneously increased the flexibility of public administration and the possibility of using political criteria in personnel practices. There was an erosion of bureaucratic criteria for hiring and promotions within the public sector, but an offsetting concern with efficiency and technical criteria. From 1964 until the late 1970s, the technocratic character of decision making partially compensated for the deinstitutionalization of personnel practices.

Decentralization within some spheres of the state sector, especially public enterprises, was intended to ensure that heads of state agencies and enterprises could manage without political pressures (Martins 1985; Trebat 1983). This move strengthened bureaucratic insulation in the short term, but one side effect was that public accounts became less transparent. Within the executive branch the budget was decentralized, and there was no unified detailed record of government expenditures. The ministries had significant autonomy, and there were few controls over their spending. This made it difficult for Congress or other bodies to oversee government spending. Public resources were centralized at the federal level, but the accounting of them was not. This lack of transparency gave rise to corruption and fostered the use of public resources to obtain political influence.

In one respect, the absence of open political competition and choice under military rule favored political manipulation of public resources (Diniz 1982; Hagopian 1996). Because the military controlled the federal government and overwhelmingly favored its supporters in the distribution of resources, there was an incentive to vote for politicians well connected to the regime. This was especially true in the poor regions of the country, which depend more heavily on government resources. If they had voted for the opposition, local communi-

ties would have lost their ability to extract resources from the federal government without effecting any policy change whatsoever, given the fact that alter-
nation in power was not a possibility.

Moreover, because of the emasculation of legislative authority from 1964 until
1988, politicians had incentives to focus primarily on serving clients and neglect
policy matters. The legislature was insignificant in policy making, so Arena/PDS
politicians had no incentive to dedicate themselves principally to policy considerations. Because the bureaucracy rather than the legislature generally made the
most important decisions, politicians perceived that the appointments they
made in the bureaucracy had more impact on government than did policy
debates.

Around 1979, with the transition from the Geisel to the Figueiredo administration, party competition became more important, the era of the technocrats
came to an end, and a new period of ascendancy of politicians began (Abrúcio
1998). With the extinction of Institutional Act V, the gradual restoration of some
legislative powers, and the end of the artificially imposed biparty system, the
government lost several mechanisms of political control, so it needed to win the
support of citizens and politicians. Consequently, the Figueiredo administration
made more concessions to political criteria, and politicians assumed increasing
power. With these changes, the doors to more extensive reliance on public
resources opened. Patronage became the government's way to win votes and
build support in a more competitive environment. The government's reliance
on patronage and clientelism was reflected in changes in the composition of
cabinets, as noted above, and a variety of other indicators, including growing
empreguismo.

The 1982 gubernatorial elections were a key moment in the acceleration of
clientelistic pressures (Abrúcio 1998; Andrade 1985; Castro 1987; Medeiros 1985).
The federal government was anxious to win the elections for state governors,
and it relied on patronage to secure votes. State governors and local officials were
even more willing to resort to *empreguismo* to facilitate their political futures.
Many governors resigned in May–June 1982 so as to be eligible to run in the
November elections. Before resigning, they packed the state bureaucracy with
political allies. Governor João Castelo of Maranhão, for example, increased the
state bureaucracy from 26,000 to 52,000 in only three and one-half years in
office.[42] According to the estimate of the minister of public administration, in
1982 alone the governors added 500,000 people to the states' public payrolls.[43]
State governors had more autonomy vis-à-vis the federal government, and they
freely hired public servants to bolster their own political situation.

PDS politicians expanded their clientele networks by putting more people on
public payrolls after 1979. Between 1979 and 1985, employment in public admini-

stration increased over 40 percent, from 3,133,000 people or 16.1 percent of the full-time formal sector labor force, to 4,395,000 people or 21.4 percent of the force. Most of this increase came at the state and municipal levels; the federal public administration grew only marginally (Ministério do Trabalho 1987).

Another wave of *empreguismo* occurred in 1985, when in response to the military government's defeat, high-ranking federal officials took advantage of a final opportunity to pack the bureaucracy with allies. Later that year, the municipal elections again occasioned more *empreguismo* as incumbents hired people on state payrolls to expand their clientele networks. In one extreme case, in São Luís do Maranhão, the outgoing administration hired 14,500 people illegally in its last months in office, leading to a situation in which the payroll alone was more than three times the city's revenue. In the second semester of 1985, the number of city employees in São Luís quadrupled.[44]

Particularly in the poor states, which from 1982 until 1984 were generally still dominated by the PDS, political criteria became more important in determining public hiring. The expansion of public employment was more acute in the backward regions, reflecting the greater preponderance of patronage politics. In the relatively wealthy Southeast and South, employment in public administration increased 25.6 percent between 1979 and 1985. In the North, public employment increased by 80.9 percent in six years; in the Northeast, by 64.0 percent during that same period. By 1985, in the North, Northeast, and Center-West regions of the country, more than 35 percent of the labor force in the formal sector was employed in public administration, a figure about twice as high as in the South and Southeast (Ministério do Trabalho 1987).

In the four-year period from January 1982 to December 1985, the economy generated 1.9 million new jobs, of which 59.3 percent were in public administration. As a government document with an apposite title—"The Tragedy of Employment in Direct Public Administration"—observed, "The extraordinary expansion of employment in public administration in the northeast, especially in the *municípios*, is the most transparent evidence of the use of the state machinery for *empreguismo*, for strictly political-electoral purposes."[45] There was an inverse correlation between the size of the public sector and quality of public services, suggesting that *empreguismo* was politically motivated.[46]

Reliance on *empreguismo* to build political support remained rampant after 1985. Despite frequent promises of fighting the fiscal deficit, cutting jobs in the bureaucracy, banning all new public hiring, and undertaking administrative reform, during the Sarney government political manipulation of the bureaucracy was acute. The President of the National Accounting Court estimated that 100,000 new jobs in federal public administration were created between March 1985 and August 1987. "This is an outrage," he decried. "The bureaucracy was already bloated."[47] Between January 1985 and January 1988, personnel expenditures for employees of the direct public administration increased a staggering 90 percent in real terms.[48] Between January 1987 and January 1988, the percentage of government revenue consumed by salaries and wages of public employees increased from 37 percent to 61 percent.[49] In several states of the Northeast, salaries and wages of public employees accounted for over 100 percent of government revenue by the late 1980s, leaving state governments bereft of resources for public investments. As proof of Congress's clientelistic proclivities, personnel costs for people on the congressional payroll nearly tripled in real terms between 1980 and 1988.[50]

Empreguismo was not the only manifestation of growing clientelism. In many state agencies, the influence of politicians increased, and public expenditures became more oriented toward clientelistic purposes. Politicians assumed greater control over nominations for bureaucratic posts than they had between 1968 and 1979.

The question of how to manage the bureaucracy under democratic government in a clientelistic polity was complex. If democratically elected state leaders are to implement policies of their choice and be responsive to the electorate, state agencies must act in consort with their policies. This problem was especially acute in Brazil because of the expansion of the state and the longevity of authoritarian rule. As a result, bureaucrats chosen by the military were in leadership positions in most state agencies. The question, therefore, was how to establish a bureaucracy responsive to democratically elected leaders when the bureaucrats were often sympathetic to the military government.

In the early years of the New Republic, most political leaders faced this issue by turning the bureaucracy into a spoils system. Individual politicians appropriated the right to name people to various state posts. Frequently they gave little attention to merit and efficiency, with deleterious results in terms of the state apparatus.

Between 1985 and 1992, the concern with efficiency and technical criteria diminished within the state. Political influence became the decisive criterion in personnel decisions in most parts of the state. The domain for technocrats diminished while that of politicians expanded. Many ministries and state banks, agencies, and public enterprises became tools for furthering the designs of clientelistic politicians who make their career dispensing state favors. Under Sarney, the Ministry of Planning, which had been entrusted with long-range planning and economic policy during the military period, became notorious for arrant clientelism and corruption (Dimenstein 1988). Also notorious for their declining standards of efficiency during the Sarney government were the ministries of finance and education.

For posts such as the local Funrural agent, police commissioners, local INAMPS directors, school directors, and directors of clinics and hospitals, in most states the federal deputy who had voted for Tancredo Neves and who had the most votes in a *município* made the appointment. (In 1988, the rule changed: the deputy who supported Sarney in the constitutional congress who had the most votes in a *município* made the appointment.) In a few states, politicians had lotteries to determine who would make what appointments.

Widespread nepotism accompanied this political use of the state, and it contributed to the demoralization of democratic practice. In one notorious case, Governor João Durval (PDS-Bahia, 1982–86) appointed literally dozens of relatives to state posts—including his three sons and one son-in-law as directors of large state enterprises, his wife, and two sisters-in-law.[51]

To mollify the various forces that had supported him, Tancredo Neves guaranteed each party and state a certain number and level of positions according to their political weight in electing him. He partitioned the state apparatus according to political criteria, and Sarney continued this practice. This arrangement encouraged a partition of the state apparatus based on political affiliation, beginning a period of more visible balkanization of the state.

Most politicians and bureaucrats agree that the general tendency during the 1980s was toward greater use of state patronage and less concern with meritocracy and efficiency than had been the case under military rule. Senator Luis Vianna (PMDB-Bahia) said that in his six decades of public life in Brazil, he never saw *empreguismo* like that of the Sarney period. "It is shocking. In the past *empreguismo* was more discreet. It wasn't so open. Whatever was done occurred with a certain reserve [*pudor*]. Public opinion did not accept flagrant clientelism and corruption. What is happening today is an effrontery [*desfaçatez*]. There is also a difference in magnitude. I have never seen so much clientelism."[52]

As a figure identified with the military government, Viana's opinion could be considered suspect. But many critics of the military government agreed. José Richa, ex-PMDB governor and ex-MDB/PMDB/PSDB senator of Paraná, said that *empreguismo* during the Sarney period "is much worse than it was under Figueiredo. The military government did not make administrative decisions based on political criteria. Politicians did not determine who got jobs. The government knew how to delegate administrative decisions and it delegated responsibility to the technocrats. The criterion of efficiency was important. Today, everything depends on political favors."[53]

Political use of the state is particularly widespread in the bureaucracy (as opposed to public enterprise) and in the underdeveloped regions of Brazil. In the Northeast and North, politicians, the state, and the dominant classes have constructed a political system that perpetuates pernicious cycles. Because of dismal poverty, people are dependent on the state. They vote for politicians who provide them with meager but welcome favors, ranging from tickets for free milk to jobs in the state bureaucracy. The misuse of public funds undermined the state's capacity for investment, contributing to maintaining the region in poverty.

Although the general tendency in the 1980s was toward more political use of the state and less concern with Weberian bureaucratic rationality, a few caveats are in order. The contemporary Brazilian state has hundreds of agencies. Some of them avoided the erosion of meritocracy. For example, a succession of Ministers of Welfare (Waldir Pires, Rafael de Almeida Magalhães, Renato Archer) attempted (though with limited success) to attack the clientelism that had undermined that ministry. All three undertook to modernize the ministry and to replace political criteria with efficiency and proceduralism (Weyland 1996a).

Some of the largest public enterprises and banks were also protected from clientelistic pressures. At Petrobrás, as of 1986, all but about 500 of 60,000 employees had joined the firm through a civil-service exam.[54] These companies were often weakened in the 1980s not because of clientelism, but rather because of questionable macroeconomic policies, efforts to suppress public-sector price increases in order to contain inflation, and policies regarding control of state enterprises (Kandir 1991).

In Brazil the growing influence of politicians coincided with greater political use of public resources and less concern with meritocracy and efficiency, but this is by no means a general tendency. The transfer from technocrats to politicians does not necessarily mean a decrease in efficiency, even though it did so in Brazil in the 1980s.

Costs of Contemporary Clientelism

Clientelism and patrimonialism have higher costs today than they did in the past. I will address four problems caused in part by extensive political use of the state in Brazilian politics: limited democratic legitimacy, limited representation of the poor majority, faltering public-sector performance, and low efficacy of social programs.[55]

CLIENTELISM, PATRIMONIALISM, AND LEGITIMACY

Linz's (1978: 18) definition of legitimacy is useful: "A legitimate government is considered to be the least evil of the forms of government. Ultimately, democratic legitimacy is based on the belief that for that particular country at that particular historical juncture no other type of regime could assure a more successful pursuit of collective goals" (see also Weber 1978: 31–38; 212–16).

Legitimacy, then, is expressed by supportive attitudes. Chapter 4, drawing on survey information, showed a lack of supportive attitudes for parties, politicians, and democracy. The difficulty parties have had in retaining support from one election to the next underscores the low level of legitimacy that they enjoy. They are seen as corrupt, self-serving, and uninterested in addressing the nation's problems. Political manipulation of the state and at times outright venality are partly responsible for this problem.

In clientelistic polities, most citizens do not believe in parties on the basis of conviction, but rather adhere to them for instrumental reasons, often for immediate material gain. But support on the basis of material favors is not legitimacy. Democratic legitimacy is created on the basis of perceptions that government responds to citizens' desires, that democracy is ultimately government of the people.

Legitimate governments must attempt to further *some* public good—a *res publica*. The nature of what constitutes the public good is contested in all democracies, but in legitimate democracies most citizens believe that government makes a serious effort to further some vision of the public good. In political systems based on private exchanges and appropriations of public goods, such a belief is likely to be fragile. Politicians and parties use public resources not for the public good, but for their own benefit.

Etymologically, republic means the public thing, but in clientelistic polities, those who rule privately appropriate what should be public. Under these conditions, true republican government is impossible, for the "public thing" is limited. By extension, legitimacy is limited, for citizens cannot be long deceived into believing that government is making an effort to further public goals. A republic of *padrinhos* is impossible,[56] for the public thing cannot belong to *padrinhos*, whose very being implies the negation of the kind of universalistic procedural norms that a republic implies.

Patronage can win votes, and trading favors can win political support, but clientelism does not create legitimacy (Graziano 1978). To the contrary, in Brazil widespread political use of the state discredited parties, politicians, and democracy. It contributed to cynicism and depoliticization among the population: why participate in politics when it is a private, corrupt exchange of goods and favors? Because legitimacy is limited, democratic government stands on weak foundations. Legitimacy has seemingly depended most on economic performance—a situation fraught with problems in a period of economic revamping.

CLIENTELISM AND POPULAR INTERESTS

A second liability of clientelistic political systems is their predominantly elitist character. Clientelistic parties have a conservative and status quo bias (Cammack 1982; Diniz 1982; Flynn 1974; Hagopian 1996; Scott 1969). Brazil's clientelistic parties are not conservative in the sense of the British Conservative Party or the Republican Party in the United States because they lack a clearly articulated ideology and program, and they do not have organic linkages to organized business interests. But they are conservative in the sense that they favor elite interests.

Brazil's clientelistic parties represent above all politicians' interests and privileged actors in society. Those who hold power may make concessions to co-opt or incorporate new actors, but the logic of parties of the state has been to conserve power by using the state in a patrimonial fashion (Faoro 1975). Politicians use state resources to enhance their own power: to obtain positions in the state apparatus or radio stations, to build political support by rewarding friends and punishing foes, to use the state illicitly for private material gain. Those in power use patronage to win control of their parties, then use the parties as vehicles by which to get elected. Many politicians appropriate power for its own sake or for its sinecures.

Typically, clientelistic politicians and their staffs spend considerable time running favors for poor people. But this individualistic and clientelistic representation of interests is the antithesis of broad entitlement programs that effectively address the needs of the poor. Clientelism can integrate the poor into politics, but it does so in a way that reinforces dependency rather than empowers. State resources are used for private or political benefit rather than for programs that ameliorate poverty or create new opportunities for the disenfranchised. The system dampens issues of broad-based class entitlement. Politicians run favors and obtain resources for narrow categories more than broad groups or classes. Where representation is individualistic, party programs and class issues are undermined to the detriment of the popular sectors.

Interest representation in Brazil has been fragmented and particularistic (Weyland 1996a). Clientelistic favors may resolve the problems of narrow groups, but they do not lead to mass entitlement programs (Leff 1968: 118–31). Clientelism offers benefits to individuals and particularistic groups at the expense of collective projects and programs. Such an individualistic distribution of benefits favors elites, who can more easily gain access to the cabinets of top state administrators and of deputies and senators. Politicians often depend on the financial support of wealthy elites, and in return they promote policies and pursue favors that protect those elites. For the disenfranchised, clientelistic representation is inadequate. Whereas wealthy elites often win big favors, the poor are generally limited to small ones. A politician may obtain a sewer or running water for a neighborhood, but does not fight to obtain a sewer system that will serve the popular classes in a broader fashion. In political terms, a politician may benefit less from successfully fighting for entitlement programs (for which he/she might not get personal credit) than for winning benefits for a specific clientele.

The clientelistic, patrimonial elements of the Brazilian political system do not make it impossible to address social inequalities and poverty. But they load the dice in favor of elite interests.

FALTERING PUBLIC-SECTOR PERFORMANCE

A third problem of widespread clientelism between 1979 and 1994 was its negative impact on the public sector. During this period, political considerations rather than universalistic procedures or criteria were often dominant for making a wide range of supposedly public decisions: who was hired and promoted in public administration, who got public contracts and concessions, etc. This is the antithesis of a meritocratic selection process, by which the most efficient and capable producer, supplier, or person prevails.

Clientelism is often an irrational way to allocate (supposedly) public re- sources. Where political loyalty is the dominant criterion for making decisions regarding the allocation of resources and the appointment of high-level public servants, rationality that emphasizes efficiency and meritocracy is undermined. Rather than award a contract to firm X in a competitive bid for $10 million, government officials give the contract to firm Y for $15 million by imposing regulations that only firm Y can meet. Rather than allow a private company to go bankrupt when it hemorrhages money, the government grants it a $250 million interest-free loan, thereby benefiting the owners. Rather than hire a qualified career administrator to head a public enterprise, the president appoints someone to mollify a governor to whom he owes a political debt. Each specific case of using patronage to build political support may not have an exorbitant cost, but the overall effect is an incentive system that favors political considera- tions and personal contacts. Efficiency, quality, and merit are often secondary considerations. Such an incentive system is not conducive to economic prosper- ity or to Weberian bureaucratic rationality (Graziano 1973; Soto 1989; Medard 1982; Tarrow 1977: 197–202; Scott 1972).

In Brazil, *empreguismo*, nepotism, and clientelism had corrosive effects on the public bureaucracy in the 1980s and early 1990s. Frequently political allies landed high-paying jobs for which the employee didn't even bother to show up for work. Instead of toiling for the public sector, they sometimes worked directly for the politician who had secured their position. Sometimes they were granted multiple supposedly full-time positions; the Ministry of Planning in 1989 dis- covered 120,000 cases of illegal double employment in the federal government alone.[57] Political appointees often see their first loyalty to the politician respon- sible for their posts rather than to public service. This is not surprising; they got their jobs through a connection rather than through a career in public service.

If their *padrinho* fails to get reelected, they may lose their job, and their *padrinho* probably expects them to help out in campaigns. A bureaucracy devoted to politics rather than public service does not encourage putting such service above private interests. As ex-minister Rafael de Almeida Magalhães observed, "Bureaucrats are loyal to whomever appointed them, not to public service, and they fail to serve the public as they should."[58]

In the 1980s, accompanying this private appropriation of the state apparatus was the demoralization of the technocrats who had worked to construct an efficient state. Nilson Holanda, who has occupied numerous high-level positions in the state bureaucracy, criticized the widespread use of the state apparatus for private and political gain in the 1980s. "The process that we were structuring since 1946 is being destroyed today. Today is a moment of revenge [*revanchismo*]. . . . The politicians who are in power were very hungry. They will gradually see that they went too far [in appropriating the state apparatus and ignoring criteria of efficiency]. Those who defend the public interest in today's Brazil are isolated. Few people are worried about the public interest. Those who concern themselves with the public interest are punished because they disturb the system of interests."[59]

Clientelism, patrimonialism, and corruption also contributed to macroeconomic problems in the 1980s, including public-sector deficits and, by extension, inflation. Rampant *empreguismo* was a factor in the public-sector deficits in the 1980s. President Sarney often undermined his finance ministers' plans for fiscal austerity because such plans would have limited the bases for clientelism. The president and his entourage saw to it that loans of hundreds of millions of dollars were approved for their friends and that, despite rhetoric to the contrary, *empreguismo* was cultivated. In order to grease the wheels of the clientelistic machine, Sarney and his ministers kept open some state agencies and approved some programs despite the vehement opposition of Finance Minister Luis Carlos Bresser Pereira. Bresser Pereira had argued for closing notoriously clientelistic agencies such as the National Department of Works Against Drought (DNOCS) and the National Institute of Food and Nutrition, but other ministers convinced Sarney to maintain these agencies, even at the expense of exacerbating the public deficit, the inflation rate, and ultimately, the parlous state of the economy. Bresser Pereira resigned in December 1987 because Sarney was willing to undermine economic policy in order to obtain a fifth year as president. Bresser Pereira's replacement, Mailson da Nóbrega, also complained that Sarney's willingness to spend from the public coffers for clientelistic purposes undermined the economy.[60] Collor's stabilization plan ran into difficulties because of the opposition of clientelistic politicians. Despite Cardoso's commitment to universalistic procedures, he frequently resorted to clientelism to win support for policy initiatives.

The favors that poor people win from the state cost little in financial terms, but the favors that the rich extract are costly, occasionally involving hundreds of millions of dollars at a single blow. The dealings of business executives with the state amount to dozens of billions of dollars per year. The practice of awarding public contracts on the basis of political contacts rather than competitive bidding is particularly pernicious. These practices exacerbated bureaucratic inefficiency in the 1980s.

Public-sector inefficiency results from private appropriation of public administration. In an economy where the public sector is so important, the subversion of criteria of meritocracy had significant consequences. In the 1980s, public administration increasingly became the tool of politicians for their own benefit and for the benefit of their wealthy financiers. The combination that characterized Brazil in the 1980s—a large, interventionist state whose concern with efficiency and meritocracy had eroded—was problematic. The problem is not simply the interventionist character and the size of the state, as state bashers might suggest. Throughout much of Europe, the state plays a leading role in investment, and public enterprises are central forces in the economy. But in Western Europe, the bureaucracy is closer to Weber's ideal bureaucracy than it is in Brazil, and a good deal farther from Weber's ideal type of a patrimonial state, in which the state is appropriated for personal gain.

Conversely, the problem was not one of a primitive private appropriation of an underdeveloped state. The Brazilian state had massive resources, so the patrimonial appropriation of the state had broader consequences than it would have in a society in which the state is smaller. The combination of an interventionist state characterized by pervasive clientelism distinguished Brazil in the 1980s.

In part because of rampant clientelism, the Brazilian state became a morass in the 1980s. It was centralized in that before 1988 state and local governments lacked the resources to govern effectively without federal support. It was simultaneously balkanized in that the capacity for coordinated central action that would move the bureaucracy in a more or less harmonious way to pursue some stipulated objectives had eroded. The multiplication of state agencies created competing and overlapping competencies, but such that many agencies did not manage well what they were supposed to. Because of the erosion of meritocracy, bureaucratic efficiency eroded.

From the 1930s until 1980, the state was a fundamental pillar of Brazilian development. It lost its dynamic character in the 1980s. The use of the state for personal and partisan benefit contributed to this deterioration.

The case in Latin America that most approximates the Brazilian is probably Mexico's. There, state leaders have used the state as a means of ensuring the long-term hegemony of the PRI. There are parallels in the way in which state leaders use the state to promote the political ends of the party in power, and there were also parallels in the economic problems caused by neopatrimonialism in the 1980s.

By the end of the 1980s, the crisis of the public sector in Brazil had grown so acute that in their discourse, most major actors agreed that something needed to be done to restore its efficiency. However, Collor had difficulty assembling a coalition to push through state reform and shrinking. The leftist parties were committed (at least in discourse) to greater probity in the use of public resources, but they opposed state shrinking. The catch-all parties have historically lived off state patronage, so their disposition to support measures that would reduce such patronage was equivocal. The Collor administration faced a Catch-22: in order to win congressional support, it needed to dispense patronage to congressional representatives. Such patronage, of course, partially undermined state reform.

CLIENTELISM AND SOCIAL POLICY

A final problem of clientelism is its deleterious effect on social programs for the poor. Programs intended to provide goods and opportunities for the poor end up being appropriated for private or partisan gain (World Bank 1988). As a World Bank report (1986: 22, 23) on primary education in Brazil noted, "Important decisions are largely made on political grounds. ... Important policy decisions regarding educational finance and resource allocation are not typically made by careful, objective analyses of the issues."

Widespread clientelism leads to misuse of public funds with resultant inefficiency in social programs. In northeastern Brazil, the public school system was a shambles in the 1980s. Getting a job as a teacher depended on political loyalty, and there was little effort to ensure professionalism among the teachers who were hired through *padrinhos*. In the state of Bahia, with an illiteracy rate of almost 50 percent, an estimated 37,000 teachers who were on the public payrolls as of early 1987 had never taught a single class. Money targeted for education was spent to pay *cabos eleitorais*. According to one report, clientelism was so widespread that when PMDB Governor Waldir Pires took over the state leadership in March 1987, there was not a single teacher in Bahian *municípios* with under 50,000 inhabitants who supported the PMDB.[61]

Further exacerbating the inefficiency of social programs is widespread corruption. For example, in exchange for votes and participation in party conventions, Funrural agents grant people public benefits to which they are not entitled. In early 1988, Minister of Social Welfare Renato Archer indicated that as many as one-third of the ministry beneficiaries were fraudulent.[62]

Such misallocation caused by clientelism and corruption explains why inefficiency prevails in Brazil's social programs despite substantial expenditures. In the 1980s, federal social expenditures alone accounted for as much as 10 percent of GDP (Faria and Castro 1990: 126). According to a World Bank (1988) estimate, in 1986, federal, state, and *município* social expenditures amounted to 18 percent of GDP, a hefty figure. The successes of social policy have been limited by pervasive clientelism and misallocation for political reasons (Faria and Castro 1990; Melo 1993; Weyland 1996a; World Bank 1986, 1988).

New Challenges to Political Uses of the State

Since 1988, political use of the state has been challenged on three grounds. The first challenge has come from presidents, ministers, governors, and mayors determined to run a more efficient and honest government. Although it is difficult to measure such phenomena rigorously, the Sarney administration represented the zenith of political use of the state apparatus. Beginning with Collor—and notwithstanding his own downfall as a result of corruption—some efforts to contain political use of the state have transpired.

Collor came to power with an anticlientelist, antistatist, and anticorruption discourse. He initially tried to avoid clientelistic pressures by naming a largely nonpartisan cabinet, by sidestepping Congress, and by governing by decree. His efforts to contain the political use of the state proved short-lived. His steamrolling of Congress stirred a backlash, and by early 1991 things had returned to politics as usual; Collor resorted to building congressional alliances through patronage. When his presidency was seriously threatened in 1992, he relied heavily on patronage, distributing resources in an ultimately vain effort to avoid impeachment.

The Franco and Cardoso governments earned reputations for probity. Nevertheless, both men regularly resorted to patronage politics in order to gain congressional and gubernatorial support. They reverted to a traditional Brazilian pattern of competence in peak-level state positions but clientelism to gain political support.

A second challenge to political manipulation of the state has come from the end to impunity. In December 1992, Collor resigned in order to avoid impeachment hearings in the Senate. The Chamber of Deputies had voted overwhelmingly (441 to 38) on September 29 that there was enough evidence to remove Collor temporarily from office and proceed with the hearings. Despite Collor's resignation, the Senate still went ahead and on December 29–30 voted by a seventy-six to five margin to remove the president.

A highly publicized denunciation by Collor's brother in May 1992 triggered the events that led up to the impeachment. Pedro Collor de Mello claimed that the president had collected illegal campaign contributions. More significantly, he claimed that the president's campaign manager, Paulo César Farias, had extorted millions of dollars from firms and individuals to finance campaigns of Collor allies and to subsidize the president's lavish lifestyle. Excellent investigative reporting by the Brazilian press pushed Congress to open an inquiry, and the committee reported in August that Collor was indeed culpable.

This is not the place for a detailed treatment of the saga that culminated in Collor's impeachment, nor of the factors that led up to it (see Weyland 1993; Geddes and Ribeiro Neto 1992; Brooke 1992). Collor's impeachment was a dramatic event in many respects, not the least of which was that it signaled an end to the sense of virtually absolute impunity that had been present since 1985.

In October 1993, a new megascandal surfaced, this one involving Congress. José Carlos Alves dos Santos, ex-Director of the Federal Budget Office (the Departamento de Orçamento da União, roughly the equivalent of the Office of Management and Budget), confessed that he had participated in a scam in which he implicated nineteen federal legislators, three governors, and a few ministers. After the implementation of the 1988 constitution, the congressional Budget Committee improperly allowed legislators to send public funds to phantom social agencies, often controlled by the very legislators who made the requests. In exchange for bribes, Santos facilitated approval of these venal transactions. In the ensuing months, a congressional committee investigated these denunciations. Seventeen deputies and one senator were subjected to congressional hearings. Four resigned before the hearings, and five, including an ex-president of the Chamber of Deputies (Ibsen Pinheiro), were stripped of their mandates.

Events since 1992–93 suggest that the end to impunity and the inauguration of two more honest presidents has ushered in a less corrupt period of Brazilian politics. The aura of corruption that surrounded the Sarney and Collor administrations faded during the Franco and Cardoso governments.

Still, one should be cautious in predicting a sea change in Brazilian politics on the basis of these events. Except for Paulo César Farias, all leading figures in the scandals of 1992–93, including Collor himself, got off without spending a single day in prison. Collor continued to jet around the world, living high on the hog. This outcome frustrated millions of Brazilians, reinforcing rather than undermining the sense that the most powerful get off scot-free.

Moreover, although the impeachment and the 1993 congressional hearings ended the sense of absolute impunity, they barely touched the deeply ingrained clientelistic nature of the political system. The systemic incentives for clientelism have not changed as a result of the end of impunity. Deputies and senators, presidents and governors, common citizens and mayors all have an ongoing interest in maintaining clientelistic practices. Therefore, without diminishing the significant achievement for Brazilian democracy that Collor's impeachment represented, there is little evidence that it has fundamentally changed politicians' clientelistic proclivities.

The third new limit to political use of the state comes from the slow, cautious process of state reform. Public enterprises have been privatized; the public sector has been downsized slightly; and the state has ceased performing some of its former regulatory functions. Assuming that it will go forward, state reform reduces the availability of "pork" and the centrality of state controls in the economy. Some public-sector reforms could lead to greater meritocracy, diminishing the number of political appointments.

In the long haul, state reform could provoke a rollback of patronage politics and clientelism. But in the short term, reductions in the size and functions of the public sector are not likely to alter profoundly the patronage orientation of Brazil's catch-all parties and politicians.

Postscript: The North-South Railroad Revisited

It is now time to go back and briefly reexamine the case of the North-South Railroad. Several questions need to be addressed.

First, why did the government proceed with the railroad after the initial technical studies had recommended not to build it? Some of those involved in making this decision sincerely believed that the venture was worthwhile. But that is not the whole story.

Huge public-works projects mean jobs and resources, hence patronage and—politicians hope—votes. By building the North-South Railroad, the president, his ministers, and the governors, senators, and deputies of several states would have expanded patronage opportunities. Building the railroad would have meant a massive pouring of resources and jobs into a handful of states, including Sarney's home state of Maranhão, which helps explain the president's endorsement. The project would have created jobs both directly (to build and maintain the railroad) and indirectly, by integrating the central plains and northern regions more fully into the rest of the country. Political leaders from the states that would benefit from the railroad had compelling motives to support it. The president, his ministers, the governors, and the congressional representatives from the benefited states would have enlarged patronage pots. These in turn meant greater ability to win votes, political support, and internal control of parties. Thus the logic of patronage politics explains why the North-South Railroad was approved.

The momentum in favor of the railroad was reinforced by the logic of collective action (Olson 1965): those who directly benefited from the project mobilized on its behalf, while the losses incurred by the project were spread out.

No actor stood to gain as much by blocking the project as politicians from several states and the construction firms stood to gain by supporting it. Within government circles, mobilization on behalf of the project was intense; mobilization against it was surprisingly strong but took place outside the government.

The railroad enabled some politicians to establish close links with and get favors from the major construction firms. At its most venal, the North-South Railroad promised to enrich a small number of entrepreneurs and politicians. Brazil's biggest construction firms were involved in the bidding for the North-South Railroad. They stood to profit, and they were major supporters of the project.

Given substantial evidence to the contrary, why did the Senate commission conclude that there had been no corruption and that the project was economically sound? The logic of patronage politics, coupled with the near-certainty of impunity, prevailed. Just as the bidding for the contract was rigged, so, too, was the Senate commission entrusted with the investigation. The initial composition of the commission ensured its final verdict. Four of the nine senators on the commission were from the three states (two from Goiás and one each from Pará and Maranhão) that would benefit most from the North-South Railroad. A fifth senator had strong connections to railroad interests, having been director of a major railroad in northern Brazil. These five senators provided the votes against the initial report that claimed that corruption and nonviability had flawed the project, while four senators from states not standing to benefit from the project voted for the first report. Several of the five who supported the railroad had long-established close links to Brazil's huge construction firms. The same five senators provided the votes to approve the second report that overlooked evidence of corruption and suggested going ahead with the railroad.

The hearings themselves were not impartial. The Senate commission gathered oral testimony from eleven people, only three of whom opposed the railroad. The other eight individuals who testified stood to benefit from the construction of the railroad: the governors of two states (Maranhão and Goiás) that most directly benefited from the railroad, two ministers (Transportation and Planning) known for their commitment to the railroad, executives of two construction firms that had successfully placed bids to build part of the railroad, and two executives from the state firm that had been in charge of the overall operation.

But how did the Senate allow the commission to be rigged in the first place? Some states stood to benefit greatly if the project went forward, and the senators from these states mobilized to win control of the commission. In contrast, no state stood to benefit commensurately by killing the project. During the constitutional congress, many senators were busy with constitutional issues and/or attending to their own constituencies and would have been hard pressed to serve on the commission. Yet this does not tell the entire story. In an interview, I asked Senator Mansueto de Lavor, author of the initial report that was highly critical of the North-South Railroad, why nobody in the Senate had denounced this complicity with corruption. He responded that corruption in Congress was so widespread that senators were reluctant to blow the whistle on one another.[63]

What about the other reports that also concluded that there had been no irregularities in the bidding? The Ministry of Transportation's report was questionable because of the minister's suspected complicity in the affair. Senator Lavor's report had suggested that the minister be criminally prosecuted for corruption. Asking the minister to investigate his own possible illicit behavior was not likely to produce results. And the Federal Police's report was so "lamentable, negative, and ridiculous" in the words of Senator Lavor,[64] that the Attorney General's office did not accept its conclusions.

Thus corruption was a factor in the decision to build the railroad. The huge construction firms often bought political support, fixed bids, and gave fraudulent information so they could make large profits. The attorney general refused to cooperate with Senator Lavor's efforts to investigate the case. There were suggestions of involvement in corruption by the attorney general, the minister of transportation, the minister of planning, and VALEC, the public enterprise entrusted with overseeing the whole operation.

Corruption became a prevailing norm in Brazilian politics in the 1980s (Dimenstein 1988). The North-South Railroad was not an aberration; rather, it was the tip of an iceberg, a well-publicized incident among hundreds of cases involving billions of dollars. Fraudulent bidding in public contracts was commonplace.[65] Many incidents of corruption were well documented and publicized, but rarely did a high-ranking public official go to jail. To a surprising extent for a country that has achieved Brazil's level of economic modernization, political power was appropriated for private purposes. As politicians made personal use of public resources, private firms colonized and plundered the state, rendering the public sector less effective.

The weakness of the dividing line between private and public and the willingness of politicians to appropriate public resources for private ends contributed to widespread corruption between 1979 and 1992. The likelihood of corruption was reinforced by the expansion of opportunities for patronage because of the growth of the state and the changes in personnel practices in public administration under military rule, the weakness of the judiciary, and a political system in which parties are weak and impose few constraints on the behavior of individual politicians.

Explaining Weak Party-System Institutionalization

Macrocomparative Factors and
Post–1964 Developments

Part III of this book examines the causes of the difficulty in institutionalizing a party system in the post–1985 period. The explanation is divided into three kinds of elements: long-term historical (macrocomparative) factors, post–1964 developments, and institutional rules. I discuss the long-term historical factors and post–1964 developments in this chapter and the institutional rules in Chapters 8 and 9.

Three long-term structural, political, and cultural factors have worked against a more institutionalized party system in the post–1985 period. The first is the impact of the sequence of political developments on labor parties. Disciplined working-class parties emerged in Europe at a moment in world history that cannot be reproduced. They shaped the nature of party competition as a whole. In Brazil, late industrialization and structural fragmentation have conspired against the formation of such parties. Features of Brazil's political development instead favor more clientelistic interactions between politicians and the popular sectors. This pattern makes party-system institutionalization less likely than was the case with nations that achieved democracy earlier than Brazil.

The second macroexplanation examines the historical patterns of state and party building. Where state building occurs first, the bureaucracy tends to become the primary locus of politics, relegating parties to a secondary role. This sequence of state and party building, which characterized Brazil, makes institutionalizing a party system more difficult.

The third long-term explanation is Brazil's political culture, which continues to be marked by personalism and antiorganizational proclivities. Brazilian politicians prefer considerable autonomy vis-à-vis their parties, and as will be seen in Chapter 8, they have institutionalized this preference through electoral and party legislation.

Although long-term historical factors make institutionalization more or less difficult, they hardly determine the way party systems form and develop. It is also important to look at more recent developments. In the Brazilian case, the long-term historical factors are a necessary but insufficient part of an explanation for the low institutionalization of the post–1985 party system. In addition to these long-term historical elements, three factors that emerged in the post–1964 period have worked against a more institutionalized party system.

First, the dissolutions of party systems in 1965 and 1979 hindered the process of institutionalization. The military dictatorship not only banned particular parties, but dissolved the party systems and effectively created new systems on both occasions. The dissolution of the 1945–64 party system was particularly important; the military regime succeeded in destroying partisan identities that were modestly entrenched in society.

Second, between 1981 and 1992, the Brazilian economy performed poorly, which contributed to delegitimating governing parties. High inflation rates and declining standards of living generated disaffection with the parties supporting the various governments of the post–1979 period, particularly the PDS (1979–85) and later the PMDB (1985–90). The demise of the former and the enervation of the latter account for much of the volatility in the party system as a whole. Under conditions of protracted and profound economic crisis in a new democracy, this discrediting of governing parties is to be expected. An economic crisis of the proportions Brazil experienced between 1981 and 1992 will almost inevitably shake the party system of a new democracy.

The third post–1964 explanation focuses on the development of sophisticated modern electronic media, especially television, which has encouraged candidates to rely more on them and less on party organizations. Throughout the world, the development of the electronic media has led to the displacement of some functions previously exercised by parties. This is especially the case in Brazil because the most important elected positions are chosen through direct popular elections in which candidates make appeals through television to the electorate.

These six factors help explain why Brazilian parties are weak, but they do not provide an exhaustive account. To understand fully the difficulties of party building in Brazil, we also need to examine institutional rules, i.e., party and electoral legislation and rules that govern the structure of executive power and the state. Chapters 8 and 9 are devoted to these institutional rules because they have been studied less, because they are crucial in the Brazilian case, and because they can be altered in the short term to promote party building—though often it is difficult to assemble political support for changing them.

Long- and Short-Term Causes of
Weak Institutionalization: An Overview

Explaining the weak institutionalization of the Brazilian party system is a complex question for methodological and theoretical reasons. Methodologically, the problem is the common issue of many causes and only one case. I address this problem by examining the Brazilian case longitudinally—which has the effect of creating several cases for one country, each defined by different historical periods—and comparing it with other party systems.

The greatest theoretical difficulty in explaining weak party-system institutionalization is that this question has received little attention in comparative politics—although Lamounier and Meneguello (1986) and M. Souza (1976) have made important contributions. The closest body of literature analyzes how party systems form, but it deals only tangentially with institutionalization. As a result, there is not much of an established literature from which to reap ideas.

The first question in trying to explain party-system institutionalization is whether it results primarily from long-term structural and political factors or whether short- and medium-term issues have also been significant. If Brazilian parties have always been weak, this bolsters the case for the importance of long-term political factors. Conversely, if there were periods before 1985 when the party system was more institutionalized, this suggests that factors specific to the more recent period have contributed to weak institutionalization.

Chapter 3 showed that parties were very weak in the 1822–1945 period. The more interesting question revolves around the 1946–64 party system. This issue is pivotal in understanding the balance between short- and long-term causes of weak institutionalization, so I addressed it in some detail in Chapter 3, arguing that the system became moderately institutionalized, more so than in the post–1985 period, but nevertheless with significant limitations.

The implications of the analysis of the 1946–64 party system for assessing short- and long-term explanations of weak institutionalization are complex. On the one hand, there is something to the view, forcefully presented by Lamounier and Meneguello (1986), that Brazil has always had weak parties. This suggests the importance of some long-term factors. On the other hand, the 1945–64 system represented a dramatic advance in party building over previous periods in Brazilian history. Moreover, it was more institutionalized than the post–1985 system has been. Electoral volatility was lower in 1945–64 than it has been since 1985. A higher percentage of eligible voters identified with a party in the 1950s and 1960s than in the post–1985 period. The aggregate difference between congressional and presidential voting was less pronounced from 1945 to 1962 than in the post–1985 period. These indicators suggest that the post–1985 party system was less institutionalized than the 1945–64 system, which in turn implies that some factors specific to the post–1964 period have contributed to weak institutionalization in Brazil's new period of democracy.

The party system between 1974 and 1984 acquired some characteristics that augured well for institutionalization. Voters and organized interests became more attached to parties than previously. Party labels acquired unprecedented importance, and the opposition parties in particular gained legitimacy. Political elites were loyal to their parties except after the disruption provoked by the government's decision to eliminate the two-party system in 1979. These propitious developments suggest that the difficulty of institutionalizing a party system after 1985 was not inevitable.

Even if one agrees that Brazilian parties have always been weak, there are reasons to question whether the causes of that weakness have been constant. Before 1945, structural obstacles to developing modern parties were overwhelming. This is no longer the case. Brazil has become a moderately industrial, more literate, and more organized society (Faria 1983, 1986; Santos 1985a). Industrialization brought workers together, breaking down the horizontal isolation frequently found in the countryside. Illiteracy fell from 57 percent in 1940 to 26 percent in 1980 (Santos 1985a: 256). This not only encouraged a dramatic expansion of the electorate, but also serves as a rough indicator that more people could gain access to political information. The expansion of radio and television gave common citizens access to more information than ever before. Decades of rapid economic growth gave Brazil the eighth-largest capitalist economy in the world. These massive transformations helped erode what Santos (1979) called "regulated citizenship," i.e., citizenship that was controlled from above.

By the 1980s some barriers to effective popular presence in politics had eroded. Many analysts (Schmitter 1971; A. Souza 1978; Erickson 1977; Mericle 1977; Santos 1979) have called attention to the way corporatist institutions shackled labor. But since the late 1970s, some corporatist controls such as the prohibition of national-level organizations have been dismantled, and others have been rendered less significant by the practices of the labor movement (Keck 1989; Almeida 1983). Corporatism continues to fragment and weaken the working class, but not as much as in the past. A variety of social movements emerged outside the corporatist controls (Alvarez 1990; Boschi 1987; R. Cardoso 1983; Mainwaring 1987, 1989). Surveying these structural and organizational changes at the end of the military dictatorship, Santos (1985a) argued that the chances for creating a more modem, fluid political system were good.

Two conclusions arise from these massive social and organizational changes. First, Brazil has reached a level of modernization that is compatible with a more institutionalized party system. The interesting conundrum is precisely that Brazil has long surpassed a level of modernization that would structurally impede the institutionalization of a party system. Second, the erosion of the most significant pre–1945 obstacles to party development makes apparent that no single grand interpretative scheme can explain Brazilian party fragility throughout its entire independent history.

Party underdevelopment has persisted in Brazil, but its causes have changed over time. If party fragility has remained somewhat constant, this phenomenon deserves attention in view of the stunning demographic, social, and economic changes this nation has undergone. Given the social, economic, and political conditions of Brazil until at least 1930, it would have been surprising if solid parties had emerged. This is no longer the case: today, the intriguing issue is the difficulty of institutionalizing a party system in a country that has changed so dramatically.

What makes that difficulty in the post–1985 period notable is that Brazil has now had two sustained periods of democracy and is a middle-income country. In comparative perspective, it is unusual that party building did not progress farther between 1946 and 1964, considering the duration of the democratic government. It is the only Latin American case in which democracy lasted that long only to have all of the major parties disappear. In some cases of democratization (for example, Venezuela after 1958 and Portugal after 1974), a decade was sufficient time for the consolidation of a democracy in which parties play a central role in politics (Coppedge 1994; Levine 1973; Kornblith and Levine 1995; Bruneau and McLeod 1986). In other Latin American countries, including Peru, a strong mass party emerged in the 1930s despite an absence of democracy.

Similarly, it is unusual that a nation with Brazil's level of economic modernization has not developed more solid parties. In Latin America, all of the other middle-income countries have more institutionalized party systems than Brazil (Mainwaring and Scully 1995).

Historical Sequences, Social Fragmentation, and the Formation of Labor Parties

A first factor in explaining the nature of party formation in Brazil, and more specifically weak institutionalization, is the impact of historical sequences on labor parties (Collier and Collier 1991; Keck 1992: 11–17; Reis 1988; Weyland 1996a; Chalmers 1964; Epstein 1967; Kirchheimer 1966; Pizzorno 1981). Late industrialization makes it virtually impossible to reproduce the disciplined, centralized working-class parties with mass memberships that emerged in most of Western

Europe early this century. The tight relationship between organized labor and working-class parties helped anchor party systems in which most organized interests were linked to parties. Systems with strong party roots in society developed.

In most early cases of democratization, centralized and disciplined working-class parties with mass memberships emerged.[1] These were "parties of integration" (Pizzorno 1981); they not only integrated the masses into the political system, but also established an important basis of social identity. These parties had a catalytic effect on party building. They pioneered new organizational forms with strong extraparliamentary organizations, close linkages between party and organized groups, powerful centralized national leadership, and mass memberships (Duverger 1954: xxx–xxxvii). The electoral success of the working-class parties pushed the centrist and conservative parties to modernize their own structures and techniques to seek mass appeal. The emergence of electorally viable, disciplined, working-class parties at an early stage of democratization was partially reproduced in Chile, where the communists and socialists dominated social movements and popular-interest associations. To some degree, it was also followed in Argentina, where Peronism galvanized working-class participation in politics.

Most late-democratizing countries lacked a large labor party with mass membership that served as the partisan vehicle of the labor movement. In Brazil and in most of the rest of Latin America, such centralized, disciplined, working-class parties with committed mass memberships did not emerge or did not become major entities. These parties are now something of the past, even in those democracies where they once existed (Pizzorno 1981; Kirchheimer 1966; Epstein 1967; Chalmers 1964; Bartolini 1983), and they are not in the cards in the late-democratizing nations, including Brazil (Santos 1985b). The Communist Party in the brief period of its postwar legality (1945–47) and the PT since 1979 have aspired to be working-class parties, but neither galvanized the labor movement as thoroughly as working-class parties did in the early European cases of democratization.

The formation of disciplined, centralized, working-class parties of integration occurred at a moment in world history that is no longer reproducible (Keck 1992: 11–17). It was predicated upon four conditions that do not obtain in Brazil and the other late-democratizing nations of Latin America. First, these parties depended on the existence of an urban working class that constituted a near majority of the economically active population. In Brazil, by contrast, the comparatively small size of the working class has conspired against the formation of a working-class party with a large committed mass membership. Generally speaking, late-developing nations have followed more capital-intensive industrialization strategies than the earlier industrializers, and manufacturing has absorbed a smaller share of the labor force than in the earlier European cases. In Belgium, employment in manufacturing, mining, construction, and transport reached 51.7 percent of the economically active population in 1961; in France, it reached 42.2 percent (1962); in Germany, 64.6 percent (1961); in Britain, 60.0 percent (1911); in Italy, 45.0 percent (1964); and in Sweden, 51.5 percent (1960). By contrast, in Brazil the peak figure was only 29.1 percent, reached decades later (1980) than in these other countries (Keck 1992: 13). If one compares the figures for the early twentieth century, when labor parties became powerful actors in Western Europe, the contrast to Brazil is starker.

The comparatively small size of the industrial labor force meant a smaller constituency for a working-class party because the nonorganized urban popular sectors are less likely to vote for such parties than workers are. These sectors lack the socializing influence created by workers' institutions.

The relatively small size of the industrial labor force is part of a pattern of social fragmentation, to use Weyland's (1996a) term. Social inequalities cleave Brazilian society, laying the foundations for a polity in which popular actors have sharply different material situations and have different perceptions of their interests and diverging political demands. Under these conditions, it is difficult for parties to find a unifying discourse that cuts across the popular classes. Societal fragmentation therefore presents difficulties for forming a large working-class party (Chalmers 1972).

The parties of integration were built around powerful and cohesive labor movements. Most workers were members of unions, and in most early democracies, unions were relatively united in their positions on national politics. In Brazil, by contrast, urban unionization has historically been low. Many adults, including many workers, did not even formally (much less in practice) have full citizenship rights because the illiterate were not reenfranchised until 1985.

Some analysts (Almeida 1987; Weyland 1996a) have underscored the heterogeneity of organized labor in Brazil, and if we include other groups within the popular sectors, this heterogeneity is greater. That weakens the prospects of parties dedicated to furthering the lot of an organized, relatively homogeneous class. These conditions favor particularistic (i.e., clientelistic) exchanges because it is more difficult to represent broad cross-sections of society when they are so cleaved.

As Reis (1988) and Weyland (1996a) have argued, deep social fragmentation has been conducive to patterns of political incorporation such as clientelism, populism, and corporatism, all of which circumvent parties in Brazil.[2] With such patterns of political incorporation, the popular classes tend to have diffuse political views (Caldeira 1984).

The European working-class parties emerged at a world moment that ante-dated the proliferation of new cultural vehicles and opportunities provided by modern media. Parties were more consuming sources of identity in early-twen-tieth-century Europe than they are anywhere in the Western world today. This historical moment made possible the forging of a ghetto-party culture whose existence was predicated upon restricted recreational and cultural diversity.

In Brazil, popular-class political incorporation came later, and parties of the working class appeared at a moment in world history when there was more cultural competition for popular sympathies. Television has been a powerful source of popular entertainment, an alternative source of information and activity.

Another condition that made possible the formation of centralized, disci-plined labor parties in Western Europe and that is absent in Brazil was that parties and unions dominated mechanisms of interest representation. In most early-democratizing nations, working-class parties emerged before the prolif-eration of interest associations. They were the main channels for representing popular interests. There was little space for the emergence of an array of powerful popular groups and social movements (except for the union move-ment) before the working-class parties become important actors in the political system. Later, popular groups emerged mainly under the umbrella of labor parties, and in many cases they continued to be dominated by the parties. Only after the formation of these disciplined, centralized mass parties did more autonomous interest groups and social movements form.

The relationship between parties and organized popular groups was different in most late-democratizing countries, including in Brazil. Interest associations and social movements grew up alongside parties and maintained their inde-pendence with respect to them. In Brazil, corporatist institutions rather than parties were the major forces of integrating the working class into politics; corporatist institutions were well established before the first modern parties emerged (Collier and Collier 1991). Organized interests had more autonomy with respect to parties; the parties did not dominate organized interests, as was the case with the parties of integration. Specialized interest groups and social movements emerged, and they focused on a narrower range of issues that brought participants together. State structures acquired a complexity that they lacked in early-twentieth-century Europe, as state agencies proliferated beyond what had existed earlier in the century. Specialized interest groups and social movements targeted specific state agencies for their demands. This change in the state both encouraged and reflected the proliferation of social movements and interest groups that were less significant actors in most European cases.

The parties that won the support of the labor movement did not acquire the "ghetto" characteristics of the early-twentieth-century labor parties in Europe. Nor did they attempt to provide such a wide array of functions for their members. Parties were not such encompassing organizations; they neither undertook as many activities nor solicited the commitment found in many European parties.

A final obstacle to the formation of a powerful working-class party in Brazil was corporatism. Initially designed by Vargas in the 1930s, corporatist institutions gradually incorporated organized urban labor into the political system under the aegis of the state (Collier and Collier 1991). Corporatist arrangements strengthened state control over unions in a variety of ways. National umbrella organizations open to all workers were banned, making it difficult to unify workers across categories. Worker organization at the plant level was not legal, so grassroots labor organizing was difficult. Unions recognized by the state were given a monopoly of representation for each occupational category, giving the state potential control from above. The state controlled union financing and other internal mechanisms. It had the right to intervene in unions and remove the leadership. Union leaders depended on state resources, and unions were financed through state-controlled payroll taxes. The government supervised leadership elections, internal union administration, collective bargaining, and the right to strike. These mechanisms gave the state considerable control over union leadership, and the leadership in turn exercised control over the rank-and-file members. As a result, the labor leadership was often more responsive to and dependent on government authorities than on the members (A. Souza 1978: 118–56; Schmitter 1971; Mericle 1977; Erickson 1977). Unions were organized by industry rather than by trade, a fact that intensified the social heterogeneity within the unions (A. Souza 1978: 219–70).

Between 1946 and 1964, these corporatist controls functioned with flexibility because politicians needed to court popular votes and the support of unions. Labor acquired some political clout (Erickson 1977). But before the 1980s, it did not shed the corporatist shackles that gave the state considerable power over unions.

Under military rule, these mechanisms of corporatist control, in conjunction with widespread repression of militant labor leaders, gave the state even greater control over labor organizations between 1968 and 1977. Most workers perceived the unions as adjuncts of the state rather than as associations to defend working-class interests (A. Souza 1978: 271–324; Cohen 1989).

Corporatist controls over unions have eroded since the late 1970s (Almeida 1983, 1987). Even so, internal segmentation of the working class has continued to hamper labor's ability to organize nationally and act cohesively (Almeida 1987;

Weyland 1996a). Many of the strongest unions have been linked to the PT, but labor support for the PT has been highly contested; prominent CGT and Força Sindical leaders advocate the separation of unions and parties. The largest national association, the socialist-oriented CUT (Central Única dos Trabalhadores), has a radically different view of labor-capital relations compared to the other two natural associations, the procapitalist, antistatist Força Sindical, and the procapitalist CGT. These differences spill over into party politics. Notwithstanding the PT's desire to serve as the partisan representative of organized labor, the union movement is deeply divided along party lines (Keck 1989: 272–82). Ever since the emergence of national labor organizations in the early 1980s, the movement has been sharply divided into two or more national organizations, with competing beliefs about what the movement should do and competing party sympathies.

This pattern of labor-movement development, which was facilitated by the structural effects of late industrialization, had consequences for party-system formation. During the formative decades of the labor movement, corporatism tethered unions, dampened popular political consciousness, and fragmented the working-class movement. In these ways, it inhibited the formation of a strong working-class party. A party that cast its appeal strongly in class terms would have won votes only among those workers who thought of themselves as part of the working class (Przeworski 1985; Przeworski and Sprague 1986). Because of corporatist mechanisms of control, many workers did not strongly identify themselves as members of a class (A. Souza 1978).

Parties had less incentive to serve as the conduits of popular demands because the popular classes were comparatively weak politically and were fragmented by corporatist institutions. The weakness of popular political organization favored clientelistic exchanges. Politicians had little incentive to promote mass entitlement programs given weak collective popular action on their behalf. Therefore, the weakening of unions by corporatist controls and by the fragmentation of the popular sectors made the emergence of a strong working-class party less likely.

In Brazil and most other Latin American countries, the absence of a galvanizing working-class party had important consequences for party-system formation. Throughout northern Europe, the formation of disciplined working-class parties promoted close party linkages to organized interests and deep identification of citizens with parties. Parties became the fundamental conduits of political life, creating a new model for well-organized and disciplined parties, with an extensive network of grassroots party organizations (Duverger 1954, Michels 1959, Ostrogorski 1902). The other parties never duplicated the way labor parties were structured, but in response to the challenge they became more organized.

In most of the later-developing countries, class-based (in the narrow sense) appeals have been less common, and more diffuse appeals have been the norm (Reis 1983, 1988). The other parties did not have the stimulus of matching the organization, cohesion, and discipline of strong labor-based parties. The comparative weakness of labor parties allowed the other parties to retain more rudimentary organizations.

The different historical conditions that prevailed in the early-democratizers and the third-wave democracies, leading to the creation of strong labor parties in the former and weaker ones in the latter, help explain two of the central points in Chapter 2 regarding first- and third-wave party systems. With parties that had strong identities and roots in society, first-wave systems were more likely to be well institutionalized. The close linkage between social groups and parties in first-wave cases also accounts for the greater utility of the social-cleavage model.

Sequences of State and Party Building

In her seminal book, M. Souza (1976) argued that the state has exercised a decisive impact on party formation in Brazil. She averred that party weakness derives above all from the relationship between parties and the state: "The structure of the state is a crucial factor in the nature of politics in different societies. The prior existence of a strong state organization has considerable impact on the development and later configuration of the party system. The functional weight of the party system will be greater where the bureaucratic organization of the state is less active. . . . The existence of a centralized state structure before the emergence of a party system constitutes, in itself, a difficulty for the institutionalization of the party system and a stimulus to clientelistic politics" (31, 36).

The sequence of state and party building in Brazil has been conducive to clientelistic patterns of representation and has been an obstacle in party-system institutionalization. Historical sequences of state formation and interest representation are important because once they are established, political institutions occupy "spaces" in the political system. Once the major political institutions are consolidated, the actors in the political system function according to their logic. The identity of actors is established in interaction with these institutions and other actors.

If parties and legislatures emerge as major agents of interest aggregation and representation before the phase of major state expansion, political actors are likely to pursue their objectives through parties (M. Souza 1976; H. Daalder 1966: 58–64). This option favors party-system institutionalization. But if the state expands before the institutionalization of mass parties and becomes the major locus of political activity, political actors are more likely to pursue their objectives through bureaucratic channels. Parties are likely to be more dependent on the state and to be less central players. And in Brazil, state building preceded the emergence of the first mass parties, so actors had incentives to channel demands through state agencies rather than parties.

From the vantage point of "spaces" occupied in the political system, the expansion of the state apparatus during the military regime created renewed barriers to party development. This expansion, which occurred despite occasional antistatist rhetoric, had multiple dimensions, ranging from the state as producer to regulatory functions. Government spending and revenue reflected this expansion of the state. Public expenditures grew to about 25 percent of the GNP in the 1970s (Trebat 1983: 13).

Public enterprises have been important in Brazil since the early 1940s, but their number and size grew dramatically under military rule. In addition to publicly owned productive enterprises, there are hundreds of public autarchies and foundations, including universities, hospitals, highway and road commissions, public-works commissions, social-welfare agencies, and a panoply of other entities. The power of planning agencies also expanded under military rule (Abranches 1978; L. Martins 1985). Most public policy was formulated within state agencies and the executive branch, bypassing Congress and the parties.

The state's regulatory powers also expanded greatly under military rule. State agencies controlled the import and export of many goods, provided many fiscal incentives for private investors, set tariffs, approved investment decisions of private investors, and established export incentives. They also set a wide array of prices for many goods, as well as the magnitude of wage increases, rent increases, and interest rates for savings accounts (Hagopian 1996: 140–77; Baer 1989: 238–73).

This expansion of the state enhanced decision arenas in which parties and Congress had little influence. Between 1964 (especially after the administrative reform of 1967) and roughly 1979 most state agencies became more autonomous with respect to political controls and less subject to centralized controls (F. H. Cardoso 1975a: 181–207; Abranches 1978; Schmitter 1971: 282–314). Under military rule, virtually no public firms and agencies were overseen by the legislature or parties.

Since the reestablishment of democracy and the promulgation of the 1988 Constitution, parties and Congress have become more important loci of decision making. Nevertheless, the historical legacy of state-led development and weak parties has not fully receded. More so than the legislature and parties, the bureaucracy continues to be the focal point of most interest associations and social movements.[3] Most powerful decision-making posts are inside the state, and parties have comparatively little impact in determining who gets those posts.

As M. Souza argued two decades ago, this situation poses barriers to party-system institutionalization.

An Antiorganizational Political Culture

A third historical factor that has contributed to weak institutionalization in the post–1985 period is Brazil's antiorganizational political culture. Political leaders prefer to function with considerable autonomy vis-à-vis the constraints that powerful centralized parties would impose. They build and dominate parties for their own ends. When the parties no longer suit them, they are more willing to abandon ship than politicians in the other middle-income countries of Latin America.

This pattern forms part of Brazil's political culture. Personalistic and antiorganizational attitudes have persisted in politics, nurturing a political system in which parties are relegated to a secondary plane, while personal connections and individualistic patterns of representation reign supreme. Formal regulations and laws are important, but they are often superseded by personal connections and loyalties.

The importance of personal connections and antiorganizational attitudes in politics is an old theme, developed by such famous figures in Brazilian political thought as Alberto Torres (1933) and Oliveira Vianna (1949), and more recently by Roberto DaMatta (e.g., 1979: 139–93, 1985) and Guillermo O'Donnell (1986: 121–55). According to this view, formal institutions have become more important over time, but they have not replaced personal connections. Personalism has persisted despite decades of high social mobility. Even today in many spheres of political, social, and economic life, what matters is not competence or party loyalty, but personal connections (see Chapter 6). People cultivate friendships and make connections more than they try to build organizations.

For anthropologist Roberto DaMatta, the domain of formal politics is not isolated from the world of personal connections, but is permeated by it, even though the formal discourse of the political world downplays the ways in which personal connections affect public life. Despite its rigid, formal, universalistic discourse, the political world is shaped by personal connections. Formal political processes are affected by these informal relationships, and they are often undermined by personal connections. Although DaMatta does not specifically discuss parties, it would be easy to extrapolate that one of the reasons why parties are weak is that what really matters is personal connections, not formal organizations. These themes have been echoed by some political scientists and historians (Lewin 1987; R. Graham 1990; Schmitter 1971).

To understand contemporary Brazilian party politics, the element of political culture that is most relevant is the engineering of rules that institutionalize weak parties. As is argued in Chapter 8, political elites have chosen formal institutions that reinforce the personalistic dimension of politics. Many politicians continue to subordinate parties to their personal benefit. Political elites have preferred weak parties and adopted institutions that fostered them. With weak parties, the elites can operate free of the constraints that disciplined and nationalized central parties would create.

Brazilian politicians of the catch-all labels try to ensure that parties do not greatly impinge on their autonomy. They do not profess or practice great loyalty to their organizations. They campaign in individualistic style, rely on their own financing schemes, vote as they please in Congress, and change parties when expedient. The national party leadership avoids imposing its will on individual legislators. To the extent that loyalties exist, they are usually to state-level political bosses more than national party organizations.

Organized interest groups work through individual politicians rather than parties. The catch-all parties are too diffuse, too undisciplined, and too hetero-geneous to be effective targets. Clientelistic exchanges, which are based on individual connections, prevail over more collective patterns. To a surprising degree for a middle-income nation, parties are still subordinated to individuals. Persistently antiorganizational in its consequences, this aspect of Brazil's politi-cal culture leads to attempts to build personal connections at the expense of building powerful party organizations. Often the emphasis on personalism has led to explicit antiparty attitudes, to which a host of authoritarian antiparty thinkers from the past bear witness (M. Souza 1976: 63–82; Lamounier 1974).

The Limits of Long-Term Explanations

Structural features and historical legacies make party building more or less difficult. On balance, Brazil's structural features and historical legacies work against the institutionalization of a party system. The sequence of party and state building, the country's political culture (especially as institutionalized in party and electoral legislation), and social fragmentation are obstacles to party building.

Nevertheless, these long-term factors do not fully explain the difficulties in institutionalizing a party system in the post–1985 period. For example, social fragmentation and the lateness of labor-party formation, while contributing to the weak institutionalization of Brazil's party systems, are not a sufficient explanation. This is obvious in the fact that Brazil's party system between 1945 and 1961 became moderately institutionalized despite lower levels of unioniza-tion and industrial employment than prevailed in the 1980s. Moreover, in Latin American countries where labor parties have been historically weak—including Uruguay and Costa Rica—the party system has been quite institutionalized for long stretches of time.

Exclusive emphasis on long-term causes of weak institutionalization in the post–1985 period could lead us to overlook propitious opportunities that were lost not because of long-term historical reasons but because of institutional design, poor leadership, or inappropriate party strategies. As Chapter 4 noted, some positive trends in party building emerged during the second half of military rule: the growing percentage of party identifiers, stronger linkages between social organizations and parties, a stronger commitment to building parties, the PMDB's potential to become a modern reformist party with broad support, and the emergence of the PT.

A second problem with exclusive attention to long-term historical explanations is that similar barriers to party building existed in other societies where reasonably institutionalized party systems emerged quickly and anchored consolidated democracies. Venezuela, Spain, Portugal, and Greece had sequences of state and party building relatively unfavorable to the emergence of parties as central political actors, yet parties became the linchpins of consolidated democracies.

If we look only at structural conditions and leave aside political characteristics, the differences between Brazil, Chile, and Venezuela are not extraordinary, yet Brazil's party system has been significantly less institutionalized than Chile's and Venezuela's from 1958 until the early 1990s. Social inequalities have historically been less pronounced in Chile than in the other two countries, but the difference is not overwhelming. In terms of per capita income, Brazil lagged behind Chile throughout this century and behind Venezuela after the oil boom began, but by the 1960s Brazil was catching up to Chile. Throughout most of the twentieth century, Brazil has been a more rural society than both Chile and Venezuela, but the rapid urbanization of the post–1945 period reduced the differences.

Exclusive attention to long-term historical factors also understates the impact of institutional rules in shaping party-system institutionalization. Formal institutional arrangements help configure how party systems develop. As is shown in Chapters 8 and 9, the electoral system and party legislation have an impact on the number and nature of parties and the behavior of politicians.

Long-term or structural explanations also fail to take into account the importance of party strategy and political leadership. Party strategy is conditioned by an array of structural, cultural, and institutional factors, but it cannot be fully reduced to such factors, nor can it be reduced to a vote-maximizing effort, as some theorists (e.g., Downs 1957) suggest. Just as the fate of democratic and authoritarian regimes often depends on what strategies parties, party leaders, and government leaders pursue, so too does the fate of party building. Some strategies have positive consequences for party-system institutionalization; others are deleterious.

The final problem with an exclusive focus on long-term factors is that it cannot explain radical shifts in party building. Until the Fifth Republic, France had a gaggle of undisciplined parties, most of which had short-lived existences. But in the forty years since the inauguration of the Fifth Republic, France has developed a reasonably stable party system based on parties with clear identities, reasonably strong allegiances among the political elite, and moderately strong roots in society. Anyone who had focused exclusively on structural obstacles to party building in France would not have anticipated such a development (Suleiman 1994). In a similar vein, Portugal developed disciplined parties with strong roots in society within a decade after the 1974 revolution (Bruneau and McLeod 1986), despite a tradition of weak parties.

Latin America also offers examples of countries with rupture points in party building. Some countries (e.g., Argentina) had relatively auspicious beginnings that resulted in later protracted failures, while in Venezuela, a polity with almost no democratic experience before 1958 gave rise to one with parties that dominated democratic politics and enjoyed considerable legitimacy (Coppedge 1994; Kornblith and Levine 1995). Past patterns in party building are important, but they do not completely determine future prospects. The Venezuelan party system became institutionalized quickly after the transition to democracy in 1958, notwithstanding many macro obstacles including sharp inequalities and a lack of democratic traditions.

In some countries (Venezuela, Greece, Spain, Portugal), the institutionalization of the party system occurred late, but parties have still emerged as central political actors. Conversely, in a few cases early developments appeared favorable to party-system consolidation, but later events aborted it. In Argentina, the emergence of a competitive political system with fairly broad participation occurred fairly early, 1916 being a key turning point. A high standard of living, significant urbanization, and considerable popular participation all could have favored party development. Beginning with the 1930 coup, however, this potential was consistently aborted.

None of this is to downplay the significance of the structural problems to party development in Brazil. But some important contributing factors and formal political institutions in the post–1964 period also account for weak institutionalization of the post–1985 party system.

Post–1964 Developments: The Impact of
State Dissolutions of Party Systems

The second step in the analysis of the weak institutionalization of the Brazilian party system is to focus on some post–1964 developments, which help explain not only the weak institutionalization of the Brazilian case compared to other middle-income countries in Latin America, but also the lower institutionalization of the post–1985 period compared to 1946–64.

One of the significant post–1964 developments is the dissolution of the party systems in 1965 and 1979. Because the 1945–64 party system was moderately institutionalized, its dissolution was more disruptive than would have been the case with a weakly institutionalized system. The authoritarian regime's successful attempt to implant a new party system contributed to the lasting effect the dissolution of the 1945–64 system had. Had the military not imposed a new party system that began to develop roots in society, the major pre–1965 parties would almost surely have reestablished themselves after the dictatorship. As the MDB and Arena became important actors during the process of political liberalization, the identities of the pre–1965 parties faded.

Despite the purportedly "artificial" character of the 1966–79 party system, the two parties established clearly differentiated and relatively stable social bases (Lamounier 1980; Reis 1978; von Mettenheim 1995). By 1974, the MDB represented a threat to the military regime's project of gradual liberalization via electoral politics while trying to remain firmly in control. For this reason the government ultimately dissolved the party. The dissolution of the MDB and Arena again disrupted a process of sedimentation of partisan identities. In 1981, the government again intervened against the party system with the November "electoral package," which led to the decision of Popular Party (PP) leaders to merge with the PMDB, disrupting a process of establishing party identities. As a result, the PMDB became extremely heterogeneous. This heterogeneity led to problems during the Sarney government; the party was so divided over key issues that it could not govern effectively. In turn, this incapacity led to the party's implosion in 1988.

Although the Southern Cone military dictatorships undertook more brutal attacks on parties and politicians than the Brazilian military regime, they did not alter the party systems as markedly as the Brazilian rulers. In part, this is because the Brazilian regime permitted the creation of a new party system; parties and elections functioned during the entire military period, enabling voters and political elites to develop new allegiances that superseded the old.

Television and Political Parties

There is a surprising paucity of work on how television has affected parties and politics in Latin America (but see Waisbord 1992; Skidmore 1993). But the broader literature on the demise of parties has looked at this issue (Ware 1985: 175–208; Sartori 1989), and it is especially germane in Brazil.

The development of radio and especially television has enabled candidates to bypass party channels and market themselves directly to the public. As a result, party organizations have become less central in mediating the relationship between voters and candidates. Parties have lost some of the control they once exercised over campaigns. More sophisticated campaign techniques, especially polls and electronic media, have led political consultants to replace party professionals in important campaign functions. As is the case in the United States but in contrast to the situation in Argentina (Waisbord 1993), most consultants in Brazil are not firmly attached to any specific party, and they may even see parties as obstacles. Consultants have a facility in these technical areas that most party professionals lack—although more party professionals are becoming versed in polling and media techniques.

Moreover, the development of television has diversified leisure activities. The early-twentieth-century parties of integration sponsored a wide array of activities, and members identified with the parties because so much of their lives was wrapped up in the parties. Working-class parties acted as social clubs, served an amalgam of welfare purposes, and were a prime source of information and political education for workers (Chalmers 1964).

By contrast, today with the flick of a knob people can tune in to a world of modern entertainment. A press independent of parties has burgeoned, so citizens are not dependent on parties for political information or entertainment. This diversification has caused a withering of leisure, recreational, and educational activities sponsored by parties. Parties lack the expertise, interest, and financial resources to compete successfully with the panoply of recreational and leisure opportunities that exist in middle- and high-income nations. The old party media receded as a sophisticated and accessible modern media evolved. These changes have contributed to declining involvement with parties.

Television has had a particularly pronounced impact on politics in Brazil. In the advanced industrial democracies, parties were already well established when television came on the scene. In Brazil, by contrast, television established itself as a major electoral vehicle before the establishment of enduring political parties. Rather than prompting changes in well-established institutions, television emerged as a major force before most of the current parties were created.

Television blossomed in Brazil under military rule, and it emerged as a major political force in the 1980s. Beginning with the 1985 mayoral races, television became a major force in elections for the crucial executive posts. With weak party organizations and a low percentage of partisan identifiers among the electorate, candidates for executive posts do not rely primarily on party labels to attract support. Most citizens' primary exposure to candidates for executive posts comes through television. Candidates for president and governor have ample television exposure, and their ability to cultivate a favorable image makes or breaks them.

Politicians and the mass public alike acknowledge television's tremendous impact. The octogenarian traditional politician, Senator Luis Vianna of Bahia (UDN-Arena-PFL-PMDB), who was politically active from the 1920s until his death in the early 1990s, commented in an interview on political changes he had witnessed. Regarding political campaigns, he said that the biggest change in his life had been caused by television. "Television has displaced rallies. Today you can establish direct communication (with the people) through the TV. In the old days we traveled through lots of cities putting together rallies; that's a big difference from today. . . . Today campaigns are completely different because you can see everything at home on your TV. . . . In a country where the means of communication were precarious, the advent of television has meant an especially big difference. What used to take eight or ten days of intensive campaigning, today you can accomplish in a few minutes on the TV."[4]

The mass public shares the perception that television is a powerful political force. A *Folha de São Paulo* survey (March 29, 1987) in São Paulo, Rio de Janeiro, Brasília, Belo Horizonte, Salvador, Recife, and Porto Alegre asked 3,316 respondents to rank twenty-two institutions in power and prestige. Television, radio, and the printed media ranked first, second, and third, respectively, in terms of prestige, and first, six, and fifth, respectively, in terms of power (M. Souza 1989: n. 46, pp. 389–90).

Television is a key source of political information. A 1987 IBOPE survey of 5,000 people asked where they obtained their information about the country's situation: 82.8 percent responded through television, compared to 40.1 percent for radio, 37.6 percent through newspapers, 34.7 percent through conversations, and 13.6 percent through magazines.[5] As of the mid-1980s, only two Brazilian newspapers sold more than 250,000 copies per day, and the largest sold 320,000 per day (Chacon 1985: 362). *Veja* easily has the largest circulation among weeklies, with more than a million copies sold per week. In contrast, by 1989 72.6 percent of Brazilian households had televisions.[6]

One of the reasons that television has assumed such importance in campaigns for executive posts is the paucity of other sources of political information for a majority of voters. Given precarious incomes and educational backgrounds for the masses, only a minority have access to written media. The ability of common citizens to conceptualize political information is limited by low education levels (A. Souza 1978; Reis 1983, 1988; Cohen 1989). Labor unions, churches, and neighborhood associations have had only a secondary impact in disseminating political information (Straubhaar, Olsen, and Nunes 1993). Brazilian television is sophisticated and has a well-developed market, features that enhance its political impact. In terms of technological sophistication, it is the leader among third-world television systems.

Not only has television overshadowed parties as a means of disseminating political information and orienting the electorate, television's portrait of parties has been generally negative. The media have denigrated the images of parties and Congress, thereby contributing to depoliticization, cynicism about parties, and antiparty attitudes (M. Souza 1989: 366–68).

In brief, television has played a central role in political campaigns in Brazil since 1985, enhancing the importance of individual candidates at the expense of party labels. In this way, television has contributed to the difficulties of institutionalizing a party system.

The Economic Crisis and the Party System

Poor economic performance between 1981 and 1993 added to the difficulties of institutionalizing a party system in the post–1985 period. Throughout Latin America, the poor economic performance of the 1980s contributed to electoral volatility (Remmer 1991). This was the case in Brazil.

In Brazil, the overwhelming share of downside electoral volatility occurred among parties associated with the governments that oversaw the poor performance of the 1980s. The combination of zero per capita growth and runaway inflation weakened the parties that were once dominant: the PDS until 1984 and the PMDB in 1985–89. The demise of the PDS and the PMDB (even though the latter remained the largest party) accounts for most of the electoral volatility of the 1980s. For both the PDS and the PMDB, being associated with a government that governed ineffectively was the precipitating factor in electoral demise. This is hardly surprising; in most democracies, the parties associated with governments that fail badly pay a price at the ballot box.

Survey data from the time of sharpest decline in party identification with the PMDB show that the dominant concerns of Brazilians were economic. For example, a nationwide IBOPE survey in August–September 1987 asked 5,000 respondents, "Please tell me the three areas in which Brazil is facing most serious problems." The four most frequent responses were economic issues: workers' wages (35.3 percent), unemployment (31.5 percent), inflation (20.2 percent), and control of prices (20.0 percent).[7] The political saliency of economic issues lends further credence to the view that economic mismanagement discredited the ruling parties.

Although poor economic performance contributed to the delegitimation of governing parties in the 1980s and early 1990s, it would be misleading to see economic performance as the dominant explanation for Brazil's difficulties with institutionalizing a party system. The delegitimation of the governing parties accounts only partially for the weakness of the system as a whole. Although the

PMDB lost political capital and votes in the late 1980s, it remained the largest party.

Moreover, crossnational comparison shows that economic crisis does not always immediately lead to the demise of the governing party and to the unraveling of a party system. In Argentina under Alfonsín (1983–89), economic results were worse than at any time in Brazil. Per capita income declined 21 percent in Argentina during the 1980s, compared to a 5 percent fall in Brazil. Argentina's hyperinflationary episode in 1989 (4,923 percent for the year) surpassed Brazil's worst burst of inflation.[8] The governing Radical Party suffered as a result, but until 1994, it retained over 30 percent of the vote—roughly equal to its share prior to 1983. The party system as a whole did not unravel. Still, the demise of the Radicals after 1989 also supports the argument that even old, well-established major parties that govern disastrously may suffer severe electoral consequences.

In Venezuela, economic decline in the post–1982 period was steeper than in Brazil; per capita income dropped 19 percent during the 1980s. The party system eventually (in 1993) deinstitutionalized, but only after a longer period of economic decline, a series of political scandals, and—significantly—an amalgam of political reforms engineered to weaken parties (Kornblith and Levine 1995). Like the Argentine case, Venezuela shows the vulnerability of even old, well-established parties when they preside over bad governments, but both cases also show that party systems that started off more institutionalized were more resistant to extreme volatility than the Brazilian example. In sum, economic crisis makes it more difficult for a nascent party system to institutionalize and renders even an established system vulnerable to deinstitutionalization, but it does not inevitably bring about the deinstitutionalization of an established party system.

Brazil's poor economic performance of the 1980s and early 1990s also obviously fails to account for the limited institutionalization of the pre–1979 party systems. Between 1946 and 1961, economic growth was brisk, yet the party system was not highly institutionalized. Nevertheless, the poor economic results of the 1981–93 period help explain why the post–1985 system was less institutionalized than the system of 1945–64. During the earlier democratic period, rapid economic growth buffered governing parties from setbacks comparable to those the PDS and PMDB experienced in the 1985–86 and 1988–90 elections.

Conclusion

The explanation of weak party-system institutionalization in the post–1985 period began with three long-term historical factors. Although they remain important in contemporary Brazil, they do not fully explain the weak institutionalization of the contemporary party system. The lingering disruptive effects of the dissolution of the party systems in 1965 and 1979, the emergence of television as a powerful force, and the delegitimating effect on parties of the 1981–92 economic slump are necessary ingredients in understanding weak post–1985 institutionalization. The next two chapters show that formal political institutions have also contributed to weak institutionalization since 1985.

CHAPTER 8

Institutional Rules and Weak Institutionalization: Incentives for Legislators

The preference of political elites for loose parties has been a major contributing factor to weak party-system institutionalization in the post–1985 period. Political elites institutionalized their preference for loose, decentralized parties through electoral and party legislation. Once these rules were established, they were not easily changed; whether this is because the underlying interests remained the same or because of the sticking power of the rules themselves is immaterial. The most important institutions for understanding the party system—a presidential system with strong presidential powers, robust federalism, a permissive electoral system (i.e., one with low entry barriers), and rules that favor loose, decentralized parties—have existed with minor modifications since 1985.[1] Depending on the constitutional provisions for changing the rules, they can far outlive the constellation of interests that inspired their genesis. Institutional rules initially constitute an important intervening variable; they themselves are explained by the preferences of political elites, and in turn they institutionalize the kinds of parties and party systems these elites prefer—with some unintended consequences. Institutional rules then constitute an independent variable because they often have staying power even if the interests that initially led to their genesis changes.

Institutional rules and arrangements and their impact on the party system are the focus of this chapter and the next. This one focuses on incentives for legislators, showing that the electoral system, the mechanism of candidate selection, and some party rules create incentives for individualism among legislators. Chapter 9 examines the impact of presidentialism, federalism, and malapportionment.

The institutional rules discussed in this chapter help explain how Brazilian politicians and parties function, why parties are weak, and why it has been difficult to institutionalize a party system. Institutional arrangements have created incentives for politicians to engage in individualistic, antiparty behavior. With different institutional rules, Brazilian politicians and parties would function in different ways, and parties would be stronger.

Incentives and Politicians as Rational Actors

A fundamental assumption of this chapter is that politicians' behavior is molded by incentives created by party and electoral legislation. This effect of institutional rules occurs because politicians purposefully pursue some political goals and because institutional rules shape how they pursue their goals. These assumptions and the analysis that follows rely on rational-choice approaches to politics.

Among scholars who employ such approaches, the notion of rationality as applied to politicians often indicates that their sole or primary motive is to win elections (Mayhew 1974; Katz 1980; Schlesinger 1991). This assumption has the advantage of parsimony, and it is reasonable to assume that winning elections is a major motivating force for most politicians. Nevertheless, it is too restrictive for the Brazilian context, and must be modified in four ways.

First, in thinking about the U.S. case, analysts (e.g., Mayhew 1974) have collapsed two different issues into the category of winning elections: securing candidacy and winning the general election. For the United States, collapsing these two issues is defensible because in most states securing candidacy depends on a popular election—a primary. Winning candidacy is similar in this respect to winning a general election. Therefore, for purposes of both winning candidacy and getting elected, a U.S. politician needs to cultivate a personal following.

In most democracies, including Brazil, winning candidacy and getting elected must be separated because the former does not rest on a direct popular election. Usually, party leaders exercise more control over candidate selection than in the United States. Therefore, in thinking about politicians' incentives in Brazil, as in many other countries, gaining candidacy deserves more independent attention than in the U.S. case. An exclusive focus on winning elections could wrongly deflect attention from important intraparty political struggles and incentives. The comparative literature on incentives that structure politicians' careers has not sufficiently considered this point.

Second, emphasizing reelection as the paramount objective of legislators makes sense primarily in a context where politicians repeatedly aspire to reelec-

TABLE 8-1
Reelection in the Brazilian Chamber of Deputies, 1978–94

Initial election year	A No. of deputies elected	B No. of deputies listed[a]	C Ran next time for federal deputy	D Ran for some position[b]	E Pct. who ran (D/A)	F Reelected federal deputy next time	G Pct. reelected (E/C)
1978	420	442	322	n.a.	72.9[c]	221	68.6
1982	479	—	304	350	73.1	181	59.5
1986	495[d]	—	324	355	71.7	185	57.0
1990	503	—	354	408	81.1	217	61.3
TOTAL	1,897	—	1,282	1,113[e]	76.5	804	62.7

SOURCE: 1978 data compiled from information in Câmara dos Deputados, Centro de Documentação e Informação, *Deputados Brasileiros—46a Legislatura, 1979–1983* (Brasília 1981); Câmara dos Deputados, Centro de Documentação e Informação, *Deputados Brasileiros—47a Legislatura, 1983–1987* (Brasília 1985). 1982–90 data: Figueiredo and Limongi 1996, 20–21.
[a]Number of deputies listed in the source book.
[b]Federal deputy, governor, vice-governor, senator, or *suplente* for senator.
[c]For 1978, number who ran for federal deputy as a percentage of the number of deputies listed in the source book.
[d]Includes eight deputies elected in 1988 from Tocantins.
[e]1982–90 only; excludes 1978 data.

tion. Politicians who serve for a short period and move on to other activities behave in ways inconsistent with the assumption that their behavior is geared toward reelection. Mayhew shows that his assumption is reasonable in the United States, but in Brazil the situation is less clear-cut.

To evaluate how committed Brazilian legislators are to reelection, I used data from Figueiredo and Limongi (1996) for deputies elected in 1982, 1986, and 1990 and compiled data from the Chamber of Deputies for 1978. The rate at which incumbent federal deputies ran again in the next election was examined.[2] Table 8-1 provides the results.

Column A gives the actual number of deputies elected in a given year. For 1978, Column B gives the number of deputies for whom the source book provides information. For the 1979–83 legislature, this number is higher than the number in Column A because it includes *suplentes* (substitutes) in addition to the deputies who had relinquished their seats temporarily to take another public position. Column C gives information on the number who ran again for federal deputy in the next election, and D gives the number who ran for governor, vice governor, or senator. Column E provides the percentage of deputies who sought election as a deputy, senator, governor, or vice governor. This proportion has consistently been above 70 percent. Column F provides information on the percentage of those who won reelection.

Roughly three-quarters of the deputies aspired to win reelection. If we add to this the number who relinquished their position as deputy to become mayor or run for state deputy and delete the number who died in office, the resulting picture indicates that a large majority of Brazilian national legislators desire to remain in politics from one legislature to the next. More than is the case in many Latin American democracies, Brazilian politicians can enjoy expansive political careers—and many do so. Enough politicians seek reelection to regard it as a powerful motivation in politics. Reelection is a stronger inducement in Brazil than in Costa Rica, where immediate reelection is banned and where only 14 percent of legislators in the post–1949 period have served more than one term (Carey 1996: 77); in Mexico, where immediate reelection is banned and where only 9 percent of the deputies between 1933 and 1994 were reelected (Lujambio 1995: 176); or in Argentina, where only 22 percent of deputies elected in 1993 had served in the lower Chamber between 1983 and 1993 (Jones 1997: 277).

Although further research would be needed to find a definitive answer to why Brazilian politicians value extended legislative careers more than Argentine politicians, some reasons for the desirability of such careers in Brazil seem evident. Legislative careers are the main springboard for vaulting into higher executive positions. Immediate reelection for executive posts was barred until 1998, so governors and mayors of major cities often circulated back into the National Congress, often with an idea of rerunning for governor at a later date. National legislators are well paid and enjoy ample perks. In addition, notwithstanding the limitations of the Brazilian National Congress as a policy-making body, it is a relevant political actor.

On the other hand, reelection is a less central motivation for Brazilian deputies than for members of the U.S. House of Representatives. Why do fewer deputies seek reelection in Brazil than in the United States? Being a legislator offers less power in Brazil than in the United States. The legislature is often a way station on the road to competing for executive power. Being a mayor of a city of several hundred thousand inhabitants affords more power and prestige than being a federal deputy. This explains why in 1988, about 120 members of congress—more than one in five—ran for mayor, indicating a willingness to relinquish a seat in the national legislature (Power 1991: 82, citing DIAP 1988: 27).

This information on the lower desirability of legislative posts in Brazil suggests a minor modification to Mayhew's argument on the United States. Rather than focusing solely on winning legislative reelection, in Brazil it is important to think in terms of advancing a political career. Doing so requires winning elections, but it means more mobility from one position to another—in particular, from legislative to executive positions.

Third, Mayhew argues that for U.S. congressional representatives, it is more appropriate to think of winning an election than of vote maximizing. Politicians want to win comfortably, but they need not maximize votes. In Brazil, vote maximizing is more important than in the United States because of the electoral system and different career patterns. Brazilian candidates for deputy have several incentives to maximize votes. They run against dozens or even hundreds of competitors rather than merely one as in the United States, and the number or share of votes needed to win is not clear beforehand. In the United States, in most House and Senate races, candidates know that they need approximately 50 percent of the vote. In a two-way race, all that is unknown regarding what it takes to win is the turnout, hence the raw number of votes. In Brazil, a candidate can win an election with fewer votes than a competitor from a different party. This often occurs because of the electoral system. The level of uncertainty regarding outcomes is higher, and the need to maximize votes to be assured of winning is therefore greater. In addition, the deputy of the governing coalition with the most votes in a given *município* is usually granted valuable patronage privileges. The importance of patronage provides an incentive to maximize votes; merely winning an election does not suffice. Finally, amassing a large number of votes enhances one's chances of becoming a state secretary, a minister, a head of a major public agency or enterprise, or a candidate for governor or senator. Vote maximizing is a good way to advance one's political career.

Fourth, there are some general (as opposed to specific to the Brazilian case) objections to the assumption that politicians' behavior can usefully be understood in terms of self-interest, and these general objections are more important in Brazil than in the United States. Some politicians are driven by ideological and policy considerations above and beyond any calculation of self-interest (Wittman 1973). Most politicians believe in most of the causes they espouse, and many are willing to forego some votes to be true to their causes. Some politicians are motivated more by a desire to propagate a message than to occupy public office. Putting a normative commitment above one's political career is especially common among issue-oriented politicians.

Some distinctive features of the U.S. political system diminish the importance of these general objections. Among political contenders who have a chance of gaining office, policy differences are less pronounced than in virtually any other democracy. Major contenders care deeply about winning elections, so the assumption that they base their behavior exclusively on the effort to gain office is more reasonable.

In Brazil, that assumption is less reasonable for the leftist parties, which are more ideological and less pragmatic than the U.S. parties. They more frequently adhere to ideological or policy principles even at the cost of votes and winning office than U.S. parties. Therefore, there are more politicians in Brazil than in the United States whose behavior deviates markedly from what one would expect based on the assumption that politicians orient their behavior toward winning an office.

Are these qualifications to Mayhew's arguments so powerful that we should drop the assumption that politicians are rational actors whose behavior can be predicted on the basis of institutional rules? I would modify rather than scrap Mayhew's perspective because successful Brazilian politicians care a great deal about winning elections. In order to implement their preferred policies, politicians must first win candidacy and get elected. Even in ideological parties, for successful (and therefore more relevant) politicians, securing candidacy, establishing a strong position within the party, and winning votes and elections are key motivating factors. Therefore, I assume that the behavior of most Brazilian politicians can be understood in terms of how they gain candidacy, get elected to office, and advance their political careers.

Politicians must pay attention to a wide panoply of rules in order to further their careers, but two main issues are paramount: the electoral system and candidate selection. These two issues affect their behavior and the nature of linkages between parties and politicians. Politicians' actions are affected by the incentives established during the selection, campaign, and electoral processes. Some rules make political careers heavily dependent on loyalty to the party, while others promote individualism. For example, a closed party list with proportional elections makes politicians dependent primarily on having a good position on the party list and secondarily on a good collective (party) performance at the polls. Consequently, it is in politicians' self-interest to maintain good standing with the party leaders who draw up the order of the list. Otherwise, their chances of being elected suffer. If parties control candidate selection, campaigns, and the order of the ticket, individual representatives must be loyal to the organization; otherwise, their own political careers will suffer. Under these conditions, discipline and cohesion are likely to be strong.

Conversely, if winning nomination and election depends mostly on individual initiative, then politicians have less incentive to abide by the wishes of the party leadership (Carey and Shugart 1995). Organization is likely to be looser, less cohesive, and less disciplined.

The Open-List Electoral System, Autonomous Politicians, and Weak Parties

Electoral rules provide incentives for politicians that structure their actions and logics. Some electoral systems require that politicians cooperate with other parliamentary representatives and candidates because such cooperation is necessary in order to win party backing, which in turn is essential to election and promotion. With such electoral systems, politicians have incentives to toe the party line; it is in their self-interest to appear to sacrifice their own individualism. Self-interested logic leads to focusing on the collective enterprise. The primary example is proportional systems in which the party leadership designates the order of the ticket.

Other electoral systems encourage politicians to develop personal constituencies because election depends above all on individual effort (Cain, Ferejohn, and Fiorina 1987; Carey and Shugart 1995). In Japan, for example, with the single nontransferable vote (replaced in 1993), politicians were elected exclusively by their own personal votes, so they had powerful incentives to campaign in individualistic fashion (McCubbins and Rosenbluth 1995). The single transferable vote (STV), which is used in Ireland, Malta, Tasmania, and Australian Senate elections, also rewards politicians' ability to attract personal votes (Lakeman 1974: 111–50). In turn, the incentives created by the electoral system, along with the nature of candidate selection, help explain how parties function (Katz 1980).

Brazilian electoral rules encourage politicians to develop a personal vote and avoid relying extensively on the party for election. The electoral system helps explain the individualistic behavior of politicians and has contributed to the weak institutionalization of the party system. The low degree of loyalty found in the catch-all parties is encouraged by the electoral system.

Brazil has a system of proportional representation that gives the electorate broad choice in choosing individual candidates and weakens party control over candidates. In most countries with proportional representation, party leaders have considerable authority in determining which individual candidates will fill seats. In other proportional systems, including the Brazilian, Italian (until 1993), Greek, Chilean after 1958, Finnish, Peruvian (since 1985), Ecuadorean (beginning in 1998), Polish, and, for some seats, Estonian and Latvian, preference voting completely determines the intraparty order of candidates. These open-list systems offer voters broad intraparty choice at election time. A citizen casts a vote for one deputy only, and this vote cannot be transferred to other individuals. In Brazil, voters are allowed to select a party without specifying an individual, but only a small minority exercises this option (Samuels 1996). Seats are first distributed to parties according to the total number of votes their candidates get (plus party-label votes), and then within parties according to the number of individual votes. Which individuals are elected from any given party depends completely on the candidates' ability to obtain individual votes.

This system provides an incentive to individualism in campaigns, especially because a politician's prestige and power are enhanced by a massive vote total. "Winning big" paves the way to higher political office. This system and others in which preference voting completely determines the order of candidates require politicians to develop personal votes. In the absence of other mechanisms that give the party leadership control over rank-and-file legislators, such systems can weaken the leadership and create an incentive to individualistic behavior among politicians (Lamounier 1986).

Because there is a premium on individual campaigning and because significant benefits accrue to winning, proportional representation (PR) with an open list has been conducive to profligate individual campaign spending in Brazil. A PR system with greater party control over the list would reduce incentives for individual candidates to spend. Potential financial supporters are not inclined to spend money that has little effect on their candidate's chances, and politicians have limited incentive to raise money for their own campaigns.

Where preference voting completely determines which candidates from a party get elected, politicians have incentives to develop personal constituencies and engage in individual campaign efforts (Katz 1986; Ames 1995b; McCubbins and Rosenbluth 1995; Carey and Shugart 1995). Under such conditions, party leaders are less likely to control campaigns and may have less power over elected representatives.

Even though cohesion and discipline sometimes suffer and campaigns are generally more individualistic when preference voting completely determines the order of candidates within a party, one should not exaggerate the effects of the electoral system in isolation. Other democracies in which preference voting determines the order of candidates are not characterized by individualism among politicians or by a lack of discipline. In some countries (Finland, Chile, Italy before 1993) in which preference voting completely determines the order of the list, parties are more organized, have more influence over who gets elected, and allow less autonomy to politicians. In part, the reason is that several other features of the Brazilian institutional system give politicians incentives to retain autonomy vis-à-vis their parties.

Candidate Selection and Loose Parties

Candidate selection is a crucial process for politicians because to have careers as elected public officials, they must seek and win candidacy within a party.[3] The rules that determine candidate selection therefore establish powerful incentives for politicians. The way candidates are chosen shapes linkages between politicians and parties, the way politicians seek to promote their political careers, the kinds of campaigns they run, how they attempt to win votes, how they function once they are elected, and therefore how parties and politicians attempt to represent their constituencies (Ceaser 1979; Epstein 1967: 201–32; Gallagher and Marsh 1988; Morgenstern 1996; Ranney 1981; Schattschneider 1942). Without understanding how candidate selection works, we cannot comprehend some aspects of how parties function. Yet we know little about candidate selection in most of Latin America.

How dependent are politicians upon the support of party leaders in their quest to become candidates? The answer varies from one democracy to another. In most democracies, candidate selection is controlled by a small number of party leaders, and the public does not participate in the process. Potential candidates must be on good terms with party leaders to win a place on the slate. The leadership has a powerful means of influencing politicians' behavior: if they do not follow the party line, they can be denied candidacy. Control of candidate selection makes it easier for party organizations to impose discipline. Politicians have incentives to be loyal to the party, and parties (rather than individuals) tend to be more prominent in campaigns.

In other democracies, party organizations have relatively little control over candidate selection. Individual politicians must rely on their own resources and public support to become candidates. The United States, where the widespread introduction of primary elections removed control of candidate selection from party organizations and gave it to the electorate at large, represents this end of the spectrum. Most U.S. states use primaries to determine candidate selection for local, state, and presidential office. The party organizations may have a preferred candidate, but the selection process virtually bypasses the leadership. Politicians secure nomination because of their own resources, so they have less incentive to toe the party line.

In Brazil, parties have more control over candidate selection than in the United States, but less than in most democracies. In the Brazilian catch-all parties,[4] winning nomination depends mostly on politicians' individual initiatives, although being well connected to top state-level party leaders is more helpful in winning candidacy (and election) than in the United States. Candidates have incentives to develop their own political bases.

For legal purposes, Brazilian politicians need to run on a party ticket, so they cannot entirely dispense with parties. Yet the need to go through a party to secure a position on the slate is not very confining. The large number of parties and their heterogeneous character, plus the large number of positions available on the slate, ensure that most politicians can fit into several parties. If they become uncomfortable in a party, they can usually change to another without high political cost. For politicians who are good at winning votes (*bom de voto*), there is no dearth of parties willing to offer them candidacy.

As with the United States, but in contrast to most other Western democracies, in Brazil until 1995 the state regulated how candidate selection within parties took place. In contrast to the United States, where such regulations are established by state governments, in Brazil they were set by the federal government through the Organic Law of Political Parties of 1971 and hence were uniform throughout the nation. Law 9096 of September 1995 reduced state regulation of candidate selection, and parties now have more autonomy to determine how to select candidates. As of 1997, however, the catch-all parties had roughly similar mechanisms of candidate selection.

Candidate selection for all candidates begins at the local (district or *município*) level. Local party conventions directly chose the local directorate, delegates to the state convention, the slate for councillors, and the candidates for mayor and vice mayor. This arrangement gives party members complete control of candidate selection at the local level.

Local candidate selection involves greater popular participation and conversely affords less leadership control than is the case in most democracies. Any member of a party has the right to attend and vote in local party conventions. Party membership is fairly extensive and relatively easy to obtain. In 1990, the number of party members in the state of São Paulo had increased to 2,013,916, counting only the twelve largest parties (Kinzo 1993: 34). In 1995, the PMDB had six million members nationally, the PFL three million, the PSDB and PT 700,000 each.[5] Candidate selection was formally open to many more people than in most countries, though far fewer than in the United States.

Although party membership in Brazil is extensive, fewer people are involved in local conventions in Brazil than in U.S. primaries, mostly because becoming a member in Brazil is more involved than voting in a primary is in the United States. To become a member, a person must take proper legal documentation to party headquarters in the *município* or district in which he/she resides. Members typically agree to participate in party meetings and activities, support the party's candidates, participate in electoral campaigns, defend the party's program, work for the party, and contribute financially. Most parties also require programmatic commitments. PMDB members, for example, agree to a litany of substantive commitments, including "working for the unity of popular forces, . . . joining the struggles of the great masses of the marginalized and workers, . . . working for the prestige and unity of the party."[6] Even though such obligations are not enforced, their existence indicates that party membership is intended to be restricted to individuals committed to the parties rather than, as in the United States, open to individuals whose only tie to a party is electoral support every four years.

All other party positions and candidacies are ultimately determined by the system of indirect elections described in Chapter 5. At the state level, control of candidate selection rests formally in the hands of several hundred (or at most a couple of thousand, for the large parties in the large states) delegates, most of whom are party activists and professional politicians. Although the conventions have ultimate formal authority over candidate selection, they almost always ratify agreements reached by top party and government officials in advance of the conventions. Usually, conventions are presented with a *chapa única*—an already determined ticket. In these cases, the decisions regarding candidate selection precede the convention. Only when there is a close balance between competing forces is the convention likely to decide the composition of the ticket. The party conventions then might appear to be a formality behind which the "real" mechanism of candidate selection is controlled by a small group of party leaders.

Top party and government leaders can (and usually do when possible, especially in the catch-all parties) exercise sway over candidate selection through patronage. At first glance, this situation appears favorable to the party leadership's ability to control candidate selection and thereby acquire leverage vis-à-vis legislators. Yet this impression is only partially correct. Even though party conventions ratify preestablished agreements, what takes place at local and state conventions is important for internal party control. The relative power of party leaders hinges on how many delegates they control; as a result, battles over municipal and state politics are intense. To promote their political careers, politicians need to fare well in conventions, which ultimately determine who controls the party. As a result, popular input into candidate selection is crucial. By locally electing delegates who in turn choose leaders at the state and ultimately the national level, party members shape candidate selection at higher levels as well. Politicians seeking key executive posts must have broad support in local conventions.

Therefore, the process of candidate selection creates incentives for politicians to develop their own political constituencies—their "personal vote" (Cain, Ferejohn, and Fiorina 1987). Especially to become candidates for the crucial executive posts, Brazilian politicians need their own popular constituencies. This is particularly true in the larger catch-all parties; in smaller parties, there is less competition to get on the ballot as a candidate for deputy.

The incentives to individualism generated by candidate selection are less pronounced than in the United States. In Brazil, common party members do not participate directly in the selection of candidates for state and national office. Instead, candidate selection beyond the local level is controlled by delegates chosen through indirect elections. Delegates to state and national conventions are party regulars, so candidate selection at these higher levels is controlled by a moderate number of activists and professional politicians. By contrast, in most U.S. states, common citizens can participate in the selection process for choosing candidates for congress and the president. In addition, Brazilian governors exercise more influence over candidate selection within their party than do their U.S. counterparts.

In summary, Brazilian party leaders control the selection process for congressional candidates more than leaders in the United States do, but they have less control than in most other democracies. Brazilian candidate selection for congresspeople is neither a situation of party control over candidate selection, as exists in most Western democracies, nor a situation in which the broad electorate makes the decision, as exists in most U.S. states. The state conventions neither remove control of candidate selection from the party, as direct primaries do, nor give it to a handful of leaders. They are somewhat akin to the caucuses that determined candidate selection in the United States before the advent of direct primaries. The process of candidate selection is more open to common citizens than in most democracies, where common citizens cannot participate at all.

The catch-all parties generally accept a broad range of candidates without making ideological or organizational demands. In the major parties, there is competition to appear on the ballot even for lesser positions, but leaders generally accept well-known or wealthy candidates regardless of their ideological positions if these candidates can attract votes. This willingness to accept candidates of various hues stems partially from electoral legislation, which provides incentives to run a large number of candidates. Even if a candidate does not win many votes, he/she still adds to the party's total, and hence can contribute to the number of seats the party wins.

The need to form electoral coalitions to win executive positions can also serve as an incentive not to impose demands on candidates. Many gubernatorial and mayoral candidates encourage the formation of broad electoral alliances to enhance their own prospects. Gubernatorial and mayoral candidates usually carry considerable weight in party deliberations about candidate selection and electoral coalitions. Stringent criteria for the selection of candidates for proportional positions would undermine the possibilities for constructing broad party alliances. Thus most gubernatorial candidates prefer a nonrestrictive candidate selection because it enhances their own chances of getting elected.

So far I have described the "normal" process of congressional candidate selection, which pertains for everyone except incumbent state and federal deputies and councillors, who bypass this process because of a provision that further reduces party control over candidate selection: the *candidato nato* (literally, "birthright candidate"). This is a rule by which federal and state deputies and councillors (and until 1986 senators as well) automatically have the right to be on the ballot for the same position in the next election unless the party leadership makes a deliberate decision to exclude the individual. The catch-all parties hardly ever deny incumbents a place on the ballot. A politician can violate the party's programmatic concerns, vote against the leadership, and still virtually be guaranteed a place on the ballot. The *candidato nato* rule thus gives leverage to politicians who wish to operate free of the fetters imposed by party leaders. It places the burden on the leadership to prevent a candidacy rather than on the politician to secure support for candidacy.

Why do leaders of the catch-all parties rarely deny a place on the ballot to an incumbent federal deputy when they have the right to do so? In situations of conflict between a politician and the leadership, after 1984 the cost for the politician to switch parties was low. The option of joining another party diminished deputies' need to invoke the *candidato nato* rule. Party leaders faced some cost (time, effort, and controversy) to block a candidate, and they probably calculated that they would prefer not to incur this cost in a situation of little or no gain. On balance, party leaders would have little reason to prefer that a legislator move to another party because his/her votes—assuming they are mostly transferable—would then benefit that competitor.

The great majority of candidates for proportional positions are *not* covered by the *candidato nato*; they must win candidacy through the convention process described above, in which party and government leaders can exercise considerable influence. Therefore, it might seem that the *candidato nato* rule has only a marginal effect. However, a sizable minority of federal deputies elected are seated incumbents, as can be seen from rearranging data in Table 8-1. Of those elected federal deputy in 1982, 46.1 percent (221 of 479) were seated incumbents; the comparable figures for 1986 and 1990 were 37.2 percent (181 of 487) and 36.8 percent (185 of 503), respectively. These incumbents bypassed party channels and therefore owed no allegiance to party leaders for their candidacies.

The selection process for governor is the same as for Congress in most parties; the state convention is the decisive locus. The PT, however, has a process of primaries for governor.

The presidential candidate selection process follows roughly similar contours. National conventions formally make the decision, but in practice, the input of a small number of party leaders is usually decisive. They have greater control over the formal aspects of the selection process because the national convention is one step further removed from direct popular input. Some parties have experimented with primary elections restricted to members.

Decentralization of Candidate Selection

Another important factor in how politicians and parties function is the degree to which the selection process is centralized. This aspect of candidate selection has an impact on parties because if local party leaders control candidate selection, elected representatives will not necessarily have incentives to follow the national leadership. The possibilities range from the centralization of candidate selection of national legislators at the national level to decentralization at the local or state level, with no national leadership control.

Brazil fits the decentralized pattern with essentially no control by national party leaders. With the exception of president and vice president, selection of candidates for all elected public positions occurs at the state (governor, vice governor, senator, federal and state deputy) or local (mayor and councillor) level. Winning a nomination thus requires that candidates build strength at the local and state levels. The national leadership almost never interferes with state decisions on candidate selection even though it formally has the authority to do so. The national organizations play no role in candidate selection except for the president and vice president. Even for those nominations, such a role is diluted by the fact that the national organizations are to some degree federations of state organizations.

With the exception of the United States, all the advanced industrial democracies have a more centralized process of candidate selection than Brazil. Elsewhere, national party organizations generally play a central role in candidate selection for members of the National Congress. Venezuela, for example, has a particularly centralized process of candidate selection, in which a small group of national party leaders determines candidates for president, governor, and Congress (Coppedge 1994; Crisp 1997).

Although the national organizations have a weaker role in candidate selection in Brazil than in most democracies, candidate selection in Brazil is somewhat more centralized than in the United States. In Brazil, governors exercise sway over candidate selection within their own party—especially if they are willing to use patronage to retain control of the party. Moreover, at the state level, greater centralization occurs in Brazil than in the United States: candidate selection for the lower chamber takes place at the local level, while in Brazil it takes place at the state level. Even though formally national conventions determine presidential candidate selection in both countries, in reality primaries are now the principal means of selecting presidential candidates in the United States. In Brazil, the party leadership has more influence over candidate selection for president than in the United States.

The irrelevance of the national party organizations in Brazil for candidate selection (except for president) has an impact on party politics. The fact that the national organizations do not influence congressional candidate selection helps explain why the catch-all parties have congressional delegations that are ideologically heterogeneous and why the national leadership has limited power over individual representatives.

Decentralization of candidate selection shapes the logic of Brazilian politicians. In order to win and maintain power, politicians must focus on the state and local arenas. Winning and retaining local support is crucial. Having national prestige is no antidote to a lack of support at home, as several politicians observed in interviews. For example, former Federal Deputy José Freitas Nobre, a prominent (P)MDB leader during the period of resistance to authoritarian rule, attributed his defeat in 1986 to his leadership role in the National Congress. "I was elected leader of the PMDB in the Chamber of Deputies five times, and as a result I didn't have time to attend to my clientele [*bases*] here in São Paulo. It was impossible to spend more time here in São Paulo. . . . The electorate is used to having personal contact [with its representatives]. You will not get elected if you can't be here in São Paulo."[7]

In order to attain power within the national party, politicians must be powerful within their own state party. The careers of Brazilian politicians depend in good measure on what takes place at the local level. Politicians need to retain sympathies—and control—of their local constituencies. This helps explain why politicians spend a great deal of time in their home states. Local politics remains quite important and did so—counterintuitively in view of the centralization of policy making—even under military rule. Even in small *municípios* in the interior, local politics is a battleground for national level politicians. This system induces a strong concern to maintain close connections to local constituencies, and it also often induces putting patronage politics above legislative responsibilities.

Most members of Congress spend considerable time attending to local clienteles. Even those who are most concerned with legislative tasks spend considerable time in the *município*, where they garner votes. Ex-Federal Deputy João Gilberto (PMDB-Rio Grande do Sul) stated in an interview, "As a deputy, I never failed to go to my region twice a month. My work was both national and local. I would spend several days, four or five days each time, in my region. I represented 256 *municípios* and I visited each one of them four times per year."[8]

Politicians make every effort to ensure that they retain control of their bases and expand to new areas. The battle for control of local directorates and executive committees, and especially of the delegates chosen for the state convention, is crucial for ambitious politicians. Local conventions determine who the prevailing local political bosses will be, and they also affect the political strength of national political figures.

Weak Mechanisms of Party Discipline

Between 1985 and 1988, politicians also faced institutional choices that would encourage party discipline or allow for comparatively undisciplined parties. The legislation inherited from the period of military rule was favorable to moderately disciplined parties. Under democracy, politicians quickly eliminated some important mechanisms that encouraged party discipline.

Constitutional Amendment #25 (May 1985) revoked some measures on party discipline and loyalty established by the dictatorship. By abolishing these mechanisms, it weakened party leaders and reduced executive control over parties. The amendment enabled (and as noted earlier, under some conditions even required) deputies and senators to change parties without sanctions. Previously, parties had the right to refuse membership to anyone; with the promulgation of the amendment, they lost this authority and citizens acquired the right to join whatever party they wanted to.

The rejection of mechanisms of party discipline continued in the constitutional assembly of 1987–88. That body discussed but rejected proposals that would have strengthened party control over politicians, retained the open list system, and maintained the mechanism for candidate selection. It overwhelmingly rejected an amendment (#160) that called for terminating the mandate of officeholders who switched parties. This amendment would have given the party leadership greater control over the rank-and-file legislators by effectively denying them the chance to switch parties; the leadership could then have imposed sanctions without fear that doing so would cause a politician to bolt to another party.[9]

Why have Brazilian politicians chosen measures that allow for loose parties? One reason is that a large number depend on patronage for survival and success (Hagopian 1996; Ames 1995a). The importance of delivering material goods for securing reelection makes many politicians dependent on the president and the governor of their state. Their insistence upon not being tied down by a party is partly a reaction against this dependence on presidents and governors. It has a compelling logic: many governors dominate the parties that support them (Abrúcio 1998). In a system in which political competition involves access to patronage as much as disputes among parties with different ideological proposals, allegiance to national party leaders would compete with allegiance to governors and presidents, who control the purses.

Politicians believe that loose parties best enable them to represent their local constituents. Brazilian politicians federalize the parties in practice by limiting their power over congressional representatives. Under these circumstances, politicians can represent their local clienteles with limited interference from national parties. Only where politicians are relatively free of national party obligations can they represent their local and statewide clienteles as they wish to.

The desire for autonomy to attend to the interests of local elites and needs is acute in Brazil because of enormous regional differences. Few countries in the world are characterized by such profound social, economic, and regional disparities. In 1985, the state of São Paulo had a per capita income 6.8 times greater than that of the poorest state (Piauí). (When it was created in 1988, Tocantins replaced Piauí at the bottom of the scale. São Paulo's 1985 per capita income was 7.9 times that of the *municípios* that three years later formed Tocantins.) São Paulo's 1985 per capita income was substantially higher than that of Argentina and South Korea and close to Venezuela's; Piauí's 1985 per capita income hovered around that of very poor African and Asian countries such as Ghana, Pakistan, Sri Lanka, Zambia, and Mauritania, and was significantly lower than Bolivia's, which is one of the poorest Latin American countries.[10] The North, Northeast, and Center-West regions are much poorer than the South and Southeast.

Differences in education, health, and other social indicators are commensurate. For example, according to 1991 census data, 88.7 percent of heads of household in the state of São Paulo were literate; in Piauí, only 48.5 percent were literate. In São Paulo, 8.4 percent of heads of household had at least fifteen years of schooling—the number that would usually be required for a college degree. In Piauí, the comparable figure was only 1.9 percent. In terms of per capita income, education, health, and other social indicators, the states of the North, Northeast, and Center-West are vastly poorer than those of the South and Southeast. A chasm separates the wealthy and the poor regions of Brazil in cultural, social, economic, and political terms.

Because of these disparities, politicians represent very different social realities. The class and regional differences the Brazilian political elite represent are so great that they provide politicians with a motive to prefer undisciplined and decentralized parties. A powerful, centralized national leadership would impose a unified line on politicians, impeding the autonomy legislators need to respond to such heterogeneous social realities and interests.

Politicians have helped create a political system in which they can deal in comparatively independent ways, free of the fetters that centralized parties would impose. They have prevented centralized national parties from emerging, believing that party loyalty and more disciplined parties would limit their ability to attend to their clienteles. With loosely organized parties, politicians are free to attend to their own clienteles without being bound to national programmatic concerns.

This "solution" to the problem of representing different interests and social realities in a nation of continental size with great disparities is not new. Political elites in the Old Republic deliberately built an extremely decentralized political system with weak parties and powerful executives. In attenuated fashion, the 1946–64 period had similar characteristics. Much has changed in Brazilian politics, but the combination of decentralization, strong federalism, and weak national parties has persisted, with the partial exception of some periods of authoritarian rule.

Incentives, Politicians, and Parties

Since 1985, Brazilian electoral and party legislation has had several incentives for politicians to develop their personal constituencies and maintain autonomy in most of their dealings. Electoral and party legislation has contributed to the weakness of Brazilian parties by creating incentives for politicians to act as free-wheeling agents.

Faced with the incentives created by the Brazilian electoral system and the process of candidate selection, how would rational self-interested politicians behave? They would be individualistic and would have limited reason to heed national party leaders. They would compete against members of their own parties for votes. They would focus on local and state politics and political constituencies. They would attempt to get loyal retinues to attend party conventions.

Given this behavior by individual politicians, parties would be loosely organized. The national organization would be weak, and state and local politics would be the focus of most party activity. The national party would be ideologically heterogeneous; the glue binding politicians of the same party but from different states would be weak.

Chapter 5 provided evidence that Brazilian politicians of the catch-all parties behave as one would expect on the basis of rational-choice logic. Limited party control over political campaigns and who gets elected means that politicians win primarily because of their own initiatives. This factor, in conjunction with others, gives representatives autonomy vis-à-vis the party in Congress. The catch-all parties hold little authority over their members, including members of Congress. Politicians of the catch-all parties generally vote according to their own interests and perceptions.

The effects of the electoral system and candidate selection begin with individualistic campaigning but go beyond it. Once elected, representatives can act independently of the national party leadership with little fear of sanctions.[11] They do not owe their mandates primarily to the party, but to their own initiative. The catch-all parties put up with violations of party programs and organizational commitments if a politician brings a lot of votes.

Since 1985, politicians of the catch-all parties have perceived parties as vehicles to get elected, but have generally felt limited allegiance to them. By contrast, in Argentina, Mexico, Uruguay, and Venezuela, even though the major parties are not very ideological, they command deep allegiance from professional politicians, much as in the United States. The most salient measure of this loose relationship in Brazil is the frequency with which politicians changed parties. The fact that politicians could switch parties without facing sanctions—possibly excepting that of the electorate in the next elections—enhanced their negotiating power vis-à-vis their parties. If a politician's demands were not met, he/she could transfer to another party. In brief, most Brazilian politicians act as a rationalistic model would indicate.

The qualifications introduced earlier to Mayhew's argument to make it more accurate in the Brazilian context are important. If we failed to disaggregate Mayhew's notion of winning elections into two discrete phases, we would overlook how crucial the process of candidate selection is in Brazil. Candidate selection provides a powerful incentive for focusing on local constituency service. It also provides an incentive for individualism. If the national leadership controlled candidate selection, the incentive structure of Brazilian politics would be different, even under the same electoral system.

The assumption that politicians' behavior is predicated upon the desire to gain office may be less realistic for the leftist parties than for the catch-all parties. The leftist groups follow a different logic from the catch-all parties, and it is a logic that would not be expected on the basis of the system-wide rules. The leftist parties are very disciplined, and the leadership has more authority over individual representatives. Politicians of the leftist parties behave rationally according to *internal* party rules and incentives (Samuels 1996)—but their behavior differs significantly from that of politicians of the catch-all parties.

The main mechanism of the traditional elites for institutionalizing their autonomy has been party and electoral legislation. An open-list proportional system and a decentralized mechanism of candidate selection have been important ingredients in preserving such autonomy. Despite many changes in other aspects of Brazilian party and electoral legislation, these features have remained constant in both democratic periods.

These aspects of electoral and party legislation have contributed to the weak institutionalization of the post–1985 party system. Politicians have the autonomy to seek better deals for themselves regardless of the consequences for their parties, and they have done so. The constant party switching has had deleterious consequences in terms of institutionalizing the system.

The autonomy of Brazilian politicians could be curtailed by implementing some changes in electoral and party legislation. The fact that these changes have not been adopted indicates ambivalence on the part of politicians about the desirability of strengthening parties. This ambivalence stems ultimately from the fact that Brazilian politicians want to preserve their autonomy vis-à-vis parties even at the cost of prolonging a tradition of party underdevelopment.

The final point to make is the importance of paying more attention to the incentives created by party and electoral legislation in studies of Latin American politics. Formal political institutions help explain part of the puzzle of why Brazilian politicians function as they do and why Brazilian national parties are weak. They institutionalized the preferences of political elites, who desired many of the features they got in the parties and party system.

Institutional Rules and the Party System: Federalism, Malapportionment, and Presidentialism

This chapter argues that federalism, malapportionment, and presidentialism have shaped features of the parties and contributed to limited system institutionalization. During periods of democracy, Brazil has had a decentralized federal system. Federalism influences the party system because most key decisions are made at the state level and abundant resources are allocated at this level. Decisions about electoral coalitions and about candidate selection for everything but the president and vice president are made at the state or local level. When their party is part of the governing coalition at the state level, members of Congress affiliated with catch-all parties often are as loyal to the state governor as to national party leaders. Decentralized federalism is an obstacle to the creation of disciplined national parties that project a more or less homogeneous image across state lines. Federalism is a key ingredient in the decentralization of Brazilian parties and in the focus of politicians on local and state issues.

Malapportionment, which in Brazil is a product of federalism, has affected party politics and has contributed to the weak institutionalization of the party system. Brazil has among the most pronounced malapportionment of any democracy in the world. The small states are overrepresented in both the upper and lower houses, and large states are commensurably underrepresented. The smaller states on average are poorer, and politics has a more clientelistic and patrimonial hue there. Politicians in the overrepresented states tend to be less attached to parties and to be more antiparty in attitude. The effect of the overrepresentation of small states is pronounced. With more equal representation, the left would be better represented in the National Congress, and proparty attitudes and practices would be more prevalent.

Two general features of presidentialism work against party building. Presidents are elected by direct popular elections or by an electoral college that has little autonomy vis-à-vis the popular vote. This method of election encourages candidates and presidents to cultivate personal linkages to the electorate and to develop their own political constituencies. Parties have less control over the formation of executive power than in parliamentary systems. Presidents do not always have strong ties to parties, and candidates with antiparty proclivities can get elected in some presidential democracies. In office, such antiparty presidents often deliberately weaken parties. In addition, because parties are not responsible for maintaining governments in office, legislators lack an incentive to maintain discipline that is found in parliamentary systems. Legislators are not held responsible for supporting the government, and they do not face new elections, as they would with a parliamentary system in the event that government support erodes.

These *general* features of presidentialism need not impede the emergence of an institutionalized party system. Brazilian presidentialism, however, has some specific features that have reinforced the incentives against party building. The 1988 constitution gave Brazilian presidents sweeping legislative and nonlegislative authority. Because the executive is so powerful and because presidents can win office without strong ties to major parties, there is less incentive to build parties. Parties per se are less central in the struggle for power than in cases where ambitious politicians need to build and work through a party in order to achieve powerful positions.

Federalism

Along with Argentina, Mexico, and Venezuela, Brazil has one of the four nominally federal systems in Latin America, and its federalism is the most powerful of the four along both political and economic dimensions. Federalism has fostered party decentralization and heterogeneity in Brazil, as it has in the United States (Hagopian 1996; Lima Júnior 1983; Mainwaring and Samuels 1997; Nicolau 1996a).

Since the proclamation of the republic in 1889, Brazil has formally been a federal nation, and federalism has shaped party development. During the Old Republic, parties existed only at the state level, with one party per state (with the exception of Rio Grande do Sul), and each party was limited to a single state. Subsequently, even during periods of political centralization such as the *Estado Novo* and the military regime, state politics remained important.

Despite increasing centralization during military rule, states and *municípios* continued to control significant financial resources. L. Graham (1987: 130) concluded that even under military rule, "after a decade of erosion of state autonomy and centralized rule from Brasília, Brazil continued to function not as a unitary state in terms of public finance, but as a federal republic." Graham noted that this situation represented a contrast to the other federal republics in Latin America, which had de facto unitary public financing. Graham made these observations before the promulgation of the 1988 Constitution, which mandated a massive transfer of fiscal resources from the national to the state and local governments (Dain 1995). As politicians became more important as the political system was liberalized, one of the first things they did was to insist on a larger share of tax revenue (Abrúcio 1998). The tendency to empower local and state governments by providing them with a larger share of revenue continued through the constitutional congress.

Federalism shapes the Brazilian party system in several ways. Political careers revolve around state and local, in addition to national, politics (Samuels 1998). Many members of the National Congress take leaves to run for mayor or serve as state secretary, demonstrating a preference for local and state positions over a seat in the national assembly. Because politicians have incentives to build careers at the state level, party dynamics revolve significantly around what transpires there.

The resource base of state and local governments as a share of total public-sector resources is greater in Brazil than in any other Latin American country. According to data of Gorman, Haggard, and Willis (1996: Table 4), in 1988, state and local governments in Brazil collected 53.0 percent of total tax revenue, compared to 0.0 percent in Chile (1992), 3.1 percent in Venezuela (1989), 17.3 percent in Mexico (1992), 18.4 percent in Colombia (1991), and 20.0 percent in Argentina (1992). Similarly, state and local governments were responsible for 63.5 percent of total government expenditure in Brazil (1993) compared to 12.3 percent in Chile, 22.2 percent in Venezuela, 12.3 percent in Mexico, 33.0 percent in Colombia, and 48.1 percent in Argentina. In Brazil more than anywhere else in Latin America, states and *municípios* have the resources to make state-level political careers valuable.

Not only do Brazilian governors wield power over state government, but they exercise some influence over national legislators. They control jobs and re-sources that are important to national legislators, and they also have some influence over who runs for what positions. These assets give them leverage over the members of Congress who belong to parties in the state-level governing coalition. This leverage of governors over national legislators contributes to the decentralization of Brazilian parties (Abrúcio 1998). Moreover, candidate selection follows federal lines.

The logic of politicians and parties is still guided as much by state as national considerations.[1] Brazilian catch-all parties are decentralized, and parties and politicians generally follow a logic of federalism. Many of their actions are determined more by what goes on in their own states than by what goes on in national politics. In fact, the national parties are still to a considerable extent federations of state parties. This was generally overlooked by analysts of Brazilian politics for the 1964–85 period; most scholars properly emphasized the high concentration of power and financial resources in the hands of the national government (especially the executive), but overlooked the ongoing decentralization of parties. Even during military rule, the logic of party organizations and politicians centered around states (Hagopian 1996).

In unitary political systems, the national executive appoints many subnational officials, creating an incentive to party centralization. In Brazil, by contrast, the fact that local and state officials are elected and have significant powers generates incentives for organizing at the local level to win elections. Because local and state governments are elected by popular vote, and because local and state executives have important resources, politicians have reason to focus on state and local politics.

State party organizations make most of the important decisions, and the national organizations do not have much power over their state counterparts. There are twenty-seven groups of party bosses, one per state (plus the Federal District), rather than one centralized group. Coordinating ideas and plans among twenty-seven different groups is more difficult than doing the same in one centralized party leadership. As has occurred in the United States, federalism in Brazil has worked against party unity, has obliged national leaders to tolerate diversity and autonomy for state organizations, and has favored the autonomy of politicians vis-à-vis the national leadership.

One final effect of the importance of state-level dynamics on the party system is its low degree of nationalization—meaning that voting patterns vary markedly across states rather than following a modal national pattern. For example, in the 1994 lower-chamber elections, the largest party, the PMDB, won vote shares for federal deputy ranging from 2.1 percent in the Federal District to 50.8 percent in Paraíba. The second-largest party, the PSDB, won shares ranging from 1.3 percent (Acre) to 46.9 percent (Ceará). The other major parties won shares from 1.4 percent to 29.3 percent (PT), 0.1 percent to 35.7 percent (PPR), 0.0 percent to 44.0 percent (PFL), 0.3 percent to 18.0 percent (PDT), and 0.0 percent to 46.4 percent (PTB). These are stunningly high cross-state variances, and they are consistent with results since the late 1980s.

Malapportionment

Malapportionment in Brazil is inextricably intertwined with federalism, and it stems from deliberate overrepresentation and underrepresentation of federal units. Most federal systems are bicameral and allow for malapportionment in the upper chamber (Lijphart 1984: 90–105; Stepan 1997). This holds as well for the Brazilian Senate. What distinguishes Brazil in comparative perspective is (1) malapportionment in the upper chamber is egregious; (2) there is significant malapportionment in the lower chamber as well; and (3) malapportionment and economic and social disparities go hand in hand.

Brazil has one of the most malapportioned upper chambers in the world. Among the fifteen (including Spain) federal democracies in the Stepan/Swenden Federal Databank, Brazil has the second-most-malapportioned upper chamber after Argentina. The most populous state in Brazil has 144 times more inhabitants per senator than the least.

Because of the minimum of eight deputies per state and the maximum of seventy, the lower chamber is also characterized by significant malapportionment. The less populous states are overrepresented, while the state of São Paulo is underrepresented because of the maximum. São Paulo has sixteen times more inhabitants per deputy than the state of Roraíma; in this sense, one vote in Roraíma is worth sixteen in São Paulo. This gives Brazil one of the most malapportioned lower chambers in the world, although both Argentina and Bolivia have slightly worse malapportionment (Jones 1995: 142).

Egregious malapportionment would have insignificant consequences if political preferences were similar across territorial lines. To the extent that political preferences vary from one subnational unit to the next, the consequences of malapportionment increase. Therefore, the degree of variation of political preferences across territorial lines assumes importance in assessing the impact of malapportionment.

Before directly addressing this question, let us note that malapportionment in Brazil follows regional lines. Table 9-1 shows the number of senators and deputies of each of the five regions of the Brazilian federation in the 1995–98 legislature and the number they would have in proportion to the population. The Center-West, North, and Northeast combined for sixty of eighty-one Senate seats, giving them 74 percent of the seats with only 42 percent of the population. With 58 percent of the population, the South and Southeast have only 26 percent of the seats. The three poor regions have 257 of 513 lower-chamber seats; with exact proportionality, they would have 216 seats. The North has nearly twice as many deputies as it would based on exact proportionality in a chamber supposedly based on the proportional principle.

TABLE 9-1

Actual and Proportional Number of Congressional Seats by Region

Region[a]	1991 Population	Lower Chamber 1994			Senate 1994		
		Actual seats	Proportional seats	Actual seats/ proportional seats	Actual seats	Proportional seats	Actual seats/ proportional seats
North	10,030,556	65	35.05	1.85	18	5.53	3.25
Northeast	42,497,540	151	148.48	1.02	27	23.44	1.15
Southeast	62,740,401	179	219.21	0.82	12	34.61	0.35
South	22,129,377	77	77.32	1.00	9	12.21	0.74
Center-West	9,427,601	41	32.94	1.24	15	5.20	2.88
BRAZIL	146,825,475	513	513.00	1.00	81	81.00	1.00

SOURCES: Population figures from *Censo Demográfico 1991* (Rio de Janeiro: Fundação Instituto Brasileiro de Geografia e Estastística, 1991), Vol. 1, 137–38; numbers of deputies from *Deputados Brasileiros: Reportório Biográfico, 49a Legislatura 1991–1995* (Brasília: Câmara dos Deputados, 1991).
[a]North: Rondônia, Acre, Amazonas, Roraíma, Pará, Amapá, Tocantins; Northeast: Maranhão, Piauí, Ceará, Rio Grande do Norte, Paraíba, Pernambuco, Alagoas, Sergipe, Bahia; Southeast: Minas Gerais, Espírito Santo, Rio de Janeiro, São Paulo; South: Paraná, Santa Catarina, Rio Grande do Sul; Center-West: Mato Grosso do Sul, Mato Grosso, Goiás, Distrito Federal.

Malapportionment is particularly important in Brazil because of the correlation between overrepresentation, poverty, traditional forms of political domination, and weak parties. The poor North and Center-West are greatly overrepresented, while the comparatively wealthy Southeast is underrepresented. Malapportionment in Brazil has evolved over the years, but less-populous, poor regions have always been overrepresented, particularly during democratic periods. Although regional inequalities have diminished in recent decades, tremendous regional disparities continue to exist. Per capita yearly income in the state of São Paulo approaches US$6,000, while in Piauí, the poorest state, it lags at only US$1,000. Overall, per capita income in the Southeast is 2.7 times greater than that in the Northeast. Thus a distinctive characteristic of Brazilian federalism is the overrepresentation of less-populous and poorer regions in both houses of Congress.

If malapportionment existed but the overrepresented regions had a small share of congressional seats, its effects would be diminished. However, the poor regions account for a slim majority of seats in the lower chamber and nearly three-quarters of the senate seats.

Politically, the differences between the poor, generally overrepresented states, and the wealthier, generally underrepresented ones, are sharp (Schwartzman 1982; Reis and Castro 1992; Soares 1973). The poor states are more permeated by clientelistic, patrimonial styles of politics than the wealthier states. Personalistic domination still is the rule in many parts of the Northeast and the North. Party organizations are weaker and citizens are less informed and less attached to parties.

The political differences between the overrepresented and underrepresented states can be seen in a variety of ways. The clientelistic parties are generally stronger in the overrepresented states, while the left is stronger in the underrepresented states. According to the 1991 census, about 42 percent of Brazil's population lived in the three largest states (which are politically the most underrepresented): São Paulo, Minas Gerais, and Rio de Janeiro. Although these three states accounted for only 33.4 percent of federal deputies in 1982, 32.9 percent in 1986, and 31.4 percent in 1990, until 1994 they consistently accounted for a majority of PT deputies: all eight in 1982, thirteen of sixteen in 1986, and nineteen of thirty-five in 1990. In 1994, these three states elected twenty-three of the forty-nine PT deputies. If these big states were less underrepresented, the PT share of seats in the National Congress would be higher. In 1994, the PT won almost as many votes for federal deputy as the PFL (both got 12.8 percent of the total), but it captured only forty-nine seats compared to eighty-nine.[2] Several parties—especially the PMDB—are more clientelistic in the North and Northeast than in the South and Southeast. Thus both the party composition of Congress and the physiognomy of some parties would differ under conditions of more equal representation.

Responses to surveys of the National Congress show strikingly different patterns by region. For example, my 1988 survey asked, "In your work, how important is it for you to obtain resources for your region?" Twenty-four of fifty-five legislators from the South and Southeast (43.6 percent) said that it was quite important compared to 75.6 percent (thirty-four of forty-five) from the North, Northeast, and Center-West. Clearly, obtaining resources for their regions or constituents is more important for legislators of these poorer, overrepresented regions. Asked whether legislators should lose their mandate for switching parties after the election, 49.1 percent (twenty-eight of fifty-seven) from the South and Southeast agreed, compared to only 21.1 percent (eight of thirty-eight) from the three overrepresented regions, suggesting weaker attachment to parties in the latter. Asked how important party positions were for legislators' congressional behavior, 64.8 percent (thirty-five of fifty-four) from the South and Southeast said quite important, compared to 37.8 percent (seventeen of forty-five) from the Northeast, North, and Center-West. When there is a conflict between the needs of a legislator's region and his/her party's position, 85.7 percent (thirty-six of forty-two) from the poorer regions said they usually voted according to the needs of the region, compared to only 34.7 percent (seventeen of forty-nine) of legislators from the wealthier regions. Twenty-eight of fifty-two legislators from the South and Southeast (53.8 percent) agreed that

"A political party should expel a legislator who votes against a (formalized) party decision"; only 27.9 percent (twelve of forty-three) from the poorer regions agreed with this statement. Twenty-eight of forty-seven respondents from the South and Southeast (59.6 percent) agreed that "The party leadership should have more weight within the party," compared to 31.6 percent (fourteen of forty-three) from the poor regions. Cumulatively, the responses show sharp attitudinal differences between legislators of the poor and wealthy regions. If the wealthy regions were not underrepresented, proparty attitudes in the Congress would be more prevalent, and clientelistic proclivities would be dampened.

Voting patterns in the legislature also frequently show pronounced differences in political patterns in the underrepresented compared to the overrepresented states. Table 9-2 presents the distribution of voting by region on some issues in the constitutional congress of 1987–88. Amendment #160 called for terminating the mandates of members of Congress who switched parties. In a country with rampant party switching in the post–1984 period, this amendment would have enhanced leadership control over rank-and-file members. Legislators from southern and southeastern Brazil were much more likely to be favorable to this amendment than members from the poor and overrepresented regions. Amendment #315, one of the two most polemical in the constitutional congress, instituted a presidential system. Members from southern Brazil voted predominantly (57 percent) against it; members from the poor regions voted overwhelmingly for presidentialism. Amendment #5 reworded the preamble of the constitution, eliminating a reference to direct democracy. Members from the poor regions were much more likely to endorse it. Amendment #624, also highly polemical, granted President Sarney a five- (as opposed to a four-) year term. Members from the poor regions were much more likely to be favorably disposed, reflecting their greater dependence on the federal executive and their vulnerability to presidential threats to shut off the flow of patronage. Amendment #320 instituted a five-year term for future presidents; again, members of the poor, overrepresented regions were more likely to favor it.

Not only are the poor states overrepresented, they have a majority in both chambers of Congress; thus we are not dealing with significantly overrepresented states that nevertheless have a minor weight in the national legislature. Combined with the striking divergences in policy preferences across regions, malapportionment shapes many policy outcomes. This holds not only for outcomes that actually reach the floor: Important issues are framed from the outset by the combination of malapportionment and different policy preferences across territorial lines.

Because the poor regions where clientelism is pronounced and party weakness is accentuated are overrepresented, malapportionment has contributed to party weakness. The overrepresentation of the poor states helps explain the disjunc-

TABLE 9-2
Voting by Region in the Constitutional Congress, Select Issues

Region	Amendment No. 160		Amendment No. 624		Amendment No. 320		Amendment No. 315	
	Pct. yes	No.	Pct. yes	No.	Pct. yes	No.	Pct. yes	No.
Center-West	10.8	37	62.3	53	64.7	51	54.7	53
North	7.3	41	85.0	60	80.0	60	82.0	61
Northeast	11.6	121	65.7	175	64.9	168	63.5	178
South	42.9	70	47.1	85	42.0	81	43.0	86
Southeast	20.9	134	49.4	180	47.1	170	63.5	181
Three poor regions	10.6	199	69.1	288	68.1	279	65.8	292
Two wealthier regions	28.4	204	48.7	265	45.5	251	56.9	267
TOTAL	19.4	403	59.3	553	57.4	530	61.5	559

SOURCE: Calculated from Ames and Power 1990.
NOTES: Amendment #160: A yes vote means that the mandate of an officeholder who switched parties would be terminated. Statistically significant at the .001 level. Amendment #624: A yes vote is favorable to a five-year mandate for President Sarney. Statistically significant at the .001 level. Amendment #320: A yes vote is favorable to a five-year term for presidents. Statistically significant at the .001 level. Amendment #315: A yes vote is favorable to instituting a presidential system of government. Statistically significant at the .001 level.
   The differences in levels of support between the three poor regions and the two wealthier ones are statistically significant at a .001 level for Amendments 160, 624, and 320, and at a .05 level for Amendment 315. Chi^2 tests.

ture between Brazil's economic development and the underdevelopment of its political institutions. The poor states are overrepresented, so it is not surprising that the predominant political style is based on weak democratic institutions.

   Brazil's poor states and the parties that are overrepresented through malapportionment have historically depended more on patronage than the wealthy states. Legislators and governors from the poor states have been more likely to support the president. Thus, as is the case in Menem's Argentina (Gibson 1997), severe malapportionment has usually helped Brazilian presidents build a base of support. However, presidents typically pay a cost to obtain support from the overrepresented areas: politicians from these regions are usually more clientelistic and extract a patronage cost for their support for presidential policies. In brief, the overrepresentation of poor states has had important political consequences, including significant effects on the party system.

Presidential Elections and Party Building

   Presidential systems lack some incentives for party building that are present in parliamentary systems. In the latter, party politicians directly control access to executive power; they determine who becomes the party leader, and hence who would be prime minister. If there is no majority party in the legislature, members of parliament determine what parties will form the governing coalition and who will become prime minister. Prime ministers are directly tied to their parties; they are not elected by popular vote; and they have usually had lengthy careers in the parties, culminating in their selections as party leaders (Suárez 1982). Because parties monopolize channels of political recruitment for prime ministers, chief executives in parliamentary systems usually have a past intertwined with the party. Whereas presidents are elected to a significant degree on the basis of their own personal appeal, most prime ministers are political insiders who need not build up personalistic linkages to the mass electorate.[3]

In parliamentary systems, the prime minister usually has less autonomy with respect to the parties. Especially where a multiparty coalition is ruling, his/her position directly depends on the support of the parties. Implementing major policy decisions without the support of the parties is difficult. Both because of their past socialization in party organizations and their present needs, most prime ministers have a stake in party building.

This contrast between presidential and parliamentary systems is especially vivid with multipartism. In multiparty parliamentary systems, postelection negotiations among parties rather than popular votes usually decide who will be prime minister. Citizens' votes do not play a direct role, so there is less incentive for personalistic campaigning. From the perspective of empowering parties, parliamentary governments are advantageous because they give ambitious politicians incentives to work through parties and they promote citizen loyalty to parties rather than individuals.

In presidential systems, the head of government is elected by direct popular vote or an electoral college that exercises little autonomy with respect to the popular vote. Because parties have less control over the formation of executive power, there is less incentive to focus on party building. Becoming party leader is usually not as important in presidential systems, and politicians who aspire to the presidency may have less incentive to become party loyalists.

Because they are elected by popular vote or by an electoral college whose composition is determined by the popular vote, presidents do not always have a strong stake in party building, and they frequently have limited congressional experience. In the age of the mass electronic media, it is easier than ever for presidents to make appeals directly to the population, thereby increasing their autonomy vis-à-vis the parties. Presidents sometimes enjoy an independence from the political parties that is unknown in parliamentary regimes. They may have limited experience as party people (Rose 1980; Suárez 1982: 131–37), and may even run against the parties. Depending on the candidate selection process, presidents can win nomination and office despite the opposition of most party professionals. This argument does not imply that all presidential systems are characterized by weak parties (and much less that all parliamentary systems have strong parties).

In Brazil, several presidents have been uninterested in party building; a few have even attempted to undermine parties. Several have been recruited from outside or above party channels, have had an antiparty discourse, and have engaged in antiparty actions. The absence of strong ties between presidential candidates and parties during the nomination process and the campaigns has shaped the linkages between presidents in office and parties. Having won office on their own, presidents have been less inclined to attempt to govern with parties and more inclined toward plebiscitarian appeals.

Formally, Brazilian parties control presidential nominations; the national organizations choose presidential candidates. But in practice, party organizations have been overshadowed by personalities. In order to better their chances of winning, parties frequently have run candidates who had not built their political careers through the party.

Presidents and presidential candidates have generally downplayed their connections to parties. Campaigns have emphasized personal qualities as much as issues and have relied on personal linkages more than on party organizations. To be elected, candidates need support from a wide range of the public, so strong identification with a single party could be a liability.

After 1985, Sarney and Collor carried on the tradition of antiparty presidents. Once he assumed the presidency, Sarney reproduced many of the antiparty attitudes and practices of his predecessors and entered on a collision course with his official party, the PMDB. Supported by a small party essentially created to enable him to run for the presidency, Collor was never committed to parties. Throughout his political career, he flip-flopped from the conservative promilitary Arena and the PDS to the PMDB and then the PRN. During his campaign he often criticized politicians and parties and tried to paint himself as a political outsider. He also initially attempted to govern above parties.

Throughout the 1970s and first half of the 1980s, Itamar Franco was a leading MDB/PMDB politician. However, when he lost he PMDB's gubernatorial nomination in Minas Gerais in 1986, the mercurial Franco bolted to the PL, even though the party was markedly more conservative than he. As Vice President he resigned from the PL and remained without a party affiliation. Thus, Franco had some history as an antiparty politician by the time he assumed the presidency.

Although antiparty campaigns and presidents are not an inevitable result of presidentialism, a presidential system makes it more likely that antiparty individuals could assume the chief executive office. In Brazil, winning the presidency has not depended upon parties as much as upon individual politicians, whose personal campaigns, followings, resources, and organizations are more significant than those of the parties. Presidentialism has contributed in this way to the election of chief executives who have worked to weaken rather than strengthen the parties.

Incentives and Party Building in Presidential Systems: Government Maintenance

Presidential systems are characterized by fixed terms of office, whereas in parliamentary systems, the government retains office only as long as it maintains the confidence of the assembly. This difference in patterns of government maintenance affects the logic of politicians and parties.

In parliamentary systems, *ceteris paribus*, legislators' incentives to follow the party line are stronger when their parties are in power. Individual legislators are more or less bound to support the government unless their party decides to drop out of the governing alliance. They risk losing their seats in new elections if the government is dissolved. When members of parliament cease supporting the government, there is a chance that new elections will be called in most parliamentary systems. The coalition that brings the parties together is binding for the postelection period. This helps ensure that there will be either parliamentary support for the executive or a means of toppling the government, and it promotes party responsibility for supporting governments.

By contrast, in presidential systems the parties per se are not held responsible for supporting governments. Legislators thus lack an incentive for party discipline that is found in parliamentary systems, namely, the possibility of dissolution and new elections in the event that the governing party or coalition ceases to support the government. A congressional representative can vote against the leadership without affecting the party's position in government. Legislators are not bound to support the president merely because their party or coalition does. Thus presidential systems lack one mechanism that promotes party discipline (Epstein 1964).

Strong Constitutional Presidencies, Weak Parties

It must be pointed out that several presidential systems do indeed have institutionalized party systems, and most (including Argentina, Chile, Costa Rica, and Venezuela) have disciplined parties. Therefore, although presidentialism can affect party building, its effect in this respect is usually secondary. More important in shaping party building are specific institutional mechanisms that affect how it functions.

Two features of Brazilian presidentialism diminish the importance of party building for politicians: executive posts dominate initiative capacity in the political system, and presidential (and gubernatorial) candidates can win election without belonging to major parties. If the legislature were more powerful or if belonging to a large, well-established party were a *sine qua non* for the presidency, politicians would have more reason to invest in party building. For this reason, strong presidential powers have served as an incentive against party-system institutionalization.

Brazilian presidents have had broad powers, especially under the 1988 Constitution. Their constitutional legislative powers can be divided into three broad categories: (1) reactive legislative powers, that is, those that enable presidents to block legislation—above all, vetoes and partial vetoes; (2) proactive legislative powers, that is, those that enable presidents to legislate; and (3) agenda powers, that is, their capacity to shape the congressional agenda. As has been documented elsewhere (Shugart and Carey 1992; Figueiredo and Limongi 1994, 1996; Mainwaring 1997; Power 1998), Brazil's 1988 Constitution gives the president exceptionally strong leverage in the second and third broad categories as well as some important reactive powers.

In many respects, the 1988 Constitution approximates the often misleading portrayal of Latin American executive power—the imperial presidency. A constitution with executive powers that dwarf legislative powers magnifies the importance of the presidency and diminishes the policy-making importance of legislatures. Because power in the Brazilian political system is concentrated in the executive branch, executive positions are the most desirable. Presidents, state governors, and mayors have enormous proactive powers relative to the respective legislative bodies. For many ambitious politicians, serving in the legislature is a means to an end—executive position—rather than an end in itself. When they are denied the opportunity to run for such positions, ambitious politicians sometimes switch parties so they can do so on another label; they prefer to give up their party rather than relinquish their ambitions for an executive post (Power 1991). This practice has had disruptive effects on party building.

Congress is important primarily as a mechanism for building political careers, for constituency service, for modifying executive initiatives, and at times for blocking executive initiatives. Brazilian legislatures at all levels have little autonomous policy-making capacity compared to legislatures in several other Latin American countries. Congress's policy role has been predicated more upon blocking and moderating presidential action than upon becoming an effective policy initiator. Politicians have less reason to invest in party building and more reason to focus on executive positions than they would if the president's powers were more limited.

Nonconcurrent Elections, 1985–90

The 1988 Constitution created a five-year term for presidents, four-year terms for federal deputies, and eight-year terms for senators. This format was modified by a constitutional reform in June 1994 that established a four-year presidential term concurrent with the legislature's.

In 1989, the nonconcurrent electoral cycle facilitated populism and anti-institutional campaigns. No other post except the presidency and vice presidency was disputed, and nonconcurrence surely helped Collor win as an outsider with no significant party. Other politicians, from councillors to state governors and federal legislators, were not campaigning, so they were less invested in the outcome of the contest. Party organizations were less involved in presidential elections. The lower degree of involvement of party organizations and legislators made it easier for anti-institutional candidates to become prominent.

Because they could not affect legislative outcomes during their own campaigns, candidates had no incentive to campaign for the party. Parties were thus less important to the outcome of presidential elections. Therefore, nonconcurrent elections contributed to a system that lacked incentives for party building.

This lesser degree of involvement by party organizations may be one reason why, when presidential elections are not held concurrently with national legislative elections, party-system fragmentation tends to be greater (Shugart and Carey 1992; Jones 1995). With less involvement by the legislators and state and local executives in presidential campaigns, parties have less influence over citizens and hence are less likely to sway presidential voting.

Hypothesized Effects of Electoral Legislation on Voters

Chapters 8 and 9 have focused on the incentives political institutions create for politicians. Institutions also affect voters. On balance, Brazil's electoral legislation creates incentives for voters to focus on individuals rather than parties and may thereby impede the process of establishing deep party roots in society. Although this study does not provide firm empirical support for the following propositions—doing so would require more extensive investigation into voting behavior than I undertook—they indicate some likely effects of Brazil's electoral legislation on voters.

1. Between 1985 and 1994, major elections were held with great frequency. Brazil was characterized by "hyperelectoralism"—seemingly incessant major elections. Municipal ballots were held in most major cities (all capitals and those that had been classified as "national security cities" under military rule) in 1985; elections for governors, senators, federal deputies, and state deputies in 1986; municipal polls in all *municípios* in 1988; two rounds of presidential elections in 1989; contests for governors, senators, federal deputies, and state deputies again in 1990, with a runoff for governor in most states; municipal elections in 1992 with a runoff for mayor in many major cities; a plebiscite on presidentialism in 1993; elections for president, governors, senators, federal and state deputies in 1994, with a runoff for governor in many states; and municipal polls again in 1996, often in two rounds.

The country rarely enjoyed a respite from campaign activity between the advent of civilian rule in 1985 and 1994. Constant campaigning and elections probably reinforced popular cynicism regarding politicians and parties. During campaigns, politicians presented themselves as striving to address major problems, but governments consistently failed to resolve pressing economic and social maladies until 1994.

2. Because of the electoral system, most voters choose individual candidates for all positions rather than parties. In 1994, party labels did not even appear on the ballot alongside the candidates' names. Presumably, having to choose individual candidates focuses voter attention more on individuals and less on parties.

In most Western European parliamentary systems, voters choose a party even if in some countries they also choose an individual. In some Latin American countries (e.g., Argentina), voters select a party rather than individual for the lower chamber. In others (Mexico, Bolivia, Venezuela), voters have two ballots for the lower chamber, one of which goes to a party and the other to an individual. In Uruguay, voters choose a faction within a party, but not individual candidates. These alternative electoral systems focus voters' attention on parties, presumably fostering greater likelihood of developing attachments to parties.

3. The large number of parties in conjunction with high volatility and relatively frequent party splits and mergers is likely to make it more difficult for most voters to grasp what the various labels stand for, further contributing to parties' difficulties in establishing deep roots in society. Other things being equal, one would presume that it is easier for the average voter to get a bead on a handful of parties rather than twenty. Even if one excludes minor parties on the debatable grounds that they are not relevant actors, there have been as many as eight or nine significant parties in Brazil since 1988. Lamounier and Muszynski (1986) argued convincingly that the switch from bipartism to limited multipartism by 1985–86 made it harder for citizens to identify with parties. Thus the transition to highly fragmented multipartism adds another layer of complexity for voters.

4. The long lists of candidates for proportional positions make it difficult for voters to find out much about candidates. Banck (1994: 150) reports that in the 1992 municipal elections, there were more than 1.6 million candidates nationwide, throughout 5,000 *municípios*. In 1990, there were 3,923 candidates for federal deputy, an average of 145 candidates per electoral district, and 11,169 candidates for state deputy, an average of 414 per district (Lamounier 1991: 57). Because most voters have little information about the candidates for proportional positions, they rely on the input of local politicians. This system dilutes linkages between voters and their representatives. The low percentage of voters who remember whom they supported for proportional positions suggests that

the electoral system does not foster strong linkages between voters and their representatives—notwithstanding the personalistic character of the electoral system. Interestingly, candidates for federal and state deputy cultivate personal reputations, but voters do not remember for whom they voted. An electoral system that provides deputies with strong incentives to cultivate personal votes nevertheless fails to encourage strong bonds between voters and deputies. As a result, both party and individual mechanisms of representation and account-ability are vitiated.

5. Insofar as electoral rules are responsible for extensive party switching, they are likely to have the indirect effect of delegitimizing parties. Frequent party switching by political elites is likely to enhance voter skepticism regarding party labels. When party switching is commonplace, professional politicians signal that they are not particularly loyal to labels. In a context of such frequent switching, it would be surprising if voters developed strong loyalties to parties. The practice is more widespread among catch-all than leftist parties, so the effect would presumably be greatest among voters of the center and right.

In sum, Brazil's electoral rules encourage voters to focus on individual candidates more than parties. The large number of parties and frequent mergers and splits make it harder to grasp what the parties represent than is the case in most democracies, and the large number of candidates also might place com-paratively high informational demands on voters. In terms of voter range of choice, both among and within parties, the system has a lot to offer. On the other hand, the electoral system makes it comparatively difficult for voters to develop attachments to parties.

Conclusion

The last two chapters have discussed institutional rules that affect whether politicians have powerful or weak incentives to invest in party building and whether parties will be more or less disciplined and centralized. These rules shape the nature of parties and party systems. None of them in isolation explains weak institutionalization. But it is noteworthy that many institutional rules in Brazil favor decentralized parties with comparatively high autonomy for indi-vidual politicians. They tend to work against institutionalizing a national party system.

For decades, analysts have decried the personalism that permeates politics in most Latin American countries. Often this personalism is attributed to features of Latin American culture. However important the cultural aspects of person-alism in politics may be, Brazilian political institutions have reinforced them. Given the institutional rules described in Chapters 8 and 9, it would be surprising if most parties were disciplined, cohesive, and programmatic.

These institutional rules are shaped by the historical factors discussed in Chapter 7 but in turn have an independent impact. Political institutions have reinforced the historical factors and can, in some cases, endure well beyond the events that led to their creation. Historical sequences are important, but they are counteracted or reinforced by institutional arrangements. In Brazil since 1985, weak institutionalization has been the product not only of long- and medium-term obstacles, but also of incentives created by institutional rules.

The effect of such rules in exacerbating the difficulties created by late party development can be appreciated in comparative perspective. In several second- and third-wave democracies, party-system institutionalization occurred much more rapidly than in Brazil, partially because institutional rules were more favorable to party building. Late party development is a hindrance to party-system institutionalization, but this is especially true where institutional rules impede party building.

Institutional rules have reinforced and institutionalized the personalistic aspects of Brazil's political culture. If Brazil's formal political rules provided strong incentives for politicians to rely on a collective (party) reputation, the behavior of political elites would change. For example, if the electoral system called for closed party lists or if politicians lost their mandates for switching parties, legislators would have powerful incentives to follow the party line. It is implausible that a cultural predisposition toward personalism would prevail over self-interest in winning the support of the party leadership. Similarly, if a parliamentary system were adopted, parties would become key actors in affording access to executive power. These institutional changes would affect politicians' behavior.

Cultural attitudes and practices are especially important when they are reinforced by formal institutions. Then politicians' self-interest leads them to behave in ways that reinforce the cultural dispositions. Conversely, when cultural attitudes are undercut by incentives created by institutions, they are unlikely to have as powerful an effect. Cultural attitudes may still operate in other domains of the political system, but politicians are more likely to be guided by the logic of self-interest.

In Brazilian party politics, the historic personalistic, antiorganizational tendencies have been sustained by formal institutions. Direct popular elections for the crucial executive posts encourage candidates to develop personalistic linkages to the masses. Brazilian presidentialism offers particular incentives to personalized forms of power because candidates can win the presidency without strong party organizations. The electoral system offers incentives to individualism on the part of politicians and reinforces the personalistic cultural dispositions.

Formal rules help explain why politicians in Brazil and Venezuela behave very differently. Like Brazil, Venezuela before 1945 had an authoritarian heritage in which parties had been minor actors. But with the restoration of democracy in 1958, Venezuelan politicians opted for rules that strengthened parties (Coppedge 1994; Kornblith and Levine 1995; Levine 1973). In Venezuela, political elites designed rules that made parties the central institutions of democratic processes. Discipline was ensured by having a closed party list, which enabled national leaders to promote loyal followers while undercutting those who were less loyal. Giving the central party control over the candidate selection promoted strong central leadership. Giving the president the authority to name governors and mayors further promoted discipline and a powerful central leadership. These formal rules established a logic that prevailed over the individualism and personalism stereotypically associated with Latin American political systems.

Television's impact on parties in Brazil has also been mediated by formal institutional rules. Television's impact on campaigns and elections is greatest in democracies where there are direct popular elections for top political offices and where, as a result, politicians' ability to project a favorable media image to the mass public is especially significant.

Chapters 8 and 9 argued that institutional rules in Brazil created incentives for politicians to cultivate personal votes and focus on state and local politics. The logic was explicitly comparative across cases, underscoring what is distinctive about Brazil's party and electoral legislation and showing how these features have created distinctive incentives.

The argument is also comparative across time. Some of the institutional arrangements that foster weak institutionalization were chosen after 1985. If my argument about the importance of institutional incentives is correct, one would expect some of the manifestations of weak party-system institutionalization to be more acute after the implementation of these new incentives. This is in fact the case.

As of 1985, despite the sharp decline of the PDS, many manifestations of weak institutionalization that characterized the system after 1985 were less pronounced. Party switching among national legislators was uncommon until 1984, when the PFL split from the PDS; discipline seemed greater; the constant forging of new parties was still unknown. It was only after changes in electoral and party legislation were introduced in 1985–88 that party switching increased, that new labels proliferated, and that party identification declined steeply. In many respects, documented in Chapters 4 and 5, the party system unraveled after 1985. Temporal coincidence does not prove causal impact, but many expressions of system deinstitutionalization could not have occurred without changes in party and electoral legislation.

PART IV

The Party System, Economic Reform, and the Quality of Democracy

CHAPTER 10

Political Institutions, State Reform, and Economic Stabilization

One of the three theoretical approaches this study draws on is institutionalism. Its practitioners believe that institutional design has an independent impact on political outcomes, that is, an impact that is not reducible to the result of a particular configuration of social forces. If such arguments are correct, then the design of formal political institutions should shape policy outcomes. One set of institutions should make some outcomes more likely than would be the case with different institutions.

This chapter examines the impact of political institutions on policy reform. Brazil's political institutions—of which the party system is an anchor—have a contradictory effect in terms of fostering or hindering policy reform. The fragmented party system, robust federalism, and symmetrical bicameralism make it difficult to implement major policy changes. They create a large number of what Tsebelis (1995) has called "veto players," that is, actors who can block or undermine policy reforms. On the other hand, sweeping presidential powers partially offset these institutions by concentrating power in the president's hands. Strong constitutional powers for the president facilitate policy reform by enabling him to push forward some agenda items without active congressional support. Between 1985 and 1994, the institutional obstacles to policy reform outweighed the capacity to implement reform via presidential decrees.

This chapter analyzes the proposition that political institutions affect the policy process, looking at two policy areas, stabilization policies and state reform. In post–1985 Brazil, policy reform related to stabilization involved, inter alia, trimming public spending, raising public revenue, retaining a greater share of tax revenue for the central government, restraining the debts of subnational governments, and encouraging subnational governments to assume more fiscal responsibility. State reform included the privatization of public enterprises, administrative reform, social-security reform, and cutting public payrolls. The chapter focuses on the president's capacity to implement reforms in these two policy areas.

As Tsebelis (1995) has argued, a greater capacity to implement reforms need not be desirable in and of itself; some might prefer a polity that is insulated from major policy shifts and upheavals, and thus might prefer institutions that make major reform difficult. However, in the context of democratic Brazil, most scholars believe that stabilization and state reform were important and that other key objectives were unattainable without them.

There is widespread agreement that Brazil was a regional laggard in achieving stabilization and promoting state reform (Williamson and Haggard 1994; Williamson 1990; Packenham 1994; Schneider 1991; Edwards 1995; Haggard and Kaufman 1995; Almeida 1996; Sola 1994a, 1994b). From 1991 to 1994, Brazil consistently had the highest inflation rate in the region. In 1993, Brazil's inflation rate of 2,489 percent was forty times higher than that of the second-highest rate in Latin America (Uruguay's), and in 1992 (1,149 percent) and 1994 (929 percent), it was and twenty and thirteen times higher that of any other country—despite more auspicious economic conditions than most other Latin American countries at the time of inauguration of democracy. Brazil was also a regional laggard in state reform.

From an institutional perspective, the combination of extreme party-system fragmentation, weak party discipline and loyalty, and robust federalism constrained Brazilian presidents between 1985 and 1993, limiting their results in stabilization and state reform. Because presidents lacked reliable support in Congress and from powerful state governors, it was difficult to implement major policy changes in these two areas. Sweeping presidential powers only partially offset the fragmentation created by other institutional arrangements.

Despite the constraining effects of this institutional combination, President Cardoso has been able to implement a highly successful stabilization plan and meaningful state reform. His success occurred despite institutional obstacles, and the institutional barriers to implementing major state reforms remain largely intact. But the need for major reforms has diminished now that rampant inflation is over and some state reforms have gone through.

I focus on the president as the promoter of state reform and stabilization polices for two reasons. The first is empirical: in Latin America, the president rather than Congress or organized interest groups has been the main promoter of state reform and stabilization policies. Second, for theoretical reasons presidents are better positioned than assemblies to undertake such policies; the executive branch has primary responsibility for implementing them. Presidents are elected by and responsible to a nationwide constituency; as such, they have more reason to prioritize macroeconomic results over patronage than legislators do. In contrast, when legislators are elected by personal votes, as is the case in Brazil, they become indebted to the constituencies that elect them. They have more incentives toward particularism than presidents.

Institutional Arrangements and Policy Reform

Building on arguments of Lijphart (1984), Stepan (1997), and Tsebelis (1995), this section discusses seven institutional determinants of the extent to which presidents can be expected to implement reforms they wish to undertake. Although discrete propositions for each of these seven institutions are presented, the interaction among them is crucial. With all seven propositions, the *ceteris paribus* caveat is important.

The first six institutional features involve the capacity of political actors to veto or undermine (deliberately or not) the president's reform agenda. This discussion is close to Tsebelis's (1995) notion of veto players, that is, actors who can veto policy proposals. Tsebelis's notion is broadened by including the capacity of actors to undermine a president's reform agenda; for example, state governors may not have much veto power over the president in the strict sense, but if they have enough resources and autonomy vis-à-vis the central government, they can implement policies that undermine what the president is trying to do. The analysis also parallels Lijphart's (1984) distinction between majoritarian and consensus democracy. In majoritarian democracy, there are few institutional constraints on policy reform, whereas consensus democracy rests institutionally on giving a wide array of actors veto power, hence making it more difficult for the president to implement sweeping reform.

PROPOSITION 1

As party-system fragmentation increases, the president's capacity to implement reforms decreases. Fragmentation correlates extremely highly with the share of seats held by the president's parties (Mainwaring and Shugart 1997: 405). Under normal circumstances, one would expect that the president's party would be more likely than any other to support the president. Therefore, if the party has a small share of seats, obtaining legislative support is likely to be more difficult, effecting major reforms is likely to be more problematic, and Linzian (1994)-type impasses between the executive and legislature are more probable. Conversely, if the president's party has a large share of seats, obtaining legislative support for reforms should be easier.

If other parties' policy positions are close to those of the president's party, then it should be easier for the president to offset having a small share of congressional seats. This means that the relative policy positions of the parties interact with the degree of party-system fragmentation (Amorim Neto 1995; Deheza 1997; Nicolau 1996b; Rodrigues 1995).

PROPOSITION 2

As party discipline decreases, the president's capacity to implement reforms fluctuates in unpredictable ways. A president can gain or lose from weak discipline. Although it should enable a president to win the support of individual defectors of opposition parties more easily, it also increases the chances that an individual member of the governing coalition will not support the president on a particular bill.

It is impossible to generalize whether the advantages of weak discipline for the president outweigh the disadvantages when his/her party does not have a majority. If, however, the president enjoys majority party support, party discipline should help him/her obtain the support needed to implement reforms. On rare occasions the disciplined majority party might not back the president (in which case discipline is a disadvantage), but such a wholesale defection is rare.[1]

PROPOSITION 3

As ideological distance in the party system increases, the president's capacity to implement major reforms decreases. Greater ideological distance makes it more difficult to come to compromise. Parties that are more firmly opposed on policy/ideological grounds to other major parties tend to be less malleable. With less ideological distance, the president is more likely to be able to gain support through a grand coalition or through patronage, making it easier to implement reform.

The relative ideological position of the president's party is also relevant. Even in a system with considerable ideological dispersion, a president whose ideological position is close to that of the "mean" legislator is more likely to win support for his/her reforms (assuming, for parsimony's sake, a unimodal distribution of preferences in the legislature).

PROPOSITION 4

Symmetrical bicameralism, in which both chambers of the national legislature have roughly equal powers, makes it more difficult to implement major reforms. With symmetrical bicameralism, the legislature has two veto players—the upper and lower chambers. If the composition of the two chambers varies markedly, the president's capacity to effect major reforms decreases because the likelihood that one of the two chambers will oppose reforms increases. Either chamber can refuse to pass a reform measure. Overcoming a presidential veto and thereby undermining the president's preferred agenda is also easier with a unicameral system.

The degree to which bicameralism affects whether a president can implement reforms should depend on the degree to which the upper and lower chambers converge politically. In turn, this political convergence/divergence is likely to depend on whether the two chambers are selected in a similar fashion (Jones 1995: 134–44). The more the electoral formula and district magnitude of the two chambers differ, the more likely that their political composition will diverge, hence increasing the president's difficulties in securing support for bills. In addition, if one chamber is markedly more malapportioned than the other, especially if there are pronounced political differences across states and regions, then it is more likely that bicameralism will add one more obstacle to presidents' difficulties in implementing reform.

PROPOSITION 5

If reforming the constitution takes super majorities (that is, more than 50 percent of the legislature), then a detailed constitution that determines a wide range of policies lowers the president's capacity to implement reforms. Reforms that could be implemented via ordinary law will instead require a constitutional amendment, making it more difficult to effect changes in the status quo.

PROPOSITION 6

Federalism, especially strong federalism in which local and state actors have significant resources and autonomy, lowers the president's capacity to implement policy reform. Governors and mayors then control significant resources and can block the implementation of some policies (Abrúcio 1998; Mainwaring and Samuels 1997; Samuels 1998; Stepan 1997). In a centralized, unitary system, local- and state-level actors have less autonomy and less capacity to block or undermine (by implementing policies that diverge from the president's) the executive agenda.

PROPOSITION 7

As the president's proactive legislative powers increase, his/her ability to implement reform increases. Presidents are more likely to be able to implement reforms if they can enact new legislation through decree.[2] Presidents' constitutional powers vary considerably from one democracy to the next (Shugart and Carey 1992; Shugart and Mainwaring 1997). Analytically, we can distinguish between presidents' proactive powers—those that enable the president to change the status quo—and reactive powers, those that enable the president to block changes in the status quo. In assessing prospects for implementing reforms, the president's proactive powers are especially important.

A president's capacity to implement policy reform also depends on some noninstitutional factors such as his/her leadership capabilities, whether the president is proposing major reforms or more incremental measures that would be expected to meet with less resistance, the president's public opinion ratings, the degree of policy agreement with the proposed reforms, and the strength of actors in civil society who would be adversely affected by the reforms. These noninstitutional factors may have greater weight than the institutional ones in shaping how easily a president can implement his/her policies. Nevertheless, institutional design also affects the president's capacity to implement reforms. The next sections of this chapter discuss these seven institutional features with respect to Brazil.

Extreme Multipartism, Presidentialism, and Policy Reform

Because of extreme party-system fragmentation, no party has anything close to a majority of seats. The parties of Collor (1990–92), Franco (1992–94), and Cardoso (1995–) had small shares of seats in Congress. In the lower chamber, they had 4.2 percent, 7.4 percent, and 12.1 percent, respectively, when they took office. In the Senate, they had 3.7 percent, 12.3 percent, and 13.6 percent, respectively.[3] Sarney's party, officially the PMDB, had a majority from early 1987 to early 1988, but it was deceptive because Sarney was in fact closer to the PFL than to the PMDB (Kinzo 1990). By comparative standards, these are extraordinarily low figures.

Sarney's party was the PMDB because in order to run for Vice-President, he was obliged in 1984 by the extant electoral legislation to join Tancredo Neves's party, the PMDB. Most of Sarney's close allies, including his own son, were in the PFL, which had only 20 percent of the Chamber seats and 21 percent of the Senate seats after the 1986 elections. Much of the PMDB opposed Sarney, while the PFL was the major party that most supported Sarney (Kinzo 1990). Therefore, a case could be made that Sarney's primary party base was the PFL, which would further accentuate the tendency toward presidents' parties being in a distinct minority.

Such a distinctive minority situation can limit presidents' capacity to implement reforms, since they usually need to negotiate with Congress and state governments in order to obtain what they want, and these negotiations curb their ability to undertake reforms. When their party controls a small share of seats, it is more likely that the president will have more difficulty securing support in Congress; the same applies to the president's relations with governors. In this way, party-system fragmentation can contribute to presidents' difficulties in implementing major reforms (Williamson and Haggard 1994; Haggard and Kaufman 1995). Extreme fragmentation also makes the assembling of coalitions more difficult by expanding the number of actors involved in coalition formation. More actors can defect from the governing coalition, thereby leading to a situation where executive/legislative deadlock is more likely.

Undisciplined Catch-All Parties, Weak Party Loyalty, and Policy Reform

For Brazilian presidents, limited party discipline has had an equivocal impact. Moderate discipline sometimes made it more difficult for presidents to win stable political support. Limited discipline and loyalty make executive-legislative relations less predictable. Presidents cannot always count on the support of their party or coalition, as they might with highly disciplined parties and loyal legislators. Modest discipline accentuates the instability of presidential support and reinforces presidents' proclivities toward circumventing congress or relying on patronage to build support. More so than other presidents of the post–1985 period, Sarney suffered these adverse effects as a sizable faction of the PMDB abandoned him on countless issues.

At the same time, limited discipline enables presidents to entice members of other parties to support them, and presidents usually do not face disciplined majorities determined to block them (Figueiredo and Limongi 1996; Nicolau 1996b). From this perspective, modest discipline presents advantages to presidents. During the first years of his administration, Cardoso reaped the benefits of this situation, though at the expense of providing patronage to rent-seeking politicians in exchange for their support.

For presidents, are the advantages or disadvantages of moderate discipline greater? Between 1985 and 1997, when presidents were popular, especially at the beginning of their terms, the advantages to presidents of loose discipline outweighed the disadvantages. During their honeymoon period, presidents could sway politicians of the catch-all parties to support them regardless of the party's official line.

But when presidents lost popularity, limited discipline was more of a hindrance than a help. Legislators of parties in the president's coalition bolted. This became a serious problem for Sarney in 1987 and for Collor in 1991. Overall, the disadvantages for Sarney and Collor of weak discipline offset the advantages. The only consistently disciplined major party has been the PT, which opposed the first four post–1985 governments.

Limited party loyalty has the same ambiguous effect as modest discipline: presidents benefit when legislators switch to their party or coalition, but they lose when legislators switch to a party outside their coalition. The Cardoso administration benefited by party switching to the PSDB and PFL. Sarney, however, presided over a mass migration away from his own PMDB and from the PFL toward opposition parties. By 1987, a significant part of the PMDB opposed Sarney. Conservative and clientelistic sectors of the party usually supported the government, but in June 1988 forty members of Congress split off and formed the PSDB. During the amendment phase (January–September 1988) of the constitutional congress, fifty-eight politicians left the PMDB. Forty-five went to parties more opposed to Sarney than the PMDB: thirty-seven to the PSDB, five to the PSB, and three to the PDT. Only twelve joined parties friendlier to Sarney: nine to the PTB, two to the PDC, and one to the PTR (one had no new party affiliation). Of the eleven legislators who left the PFL, five joined parties more hostile to Sarney (four switched to the PSDB and one to the PDT), while the remaining six joined center-right or right parties.

The center, center-right, and right parties were most likely to support Sarney (Kinzo 1990). If we combine the center, center-right, and right and then count all other shifts toward the left as unfavorable to Sarney and all shifts from the left to the center-left or from the center-left to the center, center-right, or right as favorable, then among eighty-one party migrations during this period, fifty-four were negative for Sarney, only fifteen were positive, and twelve were neutral. The fact that so many legislators switched to parties more opposed to Sarney reinforces the point that presidents cannot always count on the support of members of parties that are part of the governing coalition.[4]

Presidents have powerful weapons to keep members of their coalition in line, namely, patronage and policy-making positions. Presidents can win a base by offering positions and resources to legislators and governors who support them. Many legislators depend on such resources to win reelection, so this leverage is powerful. Nevertheless, toward the end of their terms, Sarney and Collor were weakened by defections. Governors and legislators distanced themselves from these unpopular presidents without having to pay a high price for defecting.

Sarney and Collor enjoyed widespread backing in Congress at moments of peak popularity, but such backing eroded with signs of plummeting public approval. Parties that initially were part of the governing coalition or that generally supported presidential initiatives defected in hard times or as positioning for the next presidential campaign began.

Even when limited discipline and loyalty enable presidents to win support from members of opposition parties, these features of the Brazilian political system increase the extractive capacity of members of Congress and governors. Legislators and governors can credibly use the threat of nonsupport to leverage concessions from the government.

In sum, during the first decade of democracy, moderate party discipline and low loyalty had mixed effects. When presidents were popular, politicians supported the government to enjoy the coattails of government prestige and to enhance their own access to patronage. When a president was unpopular, maintaining a coalition was problematic. For legislators, distancing oneself from the government was a means of avoiding the negative repercussions of supporting unpopular policies and an unpopular president.

Ideological Distance and Policy Reform

As was argued in Chapter 4, between 1985 and 1992, a large ideological distance in the party system prevailed between the PT and the rightist parties. However, the left has never held a large share of seats, and by 1995, with the migration of the PSDB from the center-left to the center, the center-left also held a small share of seats. Thus although the distance between the right and left is large, the overall dynamic in the political system has usually revolved around centrist and conservative positions. The large ideological distance between the PT and the rightist parties was also ameliorated by the patronage orientation of most centrist and conservative politicians, which dampens ideological conflict.

Although political moderation has prevailed most of the time, sharp ideological conflict was apparent at key moments between 1985 and Collor's impeachment. The 1989 presidential contest was sharply polarized ideologically, especially in the second round. Countless debates in the 1987–88 constitutional congress reflected a low degree of consensus. Disagreement about the role of the state, foreign capital, labor rights, and social policy was pervasive between 1985 and 1994 (Lamounier and Souza 1991). This disagreement contributed to the problems governments faced in reforming the state and in stabilizing the economy; as dissensus grows, the ease of reaching a compromise diminishes.

The problems posed by ideological disagreement were magnified during the constitutional congress. These problems were again acute during the Collor administration for two related reasons: Collor hoped to implement sweeping neoliberal reforms, and he was toward one end of the ideological spectrum, which made it more difficult to win a broad spectrum of support. Conversely, coalition building would logically be easier when the president comes from a centrist party; such a situation would predictably ameliorate the tensions created by a large ideological distance (Nicolau 1996b; Rodrigues 1995; Amorim Neto 1995; Deheza 1997).

After 1992, a policy consensus gradually formed regarding the necessity of stabilization and state reform; this consensus was a crucial factor in the successful stabilization and reforms of the post–1994 period. Even with robust federalism and a fragmented party system, presidents can implement reforms when there is reasonable policy consensus, as has been the case since 1994. Given the significant policy dissensus between 1985 and 1992, this task was difficult. Presidents Sarney and Collor not only had a hard time building and maintaining their own coalitions, they also faced sharp opposition on at least one pole of the party system.

Symmetrical Bicameralism and Policy Reform

Brazil is a case of symmetrical bicameralism in which the Senate possesses significant powers. As a law-making body, the Senate stands on approximately equal grounds with the lower chamber. Either the Senate or the Chamber of Deputies can initiate a bill, and both must approve it. Both must approve constitutional amendments by the same (60 percent) supermajority. The Senate also has broad powers of appointment and approval of appointments (Article 52). It must approve nominations for ministers of the Federal Accounting Court, presidents and directors of the Central Bank, the attorney general, and a host of other important positions. It must authorize external financial operations, establish the limit of total internal debt, and determine the limits and conditions of internal and external debt of the federal and subnational governments.

The combination that characterizes Brazil—symmetrical and incongruent bicameralism (with different methods of selection and marked differences in proportionality between the two chambers), while not uncommon, is far from a norm (Lijphart 1984: 90–105). As Stepan (1997) argues, it is the combination most conducive to constraining the central government.

A Detailed Constitution and Policy Reform

The 1988 Constitution is very detailed and covers a wide range of issues. In a survey of 189 constitutions in the contemporary world (Flanz 1997), the Brazilian ranked as the fifth longest, with 211 pages and 320 articles, behind only Malaysia (325 pages), India (263), Pakistan (231), and Ghana (214). It established many controversial decisions that successive presidents have wished to change. In the areas that directly affect stabilization and state reform, the 1988 constitution mandated public-sector monopolies in many spheres of the economy, ranging from telephones, telecommunications, mining, and gas (Articles 20–21 and 176–177); allowed teachers in public schools and universities to retire with full pensions after thirty years of service for men and twenty-five for women; allowed other public servants to retire with full pensions after thirty-five years of service for men and thirty for women (Article 40); granted job tenure after two years of employment to public servants who had passed a civil-service exam (Article 41); called for a substantial redistribution of tax revenue to state and local governments (Articles 157 through 159); provided job tenure for all public servants with five years of employment, even if they had been hired illegally (Transitory Article 19); provided generous subsidies to private capital at a time when the inflation rate was out of control (Transitory Article 47); and mandated certain levels of spending in education. With more parsimonious constitutions, many of these issues would be regulated by the normal policy process.

Given persistent triple- and quadruple-digit inflation rates and poor growth between 1980 and 1993, successive presidents attempted to achieve fiscal balance, reduce the size of the state, and open the economy. All three presidents between 1985 and 1994 believed that the 1988 Constitution impeded their capacity to achieve these goals because it mandated large transfers and expenditures, created rigidities in the budget process, granted what were perceived as efficiency-inhibiting public-sector monopolies, and restricted international investment.

On all of these issues, presidents needed qualified majorities in order to implement reforms. A constitutional amendment requires 60 percent approval of the total membership of both chambers of congress, and each chamber must pass the amendment twice. Given the likelihood that some members favorably disposed to an amendment might be absent, in practice this requirement imposes the need for a majority greater than 60 percent. This is a low hurdle compared to the one in the United States, but the constitution is far more detailed than the U.S. charter, and amendments require substantially more consensus than an ordinary law. Equally important, with a constitutional amendment presidents cannot employ mechanisms such as decree powers that ordinarily give them an advantage over Congress.

Federalism and Policy Reform

Federalism has advantages in a heterogeneous country of continental dimensions, but since 1988 it has also created one more mechanism of dispersion in a fragmented political system. State loyalties lead politicians to coalesce in support of projects that will benefit their own state, regardless of their party and ideology (and regardless of the cost-effectiveness of the project). Federalism has contributed to the factionalism in the catch-all parties. Politicians of the catch-all parties tend to focus more on state and local issues than on national ones, so they are less willing to toe the line of the national leadership. State loyalties make it more difficult for presidents to pull stable coalitions together; to retain the political support of a state's congressional delegation, presidents have needed to offer high-level positions and resources.

Governors and mayors of major cities are powerful political figures who compete with the president for power and resources. They command impressive political and economic resources, especially in the larger and wealthier states.

Because of their influence over deputies and senators of their party or coalition, governors (and mayors to a lesser extent) can thwart or facilitate presidential designs. Presidents need the support of legislators, so governors acquire considerable power in national politics (Abrúcio 1998). The federal government's failure to contain state and local government spending, in conjunction with the former's tendency to assume debts incurred by the latter, became a major contributing factor to the fiscal crisis under democratic government.

Brazilian federalism has also weakened party commitments to a president when the latter offers cabinet posts to members of that party. Party decisions are influenced as much by state as national issues. Following the logic of state politics, state party organizations sometimes adopt a line contrary to the dominant position of the national leaders. Deputies and senators have local and state loyalties that often outweigh their commitments to the president. These local loyalties can make it difficult for a president to capture the undivided support of the catch-all parties.

In addition to these political effects, Brazilian federalism has economic effects that limited the capacity of presidents to control monetary policy. The substantial increase in the transfer of resources to states and *municípios* mandated by the 1988 Constitution occurred without a corresponding transfer of responsibilities. The constitution is nebulous regarding what level of government has responsibility for such fundamental issues as health, education, housing, and welfare. This vagueness has fueled conflicts between federal, state, and local governments, enabling each to claim that certain responsibilities pertain to another. This situation has burdened the federal government, leaving it with diminished resources but growing demands (Almeida 1996; Sola 1994a, 1994b; Abrúcio 1998).

Brazilian federalism has given rise to powerful banks owned by state governments. The directors of these banks are political appointees, chosen by the governor. As Werlang and Fraga Neto (1992) and Novaes and Werlang (1993) have shown, after the advent of political liberalization, the state banks had incentives to operate with short-term logic, as well as a notable capacity to push the federal government to assume massive debts, leading to a situation in which federal-government control over monetary and fiscal policy is jeopardized. State banks have defaulted on their obligations, but until 1995 the federal government bailed them out, largely because presidents did not want to incur the wrath of governors. Werlang and Fraga Neto convincingly argue that this problem, which is made possible by federalism, had significant deleterious consequences: "State banks represent one of the greatest obstacles to the functioning of the Brazilian economy" (1992: 13).

The President's Constitutional Powers and Policy Reform

The broad nature of presidents' constitutional powers since 1985 has been documented by several scholars (Figueiredo and Limongi 1994, 1995, 1997; Mainwaring 1997; Power 1998; Shugart and Carey 1992). Here I focus on the most important constitutional provision that empowers Brazilian presidents and enables them to counteract to a degree the constraining effects of robust federalism and party-system fragmentation: the president's constitutional right to issue legislative decrees. This is distinctive: presidents can issue decrees that have the force of law. As a result, presidents do not always need active congressional support to accomplish their legislative agendas.

Article 62 of the 1988 Constitution allows presidents to adopt "provisional measures" [*medidas provisórias*]. Through Article 62, presidents can implement measures that have the force of law for a thirty-day period without congressional approval. In comparative terms, Article 62 gives the Brazilian president exceptional legislative powers. This measure has changed the functioning of Brazilian democracy compared to the 1946–64 period (Figueiredo and Limongi 1994; Pessanha 1993; Power 1998).

Article 62 was explicitly designed for cases of "relevance and urgency" only. In practice, however, presidents have used provisional measures to push through all kinds of bills, with little concern for whether they constitute emergencies. Between October 5, 1988, when the new constitution went into effect, and December 1995, the four presidents issued 1,249 provisional measures: 147 under Sarney, 157 under Collor, 508 under Franco, and 437 under Cardoso (Figueiredo and Limongi 1997: 144). Provisional measures have been used to legislate some of the most important bills, including the various economic stabilization plans, that have been undertaken since the 1988 Constitution.

According to the constitution, provisional measures are to be rejected unless Congress passes them within thirty days. However, presidents have regularly reissued these decrees after they expired. Of the first 1,249 Provisional Measures under the 1988 charter, 862 had previously been issued (Figueiredo and Limongi 1997: 144). The de facto practice, then, has been that presidential decrees can remain in effect unless Congress rejects them (Power 1998; Figueiredo and Limongi 1997). Presidents can use their decree powers to implement parts of a reform agenda.

A president's right to issue new laws is merely the most important of several constitutional measures that confer broad powers. Presidents also have the right to veto parts of a bill, a prerogative that enables them to fine-tune legislation they desire while blocking parts of bills they oppose. They have great power to shape the budget; until Congress approves such a bill, the president essentially controls spending, and he/she has a line-item veto. Presidents also have considerable capacity to determine the legislative agenda. On balance, the 1988 Constitution gives Brazilian presidents among the greatest powers of democratic presidents in the world.

Presidents and Governing Coalitions

The previous sections provided an overview of the institutional context that shaped policy reforms after 1985. Before discussing efforts to implement policy reforms in subsequent sections, an overview is in order of how presidents attempt to implement reform when faced with a situation in which their party usually has a small minority in Congress. When pursuing reforms, Brazilian presidents have three main strategies for dealing with Congress. They are not mutually incompatible and indeed are often coupled.

1. Presidents can issue provisional measures, which do not require active legislative support.

2. Presidents can attempt to win the support of individual legislators through selective incentives (appointments and resources). This strategy usually goes hand in hand with the third one.

Patronage often successfully induces national legislators to support the president, but it does not always ensure support for his/her agenda. There are several limits to the use of patronage in securing support for presidents' programs. First, since the redistribution of tax revenues was enshrined in the 1988 constitution, national legislators have been less dependent on the national government for patronage. They can obtain resources from the state government. Second, during periods of economic stabilization and state shrinking, there is less patronage available. Third, the costs of widespread use of patronage can be high. The Sarney years showed that it can undermine the efforts to attain stabilization and state reform. And finally, ideological issues are real in Brazilian politics; the malleability of the catch-all parties has limits.

3. Presidents can build multiparty coalitions to win majority support in Congress. Because their parties typically control a distinct minority of legislative seats, presidents need a broad coalition to secure reliable support in the legislature. They must either assemble a broad legislative coalition or deal with a situation of minority government. In either case, presidents need the support of members from other parties. This support must often be assembled in piecemeal fashion. With moderate discipline and low loyalty, governing coalitions are loose and shifting rather than hard and fast.

Since 1946, Brazilian presidents have created loose coalition governments (Abranches 1988; Figueiredo and Limongi 1996). When their own party has a minority of seats, presidents need support beyond their own parties, so they offer patronage and policy-making positions to a wide range of parties and congressional representatives. This power sharing begins at the peak level (cabinet positions and presidents of major public enterprises and executive agencies) and continues on down to minor appointments in backwoods towns and remote regions.

Between 1946 and 1964, oversized cabinets were a means of securing support from individuals affiliated with a wide range of parties (Abranches 1988; Amorim Neto 1995; Mainwaring 1997). Cabinets since 1985 have not been as inclusive as those of the 1946–64 period if we analyze the percentage of seats occupied by parties with cabinet positions, but most have still mostly been fairly inclusive. In Sarney's first ten months in office, the parties that had cabinet representatives accounted for over 90 percent of the seats in Congress. Since then, cabinets have been less inclusive; Collor's second cabinet (April to October 1992) and Franco's fourth (August 1993 to December 1994) were minority cabinets (that is, they held less than 50 percent of the seats in at least one chamber).

Presidential efforts to win broad coalition support are often successful. However, during the Sarney, Collor, and Franco (to a lesser degree) presidencies, interparty coalitions were not reliable, leading to presidential difficulties in implementing major reforms in policy areas for which they needed congressional support.

Why don't these party coalitions provide consistent support for presidents? With moderate discipline, legislators are prone to defect on individual pieces of legislation. A government may have a cabinet member from a particular party, only to face the opposition of members of that party in Congress on some bills. For example, Sarney's cabinet included many ministers from the PMDB, which was ambivalent about his government. Cabinet representation does not always ensure that the congressional representatives of that party support the government. Moreover, with weak loyalty, legislators may switch to a party more hostile to the president.

Political Institutions, State Reform, and Economic Stabilization, 1985–1994

The combination of moderately undisciplined catch-all parties and limited party loyalty, a fragmented party system, and robust federalism potentially creates a high capacity to block the president's reform initiatives. The argument in this section is that between 1985 and 1994, Brazil's political institutions made it difficult for presidents to implement stabilization and state-reform policies in a coherent fashion. Sarney, Collor, and Franco had difficulties assembling stable coalitions that would support coherent reform policies in these two broad areas.

THE SARNEY ADMINISTRATION

The main story regarding state reform and stabilization under Sarney was the president's tepid commitment to both enterprises. But an important secondary story is that political institutions made it difficult for Sarney to carry out reform. His stabilization plans ended in resounding failure, and the government made no progress with state reform.

Sarney implemented several stabilization plans, but the data underscore how badly they fared: inflation ratcheted up from 59 percent in 1986, the year of the Cruzado stabilization plan, to 395 percent the following year, 993 percent in 1988, 1,862 percent in 1989, and 1,585 percent in 1990. One of the major reasons for the failure of the successive stabilization efforts was institutional. Forging a stable base of support in a political system that disperses power is a constant challenge. Presidents rely on distributing public resources to reward allies. But massive use of public resources undermined Sarney's austerity measures.

Sarney feared that without distributing resources on a grand scale, the constitutional congress would have cut his mandate to four years. He further feared a series of setbacks on other issues. As a result, he constantly traded public resources and appointments for political support. Anxious to secure a five-year term, Sarney sacrificed policy reforms in order to buy the political support needed to attain that objective. In a context in which Sarney was dispensing jobs and resources to win a five-year term, austerity measures were politically unpalatable.

During his first eighteen months, Sarney encountered relatively little congressional opposition. This comfortable situation resulted from the weakness of the legislature, from the usually reliable support of the PMDB/PFL coalition, and from the relatively auspicious economic situation. The president possessed formidable constitutional powers. He could still govern by decree-laws, which offered a way of steamrolling Congress.

Sarney's ability to implement policy in an unfettered fashion began to wane in 1987, partly because of the larger political/economic context and partially because of a changing institutional venue. As his popularity eroded, Sarney lost a source of influence with Congress and governors. Declining popularity, increasing inflation, and an economic slowdown made legislators and governors willing to distance themselves from the president, in turn making it more difficult for Sarney to forge the support needed to implement reforms.

After the failure of the Cruzado Plan, Sarney could not always count on reliable party support in Congress. When he was immensely popular in 1986 because of the success of the plan, the PMDB and PFL supported him. With the failure of the plan, however, the progressive wing of the PMDB deserted him.

The negotiated nature of the transition to democracy forced Sarney to balance PMDB and PFL demands of appointments and resources (Hagopian 1996). But governing with a broad coalition that included those who had opposed and those who had supported authoritarian rule was difficult. Conflict among ministers was ubiquitous, often leading to a lack of coherence in policy making. To overcome this problem, Sarney attempted to forge a supraparty political base and to use his appointments and resources to sway state governors and members of congress to back him. However, after the collapse of the Cruzado Plan, he was not able to hold this coalition together. Sharp intragovernmental jostling took place throughout the balance of his term.

During the constitutional congress, Sarney forged a supraparty bloc known as the *Centrão* (literally, "big center") despite its conservative orientation. The president hoped that the *Centrão* would provide the stable support that the parties had not. Yet the *Centrão*'s devotion to Sarney was fickle, contingent upon a steady stream of patronage that undermined stabilization policies. Moreover, on many issues, the *Centrão* fell apart as a sizable faction supported measures contrary to those Sarney favored.

On issues that affected stabilization and state reform, the constitutional congress frequently voted against Sarney's predilections. As the government was pushing for greater openness to foreign markets, the constitutional congress adopted several nationalistic measures. As the government was starting to promote state shrinking, the constitutional congress approved statist provisions. The congress passed several measures that Sarney opposed: a substantial increase in the tax revenue transferred from the federal government to state and local governments; an increase in social benefits and expenditures; expanded labor rights; statist and nationalistic economic measures; and cancellation of debts that private business owed to the federal government.

The 1988 Constitution brought about important changes in presidential-legislative and presidential-gubernatorial relations. It invigorated federalism, transferred substantial resources from the federal to state and local governments, curbed presidential powers, and expanded legislative powers. These changes created a different institutional context from the one Sarney had inherited in March 1985. A stronger legislature and stronger state and local governments imposed more limits on Sarney's powers, making it more difficult for him to implement reforms. Although in most respects Brazil approximated a democracy when Sarney was inaugurated, in terms of executive-legislative relations and relations between the federal government and subnational governments, it did not; the changes ushered in by the 1988 Constitution were more significant than the minor modifications that occurred in 1985.

Nearing the end of his term, Sarney became increasingly isolated and incapable of implementing a stabilization plan. The fiscal deficit and inflation rate soared. The government attempted few important initiatives, most of which failed to win approval. For example, it introduced a bill aimed at reducing the deficit of the social-security administration by cutting back on benefits, but it did not pass. After a series of government defeats on a wage bill in congress in 1989, one member of Sarney's loyal retinue admitted, "This is the end. Whenever there is a secret vote, the government can only manage thirty-one votes [out of 570]."[5] By September, one of Sarney's defenders, Governor Newton Cardoso (PMDB-MG) said, "Nobody believes in the government any more."[6]

With the government crippled by incoherent policies, the economy deteriorated throughout 1989. The internal debt doubled between January 1988 and mid-1989, and inflation soared. The government lost control of the economy, leading to a hyperinflationary episode in early 1990.

THE COLLOR ADMINISTRATION

In contrast to Sarney, Collor was firmly committed to stabilization and state reform. Like Sarney, he was limited in his ability to implement reform because of opposition from Congress and governors and because of the need to provide payoffs in exchange for support.

Collor began his term believing that the legitimacy earned by winning 35 million votes would enable him to implement sweeping reform. In his first days in office, the youthful president initiated audacious measures aimed at stabilizing and liberalizing the economy. Most controversial among them was a temporary freeze on bank accounts; people were not allowed to withdraw more than 50,000 cruzeiros. Collor also announced a fiscal reform that would reduce the deficit by $11 billion a year, a comprehensive privatization program, the end to many subsidies, massive layoffs in the public sector, and reform of public administration.

In pursuing these measures, Collor initially circumvented the legislature; the government would not let Congress obstruct their implementation. Collor extensively used presidential decrees to govern during these early months rather than risk delays by relying on the normal legislative process. In his first sixty days in office, he issued thirty-seven provisional measures; Sarney had issued 148 in his 525 days as president after the 1988 Constitution went into effect.[7] Collor's economic plan was pronounced through provisional measures, some of dubious legality.

During his first months, Collor won congressional support for audacious reforms, in part because of the profound crisis at that moment (Brazil was on the verge of hyperinflation; see Lamounier 1991: 27–34). Yet even early on, when Congress voted on the provisional measures in April 1990, the government resorted to traditional patronage politics, offering high-level public-sector jobs to political allies. Despite such efforts, Congress altered many of the government's proposals. For example, it voted for a less-recessive wage policy, for a more liberal law regarding public employees' rights to organize, for maintaining some subsidies that the government wanted to eliminate, and for increasing access to savings accounts that had been frozen. Collor was forced to compromise a bit, and his brazen disrespect for Congress cost him support among the political elite.

As his approval ratings declined after his first few months in office,[8] Collor came under increasing congressional criticism. In early June 1990, the government suffered a defeat when Congress increased sixfold the amount that people were allowed to take out of savings accounts. Minister of Justice Bernardo Cabral admitted, "Now there's no way out except to negotiate."[9] Pressures from Congress and society softened the government's intention of carrying out massive public-sector layoffs. Days later a more significant defeat came when the Supreme Court declared illegal Collor's effort to reissue a provisional measure that Congress had rejected.

Despite occasional defeats and notwithstanding the need to negotiate on many issues, Collor was able to implement most of his initiatives during his first year in office. But by early 1991, before he had completed even a year of his term, his support had eroded so much that some opposition leaders expressed concern about a crisis of governability. Many political leaders attributed Collor's inability to govern to his weak congressional base.[10] Increasingly isolated, the government relied more on distributing jobs and resources to garner legislative support.

In May 1991, Zélia Cardoso de Mello was sacked as finance minister, above all because of the poor economic results and her personal lack of credibility, but also because most politicians perceived her and her team as unwilling to listen to or compromise with Congress. Politicians gained more influence after her fall, and the technocratic, exclusionary decision-making style gave way to negotiations and compromise. The government became more forthcoming in meeting demands from its congressional base. Tensions between Collor and Congress eased slightly and perhaps would have improved markedly had it not been for the economic problems and the succession of corruption scandals. But there was also a cost to the rapprochement between the president and Congress: having begun with great audacity, by mid-1991 the Collor government was floundering without clear direction or purpose. Its efforts to trim the state were undermined by its reliance on deputies and senators whose political careers had been made through public resources in alliance with powerful private interests. As a core part of his stabilization plan, the new finance minister, Marcílio Marques

Moreira, pushed for constitutional amendments in the areas of fiscal and tax reform, but he failed to gain support.

Beset by ubiquitous scandals, rising inflation, and a deep recession, after mid-1991 Collor rarely regained the political initiative and was no longer capable of accomplishing major reforms. The government still pushed for a fiscal reform and for an increase in employees' and employers' contributions to the social-security fund, but Congress substantially revised fiscal changes and blocked social-security reform.

By early 1992, Collor had been reduced to building political support through public resources and high-level nominations, especially cabinet positions. In the wake of a cabinet reshuffling in January 1992, the government outlined five major programmatic objectives, all of which required legislative approval: privatizing some public services, privatizing port services and ending the monopoly of unionized workers in the ports, establishing a law that recognized international patents for medicines and other products, enacting fiscal reform, and ending the monopoly of Petrobrás, the state-owned oil company. In late June, the Chamber approved the ports project, but the other four languished.

As scandal after scandal erupted after April 1992, the Collor government's support in Congress eroded. It was no longer capable of accomplishing reforms. Increasingly, Collor sacrificed the effort to impose fiscal austerity in order to buy political support to stave off impeachment. Thus a government that came into office with an ambitious agenda and high initial approval ratings ultimately failed to achieve stabilization or profound state reform. Inflation remained rampant (475 percent in 1991 and 1,149 percent in 1992), and privatization and public-sector reform proceeded slowly (Schneider 1991; Packenham 1994). This failure stemmed significantly from congressional and gubernatorial resistance to Collor's reforms. On the other hand, the Collor government achieved considerable success in trade liberalization and helped reorient perceptions of elite actors regarding the necessity of state reform (Sola 1994b).

THE FRANCO ADMINISTRATION

The story of stabilization and state reform under Franco resembles that under Sarney. The president equivocated about priorities and pursued state reform and stabilization inconsistently. As was also the case under Sarney, Franco's efforts to foster reform policies were limited by Congress and governors and were undermined by the need to trade public resources for support.

Like his predecessors, Franco assumed office with broad endorsement. Political elites were anxious to ensure governability in the aftermath of the Sarney and Collor debacles. The public and most political elites were relieved that Collor was gone and were disposed to grant Franco considerable latitude. The new president had ministers of PMDB, PSDB, PT, and PFL vintage, so the ideological spectrum supporting him was broad. But congressional opposition to Franco increased until mid-1994, and the president had difficulty getting key legislation passed on salaries, inflation, state reform, and reducing the budget deficit.

Franco hoped to bring inflation under control, yet until July 1994 he consistently failed to do so. Inflation soared to 2,489 percent in 1993 and was running even higher than that in the first semester of 1994. Franco went through a succession of finance ministers, the first several of whom lacked the political support needed to realize significant reforms. The government had difficulty enacting budget cuts, although it often proclaimed the need to do so. Like Sarney and Collor, Franco rhetorically committed himself to cutting public expenditures, but like his predecessors, until mid-1994 he made little headway, partly because he used public resources to forge political support. The government affirmed the importance of cutting expenditures, but it spent freely to win political support for other programs.

On several issues, the Franco government failed to realize its objectives because of opposition from Congress and governors. It was frequently defeated in its efforts to curb wage increases. One of the government's professed priorities was cutting the budget deficit so as to attack inflation, but Congress frequently diluted or opposed austerity measures and state reform. In their public discourse, many politicians endorsed cuts—provided their own resources were not affected.

In December 1993, Franco's finance minister, Fernando Henrique Cardoso announced a new stabilization plan (which subsequently became known as the Real Plan) involving budget cuts, a temporary (1994–95) reduction in the tax revenue sent to local and state governments, a tax increase, and ultimately a new currency. This plan was to be implemented over the next several months.

The government sent parts of the plan to Congress because it required constitutional amendment. In February 1994, the lower chamber approved a constitutional change that raised taxes and slightly reduced the flow of tax revenue to state and local governments in 1994–95. Otherwise, however, the Franco government failed in its efforts to win constitutional reform, despite a review period during which amending the constitution was easier.[11] The Franco government hoped to obtain support for constitutional amendments that would lower the share of tax revenue going to state and local governments, eliminate job tenure for public servants, end some public-sector monopolies enshrined in the 1988 Constitution, reform the welfare system, and modify the tax structure. But it was unable to muster support for any of these measures.

SUMMARY

Between 1985 and 1994, Brazil's political institutions fostered dispersion of power, making it difficult for presidents to implement stabilization and state-reform policies in a coherent fashion. Presidents Sarney, Collor, and Franco frequently were not able to implement reform policies in these areas. The combination of moderately disciplined parties, party-system fragmentation, ideological dissensus, and robust federalism made it difficult for them to command consistent support in Congress and with governors. When congressional and gubernatorial support eroded, presidents were unable to implement reforms.

Despite its difficulties overturning presidential vetoes[12] and despite its weakness as an agent of policy formulation, the Brazilian Congress can force presidents to make many concessions. When Congress does not support the president, the latter faces difficulty implementing reforms. Even when presidents are able to build a winning coalition on a particular policy, they need to make concessions—usually in the form of public jobs and resources—that compromise their ability to control the fiscal deficit, hamper public sector efficiency, and undermine state reform. This does not mean that the social and economic problems of this period were due mostly to the institutional configuration, but rather that this configuration hindered the implementation of reforms that could have resolved the problems (Sola 1994a).

Sarney, Collor, and Franco had trouble overcoming opposition from Congress and governors and implementing major policy reforms when their popularity dissipated. The presidents' lack of reliable majority support in Congress limited state reform and undermined stabilization measures, which helps explain Brazil's lag in these two areas.

The problems presidents encountered in winning support for their programs usually did not surface because of congressional rejections of bills sponsored by the executive. Rather, they appeared mainly in the guise of presidential need to secure broad-based congressional support before legislation reached the floor of the legislature. Congress dragged its feet on constitutional amendments and bills the presidents wanted, it approved bills they opposed (even though they could veto the bill with a low likelihood of an override), and it amended presidentially initiated bills in "unfriendly" ways. Legislators had incentives to extract a high price for their support: they wanted patronage. Winning congressional support was a challenge, even though presidents could dispense jobs and resources to secure support. Winning support by trading public resources often undermined other presidential reforms. This helps explain the difficulty in cutting the size of the state, reducing the fiscal deficit, and privatizing public firms. Presidents needed to negotiate with Congress and governors in order to obtain what they wanted, and these negotiations curbed their ability to implement reforms. In this way, between 1985 and 1994, Brazil's institutional combination contributed to problems of implementing reforms. Presidents were frequently unable to implement their preferred policies in the following policy areas related to stabilization and state reform:

1. Although most economists and business leaders agreed that indexation contributed to inflation until 1994, governments were unable to deindex wages and pensions because of congressional opposition. Politicians knew that their votes on wage policy were monitored by unions and that they would have difficulty explaining votes that reduced wages in the short term. Even conservative politicians who rhetorically made combating inflation a top priority often voted for "progressive" wage bills.[13] In wage policy, Congress was a key reactive actor, and it opposed measures that would have adversely affected wages in the short term.

2. Governments had difficulty cutting public-sector employment despite a consensus that it was necessary. Politicians not only protected their constituents (and by doing so, themselves) by voting against measures to cut public-sector employment, they also protected their political careers by naming allies to public positions.

The 1988 Constitution guaranteed job tenure to public-sector servants with at least two years of service, provided they had entered through a civil-service exam (Article 41). It also established (Transitory Article 19) that all public-sector employees with five years of service as of the time of promulgation of the constitution would be guaranteed tenure even if they had not entered the public sector through an examination. Thus Congress was a key actor in any effort to cut back the size of the public sector quickly. (Congress would not necessarily be an actor in cutbacks through attrition.) Governors and mayors had autonomy to hire public-sector personnel. Presidents were not able to control the hiring practices of local and state governments, and until Cardoso, they were unwilling to push governors and mayors toward fiscal discipline by refusing to roll over loans to state-level banks.

3. Through the constitutional provisions (Articles 20, 176, and 177) that made oil, gas, and telecommunications the exclusive prerogative of the public sector, presidents were limited in the privatizing of public enterprises. By refusing to endorse constitutional change, Congress limited the ability of governments to privatize public-sector firms. Sarney unsuccessfully fought against provisions guaranteeing a state monopoly in many areas of the economy. Collor and Franco then unsuccessfully attempted to obtain constitutional amendments that overturned public-sector monopolies.

In addition, Congress opposed the privatizing of public enterprises that did not enjoy a public-sector monopoly enshrined in the 1988 Constitution. Werneck (1992) notes that congressional resistance to privatization obliged the Collor government to proceed slowly. This helps account for the comparatively slow pace of privatization in Brazil. Between 1980 and 1992, the Brazilian government privatized 6 percent of state-owned enterprises, compared to 15 percent in Argentina, 62 percent in Venezuela, 87 percent in Mexico, and 96 percent in Chile (Edwards 1995: 171).

4. Congress limited the capacity of governments to increase taxes. Congressional approval is needed to create new taxes or to increase rates (Article 150 of the 1988 Constitution). The difficulty of increasing revenue made it tough to balance budgets.

5. Congress and the governors defended the share of state and local governments in federal tax revenues despite a widespread perception that this arrangement contributed to fiscal problems and inflation. This share was constitutionally enshrined (Transitory Article 34), so it could be modified only through a constitutional amendment.

After the constitution was promulgated, the federal government faced a declining resource base because of the new transfers to state and local government. Sarney and his successors sought to collect loans the subnational governments owed the federal government because state and local governments could now afford to pay these debts. But the governors and Congress blocked such initiatives. On December 7, 1988, Congress approved a measure that restricted states' payments to between 6.5 percent and 10.2 percent of their debt on a sliding scale. These amounts were only 26 percent to 41 percent of what Sarney had proposed. Congress also rejected bills that would have transferred some responsibilities from the federal to state and local governments.

6. Congress and the governors resisted federal-government efforts to curb the autonomy of state-level public banks and enterprises, even though they were not well run and contributed to the problems of national economic policy. Until Cardoso became president, state-level banks, which are under the jurisdiction of governors, had broad authority to make their own loans, and effectively had the autonomy to undermine national-level monetary and fiscal policy. They had a reputation for profligate spending to bolster the careers of the politicians who oversaw them. Despite affirming a commitment to rein in these banks and to prohibit the Central Bank from covering their deficits, the Sarney, Collor, and Franco governments did little in this regard.

The main reason for this inertia in clamping down on state banks was that all three presidents relied on support from governors and were unwilling to jeopardize it by aggressively acting against the banks. Through their control of state-level public resources and their influence over candidate selection, governors influence career prospects of members of congress. As a result, governors can influence the voting patterns of legislators who are members of the state-level governing coalition. They use this influence to block measures in the National Congress that would adversely affect states' interests.

7. Congress and the governors fought against the federal government's insistence that state governments and enterprises pay the interest on the massive loans they owed the federal government.

All three administrations announced their intention to harness state governments that spent beyond their resources and ultimately relied on the federal government to cover their deficit. The central government needed to reduce the hemorrhage of resources to fiscally irresponsible state governments. By 1993, state and local governments owed the federal government around $60 billion. As finance minister in 1993–94, Cardoso made roping in these state governments and collecting debts the states owed the central government a priority.

All three administrations consistently capitulated in the face of the resistance of governors and members of Congress. After averring that the state of São Paulo owed the federal government $13.6 billion, Finance Minister Cardoso accepted without explanation the affirmation of Governor Luiz Antonio Fleury (PMDB) that the state could pay only $1 billion. This quick acceptance was motivated by the government's desire to retain Fleury's political support. This episode prompted one journalist to conclude that "Governors are giants and the president a dwarf" when there is a conflict between the two.[14] The Franco government did obtain an agreement on renegotiating state debts—Abrúcio (1998) notes that this was its first victory over state governors on fiscal and financial matters since 1988—but it covered only 38 percent of the debts.

8. Congress sometimes blocked the federal government from collecting debts owed by private capital. For example, the 1988 Constitution forgave interest payments of most private businesses on loans contracted between February 28, 1986, and February 28, 1987, and forgave interest payments on debts contracted by all but large farmers between February 28, 1986, and December 31, 1987. This amounted to a massive subsidy of private business. A farmer who took a loan on March 1, 1986, would have had over 80 percent of the loan forgiven in real terms. The constitutional congress also canceled the interest on debts owed the government by small- and medium-size firms.

9. Until March 1996, Congress refused to pass constitutional amendments providing for social-security reform. Collor and Franco sought such amendments because the 1988 Constitution (Articles 40 and 202) enshrined provisions that the social-security system could not handle, including a low retirement age and benefits that were generous compared to the salary structure of active members of the labor force. The system was solvent, but experts projected that with the rapid increase in the number of pensioners, it soon would be in the red.

Therefore, they believed that social-security reform was an imperative (Weyland 1996b).

These nine policy areas were critical for Brazil. They fundamentally affected the capacity of presidents to balance the budget, undertake successful stabilization policies, and reform the state. Stabilization and state reform were arguably the most important problems on Brazil's policy agenda, for they were virtually essential to resuming steady growth, addressing poverty, and ameliorating inequalities.

Assessing the Impact of Institutions

Political institutions were not the only factor behind Brazil's slow pace of stabilization and state reform from 1985 to 1994. Other factors such as weak presidential leadership under Sarney and Franco and policy dissensus also contributed to Brazil's delay. Almeida (1996) makes the point that the commitment to state reform and stabilization was lower in Brazil than in most Latin American countries until Collor reached office, and this weaker commitment is a core part of the explanation for why Brazil lagged. However, Almeida also correctly attributes part of Brazil's delay to institutional factors (see also Abrúcio 1998; Abrúcio and Couto 1996; Haggard and Kaufman 1995; Sola 1994a, 1994b). There is no way of calculating exactly what share of Brazil's delay in effecting reforms between 1985 and 1994 stemmed from institutional as opposed to other causes. Nevertheless, there are means of verifying whether the institutional argument laid out here is compelling.

If my claim about how institutions shape policy reform is correct, it should have been easier for presidents to implement reforms in policy areas where Congress and governors are less-central actors. In assessing this issue, it is crucial to focus on policy implementation—whether presidents were able to implement the policies they wanted—rather than results. Whether policies succeed or fail depends primarily on a host of noninstitutional factors, whereas presidents' capacity to implement reforms depends significantly—though far from exclusively—on institutional arrangements. It is also crucial to hold roughly equal the difficulty in getting policies passed in a certain policy area; some policies have profound repercussions on much of society and are essentially zero-sum, while other policies have little or no adverse impact on powerful actors.

There is a continuum, ranging from unfettered to weaker presidential control over a policy area or, conversely, from virtually no influence on the part of Congress and governors to block reforms. For parsimony's sake, let us make a simple distinction between policy areas in which Congress and governors have substantial formal influence and those in which it is minimal.

In many major policy areas of high visibility and impact, Congress and/or governors could block the president, force him/her to change significantly an initial proposal or extract substantial concessions from him/her in exchange for support, or undertake policies that undermined presidential initiatives. However, in two important policy areas—exchange rates and tariffs—Congress and the governors were weak players. In contrast to the situation with the nine policy areas indicated above, the 1988 Constitution gave Congress and governors no formal authority over exchange rates and tariffs. The constitution explicitly (Article 153) gives the president complete authority over tariff rates (and implicitly does so over exchange rates).

Not coincidentally, Collor's most significant success in implementing neoliberal reforms was opening markets. In 1990, Collor quickly eliminated quantitative restrictions on imports, slashed average tariffs from 37 percent (in 1989) to 21 percent by 1992, and planned further reductions in tariffs (Fritsch and Franco 1992). The government began to open up the previously closed computer market to imports. As was the case with the policy areas in which presidents were institutionally constrained, trade liberalization created many short-term losers; it was not an easy policy to undertake in that sense. Throughout Latin America, trade liberalization adversely affected powerful business and labor interests that had grown up around protection from international competition. Trade liberalization probably has a more immediately negative impact on some vested interests than most other reforms because it can quickly drive inefficient domestic producers out of business. But trade liberalization was easier institutionally than other neoliberal policies because Congress and the governors did not hold veto power. Trade liberalization in Brazil occurred more gradually than in Chile, Mexico, or Peru, but more quickly and earlier than state reform in Brazil.

In a similar vein, exchange rates affect who wins and who loses in Brazilian society. An overvalued currency adversely affects exporters and most domestic producers who compete with imported goods, while it benefits importers. Altering the exchange rate is therefore not easy in terms of its impact on powerful actors in society, but Congress and the governors have no direct ability to block presidents from setting exchange-rate policy. In this respect, it is telling that the exchange rate became a major peg of Cardoso's stabilization plan in 1994. In short, presidents were able to implement reform policies when they had little institutional resistance, even when they faced societal opposition, but they were not able to do so when Congress and/or the governors were key players.

A second means of assessing the impact of institutional constraints looks at variation within a policy area. Privatization of public enterprises is an example. The institutional constraints to privatization were greatest in cases where the constitution enshrined a public-sector monopoly or where governors opposed privatization of state-level public enterprises. As was discussed above, privatization in Brazil proceeded slowly. By the Collor period, some privatizations were taking place—but none in the sectors where the constitution mandated a public-sector monopoly. Privatization in these sectors became possible only after the constitutional amendments of 1995. Despite effort, neither Collor nor Franco was able to secure support for such amendments.

If we engage in crossnational comparisons, presidents should be able to implement reforms more easily if party-system fragmentation is lower, if the constitution is less detailed or easier to amend, or if governors and mayors have fewer resources and less autonomy. Did presidents in other Latin American democracies with fewer veto players face comparable resistance in implementing equally painful adjustment policies and state reforms? If so, then the institutional claim is weakened. Conversely, that claim is strengthened if presidents who faced fewer veto players had an easier time implementing market-oriented reforms.

The evidence supports the idea that presidents who faced weaker institutional resistance found it easier to implement reform policies (although this did not ensure positive policy results). Among the large countries of Latin America, institutional constraints to reform were lower in Argentina, Colombia, Mexico, Peru, and Venezuela than in Brazil. The party system in all five countries is less fragmented; with the exception of Fujimori in Peru, presidents have consistently come from major parties with sizable congressional delegations; party loyalty is strong, again with the exception of Peru after 1990; and party discipline is strong in Argentina (Jones 1997), Venezuela (Coppedge 1994), and Mexico. Governors or their equivalents enjoy less autonomy and administer a smaller share of public-sector resources, and hence have less capacity to undermine or block reform initiatives from the center. The constitutions are much less detailed and in some cases (e.g., Colombia) easier to reform than the Brazilian.

Economic stabilization and state reform occurred more quickly and earlier in all five countries (Williamson 1990; Packenham 1994; Edwards 1995), particularly in Argentina, Mexico, and Peru. In Venezuela, President Carlos Andrés Pérez (1989–92) implemented radical stabilization and market-oriented policies after assuming office in 1989. The Pérez government quickly liberalized prices and opened markets, eliminated nontariff barriers and lowered tariffs, eliminated restrictions on foreign investment, and initiated the privatizing of some public enterprises. It was unable to achieve sweeping state reform, however, partly because of unyielding congressional resistance. Such legislative opposition may seem surprising in view of the fact that Pérez's own party (AD) had a near-majority in Congress. However, AD largely opposed Pérez's market-oriented reforms (Naim 1993). This is consistent with the general claim that institutional support or its lack is a key determinant of a president's ability to implement major reforms, but for idiosyncratic reasons it does not support the more specific contention that presidents should face less institutional resistance with less-fragmented party systems.

Brazil's delay did not result solely from a lack of will. Presidents from Sarney on were anxious to bring inflation under control, but they failed to do so, in good measure because of institutional constraints. Brazil's delay in state reform can be partly attributed to Sarney's and Franco's vacillations, but even Collor, who was adamantly committed to state reform, accomplished little. During the first three years of the Cardoso administration, state reform proceeded slowly because of constraints from Congress and governors.

A third way to approach the impact of institutions is to see whether presidents in other countries who faced high institutional constraints also had difficulty implementing their policies. Institutional constraints are significant in Bolivia and Ecuador, given the fragmentation of the party systems and the low degree of party loyalty in both countries. As in Brazil, presidents in Bolivia and Ecuador typically come from parties in a distinct minority situation in Congress, and party switching is common in Ecuador.

In Ecuador, presidents had a hard time sustaining adjustment and state-reform policies, in good measure because of congressional resistance. Such opposition helped block stabilization efforts initiated by presidents Roldós (1979–81), Febres-Cordero (1984–88), Borja (1988–92), and Durán-Ballén (1992–96) (Conaghan 1994; Grindle and Thoumi 1993). Edwards (1995: 2–3) regarded Ecuador as one of Latin America's three countries (along with the Dominican Republic and Haiti) that had not undertaken major reforms as of 1995. During the 1990s, even presidents committed to state reform (such as Durán-Ballén) were not able to implement it because of congressional opposition. Bolivia, conversely, was an early case of state reform and stabilization and thus runs somewhat counter to the hypothesis. One economic and one institutional factor are crucial in explaining the rapidity and profundity of stabilization and state reform in Bolivia. The former was the magnitude of the crisis: inflation reached 2,177 percent in 1984 and 8,170 percent in 1985, and the economy appeared to be on the verge of collapse. This created a widespread sense that dramatic change was needed even if the costs were high. The institutional factor is fully in line with the arguments presented in this chapter: Presidents Paz Estenssoro (1985–89) and Paz Zamora (1989–93) enjoyed solid and stable congressional majorities that supported their reforms, partly because of the peculiarities of Bolivia's hybrid presidential system (Gamarra 1997).

What other hypotheses could explain Brazil's delay in stabilizing and initiating state reform between 1985 and 1994? It must reflect some combination of

(1) a government rejection of or ambivalence about state reform and economic adjustment (that is, a lack of political will); (2) technical mistakes by economists in implementing policies; or (3) political resistance. The first explanation holds weight; Sarney and Franco were equivocal about state reform. However, it does not account for the difficulty in stabilization, nor does it explain the problems Collor had with stabilization and market-oriented reforms. The second explanation (technical mistakes) is unconvincing in view of the number of excellent Brazilian economists; given a committed government and weak political resistance, economists have sufficient know-how to design stabilization and state-reform measures. That leaves us with the third alternative, political resistance, but it looks at opposition from societal groups. The contention here would be that societal interests blocked the implementation of policies.

This argument is not as powerful as one based on political institutions. Congress reflects and represents interests in society, and in this sense an interpretation based on societal opposition to presidents' projects is compatible with one based on institutions. A full account of why Brazilian presidents had difficulty implementing reform would necessarily look at actors from civil society: public-sector unions that fought public-sector cutbacks, business groups that resisted lower subsidies, unions that protected workers by opposing deindexation, etc.[15]

However, the sociological and institutional approaches produce different emphases. In all societies, some interest groups opposed stabilization and state-reform measures, although counterintuitively, Bates and Kruger (1993: 461) report that in the eight countries they analyzed, "variations in the pattern of interest-group representation failed to account for variation in the success of different governments to implement economic policy reforms." The specificity of the Brazilian case resided neither in the fact that societal interests opposed such reforms, nor in the capacity of such interests to block reform. Brazilian civil society is not comparatively powerful. If it were, one could muster a compelling sociological interpretation: social actors were more capable of resisting neoliberal policies in Brazil than elsewhere.

Rather, the distinctive feature of the Brazilian case was the set of political institutions that blocked the emergence of a stable pro-reform coalition. These institutional arrangements were exceptional in several respects that would lead one to predict a low presidential capacity to implement reforms. Moreover, the sociological argument fails to explain the variance across policy areas depending on institutional constraints. Brazilian presidents were able to implement reforms in redistributive arenas such as tariffs and exchange rates when Congress and governors were out of the loop. They were not able to do so in policy areas where they depended on the support of those political actors.

Countries (Argentina, Bolivia, Uruguay) with worse initial economic conditions under democracy were able to stabilize more quickly than Brazil. Argentina and Bolivia also undertook state reform more quickly than Brazil. Brazil's initial economic conditions help account for the need to implement reforms, but not for the delay in doing so.

The problems of implementing stabilization and state reform policies in Brazil appeared directly as a result of presidents' inability to get projects approved because of opposition by Congress and/or governors. Politicians have a fair degree of latitude vis-à-vis the interests that help elect them. For these reasons, interactions between the president and legislature and governors provide a more fruitful primary explanation of presidents' difficulties in implementing policies than societal opposition.

Another alternative explanation of such difficulties in undertaking reforms focuses on fragmentation within the state (Abranches 1978; L. Martins 1985; Weyland 1996a), which hinders cohesive policy making because different agencies move in competing directions. The Brazilian state may certainly be characterized as fragmented, but this problem exists in part because presidents and governors deliberately carve up the state to gain the support of legislators and governors from a wide array of parties. Presidents assemble broad coalitions to compensate for the fact that their own parties have a minority of seats (Abranches 1988). But broad coalitions leave the government subject to significant internal jostling. This problem surfaced particularly during the Sarney and Franco administrations. Therefore, rather than provide a competing explanation of presidents' inability to reform between 1985 and 1994, fragmentation of the state complements and is related to the institutional arrangements discussed in this chapter.

The Cardoso Administration: Overcoming Institutional Obstacles?

Beginning with the approval of a new tax (the Social Emergency Fund) in March 1994, and especially with the full implementation of the economic stabilization plan in mid-1994, the Franco and Cardoso administrations were able to get much of what they wanted from Congress and governors in the areas regarding stabilization and (to a lesser degree) state reform. In 1995, Cardoso won support for constitutional amendments to eliminate state monopolies in gas, telecommunications, and petroleum. He also won an amendment to end the privileges given to national companies over foreign investment. After years during which presidents generally seemed hamstrung after short honeymoons, Cardoso's success in obtaining qualified (at least 60 percent of each chamber) congressional majorities for what had previously been highly controversial issues was remarkable. Franco had failed to get support for similar constitutional measures during the period of constitutional reform, when amendments were easier to effect; Collor, too, had unsuccessfully pushed for similar constitutional amendments. For decades until the 1980s, the state monopolies in gas, telecommunications, and petroleum had been relatively consensual, and they were enshrined in the 1988 Constitution.

Whereas previous stabilization plans had faltered for political reasons, the Real Plan finally tackled inflation. The rate fell from 2,489 percent in 1993 to 22 percent in 1995 and 10 percent in 1996. In contrast to the recessive effects caused by some stabilization plans, growth remained solid (4 percent in 1995 and 3 percent in 1996). Cardoso's predecessors had failed to rein in state banks; he did so, albeit gingerly and partially. Previous efforts to deindex wages had met congressional resistance; Cardoso was able to get through a provisional measure that brought about deindexation. In July 1997, Congress approved a constitutional amendment fostering modest reform of the public administration; previous presidents had been defeated in their efforts to obtain such a change.

These successes call into question why institutional obstacles that had prevented Sarney, Collor, and Franco from implementing reforms had not similarly blocked Cardoso. Perhaps the most important factor was the profound sense of crisis that permeated Brazil by 1994. The country, for all its promise, was the only Latin American nation that had not stabilized its economy by 1994. Brazil lagged behind the other major Latin American countries in economic adjustment and state reform. The success of neighboring Argentina and Chile in stabilizing and for several years resuming robust growth through market-oriented policies eventually had profound repercussions in Brazil, causing a revision of how actors perceived the role of the state (Almeida 1996). This, coupled with the long period of stagnation, generated a willingness to try what increasingly appeared as the only way out. By 1994, many Brazilians feared that their society was disintegrating under the weight of rampant inflation, slow growth over the previous thirteen years, declining living standards, and escalating urban violence. The depth of the crisis lent urgency to the effort to accept new measures. Under these conditions, legislators and governors gave Cardoso (first as finance minister and then as president) greater latitude to implement reforms.

Between the late 1980s and 1994, the dominant position of Brazilian elites moved from state-led development to more market-oriented approaches (Almeida 1996). The concomitant growing consensus in Brazil and more broadly in Latin America in the post–Cold War period also favored Cardoso. Under Collor, Brazil's centrist parties (PMDB and PSDB) had deep misgivings about neoliberal policies. By 1995, when Cardoso assumed the presidency, the PMDB, PSDB, and the conservative parties had shifted significantly toward acceptance of the neoliberal agenda. The successful stabilization in Argentina, the robust growth of the Chilean economy, and the regionwide trend toward a smaller state helped generate growing consensus toward stabilization, adjustment, and state-shrinking policies in Brazil. Policy convergence did not guarantee rapid success for Cardoso's state-reform agenda, but it paved the way. Policy convergence regarding stabilization and state reform emerged later in Brazil than in most of Latin America, largely because the sense of crisis in Brazil was less acute for a long time and the belief that the status quo could be maintained was more widespread.

The collapse of real socialism delegitimated the leftist statist utopia and fostered consensus about the role of the state: the most statist options were delegitimized. By 1994, the broad ideological dissensus that characterized Brazil in the 1980s had been attenuated.

In addition, Cardoso was a better leader than his predecessors. He was articulate, had a clear vision of where he wanted to go, and chose capable ministers. His landslide victory in 1994 strengthened his hand with Congress and the state governors. He won more leeway with them because Lula was the easy front-runner in the presidential race until after the full implementation of the stabilization plan in July 1994.[16] Fearful of the consequences of a leftist victory, Congress and the governors supported measures that might not otherwise have been passed. His landslide victory, with the greatest winning margin ever in reasonably fair and competitive elections in Brazil, gave Cardoso political leverage. The new president enjoyed great prestige nationally and internationally because of his role in engineering stabilization as well as his reputation as a capable and honest leader. By contrast, in 1993, Congress was delegitimized in the public's eye as a result of a widely publicized corruption scandal, which left it less able to stand up to a popular and successful president. Cardoso's successes in turn extended the honeymoon that presidents usually enjoy.

Following the Argentine example, Cardoso found a new mechanism to help bring down inflation: the exchange rate. Most previous stabilization plans in Brazil had relied on more conventional fiscal and monetary mechanisms. Fiscal policy was undermined by the need of presidents to spend to retain political support and by legislators' and governors' quest for patronage. Efforts to control the monetary supply were hindered by the autonomy of state governments and the difficulties of controlling state banks. By contrast, Congress and governors have essentially no control over exchange-rate policy.

Institutional constraints to policy reform continued to surface during Cardoso's presidency. For a protracted time, the government was not able to win support for constitutional amendments on administrative reform (until July 1997), tax reform, and social-security reform (until March 1996)—three pillars of its program. Congress may have rolled over for a time, but it did not disappear as a political actor to be reckoned with. Recognizing the government's failure to achieve more rapid and thorough reform, in a July 1997 interview, Minister of Communications Sérgio Motta said that the government always had to dilute its reforms: "We are captive to the need to win the support of three-fifths of the Congress to approve reforms."[17]

The government hoped to effect an administrative reform that would establish a ceiling for salaries and pensions for public servants, end guaranteed job stability for public servants, and mandate that local, state, and federal governments could not spend more than 60 percent of revenue on wages. The government sent a constitutional amendment to Congress in August 1995. Despite overwhelming endorsement from governors, the administration spent two years securing support for this reform. Congress approved a constitutional amendment in July 1997, but in greatly watered-down form. Preliminary assessments were that the reform would have minor impact.

In August and October 1995, the government sent two bills to Congress to reform the tax code. The government feared that without boosting revenue at the federal level, medium-term equilibrium would be jeopardized. One proposed bill would have broadened the base of contributors and simplified the tax structure. Congress thoroughly revised the bill before it was approved. The government's bill had thirty-two articles, twenty-six of which underwent substantial amending in a congressional subcommittee. Another item on the tax-reform agenda involved reducing the tax revenue flow from the central government to state and local governments. This measure requires a constitutional amendment, since the 1988 Constitution mandates that a certain percentage of tax revenue go to state and local governments. As of August 1997, the government showed no signs of being able to push the reform through. The government was not able to break the predatory relationship state governments had established with the central government after 1988 (Abrúcio and Couto 1996).

The attempt to revamp the social-security system enshrined in the 1988 Constitution began under Collor, whose multiple efforts to push through reform all failed (Weyland 1996b). Franco also sought but failed to win approval for social-security reform. In March 1995, the Cardoso government proposed a constitutional amendment to reform social security, scale back benefits, and avert the bankruptcy of the system. After an initial government defeat in March 1996, Congress approved a greatly diluted amendment two weeks later. According to *Veja*, in order to win support, the government agreed to assume $5 billion of debt the state government of Rio Grande do Sul owed plus $1.2 billion owed by the municipal government of São Paulo.[18] It also forgave $7 billion in debts owed by large landowners. Without these massive concessions, the government feared it would go down to another defeat. Renowned economist Rogério

Werneck commented in the aftermath of this process that "The government is permanently giving way. . . . It is constantly tempted to reduce the ambition of its proposals to make them politically viable. In order to go forward, the reforms have to be so mediocre . . . that very little is left."[19]

Even the Cardoso government had to negotiate with Congress—and failed to obtain much of what it sought. For example, in April 1995, Congress overrode a presidential veto of a law that postponed debt payments owed to the Banco do Brasil by landowners. The legislators linked to rural interests threatened to boycott voting on the administration's constitutional amendments if the government tried to circumvent the override. Cardoso caved in despite the high financial cost; the government agreed to defer payment on the landowners' debts, estimated at $1.8–5.0 billion, for two years. The concession was a sine qua non for the support of scores of legislators for constitutional reform. The government was forced to resort to traditional patronage politics in order to win the congressional support of the large bloc that represented the landowners.

Although the Cardoso government's stabilization plan has been highly successful, state reform has been modest. The government believes that much more needs to be done. The consensus among scholars is that, for better or worse, Brazil's state reform remains modest compared to that of the other middle-income countries of Latin America (Almeida 1996; Edwards 1995; Weyland forthcoming).

Conclusion

Political institutions have an independent impact on policy processes. They create incentives and disincentives for different kinds of action. They pave roads and create barriers for different policies, thereby affecting the rapidity and breadth of reform. Some democracies have institutions that create many "veto points" and veto players (Tsebelis 1995); others, such as the British system, have fewer ways to block sweeping reform.

Brazil's institutions make sweeping reform difficult, notwithstanding the president's decree powers. Between 1985 and 1994, Brazil's political institutions blocked presidents from implementing stabilization policies and state reforms in a coherent fashion.

What are the implications beyond Brazil? Five points deserve attention.

1. Much of the recent literature on presidentialism has focused on the important issue of regime stability. This chapter has taken a different tack, looking at the policy process rather than at regime stability, and arguing that we should look at institutional combinations. Presidentialism in Brazil is strongly affected by three features of the party system—the degree of fragmentation, the level of party discipline and loyalty, and the degree of polarization. It is also affected by

robust federalism, the president's sweeping formal powers, and the detailed nature of the constitution.

Although the literature on comparative presidentialism has not dealt in detail with policy processes, the literature on institutional economics (e.g., North 1990) has emphasized how institutions shape policy. In a similar vein, recent work by political economists (e.g., Abrúcio and Couto 1996; Almeida 1996; Haggard and Kaufman 1995; Sola 1994a, 1994b) has underscored how institutions shape policy processes.

2. Following the suggestion of Tsebelis (1995), to understand how institutions shape policy processes, it is important to look at institutional configurations rather than isolate particular institutions. Presidentialism with multipartism and robust federalism functions differently from presidentialism with bipartism and unitary government. For some time, comparative political scientists have been keenly aware of how profoundly party-system features affect parliamentarism (Lijphart 1984), and many Americanists have underscored how much federalism and the nature of the parties affect U.S. presidentialism (e.g., Mayhew 1986). Comparativists are only now starting to appreciate how much presidentialism varies according to party-system features and, in some cases, federalism.

The Brazilian case shows that presidentialism does not necessarily generate winner-take-all competition. Whether a system tends toward such competition depends more on the fragmentation of the party system, its federal or unitary character, its bicameral or unicameral nature, and the president's constitutional powers than on the system of government (Shugart and Mainwaring 1997; Tsebelis 1995).

In Brazil, federalism, balanced bicameralism, and extreme party-system fragmentation have led to dispersion of power. Through these institutional arrangements, a large number of parties representing most of the Brazilian population has some share of power: executive power at the local, state, or federal level; or power in Congress. Executive power at the federal level is divided among several parties.

3. The Brazilian case suggests that endowing presidents with strong constitutional powers does not always overcome the effects of party-system fragmentation and federalism. Article 62 was written into the 1988 Constitution with the intention of helping the president implement policies. The widespread use of decree powers has made it easier for presidents to implement reforms. Nevertheless, legislative decree powers have not always guaranteed that a president can do so.

Given sweeping presidential powers and congressional difficulty in overriding a veto, why does Congress sometimes serve as a check? First, presidents need congressional support to enact ordinary legislation, which is still an important component of governing. Attempting to govern as an imperial president without congressional support has costs, and weak legislative support makes it difficult to govern through provisional measures. Unpopular presidents probably cannot govern through presidential decree.

The 1988 Constitution grants Congress some meaningful powers even though it is a comparatively weak body proactively. Congress is a key actor in the ordinary legislative process. With the partial exception of provisional measures, which require congressional acquiescence, presidents need congressional support to enact legislation. Despite provisional measures, the majority of legislation passed between 1988 and 1995 won active congressional support. Of 1,259 laws sanctioned between 1989 and 1994, only 116 were provisional measures that Congress did not modify (Figueiredo and Limongi 1995: 184).

Congress has some authority in setting the budget. It has a panoply of other powers that potentially constrain presidents: the exclusive authority to approve all international agreements with budgetary implications; to approve presidential and vice-presidential requests to leave the country for more than fifteen days; to approve a state of defense, state of siege, or federal intervention in state-level political affairs; to oversee and control directly all acts of the executive; to approve presidential initiatives related to nuclear activities; and to authorize and convoke plebiscites. The Chamber and the Senate, as well as any of their committees, have the right to interpellate ministers of state. The Chamber of Deputies and the Senate together have ten of the fifteen members of the Council of the Republic, which formally must issue a statement on federal interventions, states of defense, and states of siege, as well as issues related to the stability of democratic institutions. The Senate must approve nominations for certain judges, governors of territories, the president and directors of the central bank, the attorney general, and the heads of diplomatic missions. It names two-thirds of the ministers of the National Accounting Court (Tribunal de Contas da União), and it must approve the members named by the president. It can set limits on Brazil's internal and external borrowing and loans. In short, Congress can curb presidents' capacity to implement reforms.

Second, provisional measures require congressional acquiescence. They can be a powerful tool for presidents when Congress is indifferent or deeply divided about a proposal. However, when the legislature actively opposes a bill, provisional measures have not allowed presidents to ram their agenda through. Congress can amend legislative decrees in unrestricted ways; of the 229 provisional measures approved by Congress in 1989–94, 113 were amended (Figueiredo and Limongi 1995: 184).

In response to its dissatisfaction with Collor, the lower chamber nearly approved a bill that would have regulated and restricted the use of provisional measures (Power 1998; Pessanha 1993). In March 1991, the Chamber of Deputies failed by a scant five votes to approve a measure that would have prohibited the president from reissuing a provisional measure that had expired. Although the opposition failed to muster the 252 votes needed, it garnered 247 votes to only 177 for the government. This served as a warning bell: if the government tried to steamroll Congress through decrees, the legislature would circumscribe the use of provisional measures. If an unpopular president abused decree powers, Congress could attempt to pass a bill that would circumscribe the use of these powers. In 1997, the legislature again discussed a bill that would limit the use of presidential decrees. If a president infringed on what Congress viewed as its prerogatives, it would react negatively, making it more difficult for the executive to win legislative support for subsequent bills.

Third, during exceptional periods, presidents need congressional support for issues around which presidential decrees do not serve their needs. During the constitutional congress, President Sarney hoped to secure certain results (above all, a five-year mandate for himself and the maintenance of a presidential system). Sarney was not able to impose his preferences. Another exceptional period occurred when Collor needed congressional support to avoid impeachment.

Another exceptional circumstance that levels the playing field between Congress and the president is a constitutional amendment. Since the promulgation of the 1988 Constitution, successive presidents have yearned for amendments that would make it easier to implement reforms. As president, Cardoso believed that the 1988 Constitution needed to be amended, and he had to bargain to obtain the votes to win approval of key amendments. Many of Cardoso's most important initiatives required such basic change. Thus "exceptional periods," meaning times when presidents could not get what they needed without active congressional support, have been common (Couto 1997).

Even outside such exceptional periods, on an ongoing basis presidents prefer congressional support to governing through decrees. Presidents may need active congressional support on other occasions, and widespread use of decrees could diminish their chances of such support.

4. The Brazilian case suggests that with extreme multipartism, giving presidents legislative decree powers and extensive control over the legislative agenda has mixed effects. On the one hand, legislators gave the executive sweeping powers because they feared that otherwise presidents would be shackled (Power 1998). The difficulties presidents had in governing between 1987 and 1994 even with great constitutional powers suggests that legislators may have been right. On the other hand, these sweeping presidential powers generate an imbalance in legislative-executive relations and weaken mechanisms of accountability,

leading to exaggerated executive authority (Figueiredo and Limongi 1994, 1995, 1997; Power 1998; Shugart and Mainwaring 1997).

5. The Brazilian case suggests that situations in which presidents' parties have a small share of seats may be problematic. In general, legislators from the president's party are more likely than those of other parties to support the executive. Therefore, if the president's party has a small share of seats, obtaining legislative support is likely to be more difficult, effecting major reforms is likely to be more problematic, and Linzian (1994)-type impasses between the executive and legislature are more probable (Przeworski et al. 1996; Mainwaring 1993).

Presidential democracies need not be engineered in a highly majoritarian way, such that the president can always implement his/her preferred policies. However, in third-wave democracies in which major reforms are needed, effective democratic governance under presidentialism is unlikely if the president's most important policies are consistently thwarted.

This observation does not mean that presidentialism with extreme multipartism is doomed. Deheza (1997), Figueiredo and Limongi (1996), and Nicolau (1996b) contend that extreme multipartism can be coupled with presidentialism, as the earlier Chilean case from 1932 until 1970 shows. However, implementing major reforms with this combination is more likely to be difficult than others.

CHAPTER 11

Conclusion

This concluding chapter undertakes four tasks. First, it analyzes some consequences of weak party-system institutionalization. Chapter 2 argued that party systems vary markedly in how institutionalized they are. But this fact by itself does not justify a call for rethinking theories of party systems. One of the assumptions behind the argument that we need to rethink theories of party systems is that the variance in institutionalization has important consequences for democratic politics. This final chapter develops that argument.

Building on the discussion in Chapter 2 of four dimensions of institutionalization, I analyze several general implications of the variance in institutionalization. With greater instability in interparty competition, the electoral market is more open and outcomes are less predictable. Other things being equal, one would expect this situation to increase actors' uncertainty about the desirability of democracy, make it more difficult for citizens to evaluate the parties, increase the chances of significant policy change, and lead to greater legislative turnover. Second, with weak party roots in society, one would expect personalism to be more predominant in electoral campaigns and outcomes. As a result of greater personalism in the political system, accountability is likely to suffer. Third, the lower legitimacy of parties makes it easier for antiparty politicians to win office. Finally, with weaker party organizations, individual leaders are likely to be more important and ad hoc practices more widespread.

The second objective is to examine the consequences of weak institutionalization, specifically for Brazil. I sequentially examine the general hypotheses formulated in the first section and argue that the Brazilian case supports most of them.

Finally, the chapter examines the implications of the Brazilian case for institutional design in democracies with fluid party systems. Institutional design can foster party system institutionalization—but within certain bounds. Seven rules can be designed to favor party building, although not all should be implemented, as this would likely create a stultified party system with oligarchical control by party leaders. However, political elites in weakly institutionalized party systems should use some of these rules to foster party building.

General Implications of
Weakly Institutionalized Party Systems

Chapter 2 argued that the level of institutionalization is a crucial feature that deserves more systematic treatment in theories of party systems. To justify this claim, one needs to show not only important variance across cases, which has already been done, but also that important differences in democratic politics are associated with this variance.

The discussion in Chapter 2 presented part of the argument for why different levels of institutionalization are important to democratic politics. A high degree of instability in party competition means that electoral outcomes are less predictable, and it is easier for new parties to come on the scene and become important contenders for power. But the consequences of weak institutionalization go beyond these features. A fuller exploration of the implications of weak institutionalization is the task at hand in this section.

The centrality of parties in democratic politics suggests new challenges for comparative thinking about democracy in cases of weak institutionalization. What happens when democratic politics unfolds within the context of third-wave party systems that differ in important respects from those that existed in the first and second wave? In what ways does weak institutionalization affect democratic politics? From the earlier (Chapter 2) discussion of four dimensions of party system institutionalization, we can derive several implications of weak institutionalization.

IMPLICATIONS OF SIGNIFICANT INSTABILITY
IN INTERPARTY COMPETITION

The dramatic differences in the stability of patterns of party competition are inherently consequential for democratic politics. With low volatility, electoral outcomes are stable from one election to the next, generating a high degree of predictability to a decisive aspect of democratic politics. Opportunities for new parties are restricted as a result of the low turnover. With high volatility, outcomes are less stable from one election to the next. Some major parties suffer large losses, while new or minor ones enjoy commensurable gains. The electoral market is more open and less restrictive, and outcomes are less predictable.

In addition to these implications for democratic politics that inhere in cases with high electoral volatility, four other consequences of high volatility seem likely. I present them as hypotheses, logically deduced but without empirical evidence that rigorously tests them. First, because the major parties in a stable system remain on the scene for decades, it should be easier for citizens to know what they stand for. Conversely, the fact that in weakly institutionalized systems parties enjoy rapid ascension and experience quick demise presumably makes them less readily familiar to citizens: people have less time to assimilate what different contenders represent. Frequent mergers, schisms, disappearances, and name changes would predictably make it harder to recognize party labels and identify positions. If Downs (1957) is right that party labels help citizens follow democratic politics without undue cost, where electoral volatility is very high, either citizens will spend more time informing themselves about parties or will be less able to grasp their positions. This is not to say that citizens under conditions of high volatility are incapable of making informed judgments, just that they are more difficult and costly. This hypothesis requires a *ceteris paribus* clause; many other factors, including citizens' information levels, the number of parties, and ballot format contribute to facilitating or hindering citizen understanding of different party options.

Second, volatility should affect policy stability. With low volatility, there is limited turnover in legislative seats (barring quirks produced by the electoral system) and in presidential voting; this situation should be favorable to policy continuity because dramatic changes in who holds power are unlikely. Conversely, high volatility presumably increases the chances of significant change in policy because it means ample change in the distribution of seats and power, making change in government composition more likely. Other things being equal, one expects more sweeping policy change with turnover in government. Again, a *ceteris paribus* clause is indispensable; the degree of policy stability reflects many factors in addition to the level of electoral volatility.

Third, the stability of interparty competition should affect legislative recruitment and turnover. In principle, there are two analytically distinct ways in which incumbents can lose seats: because of a decline in party performance or because of their own personal performance. Low volatility should make it easier for legislators to retain their seats by curtailing the first kind of turnover. At the extreme, with zero volatility in an electoral period, an incumbent could lose his/her seat only if a copartisan picked up a seat. With high volatility, legislative turnover is necessarily great. Significant legislative turnover increases the likelihood that large numbers of legislators have little experience. Although we know relatively little about the impact of legislative inexperience, this situation surely affects how legislatures function (whether for better or worse is the subject of some debate). Of course, legislative turnover depends on multiple factors, including most significantly the value that politicians attach to legislative careers and legal restrictions on reelection.

Finally, volatility may affect democratic survivability. High volatility may be associated with lower democratic survivability than low volatility. One ubiquitous ingredient in democratic breakdowns is that some powerful actors fear that the stakes of democratic politics are too high. The greater uncertainty of electoral outcomes associated with high volatility presumably increases political uncertainty, which is related to the fears that lead some actors to support coups. Conversely, if powerful actors who are coup-prone are assured by virtue of a high degree of electoral stability that "unacceptable" electoral outcomes are highly unlikely, they would be more inclined to abide by democratic rules of the game. However, given the reduced stakes of politics in the post–Cold War period, the lower degree of predictability associated with greater volatility is less of a problem for democratic survivability than it was before 1989.

IMPLICATIONS OF WEAK PARTY ROOTS IN SOCIETY

Weak party roots also have significant implications for democratic politics. In more-institutionalized systems, voters are more likely to identify with a party, and parties dominate patterns of political recruitment. At one logical end of the spectrum, all voters would vote on the basis of party sympathy. In this situation, there would be little possibility that an antiparty politician could win election. In fluid systems, a larger share of the electorate votes according to personality; antiparty politicians are more able to win office. Thus populism and antipolitics are more common in weakly institutionalized systems. Personalities rather than party organizations dominate the political scene.

With fluid party systems, there is less institutional control over leadership recruitment than in more institutionalized ones. The institutionalization of party systems affects the recruitment of political leaders. Countries with more-institutionalized party systems are less likely to have antiparty leaders. Consistent with this argument, Uruguay, Costa Rica, Venezuela, Colombia, and Chile have had few antiparty presidents and few who were not career politicians from major parties—in contrast to Brazil.

Because of the greater probability that a populist with a weak party base would be elected, institutional impasses may be more likely in democracies with fluid party systems. In institutionalized party systems, candidates from minor parties have little chance of being elected president. Most voters are loyal to a party, and they generally cast their ballots for candidates of that party.

If elections are personalistic contests, individuals cast their ballots for individuals rather than on the basis of party profile. Of course, some citizens in all democracies vote on the basis of personalistic appeals rather than party differences. But where personalistic disputes are decisive and party labels are less entrenched, those who win elections are less likely to feel restrained in how they govern (Linz 1994; Rose 1980). They are more prone to demagoguery and populism, both of which can have deleterious effects on democracy.

Weak party roots in society and a high degree of personalism enhance the role of television in campaigns, especially for executive positions. Television has become an important vehicle in political campaigns everywhere, but one would expect the effect to be more powerful where citizens are less attached to parties to begin with.

We can also expect differences in the policy style of heads of government, depending on how institutionalized the party system is and how resistant it is to populists. Because they rely on direct linkages to the masses, populist leaders are probably more prone than others to pursue policy measures with an eye toward publicity rather than long-range policy impact. Less attached to and constrained by a party, they are more likely to be erratic and to violate unspoken rules of the game. A vicious cycle can erupt; the fluid nature of the party system opens more space for populists, who then govern without attempting to create more solid institutions (O'Donnell 1994). With an fluid system, predictability declines while the potential for erratic leadership increases.

The institutionalization of party systems also has implications for democratic accountability. Given the propensity to personalism and the comparative weakness of parties in less-institutionalized systems, mechanisms of democratic accountability are usually weaker. A more-institutionalized party system helps foster accountability in two ways. First, politicians are more accountable to party leaders, who have more of a vested interest in protecting the party. Those holding executive office are more inclined to follow established party platforms. Politicians are less likely to be autonomous agents. This does not ensure accountability, but it establishes one more mechanism to generate accountability.

A more-institutionalized party system also strengthens mechanisms of politicians' accountability vis-à-vis voters. Democratic accountability revolves in part around having the opportunity to displace political leaders through the vote. Voters can seek accountability through either individual politicians or parties.

In weakly institutionalized systems, accountability through parties is hampered by the fact that they are fluid and heterogeneous. Moreover, some parties lack the organizational continuity to create a clear profile in the minds of most voters. Because party profiles are less established, they are more difficult for citizens to appraise.[1]

In more-institutionalized systems, party labels are powerful symbols, and party commitments are important. Parties give citizens a way of understanding who is who in politics without needing to read all the fine print (Downs 1957). By doing so, they help facilitate the process of accountability that is a central part of democratic politics. Accountability is enhanced because even if voters cannot evaluate individual candidates, they can assess party labels and can differentiate among the parties. It is easier to evaluate parties than individuals because there are fewer of them and because their positions are more visible than those of individual politicians.

IMPLICATIONS OF LOWER LEGITIMACY OF PARTIES

The third dimension of party-system institutionalization, the legitimacy of parties, also has important implications for democratic politics. Where parties are discredited, it is easier for antiparty politicians to win office because they find a supportive electorate. For this reason, the low legitimacy of parties explains the significant number of antiparty voters in many third-wave countries. The problems attendant on antiparty politicians, including attacks on democratic institutions and a somewhat greater likelihood of erratic leadership, are more common. If parties have legitimacy in the minimalist sense discussed in Chapter 2—that is, they are widely seen as a necessary institution of democratic politics even if individual parties are not perceived positively—it is more difficult for antiparty politicians to win office.

The limited legitimacy of parties in fluid party systems also hinders democratic consolidation, a term that implies a positive construction of beliefs and norms toward the regime. Gunther, Diamandouros, and Puhle (1995: 7) consider a democracy consolidated "when all politically significant groups regard its key institutions as the only legitimate framework for political contestation, and adhere to democratic rules of the game" (see also Linz and Stepan 1996: 5–6). Democracy is generally more consolidated when actors accord legitimacy to parties because they constitute the main mechanism for competing for state power in virtually all democratic systems.[2]

IMPLICATIONS OF WEAKER PARTY ORGANIZATIONS

The fourth dimension of institutionalization is the solidity of party organizations, differences in which also affect the nature of democratic politics. With weaker party organizations, there is greater space for personalistic leaders and greater likelihood that individuals, as much or more than parties, will be the important contenders for power.

Having looked at the implications of weak institutionalization for each of the four dimensions, a general synthesis is in order. Increasingly, and contrary to what some of the classic works on the relationship between parties and democracy posited, it has become apparent in the third-wave cases that democracy can survive despite weak party-system institutionalization. Some classic works (e.g.,

Schattschneider 1942) saw parties as so central to democracy that they seemed to suggest that without a well-formed party system, democracy would be unthinkable. In the third wave, democracy with weak party systems is common.

Low institutionalization, however, affects the way democracy functions. It is associated with certain styles of democratic politics. Guillermo O'Donnell coined the fruitful term "delegative democracy" to refer to democracies with four main characteristics: a high degree of personalism, considerable power vested in the executive, weak institutions, and weak mechanisms of horizontal accountability (that is, weak oversight). Although O'Donnell does not state the point in this way, a weakly institutionalized party system is at the core of delegative democracy. Weak party-system institutionalization is one of the primary commonalties that bind together the otherwise very diverse process of democratization in most post-Soviet and Latin American cases.

Implications of Weak Institutionalization: Brazil

How do these general hypotheses about the consequences of weak party-system institutionalization apply to Brazil? Although the Brazilian case alone cannot prove or disprove any of these hypotheses, they can illuminate the Brazilian experience, and vice versa.

CONSEQUENCES OF INSTABILITY OF INTERPARTY COMPETITION

Four hypotheses have been proposed regarding the consequences of significant instability in interparty competition. First, instability should make it harder for citizens to identify parties' positions. Although factors other than electoral volatility contribute to this outcome, many Brazilian voters have difficulty locating the positions of most parties. Moreover, more citizens have been unable to locate parties' positions in the 1990s than during the 1970s, when the system was more stable. Thus the Brazilian case appears to support this hypothesis, though further research is needed.

Second, electoral volatility should be associated with greater policy instability. Brazil has experienced considerable policy instability since 1985, but it is not apparent whether it stems from electoral volatility. The biggest policy changes occurred in the three presidential successions. However, attributing these shifts to electoral volatility is questionable because neither Sarney nor Franco was a popularly elected president.

Third, with high volatility, legislative turnover is likely to be greater. Moderately high turnover has gone hand in hand with high volatility in Brazil. Legislative turnover in Brazil is high compared to the United States, but low compared to Argentina, where it approaches 90 percent (Jones 1997). Less certain is how much of the turnover in Brazil can be attributed to high volatility. Legislative turnover has remained more or less constant since the 1970s while electoral volatility increased after 1985, which suggests that the two have varied independently. In post–1985 Brazil, high legislative turnover may be less related to high volatility than was suggested earlier because the high incidence of party switching creates a situation in which some individuals are reelected but from a different party, thus contributing to increasing electoral volatility without increasing legislative turnover. Alternatively, it is conceivable that high legislative turnover during the 1970s stemmed primarily from politicians' disinclination to serve in a legislature stripped of meaningful functions, whereas high turnover in the post–1985 period has resulted more from high volatility.

The final hypothesis related to electoral volatility is that it may have an inverse effect on democratic survivability. The Brazilian case is far from conclusive; high volatility has not prevented democracy from surviving.

WEAK PARTY ROOTS IN SOCIETY

Weaker party roots should be associated with greater personalism in politics and with problems of accountability. The Brazilian case conforms to both expectations. With fluid party systems, there is less institutional control over leadership recruitment than in more-institutionalized ones. In Brazil, this fact has been pellucid, and it has contributed to the travails of democratization.

Between 1985 and 1994, one contributing factor to Brazil's difficulties was poor leadership at the presidential level. Figueiredo, Sarney, Collor, and Franco were poor presidents. Figueiredo was indecisive and lacked vision. Sarney had a provincial mentality, relied extensively on patronage politics, was indecisive, and tolerated patrimonialism. Collor was erratic, demagogic, and corrupt. Franco alternated between moments of provincialism, populism, demagoguery, indecision, and mercurial behavior. Presidents matter everywhere, and they particularly make a difference in a country like Brazil where policy-making powers are concentrated in the executive branch. This litany of poor leaders had a deleterious impact.

This succession of poor presidents may appear to be merely a case of bad luck unrelated to the fluid nature of Brazil's party system. This is largely true for Figueiredo and Sarney, but the low degree of institutionalization of the party system was a crucial factor in enabling Collor and Franco to gain the presidency. Collor not only had an antiparty history, but also campaigned against parties and politicians. A candidate without a party would have a difficult time winning the presidency in a democracy with a more institutionalized party system because fewer voters are willing to support a maverick antiparty politician. Collor's election paved the way for Franco's ascension, so Franco, too, was more likely to be a product of an fluid party system.

It is no accident that democratic politics in Brazil has been flavored by personalism, by concentration of power in presidential hands, and by erratic shifts in policy making. Lack of predictability and institutionalization have plagued Brazil, giving rise to a resurgence of populism and personalized electoral campaigns. Candidates for executive posts are elected mostly on the basis of their own strengths and weaknesses, with comparatively little influence exercised by parties (Meneguello 1995).

Party weakness has created a lack of mediating instances between presidents and the people. Choices regarding who governs are more erratic because the parties do not define the electoral arena to a great extent, and they are also more difficult, unpredictable, and personalistic for voters. These are core ingredients of O'Donnell's (1994) delegative democracy.

The Brazilian case also supports the hypothesis about the linkage between a weakly institutionalized party system and accountability. One of the problems in Brazil since 1985 has been weak mechanisms of democratic accountability. Between 1985 and 1992, presidents, ministers, and governors ruled as though Brazil were a patrimonial state, using public resources for financial and political gain. Senators, deputies, mayors, and heads of public agencies and firms followed suit, attempting to bolster their own political careers more than to promote the public good. Billions of dollars were squandered through corruption. The corrupt enjoyed widespread impunity that was only dented with Collor's impeachment and the investigations of congressional corruption in 1993–94.

These problems result partly from party weakness. fluid party systems involve a low degree of institutionalization of party politics, so politics tends to be more personalized and patrimonial. These conditions form a fertile breeding ground for corruption (Huntington 1968: 59–71). No political system is immune to corruption, and in the 1990s, even previously well-institutionalized party systems (the Italian, Japanese, and Venezuelan) were shaken by widespread graft. Nevertheless, *ceteris paribus*, fluid party systems are less transparent and more prone to corruption.

Brazil since 1979 has been a textbook case of how fluid political situations, with fluid party systems, have fostered corruption. The weakness of mechanisms of accountability created an impunity that was only slightly shaken when Collor was impeached. The Brazilian press has been a valuable mechanism for demanding accountability, but the most important such mechanisms formally within the political system—the judiciary, the legislature, and parties—were remiss until 1992 (Weyland 1993; Geddes and Ribeiro Neto 1992).

In Brazil, paradoxically in view of the high degree of personalism in politics, individual politicians are not particularly accountable. In the case of executives, this was partly because of the prohibition of immediate reelection until 1998; this bar diminished voters' ability to reward good leaders and punish the inept or corrupt. Legislators' accountability is weakened by the fact that there are so many politicians and candidates. For example, for the 1992 municipal elections, there were an estimated 1,500,000 candidates for *vereador* and 25,000 candidates for mayor.[3] Most citizens have limited political interest, awareness, and information. They may be able to assess candidates for president and governor on the basis of media images because candidates from the major parties have ample television time. But it is difficult for most voters to assess candidates for legislative office. They have little information on the large number of candidates, the candidates have little TV exposure, and considerable legislative turnover makes for limited continuity in representation.

Since 1984, frequent party switching by elected representatives has undermined party accountability. People may vote for a candidate partially because of his/her party affiliation,[4] only to have the representative switch to another party after the election. When politicians change parties, voting against a party may not ensure a change in the form of representation if the same individuals remain in Congress. Thus after 1985 the PDS became a minor party, but many ex-PDS politicians remained in office (Power 1993; Hagopian 1996; Fleischer 1988).

Because he was not tied to a solid party, Collor was initially able to operate with considerable autonomy with respect to the PRN and the other labels that supported him. Free of party commitments, in March 1990 Collor imposed the most stringent state controls over the financial system in Brazil's history despite having campaigned on a platform of reducing state intervention. Collor acted as though his commitments to his party and voters were irrelevant. Although such a process of dramatically reversing campaign pledges has not been unique to countries with fluid party systems, it is more likely in them.

IMPLICATIONS OF LOW LEGITIMACY OF PARTIES

One would expect that cases in which parties have limited legitimacy are likely to be more conducive to antiparty populist politicians. Such politicians find more fertile breeding ground for their message if large numbers of citizens are hostile to parties. This hypothesis is borne out in Brazil, with the presidential election of Fernando Collor de Mello in 1989 serving as the paramount example. In addition, many state governors have been personalistic populists who would have had dim chances of winning an election in a democracy in which most citizens vote along party lines.

LOW INSTITUTIONALIZATION OF PARTY ORGANIZATIONS

This is closely related to a high degree of personalism in politics—so much so that it does not make sense to talk about the latter as a consequence of the former.

Thus the general discussion of this dimension generates no specific hypotheses for the Brazilian case.

Overall, the Brazilian case strongly supports the contention that the level of institutionalization of the party system has important consequences for the nature of democratic politics. To refer once again to O'Donnell's suggestive distinction, Brazil is close to the model of delegative democracy: weak institutions, great power vested in the executive, and a high degree of personalism. These features are closely related to the weak institutionalization of the party system.

WEAK INSTITUTIONALIZATION AND
THE REPRESENTATION OF POPULAR INTERESTS

The discussion so far has focused on the consequences of weak party-system institutionalization that stem logically from the four dimensions of institutionalization and for which there is solid comparative evidence. A final reflection on the consequences of weak institutionalization focuses on Brazil: weak institutionalization has bolstered elite interests and has had adverse consequences for the representation of popular interests. Although this argument is probably generalizable, it requires further comparative evidence before being presented as a general claim.

Popular interests can be voiced through a panoply of mechanisms: unions, social movements, corporatist arrangements, neighborhood associations, and other popular groups. But parties continue to be the most important mechanism of mediation between society and the state. Where parties are weak, traditional forms of elite interaction tend to prevail, enabling elites to "capture" the state apparatus. This has occurred frequently in Brazil since 1979.

Given the weakness of mechanisms of institutionalized representation, political representation in Brazil has a personalized and individualistic nature, except on the left. Individual politicians more than parties form the basis of representation; political actors rely on individual politicians more than parties to represent their interests.

This system of comparatively individualistic representation has favored those with personal contacts to politicians. Elite actors have much greater access to the informal routes to political influence than popular organizations do. Personal connections are particularly important because of the individualized nature of representation, and elites have better connections than poor people. Based on official data, Santos (1993: 94) shows that the wealthy are much more likely to report having personal contact with a politician than the poor are. The difference in frequency of contact is particularly stark if we compare the percentage of people who contacted a politician to provide a policy suggestion. In the Center-West region, for example, those in the highest income category (more than ten minimum wages) were forty times more likely to give policy suggestions to a politician than those in the lowest category (less than one-half minimum wage).

The well off are also more likely to be active party members than the poor. Data from a 1988 government household survey indicate that 4.3 percent of the upper-middle- and high-income categories (ten minimum salaries or more) were party members. This is three times the figure for those in the lowest two income categories the study used (under one minimum salary) (IBGE 1990, Vol. 2, 16).

Capitalists enjoy privileged access to politicians partly because of their role in funding campaigns. Most politicians need substantial funding to wage competitive campaigns. To finance them, politicians turn to the wealthy, especially businesspeople, who almost always sponsor individual politicians rather than parties. Because of the stringent but unenforceable legal code that supposedly regulated campaign funding, until 1993 these campaign donations were illegal, making the relationship between politicians and donors a surreptitious affair.

In a system with weak accountability, the incentive in campaign finance was not only to cheat—which everybody did because the legal code was excessively stringent—but to cheat flagrantly, because legally there was no difference between egregiously unethical practices and those that would be accepted under most legal systems. The law failed to discriminate between those attempting to buy influence and those merely seeking access, between those willing to compromise the public good and those who refused to do so. In interviews, Brazilian politicians freely alleged that graft involving campaign contributions was widespread (even if they did not admit their own culpability).

The byzantine case of Fernando Collor de Mello and his campaign treasurer, Paulo César Farias, revealed not only the ugly face of corruption in campaign financing in Brazil, but also the implications of the individualized pattern of representation for popular interests. Farias extorted at least $32 million, and perhaps hundreds of millions, out of business executives (Brooke 1992: 31). The flip side of the Collor/Farias scheme was big favors for big business. While he was still governor of Alagoas, but as he was beginning to assemble a campaign chest for his presidential campaign in 1989, Collor returned $100 million in taxes to Alagoan sugar cane barons. Reportedly, the sugar producers siphoned 20 percent of this fortune to Farias for Collor's next political race (Brooke 1992: 44). It is possible that Collor would have returned the taxes even if he had not personally benefited from the deal, but at best this situation gave the appearance of setting public policy to favor the wealthy in exchange for their campaign support. This example could be multiplied hundreds of times for the post–1979 period.

The methods of campaign financing are a manifestation of the venal network that links the interests of politicians with those of Brazil's wealthy—above all, contractors who deal with the state. Most politicians have business interests through which they develop business associates. Rodrigues's study (1987: 76–89), which was limited to federal deputies and focused on their principal occupation, showed that 32 percent of the deputies of the 1987–90 legislature were involved in business as a primary occupation before becoming politicians. Fleischer (1988: 34) included the entire Congress (rather than just deputies), and he considered up to four professional activities rather than just one. The principal occupation of 37.7 percent of legislators was some form of business owner, and another 24.9 percent were managers and high-level executives. Many other legislators had businesses but declared another primary occupation, so the total number of executives in Congress exceeded this already elevated number. A 1991 survey conducted by the weekly *Istoé Senhor* classified 201 of the 503 deputies (40.0 percent) of the 1991–94 legislature as businessmen, using only their primary occupation.[5]

One need not impute facile, self-serving motives to Brazilian legislators to believe that their backgrounds and socioeconomic positions make some difference. Not every wealthy businessperson in Congress has conservative views, but surely the high percentage of business owners and executives in the legislature affects patterns of representation. The percentage of businesspeople is significantly higher in the conservative parties: politicians who are businesspeople are more likely to support conservative positions. In Rodrigues's survey (1987), none of the PT, PCB, PC do B, or PSB deputies were business executives as a primary occupation outside of politics, compared to 58 percent of PDS and 36 percent of PFL deputies. Fleischer (1988: 34) listed only three of thirty-two (9.3 percent) leftist (PT, PCB, PC do B, PSB) politicians as business owners and two (6.3 percent) as high-level executives, compared to nineteen of thirty-eight (50.0 percent) PDS legislators who were owners and nine (23.7 percent) who were executives.

As with all democracies, but to a greater extent in Brazil, the political elite are highly educated relative to the population as a whole. In the 1991–94 Congress, of 418 members who responded to a survey, 68 percent had attended a university, and 22 percent had advanced degrees. Only 3 percent had not gone beyond primary school (DIAP 1993: 25). According to the 1991 census, 151,206 Brazilians had advanced degrees. This figure represents 0.22 percent of the population twenty-five years and older, making the conservative assumption that nobody with an advanced degree was under twenty-five years old (IBGE 1991b: 129–130, 1991a: 223). Thus Brazilian legislators were 100 times more likely than the average person to have an advanced degree. Considering that the mean age of the

Congress was considerably above the mean age of the adult population and that younger generations are better educated, this gap is even more striking.

The Brazilian legislature disproportionately reflects the interests of the backward regions, the privileged sectors of society, and a patrimonial fusion between the state and the political class itself (Hagopian 1996). The freedom of politicians to wheel and deal as and with whom they want has been a fundamental pillar in an elitist political system. Politicians can defend the sugar barons of the Northeast, the coffee kings of the South, the shoe manufacturers of São Paulo, and the massive state enterprises in Minas Gerais—with little interference from party leaders who might attempt to impose programmatic or organizational unity. Politicians, their families, and their friends have benefited handsomely from this system. So, too, has the country's economic elite, which has close personal, family, and financial connections to the political class.

With weak parties and weakly organized popular sectors, politicians can win votes on the basis of personal charisma (principally for executive positions), through patronage (providing local communities and groups with services or public works), or through the support of local notables who influence the poor. These forms of representation have a legitimate place in democratic politics, but they all provide resources to the popular classes on the basis of clientele benefits rather than broad entitlement. Resources are provided on a piecemeal basis, and they are frequently subject to forms of manipulation that favor elites more than the poor. Not only are social programs available to citizens on a fragmentary basis, they also frequently involve manipulation designed to benefit politicians and private interests more than the poor. In this way, individualized patterns of representation support a political system in which popular interests are usually not well served.

Weak parties have been a pillar of a system in which the state usually functions mostly for elites, in which these elites enjoy privileged access and favors, in which codified universalistic rules are frequently undermined in favor of personalistic favors, in which public policy is constantly undermined by the personalistic exchanges and favors, and in which, as a consequence of all the above, the poor suffer.

This argument does not imply that a reformist president committed to redressing Brazil's inequalities is doomed to fail because of the party system. The argument here is based on tendencies, not inexorable determinations. The system tends to favor elite interests, but it does not always do so.

The conservative bias generated by individualized patterns of representation helps explain one of the otherwise puzzling paradoxes of Brazilian politics since 1985: many visible and contested political processes produce "progressive" outcomes, but the behind-the-scenes processes undercut these outcomes. Most

Brazilian politicians say they are on the left or center-left. In a 1987 survey, for example, 57 percent of Brazilian deputies said they were on the left or center-left compared to 6 percent who said they were on the right or center-right and 37 percent in the center (Rodrigues 1987: 97; see also Power 1993). Moreover, many highly visible outcomes produced by the legislature have been relatively progressive. This is true, for example, of the 1988 Constitution, which in terms of social rights, labor rights, and environmental protection is progressive (Bruneau 1989).[6] Other highly visible congressional debates have also produced progressive results seemingly favorable to popular interests. Congressional debates on wage laws, for example, have generally produced "progressive" outcomes.

The pro-elite bias of the individualized patterns of representation, then, does not occur because most politicians are openly conservative. Many important decisions take place outside the public's purview. In these fora the conservative bias of a polity with weak parties comes to the fore. Here, ministers allocate millions or even hundreds of millions of dollars to rescue the private firms of friends who politically support them. For example, politicians angle to grant a huge public works project to firm X, whose directors supported their campaign. They appoint M as head of a major public agency, primarily because of M's political connections and support. Politicians supported more public spending because it will enhance their own ability to benefit their constituencies, even though the poor were consistent losers with hyperinflation, and even though more public spending exacerbated budget deficits and ultimately inflation. The visible transactions of the Brazilian Congress often are progressive, but the backroom transactions, where many vital decisions occur, largely bolster elite interests.

In short, democracy functions differently when party systems are weakly institutionalized, and other things being equal, it is more likely to function better with a relatively institutionalized system. However, this does not imply a bias toward extreme institutionalization, which can be associated with a stultified party system. (Schedler 1995). The point is not that very high levels of institutionalization are necessary or even unambiguously desirable, but rather that a low level of institutionalization tends to produce problems.

Institutional Design and Party-System Institutionalization

What does the Brazilian case tell us about institutional design in new democracies? At a time when citizen cynicism about parties and politicians is high in most democracies, and when many scholars have proclaimed the partial demise of parties, this book has underscored how important a moderately institutionalized party system is. The first and most important general implication is therefore to resist the temptation to scorn parties. Specific parties may be deeply flawed, and citizens may believe that none of the parties in a given system matches their own preferences. Nevertheless, with a weakly institutionalized party system, democracy tends to function at a less than optimum level. Nothing so far has replaced parties, and nothing is likely to in the next decades. Parties are inevitably flawed, but there are no alternatives to them, and they perform vital functions.

It would be disingenuous in the Brazilian case to suggest that parties always solve more problems than they create. From the viewpoint of presidents, parties sometimes present obstacles, and undermining them therefore may be appealing. But the systemic effects of a weakly institutionalized party system are negative, and even for presidents, there are some advantages to a more institutionalized system.

Political elites can take some steps to promote party-system institutionalization. An understanding of comparative political institutions sometimes informs political debate, just as an understanding of what policies are more likely to promote development sometimes informs policy choices. Therefore, a second key implication for other countries—and this is one of the central themes of this book—is that choices of institutional rules affect party-system institutionalization. To the extent that "political engineering" (Sartori 1968) is politically feasible—and whether or not it is depends on political skill, alliances and interests—it behooves political elites in polities with fluid party systems to design rules to promote party building. Rules favorable to party-system building do not ensure that it will occur, but systematically unfavorable rules have a deterrent effect.

Seven institutional rules and features are of particular *general* importance in shaping the prospects for institutionalizing a party system: (1) the choice of a presidential, semipresidential, parliamentary, or hybrid system of government; (2) the degree to which electoral rules encourage party-system fragmentation; (3) the extent to which party organizations control the order in which candidates are elected; (4) the sequence of elections; (5) who controls the candidate-selection process; (6) the establishment of a federal or unitary system of government; and (7) whether the president has legislative decree powers.[7] It is not necessary or even desirable to design all of these rules to favor party building; doing so could create too rigid a system, with too much control resting in the hands of a small group of party leaders. But it is important to design some rules to foster party building.

1. Other things being equal, parliamentary systems are more favorable to fostering party-system institutionalization than presidential systems. In most presidential systems, winning executive power depends to a considerable extent upon the personal qualities of the presidential candidates. Voters choose indi-

viduals, not parties, and in presidential democracies the personal qualities of
candidates have considerable impact.

The personal qualities of potential prime ministers and media politics have
become important factors in many parliamentary systems, but the fact that
voters choose a party list or a Member of Parliament (MP) rather than directly
selecting the prime minister focuses attention more on parties. The head of state
in parliamentary systems is elected by MPs, whose careers have been structured
through party organizations, and the prime minister must be an MP. As a result,
prime ministers have a history of party and legislative leadership, which often is
not the case with presidents. In presidential systems with fluid party systems,
candidates may have little party and legislative experience (Suárez 1982) and may
exhibit antiparty proclivities.

In addition, parliamentary systems have a built-in mechanism for encouraging party discipline and cohesion that presidential systems lack (Epstein 1964).
In most parliamentary systems, the legislature can be dissolved if a no-confi-
dence vote is reached. This mechanism gives MPs an incentive to toe the party
line. Parties in most presidential systems are disciplined, and parties in parliamentary systems can be fractious if other mechanisms outweigh the incentive
for cohesion created by the possibility of dissolution. But the basic incentive
structure of presidentialism is less favorable to party building. Recognition of
this, of course, does not constitute a blanket suggestion that all countries should
move toward parliamentary government.

2. In presidential systems it is best to avoid extreme party-system fragmentation, which complicates its functioning. Extreme fragmentation induces barriers to party-system consolidation.

Even with proportional representation, which has the advantage of facilitating
the representation of minorities (Lijphart 1984), there are nondraconian means
of avoiding extreme fragmentation. A low district magnitude (that is, the
number of representatives per district—say, five or fewer) makes extreme
fragmentation less likely over the medium haul. Comparatively high thresholds
can accomplish a similar effect. More important, in systems with plurality
elections for the presidency, concurrent presidential and legislative elections
usually limit party-system fragmentation. With plurality presidential elections,
concurrent legislative elections help reduce the number of effective parties
because the presidential contest induces voters to cast their ballots for legislative
candidates of the same party (Shugart and Carey 1992; Jones 1995).

3. The electoral system influences party-system institutionalization. For example, party leaders are strengthened if they have some influence over the order
in which candidates of multimember districts are elected. The combination of
multimember districts and no party control over the order of the list can unleash

sharp intraparty competition unless the leaders control candidate selection. With open list PR, with the single transferable vote, or with the single nontransferable vote, candidates owe their election to their own efforts, and are not beholden to the party. This arrangement can promote individualism in campaigning and fund-raising, and successful candidates are less likely to be disciplined when the party did not secure their victory to begin with. This combination of multimembered districts with weak party control over the order of election provides incentives for individualism (as in Brazil) or factionalism (as in Colombia and Uruguay).

Critics correctly claim that the combination of proportional representation and party control over the order of the list can lead to the emergence of an oligarchic party elite. One way to minimize oligarchic control while still vesting party elites with reasonable control over the order of the ticket is through intermediate systems such as the German or the Hungarian, both of which give parties control over the order of part of the list and give voters greater personal choice for other candidates. Another way is to allow for preferential voting, but in such a way that the initial ordering of the ticket by party leaders has some weight in determining the final order in which the candidates win assembly seats. With varying degrees of party control, this is the case in Switzerland, Denmark, Austria, Norway, Sweden, Belgium, and the Netherlands (Katz 1986: 88–91).

4. The sequence of elections affects party-system institutionalization in two ways. In new democracies with fluid party systems, it may be best to avoid too many elections. Frequent polls lead to constant involvement in campaigns and intraparty jockeying to secure the inside track for coveted candidacies. This leaves politicians with little time to devote to legislative duties and to building party organizations. At worst, it can promote internecine warfare without leaving time for the party to heal the wounds from the last round of internal struggles. Frequent elections may incur citizen cynicism and apathy: if elections occur frequently and never resolve anything, they seem useless. In cases where campaigns act as a fillip for public expenditures, frequent elections may also erode fiscal equilibrium.

With a presidential system, a case can be made for having concurrent legislative and executive elections. If executive elections occur separately, the plebiscitarian elements that inhere in presidentialism are strengthened. If they take place at the same time as congressional elections, the party organization has stronger incentives to get involved. The presidential outcome will likely have some effect on congressional races, so the party machinery is more disposed to mobilize en masse.

5. Rules regarding candidate selection also shape prospects for party building. Parties are more likely to become central actors in the political system if they

control candidate selection; then individual politicians have strong incentives to be loyal to the organization. If a political system offers broad choices among viable parties or individuals with sharply competing policies, the disadvantages of a closed selection process diminish because of the breadth of interparty choices. If, on the other hand, party competition is constricted or the differences between the parties are narrow, as in the United States or Colombia, then the disadvantages of a closed selection process increase. In that case, voters would have limited choice among parties and limited choice within parties. This is a recipe for a stifled democracy, with limited popular choice.

6. Although it is a "choice" that is virtually intractable once taken, in new nations, the unitary or federal nature of a polity also shapes the party system. Other things being equal, a federal system promotes party decentralization and party heterogeneity, whereas a unitary system encourages the formation of centralized national parties. Seen only from the point of party-system institutionalization, a unitary system is more favorable to the creation of strong national organizations. Other things being equal, this scenario is also more favorable to cohesive parties, for it reduces the conflicts created by having a multitude of state-level leaders who call the shots in their own states. Despite this, in countries where regional and ethnic or religious cleavages coincide—that is, where some ethnic or religious minorities live predominantly in specific regions—federalism has compelling advantages (Lijphart 1984: 90–105; Stepan 1997): It allows these minorities greater self-governance at the local and state levels.

7. As I argued in Chapter 8, rules that provide the president with legislative decree powers work against party-system institutionalization. They also create an imbalance in legislative-executive relations.

Conventional wisdom has held that institutional reform is difficult to implement because the politicians who design institutions have benefited from the existing ones and don't want to change them. The major institutional innovations in recent years in Argentina, Bolivia, Colombia, Mexico, and Venezuela, as well as Israel, Italy, Japan, and New Zealand belie that conventional wisdom. Of course, calculations of self-interest weigh heavily in choices of political institutions, and punctilious academic analysis of comparative political institutions rarely engages politicians. Therefore, it is important to recognize the limits of what institutional engineering can accomplish and the difficulties it usually faces. But deliberate efforts at institution building are by no means doomed to fail.

Rules favoring party organizations inevitably involve tradeoffs. Rules that promote parties as the central agents of the political process often enable them to dominate political life, subjecting them to criticisms as oligarchical organizations. Such rules reduce choices among voters; party organizations rather than voters determine intraparty candidate selection, and party organizations rather than voters determine the order of the ticket. But in fluid party systems, these disadvantages are outweighed by the importance of institutionalizing a party system. Moreover, one need not opt for draconian levels of party elite control; the important point is to avoid a set of institutional rules that systematically discourages party building.

Of course, no rules ensure that a party system will become institutionalized. This study has not advocated a facile political engineering/constitutionalism approach, whereby designing effective political systems is a matter of applying universal rules to specific cases. But institutional rules do matter, and in the short run they can be changed, whereas cultures, social structures, and levels of development cannot be. Political elites can design rules that enhance the possibilities that parties will win enduring loyalties and establish stable roots in society. An institutionalized party system facilitates many favorable outcomes in the democratic process, and for this reason political elites in fluid systems do well to design some rules to favor stronger parties.

Final Remarks

I began this book with the claim that the third wave of democratization has introduced a greater number and range of democratic party systems than ever existed before, and argued that we need to rethink some central issues in party systems theory in light of the third-wave cases. Among the three broad claims made in Chapter 2, I have focused most on institutionalization as a key issue along which party systems vary, with important implications for democratic politics.

This concluding chapter has developed some of the reasons why we need to incorporate institutionalization into the comparative analysis of party systems. The nature of democracy differs according to whether the party system is weakly or strongly institutionalized. This is not to suggest a simplistic, unidimensional causal argument according to which party-system institutionalization determines how democratic politics functions. However, party-system institutionalization is an important variable in comparing party systems, and variance in institutionalization shapes the nature of democratic politics.

Reference Matter

Notes

Chapter 1

1. When I say that institutions shape outcomes, I mean that they increase or decrease the likelihood of certain occurrences. This is a probabilistic rather than a deterministic formulation.

2. This is the conventional Weberian definition of rationality. See Weber 1968 and also Tsebelis 1990: 18–47.

3. Here and elsewhere, for shorthand I refer to actors' attempts to maximize outcomes, but in some cases, rational actors may operate on a "minimax" logic, that is, to minimize regret rather than to maximize utility.

4. It might seem contradictory that I simultaneously underscore the heterogeneous and pragmatic nature of the catch-all parties and the ideological breadth in the system. Although the catch-all parties are heterogeneous and nonideological, the existence of many parties allows the sum of the parts to express a broad range of opinion.

5. The 1945 presidential election, when the Communist Party garnered almost 10 percent of the vote, was the only exception.

Chapter 2

1. This section draws upon Mainwaring and Scully 1995: 4–16.

2. The effective number of parties is calculated by squaring each party's share of the vote (or of seats), summing the squares, and dividing one by this sum.

$$N = \frac{1}{\Sigma p_i^2}$$

where N is the effective number of parties and p_i is the share of seats (or votes) of each party. For example, if four parties won 40 percent, 30 percent, 20 percent, and 10 percent of the vote, then Nv (the number of effective parties in votes) would be

$$\frac{1}{.4^2 + .3^2 + .2^2 + .1^2} = 3.33$$

A large, effective number of parties means that seats (or votes) are widely dispersed among many parties.

3. Throughout this book, unless I specify otherwise, I mean democratic party systems—i.e., party systems in democratic polities—whenever I discuss institutionalized party systems. Repeating "institutionalized democratic party systems" is cumbersome. However, nondemocratic party systems can also become institutionalized. For example, Mexico's hegemonic party system was highly institutionalized between the 1940s and the 1980s.

4. Huntington (1968) and Panebianco (1988) see the autonomy of parties vis-à-vis organized interest groups as an expression of institutionalization. I do not share this view. Where linkages between parties and organized interests are stronger, parties are more likely to be deeply embedded in society, making the system more (not less) institutionalized.

5. Ballot structure and electoral rules also affect the difference between presidential and legislative voting. For example, the Uruguayan, Bolivian, and Honduran electoral rules impose straight ticket voting, so presidential and legislative vote results by party are virtually identical.

6. Bicameral parliamentary systems or systems that give voters two votes (Germany) afford the opportunity of ticket splitting, but it is not directly comparable with that between the president and Congress.

7. A more thorough analysis of ticket splitting than is possible here would control for the effective number of parties. As the number increases, so do options for ticket splitting, independent of the level of institutionalization. Ticket splitting may reflect the action of a rational and informed voter, but it still indicates comparatively weak citizen attachment to a particular party.

8. This idea was suggested by Dix 1982.

9. Dix (1989) makes a similar claim, but my analysis diverges from his in one respect. Dix assumed that the social-cleavages model applied well to Western European party systems, but the evidence is mixed on this score. The power of the social-cleavage model to explain the physiognomy of most Western European systems has declined since the 1960s. Moreover, for a few cases such as Ireland, the social-cleavage model was never too useful.

10. This raises questions about Gibson's (1996) definition of conservative party. He argues that "conservative parties . . . draw their core constituencies from the upper strata of society" (7). In Brazil, however, some conservative parties (e.g., Collor's PRN) have fared best among the poor and worst among the privileged. The same is true of the right-wing party, MODIN, in Argentina (Adrogué 1995: 49). The analyst must then either reach the dubious conclusion that the party is not conservative because its core constituency is lower-class, or that despite its weak showing among the privileged strata, they still constitute its "core constituency." The latter claim ultimately rests on the dubious premise that a social scientist can discern what constitutes the "true" core constituency, notwithstanding voting behavior to the contrary. This claim is difficult to falsify and even tautological because regardless of the party's electoral base, the upper class is assumed to be the core constituency.

11. An estimate of the pseudo R^2 for an equation with income, education, and size of municipality as independent variables suggests that these factors leave 68 percent of the variance unexplained.

12. This probably has not always been the case. Before the 1970s, churchgoing Catholics were almost surely more conservative than a random sample of the entire population.

13. In the October 1994 presidential election in Brazil, a different kind of nonstructural issue surfaced as the paramount political cleavage: support or opposition to the economic stabilization plan. The 1994 stabilization plan dramatically turned the election around. After trailing Lula 40 percent to 17 percent as late as May 25, 1994, Cardoso, who as finance minister was responsible for the stabilization plan, quickly surpassed his main competitor as inflation tumbled from more than 40 percent per month to about 2 percent. In a September 9, 1994 survey, 73 percent of Cardoso's supporters said that they personally benefited from the stabilization plan, compared to only 42 percent of Lula's supporters. A respondent's perception of whether the stabilization plan had helped or hurt her/him was a more powerful predictor of the vote than the sociological categories shown in Table 2-5. DataFolha national survey, September 9, 1994 (10,560 respondents): CESOP archive.

14. The reasons for this decline are not exactly the same in Western Europe and Latin America. In Western Europe, most evidence (e.g., Inglehart 1977, 1984; Clark and Lipset 1991) suggests that growing affluence led to less salience of traditional class issues and greater salience of postmaterialist concerns (Kitschelt 1989, 1994). In Latin America, declining class voting in the 1980s occurred during a period not of growing affluence, but of increasing poverty. The collapse of the developmentalist state and the search for a new development model produced a reconfiguration of political loyalties (i.e., a realignment) and dealignment.

15. The most important exception is Kitschelt et al. forthcoming.

Chapter 3

1. When I discuss modern or mass parties, I have in mind parties that organize to compete in contested elections. This excludes totalitarian parties and one-party states.

2. My notion of a modern (or mass) party draws upon Sartori's (1976) concept of mass party, but it differs from Duverger's understanding of the same term (1954: 63–71). Duverger contrasted mass and cadre parties, the latter being based on broad membership. His mass parties are generally parties of the left, closed linked to the working class, the European socialist parties being the paradigmatic examples.

3. I alternatively use 1945 and 1946 throughout the discussion in this section. The party system began to form in 1945, and the first presidential and congressional elections were held that year. However, the president and Congress took office in 1946, when the new constitution was promulgated and went into effect. Therefore, I use 1945 as the inaugural year for the party system but 1946 as the beginning point of the democracy.

4. Soares (1973: 78) calculated the correlation coefficient between percentage of valid votes for the PSD and percentage of population living in cities and villages with over 10,000(inhabitants as –.60(in 1945 and –.52 in 1947. The corresponding figures for the UDN were –.39 and –.33, and for the PTB +.68 and +.45. The figures for all three parties probably continued to decline as absolute values as the UDN made inroads into the biggest cities and the PTB expanded its organizational base to smaller *municípios*.

5. For comparative data on electoral volatility in contemporary Latin America, see Mainwaring and Scully 1995: 6–9; Coppedge forthcoming. For data on Western Europe, see Pedersen 1983; Bartolini and Mair 1990. None of the Western European cases exhibit electoral volatility as high as that in Brazil between 1945 and 1964.

6. It would be preferable methodologically to use votes, but with the exception of the 1945 and 1947 lower-chamber results, official vote totals provide data on coalitions without distingushing to which coalition partner votes should be assigned. In 1945, when the difference between the presidential and lower-chamber vote was 11.7 percent, the difference between the presidential vote and parties' share of seats was 12.8 percent. Thus, for that particular year, it mattered little whether one made the calculation on the basis of votes or seats.

Chapter 4

1. Of the opposition parties, even the PMDB lacked local organizations in many small towns in the interior. In October 1980, the PDS had a total of 2,979 local party organizations (directorates), compared to 2,127 for the PMDB, 869 for the PP, 625 for the PT, 558 for the PDT, and 334 for the PTB (Alves 1985: 216–17). The PDS was organized in the vast majority of *municípios*.

2. Until Fernando Collor de Mello assumed the presidency in March 1990, Brazil did not unequivocally qualify as a democracy. In 1985, Neves and Sarney were chosen through an electoral college whose composition was rigged to favor the PDS. In an unambiguously democratic election, Neves might have been elected, but Sarney would not have been. In addition, until 1988 the authoritarian constitution was still in effect, nothwithstanding important modifications.

3. Because of the fluid nature of party affiliations, data on the number of seats per party often differ slightly from one source to the next.

4. Fundação do Desenvolvimento Administrativo, Instituto de Economia do Setor Público, *Indicadores IESP* #34 (November 1994), 41. The IGP-DI is the indicator of inflation here. The IGP-DI is a different indicator from the one used in Table 3-1; the difference in concrete terms is minor.

5. In the state of Rio de Janeiro, the weakening of party identifications and the decline of party voting were evinced in 1982, but Rio was an isolated case. See A. Souza et al., 1985.

6. The exception is a system of "fused" voting, which imposes a straight party vote on citizens, as is the case in Uruguay, Bolivia, and Honduras.

7. CESOP archive, IBO/BR 94.jun-00348. June 2–6, 1994. N=2,000.

8. Party sympathizers were identified on the basis of a close-ended question, with a list of parties read to respondents. There were 500 total respondents, 111 of whom considered themselves PT sympathizers.

9. On the other hand, Balbachevsky (1992) convincingly argues that party identification is still meaningful in the Brazilian context.

10. DataFolha national survey, September 9, 1994. N=10,560.

11. IBOPE National Voter Survey #1, February 15–March 12, 1987. N=5,000.

12. The survey was conducted June 10–13, 1988, with 500 respondents—100 each in Rio de Janeiro, São Paulo, Recife, Belo Horizonte, and Curitiba. The distribution of responses was weighted according to the relative size of the five cities, socioeconomic class, gender, and age.

13. For 1986, complete data on the lower-chamber vote by party are not available for eleven states. For them, data on personal votes of parties that won at least one seat in the state are available. I estimated a statewide total by assuming that parties won the same

share of party votes (*votos de legenda*) in each of the eleven states as they did for the other fifteen states aggregated.

14. Harry Makler generously supplied these data from a survey he conducted in Brazil in 1990.

15. In a November 1989 IBOPE national survey (Wave 19, n=3,650), 57.5 percent agreed that "The Brazilian people do not know how to vote." Only 35 percent disagreed.

16. The one-third figure is a rough approximation because candidates' personal vote totals determine the intracoalition order of seats. Assume that parties A, B, and C form coalition ABC, which wins one seat. Fifty-five percent of the coalition votes belong to A, 35 percent to B, and 10 percent to C. However, if C has the individual candidate who wins the most votes, that candidate will get the seat. Then A and B fail to win a seat despite surpassing one-third of the threshold, while C wins one despite failing to reach one-third of the threshold.

17. Nicolau (1996b) questions whether this moderation will occur in Brazil, given the decentralization of the party system.

18. I chose the term "ideological distance" rather than Sartori's notion of ideological polarization. Sartori uses that notion in two different and not entirely consistent ways. At times, it refers to what I have called ideological distance. Elsewhere, however, he tends to conflate this usage with a situation of sharp ideological conflict among parties. The problem with conflating the two usages is that parties can hold sharply divergent ideological positions without generating intense conflict.

19. The term Rodrigues used—*radical* left and right—may have prejudiced deputies against so classifying themselves because of its negative connotation.

Chapter 5

1. Coppedge 1994 is an exception. On party organization in the Brazilian catch-all parties between 1946 and 1964, see Peterson 1962; L. Oliveira 1973; Hippólito 1985: 119–38, Benevides 1981: 160–77. On the PT, see Meneguello 1989: 65–102.

2. "A Mancha da Traição," *Veja*, August 14, 1996.

3. In both countries, party switching is so common that specific terms have been coined. In Ecuador, the term *cambio de camiseta* (literally, change of jersey) refers to politicians' practice of changing parties. See Conaghan 1995.

4. In the early 1980s, the electorate was often unforgiving of politicians who moved from the PMDB (or another opposition party) to the PDS. Between 1985 and 1994, however, many politicians who switched parties won reelection. R. Schmitt and Araujo (1997) show that the reelection rate in 1994 of Members of Congress who switched parties between 1990 and 1994 was only marginally lower than the rate of those who did not.

5. "Dinheiro no bolso," *Veja*, October 6, 1993, 18–21.

6. Interview with author, January 21, 1988.

7. Interview with State Deputy Waldemar Chubaci, March 29, 1988.

8. In 1994, *Veja* reported that "in the interior of Pernambuco, most mayors request 30,000 Reais (about US$34,000) to campaign (for a candidate for federal deputy) in their cities." "Corrida por votos e por dinheiro," *Veja*, September 7, 1994, 41.

9. Senator Mauro Benevides (Ceará), long-time treasurer of the PMDB national party and member of the party's national executive committee, stated in a January 26, 1988,

interview with the author that "In their statements to the Electoral Court regarding campaign expenses, candidates lie in flagrant and visible ways." Given his position, Benevides was among the best-informed Brazilian politicians on the subject of party finances.

10. Interview with the author, August 8, 1987.

11. Interview with the author, March 29, 1988. Chubaci estimated the average expenditures in cruzados. I converted the cruzado figures into dollars at the parallel (black) market rate for October 1986. Using the official exchange-rate conversion, the average expenditures of successful candidates for federal and state deputies would be 70 percent higher in dollar terms than the figures I have provided here.

12. "Atrás do voto," *Istoé Senhor*, August 1, 1990, 43.

13. "Quando me apoíam de graça, eu até choro," *Veja*, September 7, 1994, 43.

14. "Milhoes na revisao," *Veja*, February 2, 1994, 22.

15. "An Edge for Incumbents: Loopholes that Pay Off," *New York Times*, March 20, 1990.

16. "Atrás do voto," *Istoé Senhor*, August 1, 1990, 43.

17. *Istoé Senhor* gave no explanation of how it reached this estimate, so it should be interpreted with caution. This caveat applies to all other estimates of campaign expenditures.

18. "Corrida por votos e por dinheiro," *Veja*, September 7, 1994, 39.

19. "A matemática dos tucanos," *Veja*, November 30, 1994, 38–39.

20. "A face oculta do PT," *Veja*, December 7, 1994, 45.

21. "Prefeitos-sabonete," *Veja*, August 7, 1996, 39.

22. There have been some exceptions to this generalization. In 1986, because of his own low personal appeal and the high public-opinion ratings of his party, the PMDB candidate for governor of São Paulo, Orestes Quércia, successfully ran a campaign relatively centered around party appeals and symbols. The PT has run many party-centered campaigns.

23. In the United States, national conventions met only once every four years and their function was limited to choosing a presidential candidate, yet this function ensured the importance of the national convention until around 1970. It also gave parties that were decentralized in most ways an important moment of unity and centralization.

24. "Ulysses divide, mas ainda é o rei," *Correio Brasiliense*, April 1, 1987.

25. Interview with author, August 8, 1987.

26. Interview with author, January 26, 1988.

27. *Adesismo* refers to a practice of supporting whomever is in power; *adesista* is the adjective.

28. The PFL expelled two Members of Congress in early 1997 for selling their votes for a constitutional amendment. In 1995, the PDT expelled five deputies for failing to toe the party line on privatization. Such cases are unusual.

29. Whereas municipality in English suggests an urban area, many *municípios* are predominantly rural.

30. The state convention is called the *convenção regional*; the state directorate is called the *diretório regional*; and the state executive committee is called the *executiva regional*.

31. This is similar to how the national committees of the U.S. parties were formed for a long time. Until the 1970s, when it departed radically from the old formula, the

Democratic National Committee consisted of one man and one woman from every state, plus members from the territories. The Republican National Committee functioned in the same way until 1952, when states gained a third representative as a reward for electoral success.

32. Brazilian members of Congress do not formally represent their entire state. In practice, however, about half of the federal deputies represent well-defined regions within their states. See Ames 1995b; Kinzo 1988; Fleischer 1976.

33. Interview with the author, May 21, 1988.

34. Interview with the author, José Antonio Campoy, ex-PMDB activist and Advisor to State Deputy Wanderley Macris, PMDB-São Paulo, March 25, 1988.

35. Interview with the author, August 18, 1987.

36. Unpublished data of the Tribunal de Contas da União.

37. Author's interview with Dr. Salatiel, an official of the Tribunal Superior Eleitoral, January 13, 1997.

38. Author's interviews with Senator Lúcio Alcântara (PSDB-Ceará), January 14, 1997; interview with Dr. Salatiel, an official of the Tribunal Superior Electoral, January 13, 1997; interview with João da Silveira, ex-Secretary General of the Pedroso Horta Foundation of the PMDB, January 12, 1997.

39. Author's interview with Senator Mauro Benevides (PMDB-Ceará), January 26, 1988.

40. Author's interview with Federal Deputy Marcelo Cordeiro, September 22, 1987.

41. See also Strom's (1990) interesting discussion of parties as rational actors.

42. This assumption is not necessary for rational-choice approaches. Rational-choice theorists could postulate that parties are rational actors with multiple objectives. Strom (1990) analyzes three rational objectives of parties: vote maximization, office holding, and policy.

43. Author's interview with Federal Deputy Hélio Duque, PMDB, State of Paraná, October 28, 1987.

Chapter 6

1. "Lucena forma filas para oferecer cargos na PB," *Folha de São Paulo*, November 1, 1987. There is a play on words here, since PCB were the initials for the Brazilian Communist Party, which often was the scapegoat for Brazil's problems, just as Burity blames the other PCB (Brazilian Clientelistic Party) for the country's ills.

2. For a similar point in other contexts, see Archer 1990; Chubb 1982; Graziano 1973; Oi 1989; Tarrow 1967: 325–40; Weber 1978.

3. Graziano (1975), Tarrow (1967), and Weber (1978) argued that modern clientelism is based on party-directed exchange rather than traditional political notables. This observation applies only in part to Brazil. Because of the weakness of party loyalties and identities among the catch-all parties, individual loyalties still retain salience. The parties control patronage opportunities less than in the southern Italian case.

4. Gay (1994) shows that in a favela of Rio de Janeiro, community leaders were quick to change their loyalty from one politician to another when it appeared the latter could deliver more.

5. "Aluísio revela o caos total na administração," *Estado de São Paulo*, November 6, 1985. Brazilian public administration is divided into direct and indirect sectors. The former includes traditional state bureaucracies in charge of government services, comprising above all the agencies subordinated to the various ministries. The latter includes business and commercial enterprises, foundations, and autarchies (including most federal universities, technical schools, public banks, and regional superintendencies, among others).

6. "Aluízio assegura fim do pistolão," *Jornal de Brasília*, August 23, 1986. *Pistolão* is literally a "big gun."

7. "Empreguismo: Como na Velha República," *Visão*, July 3, 1985.

8. "Mil e uma noites," *Jornal do Brasil*, February 6, 1985.

9. "Quem não tem padrinho morre pagão." The literal translation of *padrinho* is godfather, but the term has a more expansive meaning. A *padrinho* is at the same time a godfather, a protector, and above all a sponsor or patron. In traditional Brazil, "dying a pagan meant going through life without faith and hope, only to die and go to hell."

10. "Trem alagoano tem 10 mil passageiros e 550 'marajás'," *Folha de São Paulo*, June 8, 1986.

11. Clientelism is often treated as an expression of cultural patterns. Without denying the potential usefulness of this approach, I examine the question from the perspective of incentives.

12. Chapter 5 reports higher figures for party membership. Those figures are based on data from the State Electoral Court of São Paulo, whereas the data here come from self-reported membership. Some people who are on the official lists as party members fail to acknowledge their membership when asked. Presumably, most of them were once active in a party or went to a convention to gain access to patronage, but subsequently became less involved.

13. In 1986 Vice-Governor Orestes Quércia (PMDB-São Paulo) appointed ninety people to the Basic Sanitation Company of the State of São Paulo (Sabesp), a state firm. All were either delegates, political notables who controlled the votes of some delegates, or relatives of delegates. See "Quércia troca cargos da Sabesp por apoio na convenção," *Folha de São Paulo*, November 9, 1986. Quércia's control of the party machinery, lubricated by patronage, enabled him to win the PMDB's gubernatorial nomination in 1986.

14. In a 1994 IBOPE nationwide survey, interviewers asked, "This year there will be concurrent elections for several positions. Which of these positions are you most interested in voting for?" Forty-seven percent of the respondents said the president, 21 percent said governor, 8 percent said deputy, and 3 percent senators. Twelve percent said they weren't interested in voting for any position, 6 percent were equally interested in all positions, and 5 percent didn't know or answer: CESOP archive, OPP 266/94, June 2–6, 1994. N=2,000. In a 1974 survey on the eve of the elections in the city of São Paulo, only 19.1 percent of respondents could name their candidates for federal deputy. In a similar survey eight years later, only ninety of 677 (13.3 percent) had a preference for federal deputy. In a 1976 survey in President Prudente, São Paulo, only eighty-seven of 863 respondents (10.1 percent) could remember how they voted in 1974 for federal deputy, and only fifty-four (6.3 percent) could recollect how they voted for state deputy. This information comes from CEBRAP and IDESP surveys.

15. See Lamounier 1991: 76–79 for a discussion of such practices in the 1990 elections in the state of Alagoas.

16. "Raphael sai com críticas a Saulo e Murad," *Folha de São Paulo*, October 24, 1987. See also Rafael de Almeida Magalhães's analysis of this situation in "Obstáculos à Modernização do Estado," IUPERJ, *Cadernos de Conjuntura* #14 (1988).

17. Data on resources distributed by the Ministry of Housing come from the *Folha de São Paulo*, March 23, 1988. Population figures are based on projects from the 1980 census. Fundação Instituto Brasileiro de Geografia e Estatística, *Anuário Estatístico do Brasil 1990* (Rio de Janeiro).

18. "Chiarelli divulga relatório e diz que houve apadrinhamento," *Folha de São Paulo*, April 3, 1988.

19. "CPI faz nova relação das verbas liberadas por Aníbal," *Folha de São Paulo*, April 22, 1988; "Revelando o culpado," ibid., April 24, 1988.

20. "Cidade natal de Sarney é campeão no recebimento de verbas no Maranhão," *Folha de São Paulo*, February 15, 1988.

21. "Verba não foi para obras, diz Gardênia," *Folha de São Paulo*, February 11, 1988.

22. Cammack (1982) reports that *adesismo* was so widespread after the 1972 elections that in many states, one-half to two-thirds of the mayors elected on the MDB ticket switched to Arena.

23. "Prática divide opiniões de congressistas," *Folha de São Paulo*, February 21, 1988.

24. "Dropes," *Folha de São Paulo*, February 13, 1988. *Despachante* literally means "dispatcher." In Brazil, *despachantes* are people who make a livelihood out of processing demands and paperwork through the sinuous bureaucracy. Countless bureaucratic processes are either difficult and time-consuming or virtually impossible without a *despachante*. *Luxo* is the word for "luxury"; thus, a *despachante de luxo* is a high-class *despachante*.

25. "Frases," *Folha de São Paulo*, February 15, 1988.

26. "Inclusão da família no apadrinhamento irrita Sarney," *Folha de São Paulo*, February 11, 1988.

27. "Tres baianos comandam ofensiva dos cinco anos de mandato de Sarney," *Folha de São Paulo*, January 24, 1988.

28. "Magalhães admite uso político de concessões de rádio e TV," *Folha de São Paulo*, December 6, 1987.

29. "Ministros lutam por Sarney," *Correio Brasiliense*, December 7, 1987; "Anibal sí liberava verba com apoio aos 5 anos, diz deputado," *Folha de São Paulo*, January 25, 1988.

30. "Sarney vai tratar como inimigo quem vão votar nos cinco anos," *Jornal do Brasil*, November 12, 1987.

31. "Cargos vagos deverão ser preenchidos por cincoanistas," *Folha de São Paulo*, January 28, 1988.

32. "Cincoanistas de MT querem cortar verbas para Bezerra," *Folha de São Paulo*, February 7, 1988.

33. Interview with the author, August 12, 1987.

34. "Na caça ao voto, empreguismo é arma de governador," *Jornal do Brasil*, May 18, 1986. Magalhães's statement resembled that of a famous traditional politician from Minas Gerais, Ultimo de Carvalho, who averred that "The essence of power is hiring, firing, and arresting."

35. Interview with author, September 18, 1987.

36. Interview with author, May 11, 1988. Other high-ranking economic policy makers, including ex-Finance Minister Luis Carlos Bresser Pereira (May 12, 1988) and Luis Gonzaga Belluzzo (March 18, 1988) relayed similar opinions in interviews with the author.

37. Interview with author, May 9, 1988.

38. Interview with author, February 3, 1988.

39. Senator Luis Viana (UDN-Arena-PDS-PMDB), who was minister of justice under Castello Branco and later Governor of Bahia, expressed this perspective clearly. "A government has some essential parts and some secondary parts. You need efficient elements in some departments, and in others you can tolerate less efficiency." According to him, the military tolerated clientelism in the secondary agencies, but not in the "essential" ones. Interview with the author, January 28, 1988.

40. Compiled from data in the *Enciclopédia Mirador Internacional.* See also Nunes 1978. I defined a political minister as one who had already been a councilor, state deputy, federal deputy, senator, vice-governor or governor before assuming his/her cabinet position. A person who was named minister and later won elected office was not counted as a political minister. Nor were individuals who had previously run for office but lost counted as political ministers, largely because of the difficulties in obtaining such information.

41. Interview with the author, December 10, 1987.

42. "Nomeações, herança dos Estados com a disincompatabilização," *Estado de São Paulo, June 13, 1982.*

43. "Governo federal investiga contratações sem concurso," *Folha de São Paulo,* October 12, 1985.

44. "Uma praga nacional," *Visão,* January 22, 1986.

45. "O submundo do clientelismo," *Folha de São Paulo,* October 29, 1988, citing a government document entitled *"A Tragédia do Emprego na Administração Pública Direta."*

46. Faria and Castro (1990) note that there was a real expansion of many state services in the 1980s; thus, the increase in personnel was not exclusively caused by *empreguismo.*

47. "Tribunal de Contas da União vai investigar empreguismo," *Folha de São Paulo,* August 15, 1987.

48. "Traidores e bastardos," *Folha de São Paulo,* January 29, 1988.

49. "Arroz, feijão e caviar," *Folha de São Paulo,* January 27, 1988.

50. "Os gastos do Congresso explodem," *Folha da São Paulo,* June 13, 1988.

51. "Muitos 'Carneiros' nas listas de Durval," *Estado de São Paulo,* July 18, 1985.

52. Interview with the author, January 28, 1988.

53. Interview with the author, January 28, 1988.

54. "Empreguismo nas companhias estatais lembra o serviço público," *Folha de São Paulo,* July 6, 1986. This same article reported that at Nuclebrás, a public enterprise corroded by clientelism, none of the 5,777 employees had joined via a civil-service exam.

55. For a less-negative evaluation of the effects of clientelism, see Scott 1969, who emphasizes the capacity of clientelistic machines to integrate the poor into the political system and to encourage party building.

56. This is the suggestive title of Dimenstein's book (1988) on corruption and clientelism in the New Republic. Although this title is a contradiction in terms, it is nevertheless appropriate, for it captures the contradiction of Brazilian reality during the Sarney period.

57. "Seplan apura existência de 120 mil casos de duplo emprego," *Folha de São Paulo*, February 26, 1989.

58. Quoted by Jânio de Freitas, "Os autores da impunidade," *Folha de São Paulo*, October 24, 1987.

59. Interview with the author, February 25, 1988.

60. "Assím é impossível trabalhar, desabafa Mailson," *Folha de São Paulo*, June 16, 1988; "Dívida de agricultores causa conflitos entre Sarney e Mailson," ibid., June 17, 1988.

61. "Bahia enfrenta empreguismo no ensino," *Estado de São Paulo*, April 12, 1987.

62. "Como roubar dos aposentados," *Folha de São Paulo*, February 1, 1988. In 1992, Minister of Welfare Reinhold Stephanes (PFL) gave a lower estimate of at least 1,000,000 fraudulent beneficiaries (about 8 percent of the total) of the National Institute of Social Security. "Fraude beneficia 1 milhão de pessoas," *Estado de São Paulo*, August 12, 1992.

63. Interview with the author, November 24, 1987.

64. Senate Commission hearings, mimeographed, October 15, 1987.

65. The widespread nature of this problem was underscored by a case involving the director of the State Highway Department of Minas Gerais in 1987. He offered as a justification for a fraudulent bid in which he awarded a state contract to his own private company the fact that *all* bidding in the state had been fraudulent during the previous fifteen years. Pervasive impunity is underscored by Governor Newton Cardoso's reaction. Cardoso, responsible for the director's appointment, defended his friend and attacked the deputy who denounced nepotism and corruption. See "Coisa antiga," *Folha de São Paulo*, October 24, 1987.

Chapter 7

1. The United States, of course, was an exception to this rule.

2. As was argued in Chapter 6, clientelism in many countries is party-based, but in Brazil, individual politicians rather than parties typically control patronage.

3. During the process of constitution writing, Congress was the focal point of political actors, but *qua* constitution maker and not *qua* legislator.

4. Interview with the author, January 28, 1988.

5. IBOPE nationwide survey, May 1987.

6. Data from the Instituto Brasileiro de Geografia e Estatística, reported in "Partilha Selvagem," *Istoé Senhor*, November 21, 1990, 37.

7. The survey was called Brasil 5000, Fourth Round.

8. CEPAL, "Preliminary Overview of the Latin American and Caribbean Economy 1995," *Notas sobre la economía y el desarrollo* No. 585/586 (December 1995).

Chapter 8

1. Federalism is an exception; the 1988 Constitution significantly reinvigorated fiscal federalism.

2. The 1978 information has one shortcoming: it does not tell us how many incumbent deputies did not run because they died in office, assumed a high-level executive post in the bureaucracy and did not immediately run for elected office, or ran for governor, vice governor, or senator in 1982. The information serves as a good measure of how many

deputies ran again for office—hence literally conforming to a model of the politician seeking *re*election, but it fails to tell us how many remained active in elective political posts other than federal deputy. Politicians in this latter category did not literally run for reelection, but they were committed to furthering their political careers.

3. Legally, in some democracies, candidates can run as independents. In practice, however, in most democracies, parties exercise a virtual monopoly over access to elected office. In Brazil in the 1930s, independent candidates could legally run for office, but since 1945 they have had to be members of and win nomination from a party.

4. In terms of candidate selection, the PT differs from the catch-all parties. See Meneguello 1989: 84–86 for details.

5. "O Poder São Eles," *Veja*, May 3, 1995, 41.

6. PMDB, "Código de Ética," Art. 8, ¶ 108.

7. Author's interview with José Freitas Nobre, March 9, 1988. Flávio Bierrenbach, a PMDB federal deputy from São Paulo, also attributed his 1986 electoral defeat in part to his assumption of a prominent position in Congress. As a result, he had to be in Brasília most of the time.

8. Interview with the author, July 30, 1987.

9. My emphasis on the comparative autonomy of politicians is not to claim that there is a complete lack of party discipline. As Figueiredo and Limongi (1994, 1996), Limongi and Figueiredo (1995), and Novaes (1994) have demonstrated, the Brazilian Congress has a centralized decision-making process dominated by party and congressional leaders. Party leaders exercise some control over the agenda and decision making in Congress. As is true almost universally, individual politicians have relatively little influence over the congressional agenda, though they do have unlimited power to propose bills and amendments. In other spheres, including how they vote on bills, how they divide their time, how they campaign, etc., individual politicians have considerable leeway.

10. Based on data from the *World Bank Development Report 1987*.

11. This is a comparative judgment and does not imply that there are no sanctions at the disposal of state party leaders. Those who are disgruntled with a federal deputy may encourage a state deputy with competing electoral bases to run for federal office in the next election.

Chapter 9

1. For an analysis of this point for the 1946–64 period, see Soares 1973 and Lima Júnior 1983. For the post–1985 period, see Nicolau 1996a.

2. This difference stems from both malapportionment and the effects of coalitions in proportional elections. Given the characteristics of the electoral system for deputies, a party can win a significantly lower or higher share of the coalition's seats than its share of the coalition's votes.

3. In the age of television politics, the personality and leadership skills of competing candidates for prime minister have become increasingly important in determining how voters choose. Nevertheless, personalistic linkages to the electorate remain more important in presidential than parliamentary systems.

Chapter 10

1. Venezuela under President Carlos Andrés Pérez, 1989–92, is an example in which a president was often abandoned by his own disciplined party, Acción Democrática.

2. The potential importance of presidential decree powers in overcoming institutional veto players has not been widely recognized. Tsebelis (1995) assumes that a greater number of veto players makes policy reform more difficult. Other things being equal, this is true, but it is important to examine the executive's constitutional powers. Sweeping constitutional powers, especially decree powers, can enable an executive to overcome institutional veto players.

3. Itamar Franco did not have a party, nor was he closely identified with any particular party. I have considered the PSDB Franco's party because of his linkages to it.

4. This information is compiled from data in Coelho and Oliveira 1989 and DIAP 1988.

5. Luis Eduardo Magalhães, Federal Deputy (PFL-Bahia), quoted in "Salve-se Quem Puder," *Istoé Senhor*, July 5, 1989, 25.

6. "Tchau, Sarney. Alô, Ermírio." *Istoé Senhor*, September 6, 1989, 40.

7. "Pés de barro," Istoé Senhor, May 16, 1990, 19.

8. His approval ratings fell from 71 percent in March 1990 to 36 percent three months later, 23 percent by March 1991, and 15 percent by February 1992. Data from "Sem choro nem vela," *Veja*, April 8, 1992, 20–21.

9. "Brincando com fogo," Istoé Senhor, June 13, 1990, 19.

10. See, for example, the comments of Senator José Richa (PSDB-PR) in "Oxigênio para o governo," Istoé Senhor, March 6, 1991, 12.

11. The constitutional congress established a period for constitutional reform during which the legislature could approve amendments with a single, unicameral, absolute majority. Originally this review period was scheduled for 1993, but it was ultimately put off until early 1994.

12. During the Franco presidency, Congress overrode only one veto.

13. "Progressive" is in quotation marks because inflation corroded the real wages of the poor. Therefore, a supposedly "progressive" wage bill that fueled inflation could easily have pernicious effects precisely on those whom it intended to benefit.

14. "Sócios da bagunça," *Veja*, June 30, 1993, 24–28.

15. Consistent with theories of legislators (and governors) that emphasize "the electoral connection" (Cain, Ferejohn, and Fiorina 1987; Cox and McCubbins 1993; Mayhew 1974), the reasons why legislators and governors opposed certain reforms should be understood through their links with their constituencies. For example, many legislators are financially supported by agricultural interests, and they consequently oppose cutting agricultural subsidies.

16. In two national surveys in May 1994, DataFolha registered a 42–16 percent lead for Lula over Cardoso, followed by a 40–17 percent lead.

17. Interview with Sérgio Motta, *Veja*, July 23, 1997, 11.

18. "Foi dando que FHC recebeu," *Veja*, March 27, 1996, 30–32.

19. "A gastança continua," *Veja*, March 27, 1996, 7.

Chapter 11

1. This is true compared to the advanced industrial democracies. As Kitschelt (1995) shows, even in inchoate party systems, most voters have some idea of what the major parties are, but fewer voters understand well what all of the parties stand for.

2. For a diverging viewpoint on the relationship between party-system institutionalization and democratic consolidation, see Toka 1997, who argues that the former is not necessary for democratic consolidation.

3. "Quem paga a conta," *Veja*, August 19, 1992, 30.

4. Although only a minority of Brazilian citizens has voted according to party label since 1985, some people regularly do so. During the late 1970s and early 1980s, party labels were important to a significant part of the electorate.

5. "Perfil parlamentar brasileiro," *Istoé Senhor*, March 13, 1991, 17.

6. In the labor area, the constitution shortened the work week from forty-eight to forty-four hours; gave workers an unrestricted right to strike; and provided 120 days paid maternity leave and eight days of paid paternity leave for newborns. In social policy, it obliged the federal government to spend 18 percent (as opposed to 13 percent) of total expenditures on education. It also introduced popular referenda and initiatives. In economic affairs, the constitution was nationalistic and statist. It banned foreign companies from exploring the subsoil and gave existing foreign mining companies five years to sell majority control to Brazilians.

7. The seven issues discussed here do not exhaust the list of institutional rules that affect party building, but they are issues that arise in every democracy (except the last one, which arises in all presidential democracies). In Brazil, rules not discussed in this chapter have also adversely affected party-system institutionalization.

Bibliography

Abranches, Sérgio Henrique Hudson de. 1978. "The Divided Leviathan: State and Economic Policy Formation in Authoritarian Brazil." Ph.D. dissertation, Cornell University.

——. 1988. "Presidencialismo de Coalizão: O Dilema Institucional Brasileiro." *Dados* 31 No. 1: 5–34.

Abrúcio, Fernando Luiz. 1998. *Os Barões da Federação: Os Governadores e a Redemocratização Brasileira*. São Paulo: Departamento de Ciência Política da USP/Editora Hucitec.

Abrúcio, Fernando Luiz, and Cláudio Gonçalves Couto. 1996. "O Impasse da Federação Brasileira: O Cenário Político-Financeiro e as suas Conseqüências para o Processo de Descentralização." Cadernos CEDEC.

Adamany, David. 1984. "Financing Political Parties in the United States." In Vernon Bogdanor, ed., *Parties and Democracy in Britain and America*. New York: Praeger, 153–84.

Adrogué, Gerardo. 1995. "El nuevo sistema partidario argentino." In Carlos Acuña, ed., *La nueva matriz política argentina*. Buenos Aires: Nueva Visión, 27–70.

Afonso, José Roberto Rodrigues. 1985. "Relações Intergovernamentais e Finanças Públicas de Estados e Municípios," Paper for XIII Encontro Nacional de Economia, Vol. I.

Afonso, José Roberto, and Maria Cecília Souza. 1985. "O Sistema de Relações Financeiras Intergovernamentais e Seu Papel no Financiamento de Estados e Municípios." *Revista de Finanças Públicas* XLV No. 362 (April–June): 15–32.

Almeida, Maria Hermínia Tavares de. 1983. "O Sindicalismo Brasileiro entre a Conservação e a Mudança." In Bernard Sorj and Maria Hermínia Tavares de Almeida, eds., *Sociedade e Política no Brasil pós-1964*. São Paulo: Brasiliense, 191–214.

——. 1987. "Novo Sindicalismo and Politics in Brazil." In John D. Wirth, Edson de Oliveira Nunes, and Thomas E. Bogenschild, eds., *State and Society in Brazil: Change and Continuity*. Boulder: Westview, 147–78.

——. 1996. "Pragmatismo por Necessidade: Os Rumos da Reforma Econômica no Brasil." *Dados* 39 No. 2: 213–34.

Alvarez, Sonia E. 1990. *Engendering Democracy in Brazil: Women's Movements in Transition Politics*. Princeton: Princeton University Press.

Bibliography

Alves, Maria Helena Moreira. 1985. *State and Opposition in Military Brazil*. Austin: University of Texas Press.

Ames, Barry. 1987. *Political Survival: Politicians and Public Policy in Latin America*. Berkeley: University of California Press.

————. 1994. "The Reverse Coattails Effect: Local Party Organization in the 1989 Brazilian Presidential Election." *American Political Science Review* 88 No. 1 (March): 95–111.

————. 1995a. "Electoral Rules, Constituency Pressures, and Pork Barrel: Bases of Voting in the Brazilian Congress." *Journal of Politics* 57 No. 2 (May): 324–43.

————. 1995b. "Electoral Strategy under Open-List Proportional Representation." *American Journal of Political Science* 39 No. 2 (May): 406–33.

Ames, Barry, and Timothy Power. 1990. "Research Guide to Roll-Call Voting in Brazil's Constituent Assembly, 1987–1988."

Amorim Neto, Octávio. 1995. "Cabinet Formation and Party Politics in Brazil." Paper for the 1995 meeting of the Latin American Studies Association, Washington D.C., September 28–30.

Andrade, Maria Antônia Alonso de. 1985. "As Eleições de 1982 na Paraíba: Clientelismo e Máquina Estadual." In Joaquim Falcão, ed., *Nordeste Eleições*. Recife: Fundação Joaquim Nabuco/Massangana, 187–213.

Archer, Ronald. 1990. "The Transition from Traditional to Broker Clientelism in Colombia: Political Stability and Social Unrest." Kellogg Institute Working Paper #149, University of Notre Dame (July).

————. 1995. "Party Strength and Weakness in Colombia's Besieged Democracy." In Scott Mainwaring and Timothy R. Scully, eds., *Building Democratic Institutions: Party Systems in Latin America*. Stanford: Stanford University Press, 164–99.

Arrow, Kenneth. 1951. *Social Choice and Individual Values*. New York: Wiley.

Avelar, Lúcia. 1989. *O Segundo Eleitorado: Tendências do Voto Feminino no Brasil*. Campinas: Editora da Unicamp.

Avelino, George. 1991. "Política e Políticas Sociais no Brasil: Um Estudo sobre a Previdência." M.A. thesis, University of São Paulo.

Baer, Werner. 1989. *The Brazilian Economy: Growth and Development*. New York: Praeger. Third edition.

Balbachevsky, Elizabeth. 1992. "Identidade Partidária e Instituições Políticas no Brasil." *Lua Nova* No. 26: 133–65.

Baloyra, Enrique, and John Martz. 1979. *Political Attitudes in Venezuela: Societal Cleavages and Public Opinion*. Austin: University of Texas Press.

Banck, Geert. 1994. "Democratic Transparency and the Train of Joy and Happiness: Local Politicians and the Dilemmas of Political Change in Brazil." In Jojada Verrips, ed., *Transactions: Essays in Honor of Jeremy Boissevain*. Amsterdam: Spinhius, 135–56.

Bartolini, Stefano. 1983. "The Membership of Mass Parties: The Social Democratic Experience, 1889–1978." In Hans Daalder and Peter Mair, eds., *Western European Party Systems: Continuity and Change*. Beverly Hills and London: Sage, 177–220.

Bartolini, Stefano, and Peter Mair. 1990. *Identity, Competition, and Electoral Availability: The Stabilisation of European Electorates, 1885–1985*. Cambridge and New York: Cambridge University Press.

Basáñez, Miguel, Marta Lagos, and Tatiana Beltrán. 1996. "Reporte 1995: Encuesta Latino Barometro." (May). Unpublished document.

Bates, Robert H., and Anne O. Krueger. 1993. "Generalizations Arising from the Country Studies." In Robert H. Bates and Anne O. Krueger, eds., *Political and Economic Interactions in Economic Policy Reform: Evidence from Eight Countries*. Oxford: Basil Blackwell, 444–72.

Bendel, Petra. 1993. "Partidos políticos y sistemas de partidos en Centroamérica." In Dieter Nohlen, ed., *Elecciones y sistemas de partidos en América Latina*. San José: Instituto Interamericano de Derechos Humanos/CAPEL, 315–53.

Benevides, Maria Victória de Mesquita. 1981. *A UDN e o Udenismo*. Rio de Janeiro: Paz e Terra.

————. 1989. *O PTB e o Trabalhismo: Partido e Sindicato em São Paulo (1945–1964)*. São Paulo: Brasiliense/CEDEC.

Berquó, Elza, and Luiz Felipe de Alencastro. 1992. "A Emergência do Voto Negro." *Novos Estudos #33* (July): 77–88.

Blondel, Jean. 1957. *As Condições da Vida Política na Paraíba*. Rio de Janeiro: Fundação Getúlio Vargas.

————. 1968. "Party Systems and Patterns of Government in Western Democracies." *Canadian Journal of Political Science* 1 No. 2 (June): 180–203.

Bogdanor, Vernon. 1984. "Financing Political Parties in Britain." In Vernon Bogdanor, ed., *Parties and Democracy in Britain and America*. New York: Praeger, 127–52.

Boschi, Renato Raul. 1987. *A Arte da Associação: Política de Base e Democracia no Brasil*. São Paulo: Vértice/IUPERJ.

Brasileiro, Ana Maria. 1981. "O Empobrecimento dos Municípios e o Sistema Tributário." *Revista Brasileira de Estudos Políticos* 52 (January): 129–46.

Brooke, James. 1992. "Looting in Brazil." *New York Times*, November 8.

Bruneau, Thomas C. 1989. "Constitutions and Democratic Consolidation: Brazil in Comparative Perspective." Naval Postgraduate School Paper 56–89–009.

Bruneau, Thomas C., and W. E. Hewitt. 1989. "Patterns of Church Influence in Brazil's Political Transition." *Comparative Politics* 22 No. 1 (October): 39–61.

Bruneau, Thomas C., and Alex McLeod. 1986. *Politics in Contemporary Portugal: Parties and the Consolidation of Democracy*. Boulder: Lynne Rienner.

Cain, Bruce E., and John Ferejohn. 1981. "Party Identification in the United States and Great Britain." *Comparative Political Studies* 14 No. 1 (April): 31–47.

Cain, Bruce E., John Ferejohn, and Morris Fiorina. 1987. *The Personal Vote: Constituency Service and Electoral Independence*. Cambridge, MA: Harvard University Press.

Caldeira, Teresa Pires do Rio. 1980. "Para que Serve o Voto? As Eleições e o Cotidiano na Periferia de São Paulo." In Bolivar Lamounier, ed., *Voto de Desconfiança: Eleições e Mudança Política no Brasil, 1970–1979*. Petrópolis: Vozes, 81–115.

————. 1984. *A Política dos Outros: O Cotidiano dos Moradores da Periferia e o que Pensam do Poder e dos Poderosos*. São Paulo: Brasiliense.

Cammack, Paul. 1982. "Political Clientelism and the Military Government in Brazil." In Ernest Gellner and John Waterbury, eds., *Patrons and Clients in Mediterranean Societies*. London: Frances Pinter, 53–75.

Campbell, Angus et al. 1960. *The American Voter*. New York: Wiley.

Cardoso, Fernando Henrique. 1975a. *Autoritarismo e Democratização*. Rio de Janeiro: Paz e Terra.

————. 1975b. "Partidos e Deputados em Sao Paulo: O Voto e a Representação Política," in Bolivar Lamounier and Fernando Henrique Cardoso, eds., *Os Partidos e as Eleições no Brasil.* Rio de Janeiro: Paz e Terra, 45–75.

Cardoso, Ruth C. L. 1983. "Movimentos Sociais Urbanos: Balanço Crítico." In Bernard Sorj and Maria Hermínia Tavares de Almeida, eds., *Sociedade e Política no Brasil pós-1964.* São Paulo: Brasiliense, 191–214.

Carey, John M. 1996. *Term Limits and Legislative Representation.* Cambridge and New York: Cambridge University Press.

Carey, John M. and Matthew Soberg Shugart. 1995. "Incentives to Cultivate a Personal Vote: A Rank Ordering of Electoral Formulas." *Electoral Studies* 14 No. 4: 417–39.

Carvalho, José Murilo de. 1966. "Barbacena: A Família, a Política e uma Hipótese." *Revista Brasileira de Estudos Políticos* 20 (July): 153–94.

————. 1980. *A Construção da Ordem.* Rio de Janeiro: Campus.

————. 1988. *Teatro de Sombras: A Política Imperial.* São Paulo: Vértice/IUPERJ.

Carvalho, Orlando de. 1958. *Ensaios de Sociologia Eleitoral.* Belo Horizonte: Edições da Revista Brasileira de Estudos Políticos.

Castro, Maria Helena Guimarães de. 1987. "Equipamentos Sociais, Política Partidária e Governos Locais no Estado de São Paulo (1968–82)." M.A. thesis, UNICAMP.

Ceaser, James. 1979. *Presidential Selection.* Princeton: Princeton University Press.

Chacon, Vamireh. 1985. "Os Meios de Comunicação na Sociedade Democrática." In Hélio Jaguaribe et al., *Brasil, Sociedade Democrática.* Rio de Janeiro: José Olympio, 337–92.

Chalmers, Douglas A. 1964. *The Social Democratic Party of Germany: From Working Class Movement to Modern Political Party.* New Haven: Yale University Press.

————. 1972. "Parties and Society in Latin America." *Studies in Comparative International Development* 7 No. 2 (Summer): 102–28.

Chhibber, Pradeep, and Mariano Torcal. 1997. "Elite Strategy, Social Cleavages, and Party Systems in a New Democracy: Spain." *Comparative Political Studies* 30 No. 1 (February): 27–54.

Chubb, Judith. 1981. "The Social Bases of an Urban Political Machine: The Christian Democratic Party in Palermo." In S. N. Eisenstadt and René Lemarchand, eds., *Political Clientelism, Patronage, and Development.* Beverly Hills: Sage Publications, 57–90.

————. 1982. *Patronage, Power, and Poverty in Southern Italy.* New York: Cambridge University Press.

Clark, Terry Nichols, and Seymour Martin Lipset. 1991. "Are Social Classes Dying?" *International Sociology* 6 No. 4 (December): 397–410.

Coelho, João Gilberto Lucas, and Antonio Carlos Nantes de Oliveira. 1989. *A Nova Constituição: Avaliação do Texto e Perfil dos Constituintes.* Rio de Janeiro: Revan.

Cohen, Youssef. 1989. *The Manipulation of Consent: The State and Working-Class Consciousness in Brazil.* Pittsburgh: University of Pittsburgh Press.

Collier, Ruth Berins, and David Collier. 1991. *Shaping the Political Arena.* Princeton: Princeton University Press.

Conaghan, Catherine M. 1995. "Politicians Against Parties: Discord and Disconnection in Ecuador's Party System." In Scott Mainwaring and Timothy R. Scully, eds., *Building Democratic Institutions: Party Systems in Latin America.* Stanford: Stanford University Press, 434-58.

————. 1996. "The Irrelevant Right: Alberto Fujimori and the New Politics of Pragmatic Peru." Paper for the conference on "Conservative Parties, Democratization, and Neoliberalism in Latin America: Mexico in Comparative Perspective," Center for U.S.-Mexican Studies, University of California, San Diego, May 31–June 1.

Converse, Philip. 1964. "The Nature of Belief Systems in Mass Publics." In David Apter, ed. *Ideology and Discontent*. New York: The Free Press, 206–61.

————. 1969. "Of Time and Partisan Stability." *Comparative Political Studies* 2 No. 2 (July): 139–71.

Coppedge, Michael. 1994. *Strong Parties and Lame Ducks: Presidential Partyarchy and Factionalism in Venezuela*. Stanford: Stanford University Press.

————. Forthcoming. "Freezing in the Tropics: Explaining Party-System Volatility in Latin America."

Cotta, Maurizio. 1994. "Building Party Systems after the Dictatorship: The East European Cases in a Comparative Perspective." In Geoffrey Pridham and Tatu Vanhanen, eds., *Democratization in Eastern Europe: Domestic and International Perspectives*. London: Routledge, 99–127.

Couto, Cláudio Gonçalves. 1997. "A Agenda Constituinte e a Difícil Governabilidade." *Lua Nova* No. 39: 33–52.

Cox, Gary W. 1990. "Centripetal and Centrifugal Incentives in Electoral Systems." *American Journal of Political Science* 34 No. 4 (November): 903–35.

Cox, Gary W., and Mathew D. McCubbins. 1993. *Legislative Leviathan: Party Government in the House*. Berkeley and Los Angeles: University of California Press.

Crisp, Brian F. 1997. "Presidential Behavior in a System with Strong Parties: Venezuela, 1958–1995." In Scott Mainwaring and Matthew Soberg Shugart, eds., *Presidentialism and Democracy in Latin America*. Cambridge and New York: Cambridge University Press, 160–98.

Daalder, Hans. 1966. "Parties, Elites, and Political Developments in Western Europe." In Joseph La Palombara and Myron Weiner, eds., *Political Parties and Political Development*. Princeton: Princeton University Press, 43–78.

Daalder, Ivo H. 1983. "The Italian Party System in Transition: The End of Polarized Pluralism?" *West European Politics* 6 No. 3 (July): 216–36.

Dain, Sulamis. 1995. "Experiência Internacional e Especificidade Brasileira." In Rui de Britto Alvares Affonso and Pedro Luiz Barros Silva, eds., *Federalismo no Brasil: Reforma Tributária e Federação*. São Paulo: Editora da Universidade Estadual Paulista, 21–41.

Dalton, Russell, Scott C. Flanagan, and Paul Allen Beck, eds. 1984. *Electoral Change in Advanced Industrial Democracies: Realignment or Dealignment?* Princeton: Princeton University Press.

DaMatta, Roberto. 1979. *Carnavais, Malandros e Heróis: Para uma Sociologia do Dilema Brasileiro*. Rio de Janeiro: Zahar.

————. 1985. *A Casa e a Rua*. São Paulo: Brasiliense.

Deheza, Grace Ivana. 1997. "Gobiernos de Coalición en el sistema presidencial: América del Sur." Ph.D. dissertation, European University Institute.

Delgado, Lucília de Almeida Neves. 1989. *PTB: Do Getulismo ao Reformismo (1945–1964)*. São Paulo: Marco Zero.

DIAP (Departamento Intersindical de Assessoria Parlamentar). 1988. *Quem Foi Quem na Constituinte*. Sao Paulo: Oboré/Cortez.

364 *Bibliography*

————. 1993. *A Cabeça do Congress: Quem É Quem na Revisão Constitucional*. São Paulo: Oboré.

Dimenstein, Gilberto. 1988. *A República dos Padrinhos: Chantagem e Corrupção em Brasília*. São Paulo: Brasiliense.

Diniz, Eli. 1982. *Voto e Máquina Política: Patronagem e Clientelismo no Rio de Janeiro*. Rio de Janeiro: Editora Paz e Terra.

Dix, Robert H. 1989. "Cleavage Structures and Party Systems in Latin America." *Comparative Politics* 22 No. 1 (October): 23–37.

————. 1992. "Democratization and the Institutionalization of Latin American Political Parties." *Comparative Political Studies* 24 No. 4 (January): 488–511.

Dogan, Mattei. 1967. "Political Cleavage and Social Stratification in France and Italy." In Seymour Martin Lipset and Stein Rokkan, eds., *Party Systems and Voter Alignments: Cross-National Perspectives*. New York: The Free Press, 129–96.

————. 1995. "Erosion of Class Voting and of the Religious Vote in Western Europe." *International Social Science Journal* 146 (December): 525–38.

Downs, Anthony. 1957. *An Economic Theory of Democracy*. New York: Harper and Row.

Duverger, Maurice. 1954. *Political Parties: Their Organization and Activity in the Modern State*. London: Metheun.

Edwards, Sebastian. 1995. *Crisis and Reform in Latin America: From Despair to Hope*. New York and Oxford: Oxford University Press.

Enelow, James M., and Melvin J. Hinich, eds. 1990. *Advances in the Spatial Theory of Voting*. Cambridge and New York: Cambridge University Press.

Epstein, Leon. 1964. "A Comparative Study of Canadian Parties." *American Political Science Review* 58 No. 1 (March): 46–59.

————. 1967. *Political Parties in Western Democracies*. New York: Praeger.

————. 1986. *Political Parties in the American Mold*. Madison: University of Wisconsin Press.

Erickson, Kenneth Paul. 1977. *The Brazilian Corporative State and Working-Class Politics*. Berkeley and Los Angeles: University of California Press.

Evans, Peter. 1979. *Dependent Development: The Alliance of Multinational, State, and Local Capital in Brazil*. Princeton: Princeton University Press.

Falcão, Joaquim, ed. 1985. *Nordeste Eleições*. Recife: Fundação Joaquim Nabuco/Massangana.

Faoro, Raimundo. 1975. *Os Donos do Poder*. Porto Alegre: Globo.

Faria, Vilmar. 1983. "Desenvolvimento, Urbanizaçao e Mudanças na Estrutura do Emprego: A Experiência Brasileira dos Ultimos Trinta Anos." In Bernard Sorj and Maria Hermínia Tavares de Almeida, eds., *Sociedade e Política no Brasil pós-1964*. São Paulo: Brasiliense, 118–63.

————. 1986. "Mudanças na Composição do Emprego e na Estrutura das Ocupações." In Edmar Bacha and Herbert S. Klein, eds., *A Transição Incompleta: Brasil desde 1945*. Rio de Janeiro: Paz e Terra, 73–109.

————, and Maria Helena Guimarães Castro. 1990. "Social Policy and Democratic Consolidation in Brazil." In Lawrence Graham and Robert Wilson, eds., *The Political Economy of Brazil: Public Policies in an Era of Transition*. Austin: University of Texas Press, 122–40.

Ferreira, Oliveiros S. 1964. "A Crise de Poder do 'Sistema' e as Eleições Paulistas de 1962." *Revista Brasileira de Estudos Políticos* 16 (January): 179–226.

Figueiredo, Argelina Cheibub, and Fernando Limongi. 1994. "O Processo Legislativo e a Produção Legal no Congresso Pós-Constituinte." *Novos Estudos* No. 38 (March): 24–37.

———. 1995. "Mudança Constitucional, Desempehno do Legislativo e Consolidação Institucional." *Revista Brasileira de Ciências Sociais* 10 No. 29 (October): 175–200.

———. 1996. "Congresso Nacional: Organização, Processo Legislativo e Produção legal." *Cadernos de Pesquisa CEBRAP* #5 (October).

———. 1997. "O Congresso e as Medidas Provisórias: Abidcação ou Delegação?" *Novos Estudos* No. 47 (March): 127–54.

Flanz, Gisbert H, ed. 1997. *Constitutions of the Countries of the World*. Dobbs Ferry, NY: Oceana.

Fleischer, David V. 1973. "O Trampolim Político: Mudanças nos Padrões de Recrutamento Político em Minas Gerais." *Revista de Administração Pública* 7, No. 1 (January–March): 99–116.

———. 1976. "Concentração e Dispersão Eleitoral: Um Estudo da Distribuição Goegráfica do Vote em Minas Gerias (1966–1974)." *Revista Brasileira de Estudos Políticos* 43 (July): 333–60.

———. 1984. "Constitutional and Electoral Engineering in Brazil: A Double-Edged Sword." *Journal of Inter-American Economic Affairs* 37 (Spring): 3–36.

———. 1988. "O Congresso Constituinte de 1987: Um Perfil Sócio-Econômico e Político." In n.a., *O Processo Constituinte 1987–1988*. Brasília: Agil-UnB, 29–40.

Flynn, Peter. 1974. "Class, Clientelism, and Coercion: Some Mechanisms of Internal Dependency and Control." *Journal of Commonwealth and Comparative Studies* 12 No. 2 (July): 133–56.

Gallagher, Michael, and Michael Marsh, eds. 1988. *Candidate Selection in Comparative Perspective*. London: Sage.

Gamarra, Eduardo A. 1997. "Hybrid Presidentialism and Democratization: The Case of Bolivia." In Scott Mainwaring and Matthew Soberg Shugart, eds., *Presidentialism and Democracy in Latin America*. Cambridge and New York: Cambridge University Press, 363–93.

Gay, Robert. 1994. *Popular Organization and Democracy in Rio de Janeiro: A Tale of Two Favelas*. Philadelphia: Temple University Press.

Geddes, Barbara. 1994. *Politicians' Dilemma: Building State Capacity in Latin America*. Berkeley: University of California Press.

Geddes, Barbara, and Edson de Oliveira Nunes. 1987. "Dilemmas of State-Led Modernization in Brazil." In John D. Wirth et al., eds., *State and Society in Brazil: Change and Continuity*. Boulder: Westview, 103–45.

Geddes, Barbara, and Artur Ribeiro Neto. 1992. "Institutional Sources of Corruption in Brazil." *Third World Quarterly* 13 No. 4: 641–61.

Germani, Gino. 1974. *Política y sociedad en una época de transición*. Buenos Aires: Paidos.

Gibson, Edward. 1996. *Class and Conservative Parties: Argentina in Comparative Perspective*. Baltimore: Johns Hopkins University Press.

———. 1997. "Federalism and Electoral Coalitions: Making Market Reform Politically Viable in Argentina." Paper prepared for conference on "Democracy, Nationalism, and Federalism," All Souls College, University of Oxford, June 5–8.

Gomes, Angela Maria de Castro. 1988. *A Invenção do Trabalhismo*. São Paulo: Vértice/ IUPERJ.

González, Luis Eduardo. 1991. *Political Structures and Democracy in Uruguay*. Notre Dame: University of Notre Dame Press.

Gorman, Christopher, Stephan Haggard, and Eliza Willis. 1996. "Decentralization in Latin America." Paper for the annual meeting of the American Political Science Association, August 29–September 1, San Francisco.

Gouldner, Alvin W. 1959. "Organizational Analysis." In Robert K. Merton, et al. eds., *Sociology Today: Problems and Prospects*. New York: Basic Books, 400–28.

Graham, Lawrence S. 1968. *Civil Service Reform in Brazil: Principles versus Practice*. Austin: University of Texas Press.

———. 1987. "The Role of the States in the Brazilian Federation." In Louis A. Picard and Raphael Zariski, eds., *Subnational Politics in the 1980s*. New York: Praeger, 119–39.

Graham, Richard. 1990. *Patronage and Politics in Nineteenth-Century Brazil*. Stanford: Stanford University Press.

Graziano, Luigi. 1973. "Patron-Client Relations in Southern Italy." *European Journal of Political Research* 1 No. 1 (April): 3–34.

———. 1975. "A Conceptual Framework for the Study of Clientelism." Western Societies Program Occasional Paper No. 2, Cornell University.

———. 1978. "Center-Periphery Relations and the Italian Crisis: The Problem of Clientelism." In Sidney Tarrow, Peter J. Katzenstein, and Luigi Graziano, eds., *Territorial Politics in Industrial Nations*. New York: Praeger, 290–326.

Greenfield, Sidney M. 1977. "The Cabo Eleitoral and the Articulation of Local Community and National Society in pre–1968 Brazil." *Journal of Interamerican Studies and World Affairs* 19 No. 2: 139–72.

Grindle, Merilee S. 1977. "Patrons and Clients in the Bureaucracy: Career Networks in Mexico." *Latin American Research Review* 12 No. 1: 37–66.

———, and Francisco E. Thoumi. 1993. "Muddling Through Adjustment: The Political Economy of Economic Policy Change in Ecuador." In Robert H. Bates and Anne O. Krueger, eds., *Political and Economic Interactions in Economic Policy Reform: Evidence from Eight Countries*. Oxford: Basil Blackwell, 123–78.

Gunther, Richard, P. Nikiforos Diamandouros, and Hans-Jürgen Puhle. 1995. "Introduction." In Richard Gunther, P. Nikiforos Diamandouros, and Hans-Jürgen Puhle, eds., *The Politics of Democratic Consolidation: Southern Europe in Comparative Perspective*. Baltimore: Johns Hopkins University Press, 1–32.

Gunther, Richard, et al. 1986. *Spain After Franco: The Making of a Competitive Party System*. Berkeley: University of California Press.

Haggard, Stephan, and Robert R. Kaufman. 1995. *The Political Economy of Democratic Transitions*. Princeton: Princeton University Press.

Hagopian, Frances. 1992. "The Compromised Consolidation: The Political Class in the Brazilian Tradition." In Scott Mainwaring, Guillermo O'Donnell, and J. Samuel Valenzuela, eds., *Issues in Democratic Consolidation: The New South American Democ-*

racies in Comparative Perspective. Notre Dame: University of Notre Dame Press, 243–93.

———. 1996. *Traditional Politics and Regime Change in Brazil*. New York and Cambridge: Cambridge University Press.

Heath, Anthony, and Sarah-K. McDonald. 1988. "The Demise of Party Identification Theory?" *Electoral Studies* 7 No. 2 (August): 95–107.

Hermet, Guy, Richard Rose, and Alain Rouquié, eds. 1978. *Elections Without Choice*. New York: Wiley.

Hippólito, Lúcia. 1985. *PSD: De Raposas e Reformistas*. Rio de Janeiro: Paz e Terra.

Hofstadter, Richard. 1969. *The Idea of a Party System: The Rise of Legitimate Opposition in the United States*. Berkeley: University of California Press.

Huntington, Samuel P. 1968. *Political Order in Changing Societies*. New Haven: Yale University Press.

———. 1991. *The Third Wave: Democratization in the Late Twentieth Century*. Norman: University of Oklahoma Press.

IBGE (Instituto Brasileiro de Geografia e Estatística). 1990. *Participação Político-Social*. 2 volumes. Rio de Janeiro: Instituto Brasileiro de Geografia e Estatística.

———. 1991a. Censo Demográfico 1991. *Características Gerais da População e Instrução, Brasil*. Rio de Janeiro: Secretaria do Planejamento, Orçamento e Coordenação and Instituto Brasileiro de Geografia e Estatística.

———. 1991b. Censo Demográfico 1991. Resultados do Universo Relativos às Característricas da População e dos Domicílios. Rio de Janeiro: Secretaria do Planejamento, Orçamento e Coordenação and Instituto Brasileiro de Geografia e Estatística.

Inglehart, Ronald. 1977. *The Silent Revolution: Changing Values and Political Styles Among Western Publics*. Princeton: Princeton University Press.

———. 1984. "The Changing Structure of Political Cleavages in Western Society." In Russell J. Dalton, Scott C. Flanagan, and Paul Allen Beck, eds., *Electoral Change in Advanced Industrial Democracies: Realignment or Dealignment?* Princeton: Princeton University Press, 25–69.

———. 1990. *Culture Shift in Advanced Industrial Society*. Princeton: Princeton University Press.

Janda, Kenneth. 1980. *Political Parties*. New York: The Free Press.

Jenks, Margaret S. 1979. "Political Parties in Authoritarian Brazil." Ph.D. dissertation, Duke University.

Jones, Mark P. 1995. *Electoral Laws and the Survival of Presidential Democracy*. Notre Dame, IN: University of Notre Dame Press.

———. 1997. "Evaluating Argentina's Presidential Democracy: 1983–1995." In Scott Mainwaring and Matthew Soberg Shugart, eds., *Presidentialism and Democracy in Latin America*. Cambridge and New York: Cambridge University Press, 259–99.

Kandir, Antonio. 1991. *The Dynamics of Inflation: An Analysis of the Relations Between Inflation, Public-Sector Financial Fragility, Expectations, and Profit Margins*. Notre Dame: University of Notre Dame Press.

Katz, Richard S. 1980. *A Theory of Parties and Electoral Systems*. Baltimore: Johns Hopkins University Press.

———. 1986. "Intraparty Preference Voting." In Bernard Grofman and Arend Lijphart, eds., *Electoral Laws and Their Political Consequences*. New York: Agathon, 85–103.

Katz, Richard S, and Peter Mair, eds. 1994. *How Parties Organize: Change and Adaptation in Party Organizations in Western Democracies.* London: Sage.

Keck, Margaret E. 1989. "The New Unionism in the Brazilian Transition." In Alfred Stepan, ed., *Democratizing Brazil: Problems of Transition and Consolidation.* New York and Oxford: Oxford University Press, 252–96.

———. 1992. *The Workers' Party and Democratization in Brazil.* New Haven: Yale University Press.

Kinzo, Maria D'Alva Gil. 1980. *Representação Política e Sistema Eleitoral no Brasil.* São Paulo: Símbolo.

———. 1988. *Legal Opposition Politics Under Authoritarian Rule in Brazil: The Case of the MDB, 1966–1979.* New York: St. Martin's Press.

———. 1990. "O Quadro Partidário e a Constituinte." In Bolivar Lamounier, ed., *De Geisel a Collor: O Balanço da Transição.* São Paulo: IDESP/Sumaré, 105–34.

———. 1991. "La elección presidencial de 1989: El comportamiento electoral en una ciudad brasileña." *Revista de Estudios Políticos* No. 74 (October–December): 257–75.

———. 1993. *Radiografia do Quadro Partidário Brasileiro.* São Paulo: Konrad Adenauer-Stiftung.

Kirchheimer, Otto. 1966. "The Transformation of the Western European Party Systems." In Joseph LaPalombara and Myron Weiner, eds., *Political Parties and Political Development.* Princeton: Princeton University Press, 177–200.

Kitschelt, Herbert. 1989. *The Logics of Party Formation: Ecological Politics in Belgium and West Germany.* Ithaca: Cornell University Press.

———. 1990. "New Social Movements and the Decline of Party Organization." In Russell J. Dalton and Manfred Kuechler, eds., *Challenging the Political Order: New Social Movements and Political Movements in Western Democracies.* New York: Oxford University Press, 179–208.

———. 1992. "The Formation of Party Systems in East Central Europe." *Politics and Society* 20 No. 1 (March): 7–50.

———. 1994. *The Transformation of European Social Democracy.* New York and Cambridge: Cambridge University Press.

———. 1995. "Party Systems in East Central Europe: Consolidation or Fluidity?" Centre for the Study of Public Policy, University of Strathclyde, Paper #241.

Kitschelt, Herbert, et al. Forthcoming. *Post-Communist Party Systems, Competition, Representation, and Inter-Party Collaboration.* Cambridge: Cambridge University Press.

Knutsen, Oddbjorn. 1988. "The Impact of Structural and Ideological Party Cleavages in West European Democracies: A Comparative Empirical Analysis." *British Journal of Political Science* 18 No. 3 (July): 323–52.

Kornblith, Miriam, and Daniel H. Levine. 1995. "Venezuela: The Life and Times of the Party System." "Party Strength and Weakness in Colombia's Besieged Democracy." In Scott Mainwaring and Timothy R. Scully, eds., *Building Democratic Institutions: Party Systems in Latin America.* Stanford: Stanford University Press, 37–71.

Laakso, Markku, and Rein Taagepera. 1979. "'Effective' Number of Parties: A Measure with Application to Western Europe." *Comparative Political Studies* 12 No. 1 (April): 3–27.

Lagos, Marta. 1996. "The Latinobarometro: Media and Political Attitudes in South America." Paper presented at the American Political Science Association annual meeting, August 29–September 1.

Lakeman, Enid. 1974. *How Democracies Vote: A Study of Electoral Systems.* London: Faber & Faber.

Lamounier, Bolivar. 1974. "Ideology and Authoritarian Regimes: Theoretical Perspectives and a Study of the Brazilian Case." Ph.D. dissertation, University of California, Los Angeles.

———. 1975. "Comportamento Eleitoral em São Paulo: Passado e Presente." In Bolivar Lamounier and Fernando Henrique Cardoso, eds., *Os Partidos e as Eleições no Brasil.* Rio de Janeiro: Paz e Terra, 15–44.

———. 1980. "O Voto em São Paulo, 1970–1978." In Bolivar Lamounier, ed., *Voto de Desconfiança: Eleições e Mudança Política no Brasil, 1970–1979.* Petrópolis: Vozes/CE-BRAP, 15–80.

———. 1986. "Partidos Políticos e Sistema Eleitoral." *Textos IDESP* 13.

———. 1989. "*Authoritarian Brazil* Revisited: The Impact of Elections on the *Abertura.*" In Alfred Stepan, ed., *Democratizing Brazil: Problems of Transition and Consolidation.* New York: Oxford University Press, 43–79.

———, ed. 1990. *De Geisel a Collor: O Balanço da Transição.* São Paulo: IDESP/Sumaré.

———. 1991. *Despois da Transição: Democracia e Eleições no Governo Collor.* São Paulo: Loyola.

———. 1994. "Brazil: Toward Parliamentarism?" In Juan J. Linz and Arturo Valenzuela, eds., *The Failure of Presidential Democracy,* Vol. 2, *The Case of Latin America.* Baltimore: Johns Hopkins University Press, 179–219.

Lamounier, Bolivar, and Rachel Meneguello. 1986. *Partidos Políticos e Consolidação Democrática.* São Paulo: Brasiliense.

Lamounier, Bolivar, and Maria Judith Brito Muszynski. 1983. "São Paulo: 1982: A Vitória do (P)MDB." Textos IDESP No. 2.

———. 1986. "A Eleição de Jânio Quadros." In Bolivar Lamounier, ed., *1985: O Voto em São Paulo.* São Paulo: IDESP, 1–31.

Lamounier, Bolivar and Amaury de Souza. 1991. *As Elites Brasileiras e a Modernização do Setor Público.* São Paulo: IDESP/ Sumaré.

LaPalombara, Joseph, and Myron Weiner. 1966. "The Origin and Development of Political Parties." In Joseph LaPalombara, and Myron Weiner, eds., *Political Parties and Political Development.* Princeton: Princeton University Press, 3–42.

Lavareda, Antônio. 1991. *A Democracia nas Urnas: O Processo Partidário Eleitoral Brasileiro.* Rio de Janeiro: Rio Fundo/IUPERJ.

Leal, Victor Nunes. 1949. *Coronelismo, Enxada e Voto.* São Paulo: Alfa-Omega.

Leff, Nathaniel. 1968. *Economic Policy-Making and Development in Brazil, 1947–1964.* New York: John Wiley.

Legg, Keith R. 1969. *Politics in Modern Greece.* Stanford: Stanford University Press.

Lemarchand, Rene, and Keith Legg. 1972. "Political Clientelism and Development: A Preliminary Analysis." *Comparative Politics* 4 No. 2 (January): 149–178.

Levine, Daniel H. 1973. *Conflict and Political Change in Venezuela.* Princeton: Princeton University Press.

Lewin, Linda. 1987. *Politics and Parentela in Paraíba: A Case Study of Family-Based Oligarchy in Brazil.* Princeton: Princeton University Press.

Lijphart, Arend. 1984. *Democracies: Patterns of Majoritarian and Consensus Government in Twenty-One Countries.* New Haven: Yale University Press.

Lima Júnior, Olavo Brasil de. 1983. *Partidos Políticos Brasileiros: A Experiência Federal e Regional, 1945–1964.* Rio de Janeiro: Graal.

Limongi, Fernando, and Argelina Cheibub Figueiredo. 1995. "Partidos Políticos na Câmara dos Deputados: 1989–1994." *Dados* 38 No. 3: 497–525.

Linz, Juan J. 1973. "The Future of an Authoritarian Situation or the Institutionalization of an Authoritarian Regime." In Alfred Stepan, ed., *Authoritarian Brazil: Origins, Policies, and Future.* New Haven: Yale University Press, 233–54.

———. 1978. *The Breakdown of Democratic Regimes: Crisis, Breakdown, and Reequilibrium.* Baltimore: Johns Hopkins University Press.

———. "Religion and Politics in Spain: From Conflict to Consensus Above Cleavage." *Social Compass* 27: 255–77.

———. 1994. "Democracy: Presidential or Parliamentary. Does It Make a Difference?" In Juan J. Linz and Arturo Valenzuela, eds., *Presidential or Parliamentary Democracy: Does It Make a Difference?* Baltimore: Johns Hopkins University Press, 3–87.

Linz, Juan J., and Alfred Stepan. 1996. *Problems of Democratic Transition and Consolidation: Southern Europe, South America, and Post-Communist Europe.* Baltimore: Johns Hopkins University Press.

Lipset, Seymour Martin, and Stein Rokkan. 1967. "Cleavage Structures, Party Systems, and Voter Alignments: An Introduction." In Seymour Martin Lipset and Stein Rokkan, eds., *Party Systems and Voter Alignments: Cross-National Perspectives.* New York: Free Press, 1–64.

Love, Joseph L. 1971. *Rio Grande do Sul and Brazilian Regionalism 1882–1930.* Stanford: Stanford University Press.

Lujambio, Alonso. 1995. *Federalismo y congreso en el cambio político de México.* Mexico City: Universidad Nacional Autónoma de México.

Mackie, Thomas T., and Richard Rose, eds. 1991. *The International Almanac of Electoral History.* Third edition. Washington D.C.: Congressional Quarterly.

Mainwaring, Scott. 1986. "The Transition to Democracy in Brazil." *Journal of Interamerican Studies and World Affairs* 28 (May): 149–79.

———. 1987. "Urban Popular Movements, Identity, and Democracy: Brazil." *Comparative Political Studies* 20 No. 2 (July): 131–59.

———. 1989. "Grassroots Popular Movements and the Struggle for Democracy: Nova Iguaçu." In Alfred Stepan, ed., *Democratizing Brazil: Problems of Transition and Consolidation.* New York and Oxford: Oxford University Press, 168–204.

———. 1993. "Presidentialism, Multipartism, and Democracy: The Difficult Combination." *Comparative Political Studies* 26 No. 2 (July): 198–228.

———. 1997. "Multipartism, Robust Federalism, and Presidentialism: The Case of Brazil." In Scott Mainwaring and Matthew Soberg Shugart, eds., *Presidentialism and Democracy in Latin America.* Cambridge and New York: Cambridge University Press, 55–109.

Mainwaring, Scott, and Aníbal Pérez-Liñán. 1997. "Party Discipline in the Brazilian Constitutional Congress." *Legislative Studies Quarterly* (November).

Mainwaring, Scott, and David Julian Samuels. 1997. "Federalism and Democracy in Contemporary Brazil." Paper prepared for conference on "Democracy, Nationalism, and Federalism," All Souls College, University of Oxford, June 5–8.

Mainwaring, Scott, and Timothy R. Scully. 1995. "Party Systems in Latin America." In Scott Mainwaring and Timothy R. Scully, eds., *Building Democratic Institutions: Party Systems in Latin America*. Stanford: Stanford University Press, 1–34.

Mainwaring, Scott, and Matthew Soberg Shugart. 1997. "Presidentialism and the Party System." In Scott Mainwaring and Matthew Soberg Shugart, eds., *Presidentialism and Democracy in Latin America*. Cambridge and New York: Cambridge University Press, 394–439.

Makler, Harry M. 1994. "The Persistence of Corporatist Strategies: Brazilian Banks, their Politics, and the State." Paper for the XIII World Congress of Sociology, Bielefeld, Germany, July 18–23.

Malloy, James M, ed. 1977. *Authoritarianism and Corporatism in Latin America*. Pittsburgh: University of Pittsburgh Press.

March, James and Johan P. Olsen. 1989. *Rediscovering Institutions: The Organizational Basis of Politics*. New York: The Free Press.

Martins, José de Souza. 1981. *Os Camponeses e a Política no Brasil*. Petrópolis: Vozes.

Martins, Luciano. 1985. *Estado Capitalista e Burocracia no Brasil pós-64*. Rio de Janeiro: Paz e Terra.

Mayhew, David. 1974. *Congress: The Electoral Connection*. New Haven: Yale University Press.

———. 1986. *Placing Parties in American Politics*. Princeton: Princeton University Press.

———. 1991. *Divided We Govern: Party Control, Lawmaking, and Investigations, 1946–1990*. New Haven: Yale University Press.

McCubbins, Mathew D., and Frances McCall Rosenbluth. 1995. "Party Provision for Personal Politics: Dividing the Vote in Japan." In Peter F. Cowhey and Mathew D. McCubbins, eds., *Structure and Policy in Japan and the United States*. New York and Cambridge: Cambridge University Press, 35–55.

McDonald, Ronald H., and J. Mark Ruhl. 1989. *Party Politics and Elections in Latin America*. Boulder: Westview Press.

Médard, Jean-François. 1982."The Underdeveloped State in Tropical Africa: Political Clientelism or Neo-Patrimonialism." In Christopher Clapham, ed., *Private Patronage and Public Power: Political Clientelism in the Modern States*. London: Frances Pinter, 162–92.

Medeiros, Antônio Carlos de. 1983. "Politics and Intergovernmental Relations in Brazil, 1964–1982." Ph.D. dissertation, London School of Economics.

———. 1985. "Da Mediação Burocrática à Mediação Partidária: Aspectos Políticos das Relações Centro-Periferia no Brasil." *Revista de Administração Pública* 19 No. 4 (October–December): 76–97.

Melo, Marcus André C. 1993. "Anatomia do Fracasso: Intermediação de Interesses e a Reforma das Políticas Sociais na Nova República." *Dados* 36 No. 1: 119–64.

Meneguello, Rachel. 1989. *PT: A Formação de um Partido*. Rio de Janeiro: Paz e Terra.

———. 1994. "Partidos e Tendências de Comportamento: O Cenário Político em 1994." In Evelina Dagnino, ed., *Anos 90: Política e Sociedade no Brasil*. São Paulo: Brasiliense, 151–72.

———. 1995. "Electoral Behaviour in Brazil: The 1994 Presidential Elections." *International Social Science Journal* 146 (December): 627–41.

Meneguello, Rachel, and Ricardo Márcio Martins Alves. 1986. "Tendências Eleitorais em São Paulo (1974–1985)." In Bolivar Lamounier, ed., *1985: O Voto em São Paulo*. São Paulo: IDESP, 91–123.

Mericle, Kenneth S. 1977. "Corporatist Control of the Working Class: Authoritarian Brazil Since 1964." In James M. Malloy, ed., *Authoritarianism and Corporatism in Latin America*. Pittsburgh: University of Pittsburgh Press, 303–38.

Michels, Robert. 1959 (1915). *Political Parties: A Sociological Study of the Oligarchical Tendencies of Modern Democracy*. New York: Dover.

Ministério do Trabalho. 1987. "Evolução do Emprego Organizado no Periodo 1980–1985 Utilizando a Metodologia de Paineis Fixos para Pares de Anos Consecutivos da RAIS," November.

Moisés, José Alvaro. 1993. "Elections, Political Parties and Political Culture in Brazil: Changes and Continuities." *Journal of Latin American Studies* 25 No. 3 (October): 575–611.

Moraes, Juan Andrés and Scott Morgenstern. 1995. "El veto del poder ejecutivo en el proceso político uruguayo (1985–1995)." Unpublished paper, Departamento de Ciencia Política, Universidad de la República, Montevideo.

Morgenstern, Scott. 1996. "The Electoral Connection and the Legislative Process in Latin America: Factions, Parties, and Alliances in Theory and Practice." Ph.D. dissertation, University of California, San Diego.

Morlino, Leonardo, and José Ramón Montero. 1995. "Legitimacy and Democracy in Southern Europe." In Richard Gunther, P. Nikiforos Diamandouros, and Hans-Jürgen Puhle, eds., *The Politics of Democratic Consolidation: Southern Europe in Comparative Perspective*. Baltimore: Johns Hopkins University Press, 231–260.

Moser, Robert G. 1995. "The Emergence of Political Parties in Post-Soviet Russia." Ph.D. dissertation, University of Wisconsin.

Muszynski, Judith. 1988. "O Eleitorado Paulistano em 1986: A Marca do Oposicionismo," Textos IDESP No. 25.

Muszynski, Judith, and Antônio Manuel Teixeira Mendes. 1990. "Democratização e Opinião Pública no Brasil." In Bolivar Lamounier, ed., *De Geisel a Collor: O Balanço da Transição*. São Paulo: IDESP/Sumaré, 61–80.

Naim, Moisés. 1993. *Paper Tigers and Minotaurs: The Politics of Venezuela's Economic Reforms*. Washington, D.C.: Carnegie Endowment for International Peace.

Nicolau, Jairo Marconi. 1994. "Breves Comentários sobre as Eleições de 1994 e o Quadro Partidário." IUPERJ Cadernos de Conjuntura No. 50 (July): 15–19.

———. 1996a. *Multipartidarismo e Democracia*. Rio de Janeiro: Fundação Getúlio Vargas.

———. 1996b. "Presidencialismo, Multipartidarismo e Democracia." In Eli Diniz, ed., *O Desafio da Democracia na América Latina*. Rio de Janeiro: IUPERJ.

Nie, Norman H., Sidney Verba, and John R. Petrocik. 1979. *The Changing American Voter*. Cambridge: Harvard University Press. Enlarged edition.

Nohlen, Dieter, ed. 1993. *Enciclopedia electoral de América Latina y el Cáribe*. San José, Costa Rica: Instituto Interamericano de Derechos Humanos.

Novaes, Carlos Alberto Marques. 1993. "PT: Dilemas da Burocratização." *Novos Estudos* No. 35 (March): 217–37.

———. 1994. "Dinâmica Institucional da Representação." *Novos Estudos* No. 38 (March): 99–147.

Novaes, Walter, and Sérgio Ribeiro da Costa Werlang. 1993. "Financial Integration and Public Financial Institutions." Escola de Pós-Graduação em Economia da Fundação Getúlio Vargas, Ensaios Econômicos #225 (November).

Nunes, Edson de Oliveira. 1978. "Legislativo, Política e Recrutamento de Elite no Brasil." *Dados* No. 17: 53–78.

O'Donnell, Guillermo. 1986. *Contrapontos: Autoritarismo e Democratização*. São Paulo: Vértice.

———. 1988. *Bureaucratic Authoritarianism: Argentina, 1966–1973*. Berkeley and Los Angeles: University of California Press.

———. 1994. "Delegative Democracy?" *Journal of Democracy* 5 No. 1 (January): 55–69.

O'Donnell, Guillermo, and Philippe Schmitter. 1986. "Tentative Conclusions about Uncertain Democracies." Part 4 of O'Donnell, Schmitter, and Laurence Whitehead, eds., *Transitions from Authoritarian Rule: Prospects for Democracy*. Baltimore: Johns Hopkins University Press.

Oi, Jean C. 1989. *State and Peasant in Contemporary China*. Berkeley: University of California Press.

Oliveira, Lúcia Lippi. 1973. "Partidos Políticos Brasileiros: O Partido Social Democrático." M.A. thesis, IUPERJ.

Oliveira Vianna, Francisco José de. 1987 (1949). *Instituições Políticas Brasileiras*. Niterói: EDUFF.

Olsen, Orjan O. V. 1989. "Democratic Transition in Brazil: Emerging Values and the Search for New Leadership." Paper for the World Association for Public Opinion Research conference, Stockholm, Sweden, September 1989.

Olson, Mancur. 1965. *The Logic of Collective Action: Public Goods and the Theory of Groups*. Cambridge: Harvard University Press.

Ostrogorski, Moisei. 1902. *Democracy and the Organization of Political Parties*. Garden City, NY: Anchor Books.

Packenham, Robert. 1994. "The Politics of Economic Liberalization: Argentina and Brazil in Comparative Perspective." University of Notre Dame, Kellogg Institute for International Studies, Working Paper #206 (April).

Panebianco, Angelo. 1988. *Political Parties: Organization and Power*. Cambridge: Cambridge University Press.

Pedersen, Mogens N. 1983. "Changing Patterns of Electoral Volatility in European Party Systems: Explorations in Explanation." In Hans Daalder and Peter Mair, eds., *Western European Party Systems: Continuity and Change*. Beverly Hills and London: Sage, 29–66.

Pessanha, Charles. 1993. "Notas sobre as Relações entre Executivo e Legislativo no Brasil: 1964–1992." Paper presented at the 17th annual meeting of ANPOS, Caxambu, Minas Gerais, October 22–25.

Peterson, Phyllus Jane. 1962. "Brazilian Political Parties: Formation, Organization, and Leadership." Ph.D. dissertation, University of Michigan.

Pierucci, Antônio Flávio, and Reginaldo Prandi. 1995. "Religiões e Voto: A Eleição Presidencial de 1994." *Opinião Pública* 3 No. 1 (May): 20–44.

Pizzorno, Alessandro. 1981. "Interests and Parties in Pluralism." In Suzanne Berger, ed., *Organizing Interests in Western Europe: Pluralism, Corporatism, and the Transformation of Politics*. New York: Cambridge University Press, 247–84.

———. 1985. "On the Rationality of Democratic Choice." *Telos* 64 (Spring): 41–69.

Plasser, and Ulram. 1993."Zum Stand der Demokatisierung in Ost-Mitteleuropa." In Fritz Plasser and Peter A. Ulram, eds., *Transformation oder Stagnation? Aktuelle Politische Trends in Osteuropa* 2: 46–47. Vienna: Schriftenreihe des Zentrums für angewandte Politikforschung.

Powell, G. Bingham. 1982. *Contemporary Democracies: Participation, Stability, and Violence*. Cambridge: Harvard University Press.

Powell, John Duncan. 1970. "Peasant Society and Clientelist Politics," *American Political Science Review* 64 No. 2 (June): 411–25.

Powell, Walter W., and Paul J. DiMaggio, eds. 1991. *The New Institutionalism in Organizational Analysis*. Chicago: University of Chicago Press.

Power, Timothy J. 1990. Survey of Brazilian National Congress. (Database)

———. 1991. "Politicized Democracy: Competition, Institutions, and 'Civic Fatigue' in Brazil. *Journal of Interamerican Studies and World Affairs* 33 No. 3 (Fall): 75–112.

———. 1993. "The Political Right and Democratization in Brazil." Ph.D. dissertation, University of Notre Dame.

———. 1998. "The Pen is Mightier than the Congress: Presidential Decree Power in Brazil." In John Carey and Matthew Soberg Shugart, eds., *Executive Decree Authority*. New York and Cambridge: Cambridge University Press.

Pridham, Geoffrey, ed. 1990. *Securing Democracy: Political Parties and Democratic Consolidation in Southern Europe*. London and New York: Routledge.

Przeworski, Adam. 1975. "Institutionalization of Voting Patterns, or is Mobilization the Source of Decay?" *American Political Science Review* 69 No. 1: 49–67.

———. 1985. *Capitalism and Social Democracy*. New York and Cambridge: Cambridge University Press.

Przeworski, Adam, and Sprague, John. 1986. *Paper Stones: A History of Electoral Socialism*. Chicago: University of Chicago Press.

Przeworski, Adam, et al. 1996. "What Makes Democracies Endure?" *Journal of Democracy* 7 No. 1 (January): 39–55.

Queiroz, Maria Isaura Pereira de. 1975. "O Coronelismo numa Interpretação Sociológica." In Sérgio Buarque de Hollanda, ed., *História Geral da Civilização Brasileira*, Tome III, Vol. II, 153–90.

Ramos, Guerreiro. 1961. *A Crise de Poder no Brasil*. Rio de Janeiro: Zahar.

Ranney, Austin. 1981. "Candidate Selection." In David Butler, Howard R. Penniman and Austin Ranney, eds., *Democracy at the Polls: A Comparative Study of Competitive Factions*. Washington, D.C.: American Enterprise Institute, 75–106.

Reis, Fábio Wanderley. 1978. "Classe Social e Opção Partidária: As Eleições de 1976 em Juiz de Fora." In Fábio Wanderley Reis, ed., *Os Partidos e o Regime: A Lógica do Processo Eleitoral Brasileiro*. São Paulo: Símbolo, 213–87.

———. 1983. "O Eleitorado, os Partidos e o Regime Autoritário Brasileiro." In Bernard Sorj and Maria Hermínia Tavares de Almeida, eds., *Sociedade e Política no Brasil pós-64.* São Paulo: Brasiliense, 62–86.

———. 1988. "Partidos, Ideologia e Consolidação Democrática." In Fábio Wanderley Reis and Guillermo O'Donnell, eds., *A Democracia no Brasil: Dilemas e Perspectivas.* São Paulo: Vértice, 296–326.

Reis, Fábio Wanderley, and Mônica Mata Machado de Castro. 1992. "Regiões, Classe e Ideologia no Processo Eleitoral Brasileiro." *Lua Nova* No. 26: 81–131.

Remmer, Karen L. 1985. "Redemocratization and the Impact of Authoritarian Rule in Latin America." *Comparative Politics* 17 No. 3 (April): 253–75.

———. 1991. "The Political Impact of Economic Crisis in Latin America in the 1980s." *American Political Science Review* 85 No. 3 (September): 777–800.

Rezende, Fernando. 1982. "Autonomia Política e Dependência Financeira: Uma Análise das Transformações Recentes nas Relações Intergovernamentais e seus Reflexos Sobre a Situação Financeira dos Estados." *Pesquisa e Planejamento Econômico* 12 No. 2 (August).

Riker, William H. 1962. *The Theory of Political Coalitions.* New Haven: Yale University Press.

Robertson, David. 1976. *A Theory of Party Competition.* London: Wiley.

Rodrigues, Leôncio Martins. 1987. *Quem é Quem na Constituinte: Uma Análise Sócio-Política dos Partidos e Deputados.* São Paulo: Oesp-Maltese.

———. 1990. *Partidos e Sindicato.* São Paulo: Atica.

———. 1995. "Eleições, Fragmentação Partidária e Governabilidade." *Novos Estudos* No. 41 (March): 78–90.

Rokkan, Stein. 1970. *Citizens, Elections, Parties: Approaches to the Comparative Study of the Processes of Development.* New York: McKay.

Rose, Richard. 1980. "Government Against Sub-Governments: A European Perspective on Washington." In Richard Rose and Ezra Suleiman, eds., *Presidents and Prime Ministers.* Washington, D.C.: American Enterprise Institute, 284–347.

———. 1995. "Mobilizing Demobilized Voters in Post Communist Societies." Instituto Juan March de Estudios e Investigaciones, Centro de Estudios Avanzados en Ciencias Sociales, Working Paper 1995/76 (September).

Rose, Richard, and Derek Urwin. 1969. "Social Cohesion, Political Parties, and Strains in Regimes." *Comparative Political Studies* 2 No. 1 (April): 7–67.

Rueschemeyer, Dietrich, Evelyne Huber Stephens, and John D. Stephens. 1992. *Capitalist Development and Democracy.* Chicago: University of Chicago Press.

Sadek, Maria Tereza. 1988. "A Interiorização do PMDB nas Eleições de 1986 em São Paulo." Textos IDESP No. 23.

Samuels, David Julian. 1996. "Parties and Politicians: Collective and Individual Strategy Under the Open List in Brazil." Unpublished article.

———. 1998. "Careerism and its Consequences: Federalism, Elections, and Policy-Making in Brazil." Ph.D. dissertation, University of California, San Diego.

Sani, Giacomo, and Giovanni Sartori. 1983. "Polarization, Fragmentation, and Competition in Western Democracies." In Hans Daalder and Peter Mair, eds., *Western European Party Systems.* Beverly Hills: Sage, 307–40.

Santos, Wanderley Guilherme dos. 1979. *Cidadania e Justiça.* Rio de Janeiro: Campus.

————. 1985a. "A Pós-'Revolucão' Brasileira." In Helio Jaguaribe, et al., *Brasil, Sociedade Democrática*. Rio de Janeiro: José Olympio Editora, 223–335.

————. 1985b. "O Século de Michels: Competição Oligopólica, Lógica Autoritária e Transição na América Latina." *Dados* No. 28: 283–310.

————. 1986. *Sessenta e Quatro: Anatomia da Crise*. São Paulo: Vértice.

————. 1993. *Razões da Desordem*. Rio de Janeiro: Rocco.

Sarles, Margaret J. 1982. "Maintaining Political Control Through Parties: The Brazilian Strategy." *Comparative Politics* 15 No. 1 (October): 41–72.

Sartori, Giovanni. 1969. "From the Sociology of Politics to Political Sociology." In Seymour Martin Lipset, ed., *Politics and the Social Sciences*. New York: Oxford University Press, 65–100.

————. 1976. *Parties and Party Systems: A Framework for Analysis*. New York and Cambridge: Cambridge University Press.

————. 1986. "The Influence of Electoral Systems: Faulty Laws or Faulty Method?" In Bernard Grofman and Arend Lijphart, eds., *Electoral Laws and Their Political Consequences*. New York: Agathon, 43–68.

————. 1989. "Video-Power." *Government and Opposition* 24 No. 1 (Winter): 39–53.

Schattschneider, Elmer E.. 1942. *Party Government*. New York: Farrar and Rinehart.

Schedler, Andreas. 1995. "Under- and Overinstitutionalization: Some Ideal Typical Propositions Concerning Old and New Party Systems." University of Notre Dame, Kellogg Institute for International Studies Working Paper #213 (March).

Schlesinger, Joseph A. 1991. *Political Parties and the Winning of Office*. Ann Arbor: University of Michigan Press.

Schmitt, Hermann. 1989. "On Party Attachment in Western Europe and the Utility of Eurobarometer Data." *West European Politics* 12 No. 2 (April): 122–139.

Schmitt, Rogério Augusto and Simone Cuber Araujo. 1997. "Migração Partidária, Reapresentação e Reeleição na Câmara dos Deputados." Paper for the XXI Congress of the Latin American Sociology Association, Universidade de São Paulo, August 31 to September 5.

Schmitter, Philippe. 1971. *Interest Conflict and Political Change in Brazil*. Stanford: Stanford University Press.

————. 1974. "Still the Century of Corporatism?" *Review of Politics* 36 No. 1 (January): 85–131.

Schneider, Ben Ross. 1991. "Brazil Under Collor: Anatomy of a Crisis." *World Policy Journal* 8 No. 2 (Spring): 321–47.

Schumpeter, Joseph. 1950. *Capitalism, Socialism, and Democracy*. New York: Harper & Row.

Schwartzman, Simon. 1982. *Bases do Autoritarismo Brasileiro*. Rio de Janeiro: Campus.

Scott, James C. 1969. "Corruption, Machine Politics, and Political Change." *American Political Science Review* 63 No. 4 (December): 1142–58.

————. 1972. "Patron-Client Relations and Political Change in Southeast Asia." *American Political Science Review* 66 No. 1 (March): 91–113.

Scully, Timothy R. 1992. *Rethinking the Center: Cleavages, Critical Junctures, and Party Evolution in Chile*. Stanford: Stanford University Press.

Seligson, Mitchell A. 1987. "Costa Rica and Jamaica." In Myron Weiner and Ergun Ozbudun, eds., *Competitive Elections in Developing Countries.* Durham, NC: Duke University Press/American Enterprise Institute, 147–98.

Selznick, Philip. 1957. *Leadership in Administration.* New York: Harper and Row.

Shively, W. Phillips. 1972. "Party Identification, Party Choice, and Voting Stability: The Weimar Case." *American Political Science Review* 66 No. 4 (December): 1203–25.

Shugart, Matthew Soberg, and John Carey. 1992. *Presidents and Assemblies: Constitutional Design and Electoral Dynamics.* Cambridge: Cambridge University Press.

Shugart, Matthew Soberg, and Scott Mainwaring. 1997. "Presidentialism and Democracy in Latin America: Rethinking the Terms of the Debate." In Scott Mainwaring and Matthew Soberg Shugart, eds., *Presidentialism and Democracy in Latin America.* Cambridge and New York: Cambridge University Press, 12–54.

Simão, Aziz. 1956. "O Voto Operário em São Paulo." *Revista Brasileira de Estudos Políticos* 1 No. 1: 130–41.

Singer, André. 1990. "Collor na Periferia: A Volta por Cima do Populismo?" In Bolivar Lamounier, ed., *De Geisel a Collor: O Balanço da Transição.* São Paulo: IDESP/Sumaré, 135–52.

Skidmore, Thomas E. 1967. *Politics in Brazil, 1930–1964: An Experiment in Democracy.* New York: Oxford University Press.

———. 1988. *The Politics of Military Rule in Brazil, 1964–85.* New York and Oxford: Oxford University Press.

———, ed. 1993. *Television, Politics, and the Transition to Democracy in Latin America.* Baltimore: Johns Hopkins University Press.

Soares, Gláucio Ary Dillon. 1964. "Alianças e Coligações Eleitorais: Notas para uma Teoria." *Revista Brasileira de Estudos Políticos* 17 (July): 95–124.

———. 1967. "Brasil: A Política do Desenvolvimento Desigual." *Revista Brasileira de Estudos Políticos* 22 (January): 19–70.

———. 1973. *Sociedade e Política no Brasil.* São Paulo: Difusão Européia do Livro.

———. 1982. "El sistema político brasileño: Nuevos partidos y viejas divisiones." *Revista Mexicana de Sociología* 44 No. 3 (July–September): 929–59.

———. 1984. "Uma Resenha e uma Resposta." *Dados* 27, No. 1: 93–104.

Socolik, Hélio. 1986. "Transferências de Impostos aos Estados e aos Municípios." *Revista de Finanças Públicas* No. 367 (July–September).

Sola, Lourdes. 1994a. "Estado, Reforma Fiscal e Governabilidade Democrática: Qual Estado?" *Novos Estudos* 38 (March): 189–205.

———. 1994b. "The State, Structural Reform, and Democratization in Brazil." In William C. Smith et al., eds., *Democracy, Markets, and Structural Reform in Latin America.* New Brunswick: Transaction Publishers, 151–81.

Sorauf, Frank J. 1961. "The Silent Revolution in Patronage." In Edward C. Banfield, ed., *Urban Government.* Glencoe, IL: Free Press, 308–17.

———. 1963. *Party and Representation: Legislative Politics in Pennsylvania.* New York: Atherton.

Soto, Hernando de. 1989. *The Other Path.* New York: Harper and Row.

Souza, Amaury de. 1978. "The Nature of Corporatist Representation: Leaders and Members of Organized Labor in Brazil." Ph.D. dissertation, Cornell University.

Souza, Amaury de, Olavo Brasil de Lima Júnior, and Marcus Figueiredo. 1985. "Brizola e as Eleições de 1982 no Rio de Janeiro." IUPERJ Série Estudos No. 40 (August).

Souza, Maria do Carmo Campello de. 1976. *Estado e Partidos Políticos no Brasil (1930 a 1964)*. São Paulo: Alfa-Omega.

————. 1989."The Brazilian 'New Republic': Under the 'Sword of Damocles.'" In Alfred Stepan, ed., *Democratizing Brazil: Problems of Transition and Consolidation*. New York and Oxford: Oxford University Press, 351–94.

Stepan, Alfred C. 1971. *The Military in Politics: Changing Patterns in Brazil*. Princeton: Princeton University Press.

————. 1978a. "Political Leadership and Regime Breakdown: Brazil." In Juan J. Linz and Alfred Stepan, eds., *The Breakdown of Democratic Regimes: Latin America*. Baltimore: Johns Hopkins University Press, 110–137.

————. 1978b. *The State and Society: Peru in Comparative Perspective*. Princeton: Princeton University Press.

————. 1988. *Rethinking Military Politics: Brazil and the Southern Cone*. Princeton: Princeton University Press.

————, ed. 1989. *Democratizing Brazil: Problems of Transition and Consolidation*. New York and Oxford: Oxford University Press.

————. 1997. "Toward a New Comparative Analysis of Democracy and Federalism." Paper prepared for conference on "Democracy, Nationalism, and Federalism," All Souls College, University of Oxford, June 5–8.

Straubhaar, Joseph, Orjen Olsen, and Maria Cavaliari Nunes. 1993. "The Brazilian Case: Influencing the Voter." In Thomas E. Skidmore, ed., *Television, Politics, and the Transition to Democracy*. Baltimore: Johns Hopkins University Press, 118–36.

Strom, Kaare. 1990. "A Behavioral Theory of Competitive Political Parties." *American Journal of Political Science* 34 No. 2 (May): 565–98.

Suárez, Waldino. 1982. "El poder ejecutivo en América Latina: Su capacidad operativa bajo regímenes presidencialistas de gobierno." *Revista de Estudios Políticos* 29: 109–44.

Suleiman, Ezra N. 1994. "Presidentialism and Political Stability in France." In Juan J. Linz and Arturo Valenzuela, eds., *The Failure of Presidential Democracy*, Vol. 1, *Comparative Perspectives*. Baltimore: Johns Hopkins University Press, 137–62.

Taagepera, Rein, and Matthew Soberg Shugart. 1989. *Seats and Votes: The Effects and Determinants of Electoral Systems*. New Haven: Yale University Press.

Tarrow, Sidney. 1967. *Peasant Communism in Southern Italy*. New Haven: Yale University Press.

————. 1977. *Between Center and Periphery: Grassroots Politicians in Italy and France*. New Haven: Yale University Press.

Thelen, Kathleen, and Sven Steinmo. 1992. "Historical Institutionalism in Comparative Perspective." In Sven Steinmo, Kathleen Thelen, and Frank Longstreth, eds., *Structuring Politics: Historical Institutionalism in Comparative Politics*. New York and Cambridge: Cambridge University Press, 1–32.

Tóka, Gábor. 1997. "Political Parties and Democratic Consolidation in East Central Europe." *Studies in Public Policy*, Paper #279, University of Strathclyde.

Torres, Alberto. 1933 (1914). *A Organização Nacional*. São Paulo: Companhia Editora Nacional.

Trebat, Thomas. 1983. *Brazil's State-Owned Enterprises: A Case Study of the State as Entrepreneur.* New York: Cambridge University Press.

Tsebelis, George. 1990. *Nested Games: Rational Choice in Comparative Politics.* Berkeley: University of California Press.

———. 1995. "Decision Making in Political Systems: Veto Players in Presidentialism, Parliamentarism, Multicamerism, and Multipartyism." *British Journal of Political Science* 25 No. 3: 289–325.

Uricoechea, Fernando. 1980. *The Patrimonial Foundations of the Brazilian Bureaucratic State.* Berkeley: University of California Press.

Valenzuela, Arturo. 1977. *Political Brokers in Chile.* Durham: Duke University Press.

Valenzuela, J. Samuel. 1985. *Democratización via reforma: La expansión del sufragio en Chile.* Buenos Aires: IDES.

———. 1995. "The Origins and Transformations of the Chilean Party System." University of Notre Dame, Kellogg Institute for International Studies, Working Paper #215 (December).

von Mettenheim, Kurt. 1995. *The Brazilian Voter: Mass Politics in Democratic Transition, 1974–1986.* Pittsburgh: University of Pittsburgh Press.

Waisbord, Sílvio. 1993. "Party Lines: Political Parties and Mass Media in Argentine Election Campaigns." Ph.D. dissertation, University of California, San Diego.

Ware, Alan. 1985. *The Breakdown of Democratic Party Organization.* Oxford: Clarendon Press.

Weber, Max. 1946. *From Max Weber: Essays in Sociology.* H. H. Gerth and C. Wright Mills, eds. New York: Oxford University Press.

———. 1978. *Economy and Society.* Guenther Roth and Claus Wittich eds. Berkeley: University of California Press.

Weffort, Francisco. 1978. *O Populismo na Política Brasileira.* Rio de Janeiro: Paz e Terra.

Werlang, Sérgio Ribeiro da Costa, and Armínio Fraga Neto. 1992. "Os Bancos Estaduais e o Descontrole Fiscal: Alguns Aspectos." Escola de Pós-Graduação em Economia da Fundação Getúlio Vargas, Working Paper #203 (November).

Werneck, Rogério L. F. 1992. "El primer año del programa brasileño de privatización." In Joaquín Vial, ed., *Adónde va América Latina? Balance de las reformas económicas.* Santiago: Cieplan, 264–75.

Wesson, Robert, and David V. Fleischer. 1983. *Brazil in Transition.* New York: Praeger.

Weyland, Kurt. 1993. "The Rise and Fall of President Collor and its Impact on Brazilian Democracy," *Journal of Interamerican Studies and World Affairs* 35 No. 1: 1–37.

———. 1996a. *Democracy without Equity: Failures of Reform in Brazil.* Pittsburgh: University of Pittsburgh Press.

———. 1996b. "How Much Political Power do Economic Forces Have? Conflicts over Social Insurance Reform in Brazil." *Journal of Public Policy* 16 No. 1: 59–84.

———. Forthcoming. "The Brazilian State in the New Democracy." *Journal of Interamerican Studies and World Affairs.*

White, Stephen, Richard Rose, and Ian McAllister. 1997. *How Russia Votes.* Chatham, NJ: Chatham House.

Wilkie, James W. et al., eds. 1988. *Statistical Abstract of Latin America.* Los Angeles.

Williamson, John. 1990. "The Progress of Policy Reform in Latin America." Washington, D. C.: Institute for International Economics, Working Paper No. 28 (January).

Williamson, John, and Stephan Haggard. 1994. "The Political Conditions for Economic Reform." In John Williamson, ed., *The Political Economy of Policy Reform*. Washington D.C.: Institute for International Economics, 527–96.

Wirth, John. 1977. *Minas Gerais in the Brazilian Federation 1889–1937*. Stanford: Stanford University Press.

Wittman, Donald A. 1973. "Parties as Utility Maximizers." *American Political Science Review* 63 No. 2 (June): 490–98.

World Bank. 1986. "Brazil: Finance of Primary Education." Washington, DC: World Bank.

———. 1988. "Brazil: Public Spending on Social Programs; Issues and Options." Report No. 7086-BR. Washington: World Bank (May 27).

Yashar, Deborah J. 1995. "Civil War and Social Welfare: The Origins of Costa Rica's Competitive Party System." In Scott Mainwaring and Timothy R. Scully, eds., *Building Democratic Institutions: Party Systems in Latin America*. Stanford: Stanford University Press, 72–99.

Zuckerman, Alan. 1975. "Political Cleavage: A Conceptual and Theoretical Analysis." *British Journal of Political Science* 5 No. 2: 231–48.

Index

In this index an "f" after a number indicates a separate reference on the next page, and an "ff" indicates separate references on the next two pages. A continuous discussion over two or more pages is indicated by a span of page numbers, e.g., "57–59." *Passim* is used for a cluster of references in close but not consecutive sequence.

Accountability, 6, 8, 38, 322, 326–33 *passim*
Adesismo, 155, 194, 350, 353
Advanced industrial democracies, *see* Democracies, advanced industrial
Agrarian reform, 134f, 196
Antiorganizationalism, 233–34, 276, 279
Antipartism, 33, 37–38; and parties, 67, 166, 234, 240, 322–27 *passim*, 331; and presidents, 78, 83, 104, 110, 264, 272–76 *passim*, 329, 331, 338, 357
Arena (National Renovating Alliance), 58, 84–93 *passim*, 99, 119–22 *passim*, 194, 200, 203, 237; and party switching, 102, 143, 146, 161, 194, 273
Argentina, 58, 84, 93, 140, 264–67 *passim*, 273f, 310; parties in, 5, 27–36 *passim*, 66, 74, 82, 127f, 146, 226, 236, 260–61, 310, 340; electoral arena in, 29–34 *passim*, 238, 246, 277, 328; economic policies in, 241, 306, 310–15 *passim*
Australia, 66, 249
Austria, 36, 39, 129, 339
Authoritarianism, *see* Military government

Belgium, 29–34 *passim*, 227, 339
Bicameralism, symmetrical, 283–87 *passim*, 292
Bipartism, *see* Two-party system
Bolivia, 28–34 *passim*, 76, 259, 267, 277, 311, 313, 340, 346, 348

Bosses, local political, 67ff, 73ff, 157, 173, 178, 234, 257, 266, 335
Brazilian Communist Party (PCB/PPS), 47–50 *passim*, 71, 100, 126, 137, 139, 143f, 161, 165ff, 226, 334; as leftist party, 19, 92, 133, 144
Brazilian Democratic Movement, *see* MDB
Brazilian Labor Party, *see* PTB
Brazilian Progressive Party, *see* PPB
Brazilian Social Democratic Party, *see* PSDB
Brazilian Socialist Party, *see* PSB
Brizola, Leonel, 43ff, 91, 104f, 117, 152, 165
Business interests, 125, 150f, 164, 232, 307, 309; and clientelism, 177, 183–84, 188, 195, 209, 212, 217, 333f

Campaign consultants, 138, 151f, 238
Campaign control, 136ff, 147–53 *passim*, 166f, 238, 249f, 260, 330, 339
Campaign financing, 136f, 150–55 *passim*, 164–65, 188–89, 215, 250, 333
Campaigns and television, *see* Television
Canada, 25, 66, 114
Candidate selection, 16, 37, 126–27, 153–59 *passim*, 166, 243–66 *passim*, 272, 306, 337–41 *passim*, 356
Cardoso, Fernando Henrique (Pres., 1995–), 80, 115f, 135, 150, 152, 211–15 *passim*, 313–17 *passim*; policy reforms of, 107, 182, 211–14 *passim*, 284, 288ff, 295, 306–9 *passim*, 313–

20 *passim*; stabilization policies of, 107, 111, 192, 284, 303, 305, 347

Cardoso, Newton (Gov.), 193, 195, 300, 355

Catch-all parties, 19, 40, 123–24, 147, 168–73, 198–99, 203; characteristics of, 5, 10, 18–20; decentralization of, 137, 156–60 *passim*, 168, 173, 234, 266; organizational weakness of, 137, 153–67 *passim*, 173f, 199, 250–56 *passim*, 261, 266, 294; party switching and, 142–47 *passim*, 167, 173f, 234, 251, 278; ideological heterogeneity in, 143, 148, 159–62 *passim*, 168, 234, 256, 260, 264, 296, 345; campaigns and, 147–53 *passim*, 173, 234, 251; clientelism in, 167, 172, 176–80 *passim*, 185–90 *passim*, 198, 234, 253. *See also* Leftist parties; Party discipline; Party loyalty

Catholic Church, 48–51 *passim*, 82, 91, 124f, 239, 347

Center-left parties, 133, 143f, 160, 291. *See also* PDT; PSDB; PTB

Center-right parties, 133, 144f, 161, 290. *See also* PDC; Progressive Party (PP); PSC; PSD; PTB

Centrist parties, 42, 72, 133, 144f, 226, 290f, 314. *See also* PDC; PMDB; Popular Party (PP); PSD

CGT (General Labor Confederation), 124, 230

Chile, 54–59 *passim*, 84, 93, 235, 265, 306, 309, 314, 321; parties in, 5, 31–34 *passim*, 66, 74, 82, 93, 127f, 146, 226, 274, 325; electoral system in, 29f, 76, 93, 128, 249f

Christian Democratic Party, *see* PDC

Civil society, 55, 59, 68, 72–73, 81, 138, 169, 172, 175, 312

Class and voting behavior, 21–22, 39–54 *passim*, 86, 104, 120–123 *passim*, 230f, 259, 347

Class parties, *see* Working-class parties

Clientelism, 73, 157, 167, 197ff, 214ff, 221, 253, 257, 271; consequences of, 5, 177f, 192, 201–2, 207–14 *passim*; access to state resources through, 13, 69, 146f, 179–85 *passim*, 197–206 *passim*; parties and, 19, 65–69 *passim*, 91, 102f, 189, 290, 351, 355; party-system institutionalization and, 26, 37, 81, 178–81 *passim*, 291; elections and, 37, 81, 88, 135, 176, 187–90, 203, 216, 258; Brazilian governments and, 65, 99, 177, 200–8 *passim*, 296–304 *passim*, 315; support for governing and, 74, 176f, 185, 190–97, 203, 210, 214, 247, 271, 289–99 *passim*; elite interests and, 75, 177–84 *passim*, 208–10, 257, 332–35; organized

interest groups and, 82–85 *passim*, 179ff, 227, 230, 234; party control and, 83, 176, 185–87, 209, 216; definition of, 177–80; the poor and, 179–84 *passim*, 188, 194, 202–12 *passim*, 263, 268–71 *passim*, 332–35 *passim*. *See also* Business interests; Corruption; Military government

Collective action, 181, 184, 189, 216–17, 230

Collor de Mello, Fernando (Pres., 1990–92), 104, 134, 152; antipartism of, 6, 33, 100, 104, 110, 150, 155, 273, 276, 329ff; impeachment of, 6, 106, 123, 197, 214ff, 291, 302, 320, 329f; PRN and, 27, 33, 104, 110, 115–18 *passim*, 123, 146, 331; clientelism and, 197, 211–16 *passim*, 300–3 *passim*, 333; reform efforts of, 197, 211–14 *passim*, 288–96 *passim*, 300–20 *passim*, 331

Colombia, 5, 24f, 29–34 *passim*, 76, 184, 265, 310, 325, 339f

Communist parties, 20, 50, 91, 101, 124, 161

Communist Party of Brazil, *see* PC do B

Comparative macroanalysis, 7

Concurrent elections, 30, 111, 130, 275–76, 338f. *See also* Nonconcurrent elections

CONCLAT, 124

Congress, *see* Legislature

Congressional elections, *see* Legislative elections

Conservatism, 102, 197f, 208–9, 291, 334ff

Conservative parties, 41f, 50f, 72, 89, 92, 112, 131ff, 141–45 *passim*, 158–61 *passim*, 226, 290f, 334. *See also* PDS; PFL; PL; PPB; PPR; PRN; PRONA; PSD; UDN

Conservative Party, 57

Consolidated democracies, *see* Democracies, advanced industrial

Constitution, 50, 85, 101, 287–93 *passim*, 303, 314, 320, 336; and presidency, 82, 95–96, 107, 195f, 264, 270, 275, 295, 299f, 309, 318ff; and political system reform, 100–103 *passim*, 232, 258, 270, 318ff; and state reform, 182, 185, 202, 292–93, 303–7 *passim*, 311–16 *passim*; and tax reform, 191, 197, 265, 292–99 *passim*, 303, 306, 315f

Constitutional congress, 103, 134–41 *passim*, 155, 161, 199, 258, 270, 290f, 318ff, 357

Coronelismo, 69, 73

Corporatism, 48, 60, 73f, 81, 224–30 *passim*, 332

Corruption, 208, 315, 330; in government administrations, 66, 73f, 85, 95, 104, 107, 170,

214–18 *passim*, 355; in campaign financing, 151, 188–89, 215, 333; and clientelism, 175–80 *passim*, 186, 195, 200–215 *passim*, 219f

Costa Rica, 5, 29–34 *passim*, 46, 76, 146, 234, 246, 274, 325

Cruzado Plan, 101–4 *passim*, 108, 127, 148, 199, 298f

CUT (Sole Labor Confederation), 124, 230

Czech Republic, 29, 31, 36

Debt crisis, *see* Economic crisis

Delegative democracy, 128, 328–32 *passim*

Democracies, advanced industrial, party systems in, 21–35 *passim*, 41, 52–59 *passim*, 114, 119, 131, 139f, 150, 221, 231, 238, 323. *See also* individual countries by name

Democracies, third-wave, *see* Third-wave democracies

Democratic Brazilian Movement, *see* MDB

Democratic Labor Party, *see* PDT

Democratic Parliamentary Action, 83

Democratic Social Party, *see* PDS

Democratic transitions, 6–7, 55, 64, 85, 103, 170, 236, 299

Denmark, 114, 339

Dictatorship, *see* Military government

District magnitude, 129, 287, 338

Dominican Republic, 5

Dom Pedro II, Emperor (1840–89), 49–50

Downs, Anthony, 55, 168–72 *passim*, 324

Duverger, Maurice, 19, 71, 100, 138, 167, 347

Economic crisis, 82, 89f, 240, 311–15 *passim*; in the 1980s, 94f, 101–11 *passim*, 129, 134, 177, 191f, 207–13 *passim*, 222, 240ff, 294, 306. *See also* Stabilization policies

Economic stabilization, *see* Stabilization policies

Ecuador, 28–34 *passim*, 39, 76, 146, 249, 311

Education and voting behavior, 39–47 *passim*, 73, 104–5, 112, 119, 127f, 150, 239, 259

Effective number of parties, 22f, 37, 39, 72, 109, 128–29, 277, 324, 338, 345. *See also* Multipartism; Party-system fragmentation

Elections, 11f, 66f, 93ff, 129, 176–77, 244–48 *passim*, 339; concurrent vs nonconcurrent, 30, 77, 111, 130, 275–76, 338f. *See also* Campaign control; Campaign financing; Gubernatorial elections; Legislative elections; Municipal elections; Presidential elections; Clientelism; Military government

Electoral accountability, *see* Accountability

Electoral alliances, *see* Electoral coalitions

Electoral coalitions, 6, 76–81 *passim*, 94–103 *passim*, 108, 128, 130, 146, 153–59 *passim*, 254, 263

Electoral college, *see* under Presidential elections, methods of

Electoral geography, 88, 119–23

Electoral legislation, *see* Electoral rules

Electoral participation, 63–73 *passim*, 81, 93, 101–4 *passim*, 178f, 224, 227

Electoral rules, 10, 18, 73, 91, 94, 100–4 *passim*, 188, 222, 234; and effective number of parties, 18, 58, 89–94 *passim*, 100–4 *passim*, 109, 128–31 *passim*, 278; imposed by state elites, 56, 87–94 *passim*; and incentives to individualism, 75f, 81, 234, 243–50 *passim*, 254, 260–63, 276–80 *passim*; and legislative elections, 75f, 87, 287f. *See also* Electoral system; Institutional rules; Party rules

Electoral system, 8, 10, 129, 149, 187, 189, 235, 276–80, 337ff; reforms of, 58f, 100–101, 109. *See also* Electoral rules; Institutional rules; Open-list systems; Proportional representation systems

Electoral volatility, 24–28 *passim*, 39, 54, 64, 75–76, 323–28 *passim*, 347; defined, 24, 28; in post-1979 PERIOD, 88, 108–11, 119, 135, 223, 240

Elites, *see* Political elites and shaping of party system

Emperor Dom Pedro II, *see* Dom Pedro II, Emperor

Empire (1822–89), 57f, 65–69 *passim*

Empreguismo, 184, 203–6 *passim*, 210f, 354. *See also* Clientelism

Enfranchisement, *see* Electoral participation

Estado Novo (1937–45), 65, 71, 74, 264

Ethnic cleavages, 39, 48, 52

Europe, East Central, 27–31 *passim*, 36. *See also* individual countries by name

Europe, Northern, 36, 54, 59, 66, 230. *See also* individual countries by name

Europe, Southern, 27–31 *passim*, 36. *See also* individual countries by name

Europe, Western, 3, 15–22 *passim*, 59, 212, 228; social cleavages model applied to, 22, 39ff, 52ff, 346; party systems in, 27–42 *passim*, 46–55 *passim*, 59f, 123, 131, 174, 228; electoral systems in, 108, 277, 339–47 *passim*

Executive branch, *see* Presidentialism; Presidential powers

Extraelectoral party activities, 162–67 *passim*, 171

Federalism, 18f, 69, 130, 137, 243f, 260, 264–66, 293, 337, 340; and party decentralization, 16, 160, 263, 266, 293, 340; and presidential reforms, 283–87 *passim*, 291–99 *passim*, 304–7 *passim*, 318
Figueiredo, Argelina Cheibub, 139–40, 245, 321, 356
Figueiredo, João (Pres., 1979–85), 18, 89, 95, 108, 203, 206, 329
Finland, 28–34 *passim*, 131, 134, 249f
First-wave democracies, *see* Democracies, advanced industrial
Força Sindical, 124, 230
France, 29, 32–39 *passim*, 59, 108, 227, 236
Franco, Itamar (Pres., 1992–94), 214f, 273, 302ff, 354; poor leadership of, 6, 106–7, 308, 328f; reform efforts of, 288, 295, 297, 302–16 *passim*
Fujimori, Alberto, 27, 33, 37, 59, 310

Geisel, Ernesto (Pres., 1974–79), 85, 89, 203
General Labor Confederation (CGT), 124, 230
Germany, 36, 227, 339
Goulart, João (Pres., 1961–64), 71, 80–83 *passim*, 96
Governing coalitions, 190–97, 247, 263, 265, 271–72 *passim*, 286–92 *passim*, 296–300 *passim*, 304–8 *passim*, 313
Greece, 29–36 *passim*, 235f, 249
Gubernatorial elections, 85, 94f, 101–10 *passim*, 130, 146, 150, 152, 191–92, 203, 254, 331
Gubernatorial powers, 94–95, 192ff, 203, 253–58 *passim*, 285–94 *passim*, 305–10 *passim*
Guimarães, Ulysses, 104f, 116f, 154f, 170

Historical institutionalism, 7–11 *passim*. *See also* Institutionalism
Hungary, 31, 339

Ideological distance, 22f, 37, 39, 89, 101, 103, 131–35, 349; and policy reform, 286, 291–92, 304, 308, 315
Ideological polarization, 22, 64, 82, 128. *See also* Ideological distance
Illiteracy, 64, 68f, 73, 81, 101, 213, 224, 227, 259
Independence, Brazilian (1822), 65
India, 161, 292
Industrialization, 68, 221–30 *passim*, 234

Institutional design, 16, 322–23, 336–41
Institutionalism, 7–11 *passim*, 283–84, 308–13, 317–21, 345
Institutionalization, *see* Party-system institutionalization
Institutional rules, 63, 221ff, 235, 243–44, 276–78, 337–41 *passim*; and elite preferences, 5, 75, 100, 233–34, 243–44, 278ff; as political incentives, 10, 243–48 *passim*, 260–62, 278ff. *See also* Candidate selection; Electoral rules; Electoral system; Federalism; Malapportionment; Party discipline; Party rules; Presidentialism; Presidential powers
Interest groups, *see* Organized interests
Intraclass fragmentation, 41, 54, 74, 227–30 *passim*, 234
Intraparty competition, 75, 149, 169ff, 189, 244, 260, 339. *See also* Open-list systems
Israel, 129, 340
Italy, 25, 29–37 *passim*, 129–33 *passim*, 184, 227, 249f, 330, 340, 351

Japan, 161, 249, 330, 340

Labor movement, 48, 68–74 *passim*, 82, 91, 134, 184, 234, 239, 332; parties and, 14, 41, 80, 99, 123–4, 164, 226–30 *passim*; corporatist controls of, 49, 74, 224, 229f. *See also* CGT; CONCLAT; CUT; Força Sindical; Working class; Working-class parties
Labor parties, *see* Working-class parties
Latin America, 5, 17, 53, 57, 69, 74, 83, 127–28, 137f, 278ff; party systems in, 27–41 *passim*, 58ff, 66, 92–93, 110, 127, 142–46 *passim*, 225, 230–37 *passim*, 328; social cleavages in, 46–54 *passim*, 259, 347; electoral arenas in, 76f, 108ff, 138, 149–52 *passim*, 189f, 245, 251, 277; policy reform and institutional rules in, 189, 264f, 275, 284, 308ff, 314f
Left-right scale, 131–35 *passim*, 161–62, 336
Leftist parties, 19, 50, 131–35 *passim*, 151, 185, 213, 247–48, 264; catch-all parties compared to, 19f, 40, 123–24, 147, 160–73 *passim*, 198–99, 203, 261; party organization in, 71, 89ff, 140–48 *passim*, 160–67 *passim*, 261, 278. *See also* PCB; PC do B; PPS; PSB; PSTU; PT; PV
Legislative elections, 45, 89, 94, 101–4 *passim*, 109–10, 114–15, 122, 130, 150, 204, 254
Legislature, 13, 83–87 *passim*, 94, 100, 140–41, 324–31 *passim*, 335; powers of, 94, 203, 246,

275, 290, 292, 309. *See also* Bicameralism, symmetrical; Electoral rules
Legitimacy, 26, 73, 89, 103–4, 278, 315; of parties and elections, 5, 14ff, 26, 35–36, 80, 93, 125–28, 208, 224, 332, 327, 331; of democracy, 6, 14, 85, 127f, 207–8; of military, 58, 84, 93, 95, 128; and economic crisis, 102–3, 222, 240–41
Liberal Front, 96f
Liberalization, *see* Political liberalization
Liberal Party, *see* PL
Lipset, Seymour Martin, 4, 39–45 *passim*, 123
Luiz Inácio da Silva, *see* Lula
"Lula", Luis Inácio da Silva, 42–4 *passim*, 51, 104–7 *passim*, 111, 116f, 134f, 152, 315, 347

Magalhães, Antônio Carlos, 159, 196, 198
Magalhães, Rafael de Almeida, 188, 207, 211
Malapportionment, 75, 87, 224, 263, 267–71 *passim*, 287, 335. *See also* Federalism
Maluf, Paulo, 43ff, 117, 134, 146, 194
Marxism, 183
Mass parties, 5, 7, 64–73 *passim*, 100, 181–84 *passim*, 225–32 *passim*
Mayhew, David, 245–48 *passim*, 261
MDB (Brazilian Democratic Movement), 85f, 99, 102, 146, 161, 194, 197, 273; and state control, 58, 84f, 90–93 *passim*, 100, 237. *See also* PMDB
Media, 85, 87, 132, 152, 166, 175f, 194–95, 209, 215; effect on parties of, 41, 222, 224, 228, 237–40, 272, 338
Mexico, 69, 85, 127f, 189f, 246, 264f, 277, 306–10 *passim*, 340; party system in, 5, 27–34 *passim*, 56, 127, 146, 213, 260–61, 310, 346; political elites in, 27, 32, 56, 69, 189f, 213
Military coups, 57f, 71, 74, 80–84 *passim*
Military government, 18, 50, 54, 85, 143, 229–35 *passim*, 264–65; elections and, 18, 64, 83–89 *passim*, 93f, 99, 118–19, 237; party-system interventions of, 18, 55–59 *passim*, 64, 68–71 *passim*, 82–93 *passim*, 98–99, 222, 235, 237, 258; legitimacy of, 58, 84, 93, 95, 128; opposition parties and, 89–100 *passim*, 108, 129, 154, 161, 197f, 257; demise of, 95–98 *passim*, 115, 203f; clientelism and, 99, 190–91, 200–206, 218, 257
Modern parties, *see* Mass parties
MR-8, 161
Multipartism, 23, 33, 37, 58, 89, 101, 109, 128–31 *passim*, 272, 277, 288–89. *See also* Effective

number of parties; Party-system fragmentation
Municipal elections, 45, 89, 94, 101–4 *passim*, 109–10, 114–15, 122, 130, 150, 204, 254

National Democratic Union, *see* UDN
Nationalist Parliamentary Front, 83
National Order Reconstruction Party (PRONA), 111
National parties, 63f, 68–75 *passim*, 81, 137, 153–58 *passim*, 174, 256, 260, 278, 350–51. *See also* Professionalized parties; Party organization
National Renovating Alliance, *see* Arena
Neoliberal reforms, 135, 189, 197, 291, 312–15 *passim*. *See also* Stabilization policies
Nepotism, 177, 184, 206, 210
Netherlands, 129, 339
Neves, Tancredo (Pres.-Elect, 1985), 96–100 *passim*, 206, 288
New Republic, 103, 205
New Zealand, 66, 340
nonconcurrent elections, 30, 77, 130, 275–76. *See also* Concurrent elections
North-South Railroad, 175–76, 216–18
Norway, 29–34 *passim*, 339

O'Donnell, Guillermo, 128, 233, 328–32 *passim*
Old Republic (1889–1930), 50, 57, 65–69 *passim*, 259, 264
Open-list systems, 16, 75, 149, 248ff, 258, 261, 277–80 *passim*, 339. *See also* Electoral system; Legislative elections; Proportional representation systems
Organized interests, 13f, 74, 82, 312; and parties, 28, 80, 88, 123–25, 150–51, 164, 172–73, 224–35 *passim*. *See also* Civil society; Labor movement; Popular sector; Social movements

Padrinhos, 178, 183, 188, 204, 211, 213, 352. *See also* Clientelism; Patronage
Paraguay, 30–36 *passim*, 127f
Parliamentary systems, 11, 30, 65ff, 158, 195ff, 264, 271–79 *passim*, 318, 337–38
Parties, as agents of representation, 6, 11–15 *passim*, 64, 138–39, 231f; and policy formulation, 198–99, 203, 232. *See also* Party-system institutionalization; Party systems
Parties of integration, 226ff, 238
Parties of notables, 5, 64–69, 74f

Party competition, 12–15 *passim*, 66–71 *passim*, 83–89 *passim*, 92, 94, 100–7 *passim*, 135, 197, 203, 340; stable patterns of, 3, 24–28 *passim*, 76, 88, 107–8, 322–29 *passim*. *See also* Electoral volatility; Ideological distance; Intraparty competition

Party decentralization, 10, 16–19 *passim*, 65–69 *passim*, 81, 137, 263–66 *passim*, 278, 340; and elite interests, 5, 73ff, 259; and national parties, 153–60 *passim*, 164, 255–60 *passim*. *See also* Federalism

Party discipline, 6, 12f, 48, 73ff, 125, 176, 269–70, 274, 310, 356; and institutional rules, 10, 250, 257–63 *passim*, 274–80 *passim*, 338; and national party organizations, 17, 147f, 153f, 248, 251; in catch-all parties, 18f, 136–42 *passim*, 156, 165–68 *passim*, 173f, 190, 234, 260f, 289–93 *passim*, 297; in leftist parties, 140, 144f, 165ff, 261, 289; and policy reform, 284–91 *passim*, 296f, 304, 317

Party finances, 36, 163–65

Party identification, 12, 25, 37, 54, 77ff, 88, 99–100, 112–19, 223F, 235–40 *passim*, 273–80 *passim*, 324–28 *passim*, 358; in first- vs. third-wave democracies, 30–31, 41, 84, 114f, 119, 135, 230f

Party legislation, *see* Party rules

Party longevity, 31–34, 88, 92, 107, 123, 237, 324

Party loyalty, 11, 13, 27, 31, 39f, 54, 147, 325; IN 1979–96 party system, 11, 88, 93, 110, 123; in catch-all parties, 18, 140–45 *passim*, 190, 197, 234, 249, 260, 263, 297; in Western democracies, 39f, 140, 236, 261; prior to 1965, 64f, 73–83 *passim*, 93, 180; and autonomous politicians, 136, 160, 176, 179, 184, 224, 233; in Latin America, 142, 233, 260–61, 311; and institutional rules, 248f, 255, 258, 272, 278, 280; and policy reform, 284, 289ff, 296f. *See also* Party switching

Party membership, 252, 258, 333, 352

Party of Brazilian Social Democracy, *see* PSDB

Party of National Reconstruction, *see* PRN

Party of the Brazilian Democratic Movement, *see* PMDB

Party of the Liberal Front, *see* PFL

Party organization, 8, 56, 65–75 *passim*, 80f, 93, 138, 147–55 *passim*, 162–73 *passim*, 180, 185f, 276; at national vs. state and local levels, 16f, 72, 137, 142, 153–64 *passim*, 294;

in party-system institutionalization, 27, 36–37, 136–42 *passim*, 173–74; in other countries, 36–37, 137f, 162, 173–74. *See also* Party discipline; Party switching; Politicians, autonomous; Leftist parties

Party roots in society, 26, 77, 88, 139, 174, 276f, 325–31 *passim*; and electoral patterns, 28–38 *passim*, 109, 122f, 135; in other countries, 29–35 *passim*, 226, 231, 236; and personalism, 33–38 *passim*, 322–31 *passim*; and elites, 55ff, 64f, 83, 93, 119, 237; and party identification, 113, 119, 135, 325. *See also* Electoral volatility

Party rules, 8, 18, 56, 90, 130, 144, 156f, 163; and autonomous politicians, 81, 100, 221–22, 243f, 261f, 280. *See also* Electoral rules; Institutional rules

Party switching, 27, 37, 119, 145f, 311, 331; and elite interests, 6, 11, 56, 59, 65, 80f, 130, 136, 145ff, 156, 251; in legislature, 37, 96, 100–3 *passim*, 142–47 *passim*, 161, 329, 349; and presidency, 110, 289–91, 297; in catch-all vs. leftist parties, 142–47 *passim*, 166–67, 278; and institutional rules, 156, 251, 255–61 *passim*, 270, 278ff

Party-system fragmentation, 59, 94, 100, 276, 337f; from 1945–64, 18, 59, 72, 82f; post-1985, 18, 59, 89–92 *passim*, 100–8 *passim*, 129; and policy reform, 283–95 *passim*, 304, 310f, 320–21. *See also* Effective number of parties; Multipartism

Party-system institutionalization, 47–48, 123–24, 317–18, 346; comparative perspectives on, 3, 7, 18, 323, 341; four dimensions of, 3, 26–27, 88f, 99, 107ff, 136, 147, 174, 322f, 327; quality of democracy and, 4–16 *passim*, 26, 37f, 322–36; social cleavages and, 4, 21–22, 52–55 *passim*; 1945–64, 18, 57ff, 63f, 70–83, 92f, 119, 223ff, 234–37 *passim*, 241, 347; definition of, 25; obstacles to, 63–70 *passim*, 75, 81, 221–34 *passim*; military rule and, 64, 82–89 *passim*, 93, 98–103 *passim*, 222, 235, 237; post-1985, 64, 103, 135, 221–25 *passim*, 231–41 *passim*, 280; institutional design for, 322–23, 336–41. *See also* Party competition; Party organization; Party roots in society; Politicians, autonomous; Clientelism; Legitimacy; Party-system theory

Party-system institutionalization, weak, 3–4, 8, 23, 36, 39, 88, 135; and institutional rules, 4f, 10, 233–35, 243–44, 261–64, 274–80 *pas-*

sim, 337–41 *passim*, 358; and political leadership, 6, 235, 325–30; causes of, 221–25, 241–42, 263–64, 303; historical factors in, 221–42, 277, 279; post–1964 FACTORS IN, 236–42, 280

Party-system theory, importance of institutionalization in, 3–4, 21–26, 37ff, 53f, 223, 341; "top-down" vs. "from-below" approaches in, 21–22, 54–55, 60

Party systems, elite shaping of, 4f, 22, 54–63 *passim*, 68, 83, 89, 93, 178, 222, 237, 242f, 260; international, 15, 21–25 *passim*, 36–39 *passim*, 53, 66, 234–37 *passim*, 241, 279f, 327–28; major changes in Brazilian, 18, 65, 92, 128, 180–81, 203, 277; classification of, 22–24, 38; definition of, 24–25

Party systems, fluid, 27. *See also* Party-system institutionalization, weak

Party voting, 88, 94, 100, 109–17 *passim*, 135, 149, 160, 166, 348

Patrimonialism, 49, 59, 63ff, 69, 176–80 *passim*, 189, 209–13 *passim*, 218, 329f, 335; in small states, 75, 263, 268; and corruption, 177, 180, 195, 218

Patronage, 176–80 *passim*, 285f, 317, 329, 335f. *See also* Clientelism

PCB, *see* Brazilian Communist Party

PC do B (Communist Party of Brazil), 19, 92, 133, 137, 139, 143, 159f, 165ff, 334, 345

PDC (Christian Democratic Party), 50, 72, 91f, 132f, 139, 143f, 290

PDS (Democratic Social Party), 89–95 *passim*, 113–18 *passim*, 125f, 139–42 *passim*, 161, 189, 203f, 334, 348; electoral support for, 94–109 *passim*, 119–23 *passim*, 204, 240f; party switching and, 96f, 102–3, 110, 143–46 *passim*, 159, 161, 194, 273, 280; collapse of, 101, 108f, 189, 222, 240f, 280, 331; left-right scale and, 131–34 *passim*, 144, 161f

PDT (Democratic Labor Party), 19–20, 46, 91f, 113–18 *passim*, 125f, 132f, 137, 143ff, 165f, 189, 290; and electoral outcomes, 94f, 101–11 *passim*, 266; and party discipline, 139–42 *passim*, 159, 165–66. *See also* Brizola, Leonel

Peasants, 68, 73f, 82. *See also* Popular sector

Pérez, Carlos Andrés, 310

Personalism, 33–38 *passim*, 152, 268, 272, 278f, 326, 337, 356; and politicians, 10, 12, 24, 187, 324ff, 330ff, 335; in electoral campaigns, 12, 51, 53, 88, 110, 187, 278f, 322–26 *passim*; and parties, 12, 24, 57, 65–70 *passim*, 109, 134,

273; and weak party systems, 25, 35–38 *passim*, 53, 75, 81, 83, 322–31 *passim*

Peru, 24–39 *passim*, 56, 59, 76, 93, 108, 127f, 225, 249, 309f

PFL (Party of the Liberal Front), 58, 113–26 *passim*, 147, 154f, 182–83, 189, 252, 299, 334; on left-right scale, 92, 132f, 144, 161f; and electoral outcomes, 97–111 *passim*, 266, 269; and Sarney, 98, 102ff, 288, 290, 298f; and party discipline, 139–42 *passim*, 154f, 160, 196, 350; and party switching, 142–46 *passim*, 159, 167, 280, 290

PL (Liberal Party), 125, 132f, 139, 143f, 273

Plebiscites, 82, 86, 99, 118, 128, 273, 276, 319, 339

PMB (Brazilian Municipalist Party), 111

PMDB (Party of the Brazilian Democratic Movement), 5, 58, 113–26 *passim*, 170, 199, 235, 240; alliance strategy of, 91, 94, 103, 162, 237; ideological heterogeneity of, 91, 94, 102f, 132f, 144f, 161, 237; electoral outcomes and, 95–111 *passim*, 129, 189, 266; economic crisis and, 102ff, 108f, 129, 148, 199, 222, 240F, 314–15; party switching and, 102, 142–46 *passim*, 273; patronage and, 102f, 146, 187, 189, 194–99 *passim*, 213, 266; Sarney government and, 102ff, 108, 170, 196, 199, 240, 273, 288ff, 297f; demise of, 103f, 108f, 237, 240; discipline in, 136–42 *passim*, 154f, 159, 196; campaigns and, 147–50 *passim*, 154f, 159, 170; organization of, 154–55, 162–65 *passim*, 252, 348

Poland, 28–36 *passim*, 249, 328

Polarized pluralism, 22, 37, 82

Policy reform, 283–97 *passim*, 303–4, 317–28 *passim*, 335. *See also* Stablization policies; State reform

Political coalitions, *see* Electoral coalitions; Governing coalitions

Political consultants, 138, 151f, 238

Political elites and shaping of party systems, 4–11 *passim*, 22, 54–75 *passim*, 81, 100, 234, 243, 262, 335. *See also* Military government; Institutional rules

Political liberalization, 64, 85–98 *passim*, 237, 265, 294

Political participation, *see* Electoral participation

Politicians, autonomous, 51, 285; and party organization, 4–12 *passim*, 63f, 69–70, 136–74 *passim*, 221–22, 233–40 *passim*, 250f, 258ff; and career concerns, 9–10, 244–53

passim, 257, 265, 275, 279, 325; and institutional rules, 75, 221–22, 233–34, 248–51 *passim*, 256–66 *passim*, 276, 278, 330–31, 339; and clientelism, 179, 188ff, 198–99, 209, 218, 258, 285f, 335
Popular Party (PP), 91, 94, 123, 161f, 237, 348
Popular sector, 68, 73f, 81f, 91, 166, 181–84 *passim*, 209–10, 224–28 *passim*, 332–36 *passim*. *See also* Labor movement; Organized interests; Social movements; Working-class parties
Popular Socialist Party (PPS), *see* Brazilian Communist Party
Populism, 33, 38, 41, 54, 71–78 *passim*, 91, 104, 112, 200, 227, 276, 325–26, 330
Populist parties, 72. *See also* PTB
Portugal, 29, 34ff, 225, 235f
Postmaterialism, 22, 40, 52–53
PP, *see* Popular Party
PP, *see* Progressive Party
PPB (Brazilian Progressive Party), 92, 123, 145, 152
PPR (Reformist Progressive Party), 92, 107–11 *passim*, 116–23 *passim*, 159, 266
PPS (Popular Socialist Party), *see* Brazilian Communist Party
Premodern parties, *see* Parties of notables
Presidential elections, 67, 70, 85, 103–6 *passim*, 130, 146, 152, 189, 330, 335; party-system institutionalization and, 6, 30, 33, 42–45, 72–83 *passim*, 108–11 *passim*, 115–18 *passim*, 155, 271–76 *passim*; methods of, 95–98 *passim*, 101, 264, 272, 279f, 339, 348; television and, 149–52, 170, 272, 280, 326, 331
Presidentialism, 18, 30, 129, 195ff, 243–44, 263f, 271–80 *passim*, 317–18, 329f, 337–38; and parliamentarianism, 30, 195, 264, 271–79 *passim*, 318, 337–38; and clientelism, 190–97 *passim*, 258, 270–71, 285–97 *passim*, 304, 315; and governing coalitions, 190–97, 272, 286–91 *passim*, 296–97, 304
Presidential powers, 82, 264, 274–75, 279, 283f, 288, 308, 329; institutional constraints on, 129, 197, 283–99 *passim*, 303–21 *passim*, 325; legislative, 202, 264, 274–75, 283–88 *passim*, 293–301 *passim*, 317–21 *passim*, 337, 340, 357
Presidents and antipartism, *see* Antipartism
Privatization, 124, 135, 216, 284, 300–10 *passim*
PRN (Party of National Reconstruction), 27, 92, 104–18 *passim*, 132, 142ff, 189, 273

Professionalized parties, 37, 66, 137f, 156, 163–66 *passim*, 238
Progressive Party (PP), 107, 144
Progressive Social Party, 79, 81
PRONA (National Order Reconstruction Party), 111
Proportional representation systems, 16, 75, 129–30, 136–37, 148f, 248ff, 254–61 *passim*, 277–78, 338f. *See also* Legislature
Provisional measures, 295f, 300, 314, 319–20. *See also* Presidential powers, legislative
PSB (Brazilian Socialist Party), 19, 92, 133, 139, 143f, 159, 161, 165, 167, 290, 334
PSC (Partido Social Cristão), 144f
PSD (Social Democratic Party), 57, 70ff, 78, 82, 147, 157f
PSDB (Party of Brazilian Social Democracy), 103–17 *passim*, 125, 142–46 *passim*, 159, 266, 290, 314–15, 357; on left-right scale, 92, 132, 144, 291; and Cardoso, 105, 107, 111, 314–15; and party organization of, 142, 154, 164, 252
PSP (Progressive Social Party), 79, 81
PSTU (Partido Socialista dos Trabalhadores Unificado), 144, 159
PT (Workers' Party), 91, 100, 110–18 *passim*, 143f, 156, 160–67 *passim*, 252, 255, 348; ideological commitments of, 19f, 46ff, 91, 100, 112, 165ff, 171ff, 197; left-right scale and, 19, 131–35 *passim*, 144, 291; electoral outcomes and, 20, 94, 100–111 *passim*, 189, 266; bases of support for, 46ff, 91, 119–25 *passim*, 269; labor and, 48, 91, 124, 164f, 226, 230; discipline in, 100, 112, 139–42 *passim*, 158ff, 165–68 *passim*
PTB (Brazilian Labor Party), 47f, 91f, 123, 126, 132f, 139–45 *passim*, 161, 290, 348; in pre-1965 party system, 47, 57, 70ff, 79–82 *passim*; and post–1981 electoral outcomes, 94, 101, 105–10 *passim*, 266
PTR (Partido Trabalhista Renovador), 290
Public opinion surveys, 17; CESOP (Center for the Study of Public Opinion), 17; Data-Folha, 17, 110, 113, 239; IBOPE, 17, 78, 80, 111–18 *passim*, 122–28 *passim*, 239; Latino-barometro, 31, 36, 127; IDESP, 114, 135; *Istoé Senhor*, 334
PV (Green Party), 144, 159

Quadros, Jânio (Pres., 1960–61) 71, 80–83 *passim*, 104, 109–110, 115f
Quércia, Orestes, 152, 170, 350, 352

Race and voting behavior, 46ff
Rational-choice theory, 7–11 *passim*, 138, 167–73 *passim*, 244–48, 260ff, 345, 351
Real Economic Plan, 6, 199, 303, 314
Reelection, 107, 244–48, 258, 290, 325, 331, 349, 355
Reformist Progressive Party, *see* PPR
Regional disparities and electorate, 39–48 *passim*, 52, 54, 86, 106, 119–23, 258–59, 266–67, 287, 335. *See also* Urban vs. rural cleavages
Religion and voting behavior, 39, 49–51
Renovative National Alliance, *see* Arena
Research methodology, 16–18
Revolutionary movements, 20, 161
Rightist parties, *see* Conservative parties
Rokkan, Stein, 4, 39–45 *passim*, 123
Rural Democratic Union, 161
Rural vs. urban cleavages, *see* Urban vs. rural cleavages
Russia, 6, 24, 28–39 *passim*, 146, 328

Campos Sales, Manoel Ferras de (Pres., 1889–1902), 68
Sarney, José (Pres., 1985–90), 97–100 *passim*, 199, 273, 288, 328f; and policy reform, 92, 184–85, 195ff, 204, 270, 288ff, 295–300 *passim*, 306, 311–20 *passim*; and economic crisis, 101–4 *passim*, 108, 199, 298ff, 311; and party support, 102ff, 108, 170, 189, 196, 199, 237, 273, 288–92 *passim*, 298ff; and clientelism, 175, 182–85 *passim*, 189–97 *passim*, 204ff, 211–16 *passim*, 296–99 *passim*; and five-year mandate, 195ff, 270, 298
Sartori, Giovanni, 3, 22–27 *passim*, 37–40 *passim*, 82, 131–34 *passim*, 347, 349
Slovakia, 29f, 36
Social cleavages, 4, 21–22, 39–58 *passim*, 227, 231, 259, 340. *See also* Class and voting behavior; Regional disparities and electorate; Urban vs. rural cleavages
Social Democratic Party, *see* PSD
Social fragmentation, *see* Intraclass fragmentation
Socialist left, 48, 91, 315
Social movements, 13–14, 91, 99f, 123–26 *passim*, 195, 224–28 *passim*, 232, 332. *See also* Labor movement; Organized interests; Popular sector
Sociological reductionism, 8
Sole Labor Confederation (CUT), 124, 230

Southern Cone, 89, 92, 127f. *See also* individual countries by name
Spain, 29–36 *passim*, 235f, 267
Spatial model of party-system formation, 22, 54, 60
Stabilization policies, 107, 124, 211, 283–85, 291–317 *passim*, 347. *See also* Cruzado Plan; Policy reform
State capitalism, 201
State fragmentation, 313
State reform, 107, 184–85, 213, 216, 283–85, 291–317 *passim*
States and party systems, 4–7 *passim*, 22, 54–75 *passim*, 83, 138, 221, 228–35 *passim*
Statism, 134, 178, 184, 201–2, 207, 212, 231–33, 299, 315, 331. *See also* State reform
Supraparty blocs, 83, 141, 299
Sweden, 23, 28–34 *passim*, 227, 339
Switzerland, 28–34 *passim*, 339
Systems institutionalism, 8, 11, 171–72. *See also* Institutionalism

Television, 188f, 196, 224, 238, 331, 356; and parties, 12, 41, 136, 138, 199, 228, 237–42 *passim*, 326; in campaigns, 38, 112, 136, 149–52 *passim*, 170, 188, 222, 237–40, 272, 280, 326
Third-wave democracies, 3, 13, 18–35 *passim*, 39–42 *passim*, 46–60 *passim*, 135, 138, 231, 279
Ticket splitting, 30, 76–80 *passim*
Torres, Alberto, 233
Trust in parties, *see* Party legitimacy
Two-party system, 18, 22, 50, 58, 65, 118–19, 128, 224, 277

UDN (National Democratic Union), 47, 70ff, 80, 82
Unions, *see* Labor movement
United Kingdom, 31, 163, 173, 209, 229, 317
United States, 3, 7, 15–21 *passim*, 38, 47, 59, 150–55, 164; party system in, 26–36 *passim*, 114, 131–34 *passim*, 140, 161f, 173, 261–66 *passim*, 340, 350–51; candidate selection in, 155, 166, 251–56 *passim*, 340, 350; electoral arena in, 189, 238, 252, 261, 328
Urbanization, 68, 73, 235
Urban vs. rural cleavages, 39, 45ff, 51, 71, 73, 78, 81, 85f, 112, 119, 122, 195
Uruguay, 74, 84, 93, 127f, 234, 284, 313; party system in, 5, 29–36 *passim*, 46, 66, 76, 127,

140, 146, 161, 260–61, 325; electoral arena in, 93, 128, 277, 339, 346, 348

Vargas, Getúlio (Pres., 1930–45), 49f, 57, 65–74 *passim*, 80f, 96, 229
Venezuela, 127f, 225, 235, 241, 256, 259, 274–80 *passim*, 325, 330, 357; party system in, 5, 26–36 *passim*, 46, 76, 173, 235f, 310, 325; party discipline in, 140, 173, 274, 279f, 310; party switching and loyalty in, 146, 173, 260–61, 279f; reform and institutional rules in, 264f, 280, 306, 310, 340

Veto players, 283–87 *passim*, 310, 317, 357
Voting rights, *see* Electoral participation

Weber, Max, 183, 207–12 *passim*
Working class, 47ff, 54, 74, 123–24, 224–29 *passim*. *See also* Labor movement; Popular sector; Working-class parties
Working-class parties, 41, 47ff, 66, 71, 74, 80, 225–34 *passim*, 238. *See also* Brazilian Communist Party; PT; PTB
Workers' Party, *see* PT
World Bank, 213f

Library of Congress Cataloging-in-Publication Data

Mainwaring, Scott, 1954–
    Rethinking party systems in the third wave of democratization:
    the case of Brazil / Scott P. Mainwaring.
        p. cm.
    Includes bibliographical references and index.
    ISBN 0–8047–3057–1 (cloth: alk. paper). — ISBN 0–8047–3059–8
    (alk. paper)
    1. Political parties—Brazil. 2. Political culture—Brazil.
    3. Democracy—Brazil. 4. Elite (Social sciences)—Brazil.
    5. Political sociology. 6. Brazil—politics and
    government—1964–1985. 7. Brazil—politics and government—1985–.
    I. Title
    JL2498.A1M35
    324.281′009′048—dc21   98–39078

  ∞ This book is printed on acid-free, recycled paper

Original printing 1999
Last figure below indicates year of this printing:

08 07 06 05 04 03 02 01